SUSTAINABLE FOOD SYSTEMS

Related AVI Books

SUSTAINABLE FOOD SYSTEMS

edited by
Dietrich Knorr, Dipl.-Ing.
Dr. rer. nat. techn.
Department of Food Science and
Human Nutrition
University of Delaware

AVI PUBLISHING COMPANY, INC.
Westport, Connecticut

Library of Congress Cataloging in Publication Data
Main entry under title:

Sustainable food systems.

    Includes bibliographies and index.
    1. Food industry and trade. 2. Organic
farming. I. Knorr, Dietrich.
TP370.5.S94   1983   338.1'9   82-24494
ISBN 0-87055-398-4

CONTENTS

Contributors

BATES, ROBERT P., Department of Food Science and Human Nutrition, University of Florida, Gainesville, Florida.

BRINTON, WILLIAM F., JR., Woods End Laboratory, Temple, Maine.

COLEMAN, ELIOT W., The Mountain School, Vershire Center, Vermont.

FRIEND, GIL, Governor's Office of Appropriate Technology, State of California, Sacramento, California.

GUÇERI, SELÇUK I., Department of Mechanical and Aerospace Engineering, University of Delaware, Newark, Delaware.

KNORR, DIETRICH, Department of Food Science and Human Nutrition, University of Delaware, Newark, Delaware.

LE PAPE, YVES, Institute National de la Recherche Agronomique, Grenoble Cedex, France.

LOCKERETZ, WILLIAM, Nutrition Institute, Tufts University, Medford, Massachusetts.

MAGA, JOSEPH A., Department of Food Science and Nutrition, Colorado State University, Fort Collins, Colorado.

MERCIER, JEAN-ROGER, Application de Recherches sur l'Energie et la Societe, Toulouse, France.

MICKELSEN, OLAF, retired, formerly Department of Food Science and Human Nutrition, University of Delaware, Newark, Delaware.

OELHAF, ROBERT C., Hawthorne Walley School, Ghent, New York.

OLKOWSKI, HELGA, Center for the Integration of Applied Sciences, John Muir Institute for Environmental Studies, Inc., Berkeley, California.

OLKOWSKI, WILLIAM, Center for the Integration of Applied Sciences, John Muir Institute for Environmental Studies, Inc., Berkeley, California.

PIMENTEL, DAVID, College of Agriculture, Cornell University, Ithaca, New York.

PIMENTEL, MARCIA, College of Human Ecology, Cornell University, Ithaca, New York.

RIDGWAY, RICHARD L., Science and Education Administration, Agricultural Research, U.S. Department of Agriculture, Beltsville, Maryland.

SCHAAF, MICHAEL, Costal Enterprises, Inc., Bath, Maine.

VOGTMANN, HARTMUT, Research Institute of Biological Husbandry, Oberwil, Switzerland and Gesamthochschule Kassel, Witzenhausen, Federal Republic of Germany.

WATKINS, TOM R., Department of Food Science and Human Nutrition, University of Delaware, Newark, Delaware.

Preface

In recent decades, the structure of the food production, processing, and marketing industry has changed radically. Farms are fewer, larger, more specialized, and highly mechanized. Food processing and distribution has become a sophisticated industry that occurs largely within the matrix of large-scale operations. The intensive and highly mechanized agricultural technologies now commonly utilized in Western agricultural production systems have led to greatly increased productivity and labor efficiency. In the past few years, however, there has no longer been an automatic acceptance of technological innovation but rather a move to a new concern for quality, resource conservation, and sustainability. There has been increasing discussion over problems associated with the use of agricultural chemicals, such as their potential environmental impact and the fact that they require appreciable quantities of energy.

Consumer concern over the safety and nutritional quality of foods has resulted in an increasingly widespread concept that "natural" and "organic" foods are more nutritious, safer, and of higher quality than those highly processed and/or grown with agricultural chemicals. The antagonism toward agricultural practices and the processing of foods has led some to condemn intensive, highly mechanized technologies and excessive use of chemicals. This also has led to a demand for food production systems that are environmentally sound, resource efficient, and sustainable. Currently an increasing number of food producers and food processors are responding to this call. They apply alternative farming practices and minimize the extent of processing as well as the addition of agricultural chemicals and food additives to their products.

However, these efforts have remained limited in scope, and they often provide only sporadic responses to far-reaching problems. Systematic attempts to explore existing methods and to develop new technologies of more sustainable food production systems have so far been scarce. Consequently there is a need for a systematic reevaluation of methods and technologies appropriate for the production and processing of foods on a broader basis. There is also a need for increased research activities and information exchange on the feasibility of existing and newly developed food production systems. The main objective of this book is to initiate the discussion on such further development.

Because this book is meant for several audiences, including students and professionals in food science, agriculture, environmental science, and nutrition, guidance as to which chapters are most relevant for each reader may be in order. *Sustainable Food Systems* is a collection of contributions organized around four major topics:

Part I deals with the state of art of agricultural production, the potential of an alternative agriculture, and the "new" consumers. It presents prospects of new principles in food production and discusses "new" food habits and the basis of food choice.

Part II summarizes some recent developments in rural and urban food production. It contains topics on energy and agricultural production, pest management, and economic aspects of an ecologically oriented and sustainable agricultural production.

Part III contains examples of new developments and approaches in the processing and distribution of food, such as the use of solar energy in food processing, appropriate food technology, nutrient recovery from food wastes, and a discussion on food cooperatives.

Part IV presents reviews on ecologically grown foods and nutritional considerations in planning for food production as well as descriptional screening methods to detect quality characteristics of humus and plant food materials.

Needless to say, this book would not have been possible without the ideas and contributions of the individual authors. A number of friends and colleagues had to suffer from my time constraints and aggressions during this undertaking and I have to apologize for that. I am grateful to AVI Publishing Co., especially to J.R. Ice and W.W. Tressler, for their efforts and their valuable support toward the publishing of this book. It is dedicated to my daughter Hannah Agnes.

Dietrich Knorr
Newark, Delaware

Part I

System Analysis

1

The Future of American Agriculture

David Pimentel and *Marcia Pimentel*

Introduction
Trends in population growth
The American diet
Food crop exports
U.S. food production
Meeting the challenge of the future
Conclusion
References

INTRODUCTION

American agriculture has made great advances in the past 200 years both by increasing crop yields and by reducing the expenditure of human labor in food production. What changes will the next 100 years bring to American agriculture? Specifically, will our highly mechanized productive system be able to keep our food supply in balance with human needs for adequate food? Although forecasting the future is always uncertain, possible trends can be projected based on current food demands, the availability and use of fossil energy, arable land, and water resources as well as the far-reaching effects of environmental degradation and pollution.

Food supply, based on agricultural production in America and in other parts of the world, is affected by the availability of arable land, water, energy, and labor resources as well as the status of many environmental factors that interact in the total world ecosystem (Figure 1.1). Food demand is influenced by population numbers and also by the type of diets eaten. The latter is determined not only by the nutritional needs of individuals but by diverse socioeconomic and political factors that influence food preferences of individuals.

An analysis of some of the factors that influence food demand and supply can provide insight concerning the potential changes in American agricul-

3

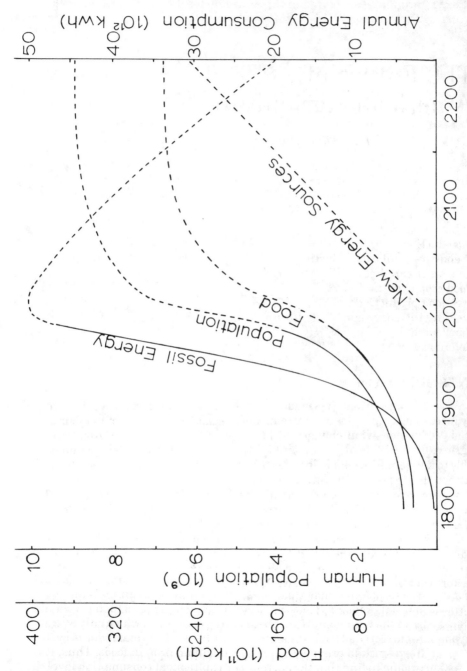

FIG. 1.1. ESTIMATED (SOLID LINE) AND PROJECTED (BROKEN LINE) TRENDS BY CENTURIES IN WORLD POPULATION NUMBERS, FOSSIL FUEL CONSUMPTION, FOOD PRODUCTION, AND NEW ENERGY SOURCES.

ture that might be expected in the future. Indeed, some change in agriculture will be necessary if our highly productive agriculture is to be sustained on our land resources.

TRENDS IN POPULATION GROWTH

First consider the trends in population growth. In 1790 the U.S. population numbered only about 4 million (Figure 1.2). Then, from 1850 to 1975, our population increased from about 23 to 215 million, an increase of nearly 10-fold. Of this increase, immigration accounted for about 38 million or about 20% of the increase.

Today the U.S. population is growing at a rate of about 0.8% per annum (PRB 1978). If this rate persists, the U.S. population will increase to about 262 million by the year 2000 (Figure 1.2). This amounts to a dramatic increase of 22% over present levels within a short 25-year period (1975 – 2000).

At present, the United States produces more than adequate amounts of nutritious food for its population. However, this does not mean all Americans are well fed. In addition, our agricultural production is large enough to support a net export of 11% of the food crop produced (USDA 1978). A major share of this export is grain and soybeans (USDA 1978). Assuming U.S. agricultural production could increase during the next 20 years, a 22% increase in U.S. population would mean that most food produced in the United States would be consumed here to maintain current diet patterns. The far-reaching effects of a major reduction in exports on the U.S. economy will be discussed in a subsequent section.

THE AMERICAN DIET

Currently, according to food disappearance statistics, the U.S. population consumes about 3300 kcal per capita per day (USDA 1978). Daily protein intake averages about 102 g, of which about two-thirds is of animal origin (USDA 1978). Although this dietary pattern is typical of many highly industrialized nations, it contrasts sharply with that of developing nations. The majority of the world population lives on about 2100 kcal per capita per day, and a major portion of its protein is from grains and legumes (Pimentel et al. 1975; Roberts 1976). For example, in the Far East, of about 56 g of protein consumed per capita daily, only about 8 g are animal protein (PSAC 1967).

Essentially this difference in protein consumption is reflected in the fact that Americans feed a major part (90%) of their grain to animals and then eat the animal products. This practice results each year in a high per-capita grain use in the United States of about 650 kg of grain, of which only 60 kg is consumed directly as food (Pimentel et al. 1980A). The remainder is cycled through livestock to provide the preferred animal protein foods. Thus, it is not surprising to find that the current per-capita meat consumption level in the United States is one of the highest in the world. In 1978, for example, the

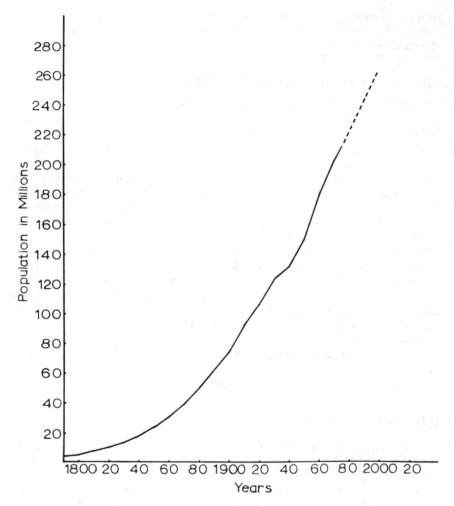

FIG. 1.2.   POPULATION GROWTH IN THE UNITED STATES, ACTUAL (SOLID LINE) AND
PROJECTED (BROKEN LINE) (FROM PIMENTEL *et al.* 1976).

annual per capita meat consumption was 115 kg (254 lbs) or about 315 g per
day (USDA 1978). Of this, beef consumption amounted to 54 kg; pork, 30 kg;
fish, 6 kg; poultry, 23 kg; and veal and lamb, 2 kg (USDA 1976). Per capita
milk and milk product consumption was 129 kg, and an average of 285 eggs
was consumed (USDA 1976).

   With population numbers increasing and assuming that these individuals will also prefer a high animal protein diet, great pressure will be felt by
our agricultural system to grow the large quantities of grain needed to
support these diets. As this will require increased inputs of energy, land,
and water, we can not be certain that our basic agricultural resources are
sufficient to meet such a demand and also continue the large food exports.

FOOD CROP EXPORTS

Over the years crops will have to become one of our major exports. As mentioned, in 1978 the United States not only supplied its own food needs but exported about $25 billion worth of grains and other agricultural products (USDA 1978). Because of these agricultural exports, the United States enjoyed a positive trade balance of about $11 billion in 1978. Thus, the fertile cropland coupled with high production yields is a major factor in helping the United States defray current trade deficits.

Presently our food export trade just offsets a small portion of our importation of oil. But imports of oil increase yearly. For example, in 1978 about 50% of the oil was imported, compared to only 35% in 1973. It is highly unlikely that we will have a dramatic decrease in oil imports in the future. Even if current oil import levels held steady, increased food needs for domestic consumption would result in a decrease in food crops available for export. Therefore, if the U.S. population increases as projected, with limited arable land resources available, it is not unreasonable to conclude that changes in the lifestyle and eating patterns of Americans may be necessary to help pay for our future oil imports.

U.S. FOOD PRODUCTION

Food production is influenced by arable land, water, climate, fertilizer, and energy. In an indirect way it is affected by pest species, public health, availability of labor, and the extent of environmental pollution. The interdependence of food production and these many factors is examined below.

Arable Land

The availability of arable land has been steadily declining in the United States because of population growth, urban expansion, and general degradation of the land already being cultivated. For example in our country, from 1945 to 1970 over 29 million hectares (ha) were lost to highway construction and urbanization, and unfortunately about half of this was fine agricultural land (USDA 1971, 1974).

An additional 40–80 million ha either have been totally ruined for crop production or remain only marginally suitable for production because of severe soil erosion (Bennett 1939; Pimentel *et al.* 1976; SCS 1977; GAO 1977). The rate of soil erosion per ha of cropland in the United States is estimated at 27 metric ton annually (Wadleigh 1968; Hargrove 1972). This high rate of erosion has resulted in a loss of at least one-third of our topsoil. Because topsoil contains the essential nutrients needed for plant growth, its loss has reduced the productivity of cropland in use today (NAS 1970).

Until now the reduced productivity of U.S. cropland from soil erosion has been offset by using more fossil energy in the form of fertilizers and other inputs (Hargrove 1972). Estimates are that 47 liters of fuel equivalents per hectare per year are being used just to offset the soil erosion loss on U.S. cropland (Pimentel *et al.* 1976). One vital question that remains unanswered is whether we can continue to expend expensive fossil energy to compensate for this loss.

The effects of soil erosion are widespread, for it also degrades reservoirs, rivers, and lakes by annually depositing about 2.7 billion tons of sediments in these water bodies (USDA 1968). Soil sediments containing nutrients (nitrogen, phosphorus, potassium, etc.) as well as pesticides have an adverse ecological effect upon stream fauna and flora (Pimentel et al. 1976). Although there is concern, little is being done now and little is planned for the future to control erosion.

In this country we have approximately 190 million ha of arable land, and about 80% is now under cultivation (USDA 1978). Approximately 300 million ha are in pasture and rangeland and about 190 million ha are forest lands. Best estimates are that only about 30 million ha of U.S. land are potentially arable. Furthermore, to develop this land, swamps would have to be drained, deserts irrigated, and mountainous areas leveled and graded. Such major reclamation projects would be expensive in both energy use and dollars.

Concern about the use and management of agricultural land is being expressed by some federal and state governments (GAO 1977; SCS 1977; Pimentel and Pimentel 1979; CEQ 1979). Whether this concern is translated into effective land use and erosion control remains to be seen.

Our arable land is the most valuable natural resource we have. In both quantity and quality it is vital to a strong agriculture. Food crops undoubtedly will become a critical resource, one with rapidly increasing monetary value as the world population continues its rapid growth in future decades.

Water

In addition to fertile land, sufficient quantities of water are necessary for growing crops. A hectare of corn, for instance, requires about 12 million liters (about 4 acre-ft) of water per growing season. Overall, U.S. agricultural production accounts for 83% of the water consumed, whereas industry and urban areas consume less than 17% (Murray and Reeves 1977).

Although 83% of the water consumed in the United States is used by agriculture, only about 10% of U.S. cultivated land is now irrigated (USDA 1978). In arid regions conflicting demands for available water among agriculture, urban population, industry, and fossil energy mining indicate that certain changes in water use are inevitable. Evidence suggests that the proportion of water allotted to agriculture will decrease mainly because the economic yields from agriculture per given quantity of water are far less than yields from industrial production and mining (Gertel and Wollman 1960).

The widespread use of irrigation to bring desert areas into production has serious limitations because it requires the expenditure of large amounts of fossil energy. About 12 million liters of water are needed just for 1 ha of corn, a fairly typical grain crop. The energy cost to pump this amount of water from a depth of a little over 90 m to sprinkle-irrigate 1 ha is about 21 million kcal (Smerdon 1974). This is nearly three times the total energy inputs needed to produce 1 ha of corn employing mechanized technology (Pimentel *et al.* 1973). Further, this input does not include the energy cost of constructing and maintaining the irrigation equipment or the environmental costs that result from soil salinization or water-logging problems associated with the continual use of irrigation.

Therefore, because of the economic factors influencing the use of water and the high energy costs of irrigation, we project little or no growth in fully irrigated crop production in the arid regions of our country. Instead, the prime use of irrigation will be to supplement rainfall in the normal rainfed regions of the nation when unusual drought conditions prevail. Often one or two water applications are all that are necessary to bring a crop through a brief dry period and maintain high yields.

In contrast to too little water, too much water and/or too rapid runoff can also be a serious environmental problem in some agricultural regions. The removal of forests on slopes, in particular, encourages rapid water runoff and subsequent flood damage to crops and pasture (Beasley 1972). An estimated $1.3 billion in U.S. crops and pasture, for example, is lost annually because of "flood water, sediment, and related watershed damage" (USDA 1965). This obviously has serious impacts on U.S. agricultural production, and ways must be found to control these losses.

Climate

Climate determines the suitability of arable land for cultivation. Consequently, changes in temperature and/or rainfall ultimately influence food supplies. These two considerations must be evaluated on two different time scales. Within any given growing season, there are likely to occur, as aberrations from the norm, irregularities in temperature and rainfall patterns that either improve crop yields or inflict enormous losses (Figure 1.3) (Thompson 1975). In addition, there are long-term climatic trends that eventually may affect agricultural production (Schneider 1976).

The mean temperature of the Northern Hemisphere reached a maximum at about 1940; since then, temperatures have declined about 0.1°C per decade (Bryson 1974; Malone 1974; Bryson and Wendland 1975). Because a mere 0.6°C drop in temperature shortens the growing season about 2 weeks (Malone 1974), yields in marginal crop growing regions can be expected to be substantially reduced as this temperature trend continues. For instance, in the U.S. Corn Belt, shortening the critical corn growing season by 2 weeks would result in a yield reduction of nearly 14 bu/acre.

On the other hand, temperature in future decades may increase because of industry, agriculture, and a rapidly growing world population. Specifically, the consumption of large quantities of fossil fuels is expected to significantly increase the CO_2 content and particulate matter (aerosols) of the atmosphere, which in turn are projected to cause a rise in tempera-

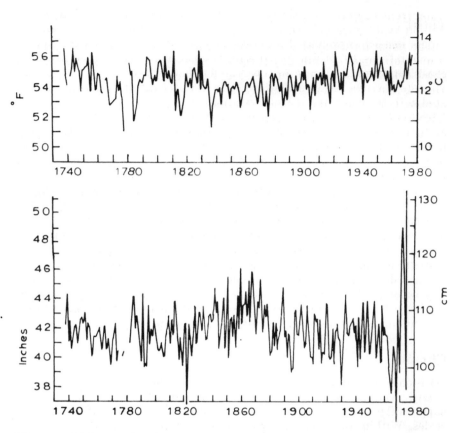

FIG. 1.3. ANNUAL AVERAGE TEMPERATURES AND PRECIPITATION TOTALS FOR THE EASTERN SEABORAD OF THE UNITED STATES FOR THE PERIOD 1738 to 1975. THE DATA ARE FROM A REPRESENTATIVE, RECONSTRUCTED SERIES CENTERED ON PHILADELPHIA FROM LANDSBURG (1970) FOR 1738 to 1967 AND FROM 1967 TO 1975 FOR THE PHILADELPHIA STATION (NOAA 1968–1975).

ture (Kellogg 1975; Singer 1975; Schneider 1978). Manabe and Wetherald (1975) project that the CO_2 content of the atmosphere will increase from 330 ppm (normal level) to about 600 ppm by the year 2100. Particulate matter is also projected to increase. The result for the United States could be a slight warming of the climate by about 2°C. If this projection occurs, the combination of the warming effect and the increased CO_2 may increase terrestrial plant productivity (Wagener 1977; Wittwer 1978). Increased plant productivity would increase crop yields, although other factors such as possible reductions in rainfall must be taken into account. It is impossible to predict whether the temperature increase due to the increase in CO_2 will offset the other changes taking place in world climate.

Fertilizers

The major nutrients that sustain plant growth are phosphorus, potassium, and nitrogen. If soils do not contain adequate levels or proportions of these elements, some way must be found to incorporate them into the soil. During this century in the United States, we have relied heavily on the use of manmade chemical fertilizer, and since 1950 total applications per year have increased nearly 10-fold (USDA 1967, 1978). This large input is one of the major reasons we have been able to offset soil erosion losses and attain high levels of production. As we look to the future we must be concerned with how to maintain high levels of essential nutrients in our agricultural land.

World reserves of phosphate and potassium are large but, as with most other mineral resources, unevenly distributed. Fortunately, North America including the United States seems well endowed with both minerals. Therefore, because of ample supplies and relatively low prices, the United States uses large amounts in contrast to other nations and will probably be able to continue this practice in the future.

Supplies of nitrogen are not so easily obtained as are phosphate and potassium because nitrogen fertilizer production depends directly on fossil energy. Although the air we breathe is 80% nitrogen, to convert atmospheric nitrogen to a form that plants can use requires large inputs of energy—about 2 liters of gasoline equivalents per kg. To produce and distribute a kg of nitrogen fertilizer requires about 14,700 kcal (Lockeretz 1980).

Another way to illustrate the seriousness of the problem is to analyze energy inputs in U.S. corn production. Corn is a typical grain crop, and use of fertilizers constitutes the single largest energy input in its production (Table 1.1). The nitrogen component of the fertilizer accounts for the large energy input. Thus, as energy supplies decrease and become more expensive, other potential fertilizer sources such as livestock manure, some agricultural wastes, and other organic wastes (leaves) must be better utilized. Estimates are that about 50% of the livestock manure that is applied to fields is now wasted because of the method of application (Slipher 1945). That is, the manure is applied during the winter and other fallow periods when the nitrogen, in particular, is leached from the manure. Some is washed into streams and lakes and causes pollution problems there. Of course, to store the manure in large holding tanks would require additional energy. Also, the manure would have to be applied to the land in the spring when the farmer is extremely busy turning the soil and planting the crop.

Therefore, it is easy to see that using manure more effectively is not as simple a procedure as it might seem. The quantity of manure applied per hectare must be relatively large to provide the needed balance of nitrogen, phosphorus, and potassium. To add the optimum amounts of about 310 kg of nitrogen, 90 kg of phosphorus, and 1660 kg of potassium per hectare per year, the manure from 7 cows, 55 hogs, or 510 chickens would be needed

TABLE 1.1.   ENERGY INPUTS PER HECTARE IN U.S. CORN PRODUCTION IN 1975

	Quantity/ha	kcal/ha
Inputs:		
Labor	12 hours	5,580
Machinery	31 kg	558,000
Diesel	112 liters	1,278,368
Nitrogen	128 kg	1,881,600
Phosphorus	72 kg	216,000
Potassium	80 kg	128,000
Limestone	100 kg	31,500
Seeds	21 kg	525,000
Irrigation	780,000 kcal	780,000
Insecticides	1 kg	86,910
Herbicides	2 kg	199,820
Drying	426,341 kcal	426,341
Electricity	380,000 kcal	380,000
Transportation	136 kg	34,952
Total		6,532,071
Outputs:		
Corn yield	5,394 kg	19,148,700
Kcal output/kcal input		2.93
Protein yield	485 kg	

Source: Pimentel and Pimentel 1979.

(Benne *et al.* 1961; Dyal 1963; Loehr and Asce 1969; McEachron *et al.* 1969; Surbrook *et al.* 1971). Of course, manure has advantages besides adding nutrients to the soil. It also adds organic matter, which increases the number of beneficial bacteria and fungi in the soil, makes plowing easier, improves the water holding and percolating capacity of the soil, reduces soil erosion, and improves the ratio of carbon to nitrogen in the soil (Andrews 1954; Cook 1962; Tisdale and Nelson 1966). Similar advantages are associated with the use of crop and other organic remains.

A strategy that can be used to increase nitrogen levels in soil is to plant legumes between corn rows in late August and plow this green manure under in the early spring. For example in the northeastern United States, Sprague (1936) reports that seeding corn hectares to winter vetch in late August and plowing the vetch under in late April added about 150 kg of nitrogen per hectare. Note that this study was conducted when average corn densities were about one-half current densities. Research at Cornell University by T. Scott and W. Knapp (personal communication, 1979) indicated that good yields of nitrogen are possible using vetch and other legumes.

The use of green manures also saves energy because they protect the soil from wind and water erosion during the nongrowing season of the soil. In addition, they add organic matter to the soil and thereby improve its texture.

Along with the advantage of planting winter vetch or any legume crop with another crop, the additional energy costs associated with producing and sowing the seed and plowing it under in early spring must be considered. Overall, though, the positive results using legume crops are most encouraging.

Pesticides

As crops grow they must contend with insect pests, plant pathogens, and weeds that vie for soil space and nutrients. Farmers use some pesticides to help control these pests and thereby insure high yields in the cultivated crops. Annually, almost one-half billion kg of pesticides are applied to U.S. agricultural lands (Berry 1979) (Figure 1.4). Despite the publicity about pesticides, the dominant methods of pest control are nonchemical, and on about 95% of our agricultural land some type of nonchemical pest control is used. Control may include host plant resistance for control of plant pathogens and insects; host plant rotations and sanitation for control of plant pathogens, weeds, and insects; beneficial natural enemies for control of insects and weeds; and mechanical cultivation control of weeds, to mention a few of the important nonchemical pest control technologies.

Some defenders of intensive pesticide use have proposed that the U.S. population would starve without the modern organic pesticides now in use. A recent analysis, however, has documented that if pesticide use were withdrawn and currently available nonchemical control substituted, additional food loss would amount to no more than 5% (Pimentel et al. 1978). It is true that yields of fruit and some vegetable varieties would be decreased.

That the U.S. population would not starve if pesticide usage was severely curtailed can be further documented by comparing food consumption patterns in the United States during the pre-pesticide era and today. For example, prior to 1945 in the pre-organic pesticide era, the per capita annual consumption of fruits and vegetables totalled 184 kg, whereas today it is 156 kg (USDA 1967, 1978). Obviously our agricultural industry in 1940 produced enough fruits and vegetables to meet consumers' needs without using the half-billion kg of pesticides that are applied to crops today. In fairness it must be admitted that the "cosmetic quality" of certain fruits and vegetables has greatly improved with increased pesticide use, but one can seriously doubt the necessity of producing perfect produce at such a cost.

Although the U.S. population would not starve if pesticide use were drastically curtailed, pesticides are certainly important in controlling major pest species. For example, with an investment of about $2.2 billion in pesticidal controls, about $9 billion worth of crops are saved from pest destruction (Pimentel et al. 1978). Therefore, at present rates of use, $1 invested in pesticide control returns about $4 in increased crop yields. This, however, is much less than some of the nonchemical controls that return from $20 to $300 in increased crop yield per $1 invested in control.

In spite of all pesticide and nonchemical pest controls employed today, pests (insects, pathogens, and weeds) destroy about 37% of all potential crops produced in the United States (Pimentel 1981). In the future, we must use all methods at our disposal to reduce this high rate of loss to pests. Both the increased use of pesticides and nonchemical controls will accomplish this goal.

On the positive side, pesticides significantly reduce pest problems in

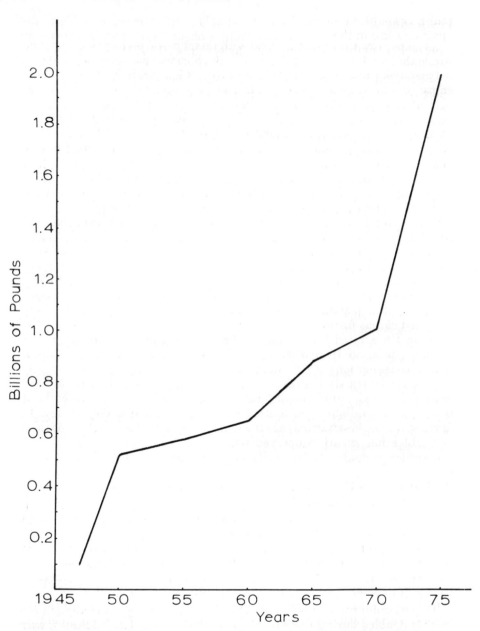

FIG. 1.4. ESTIMATED AMOUNT OF PESTICIDE PRODUCED IN THE UNITED STATES (CONVERSION OF POUNDS TO KG: 1 LB = 0.454 kg) (PIMENTEL *et al.* 1980B).

agriculture and help protect humans from insect-vectored diseases like encephalitis. But unfortunately pesticides also create serious environmental and health problems (Pimentel *et al.* 1980B). For example, each year pesticide use in the United States causes about 45,000 human poisonings, and of this number there are about 200 fatalities (EPA 1974; Pimentel *et al.* 1980B).

Beneficial biota are sometimes destroyed following the normal use of pesticides (Pimentel and Goodman 1974). When natural enemies of pests are eliminated with routine pesticide use, outbreaks of other pest species occur because their natural biological control has been exterminated (van den Bosch and Messenger 1973). In an effort to solve this problem added pesticide is usually required to control the new pests. Not infrequently this has resulted in the treated pest population evolving pesticide resistance. In fact, nearly 400 species of pest insects and mites already have become resistant to pesticides in the United States (Georghiou and Taylor 1977).

To deal with the increased pest problems created by both the destruction of natural enemies and evolved pesticide resistance, an additional $350 million is spent on pesticides needed to control the new or resistant pests (Pimentel *et al.* 1980B).

Programs of integrated pest management (IPM) that include procedures for monitoring pest and natural enemy populations are aimed at making more effective use of natural enemies while reducing pesticide use. This would help reduce pesticide resistance, farmers' costs in pest control, and pesticide pollution.

Although it is projected from previous growth curves that pesticide use may about double in the United States during the next 25 years, some agriculturalists have established a goal of reducing pesticide use by about 50% by implementing IPM programs and substituting nonchemical pest controls for pesticides whenever possible. Although we support this goal and would like to see it accomplished, we believe that pesticide use will not even be held at the current level of one-half billion kg, but will probably increase to nearly 1 billion kg by 2000.

Energy

The use of energy to manipulate and manage the diverse components of the ecosystem is one of the major factors that has enabled the world and the U.S. population to grow rapidly in the past (Figure 1.5). Note that the exponential increase of human numbers directly coincides with the use of fossil energy on a worldwide basis. Fossil energy has been used effectively to increase food production, to improve food storage and processing, to distribute food, and to improve public health.

Of particular concern is the fact that U.S. fossil energy consumption has nearly doubled during the past 20 years. Indeed, the United States, with only 8% of the world population, burns more fossil energy than any other nation. This high rate of energy consumption reflects a lifestyle highly dependent on energy both in the United States and world. The known world reserves of petroleum and natural gas that even now are being used up

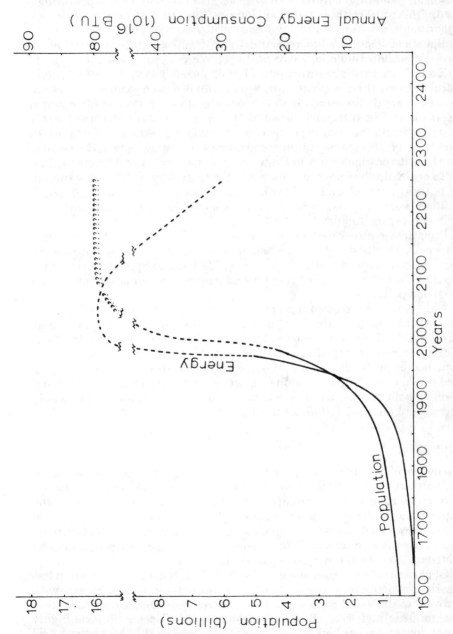

FIG. 1.5. ESTIMATED WORLD POPULATION NUMBERS (SOLID LINE) FROM 1600 TO 1975 AND PROJECTED NUMBERS (BROKEN LINE) (????) TO THE YEAR 2250. ESTIMATED FOSSIL FUEL CONSUMPTION (SOLID LINE) FROM 1650 TO 1975 AND PROJECTED (BROKEN LINE) TO THE YEAR 2250 (AFTER PIMENTEL *et al.* 1975). CONVERSION OF BTU TO JOULES: 1 BTU=1054.9 J.

rapidly are expected to be more than half depleted within the next 20 years. Further, more than half the vast coal reserves are estimated to be depleted by the year 2100 (Hubbert 1972). Genuine concern about energy supply is made more serious by the fact that the world population is projected to reach a density of 10 to 16 billion shortly after 2100. This brings us to the grave problem of how to manage our vital resources.

Today U.S. agricultural output is highly dependent upon large expenditures of energy. For example, the production of 1 ha of corn in the United States requires the equivalent of about 760 liters (6 million kcal) of fuel (Table 1.1) (Pimentel and Pimentel 1979). More than half of this energy input is for fuel to run machinery and to make nitrogen fertilizer. On the positive side, the substitution of machinery for human labor has reduced the man-hour input to only about 12 hours per hectare compared to 1144 man-hours per hectare required to produce corn primarily by hand (Table 1.2).

TABLE 1.2.   ENERGY INPUTS IN CORN PRODUCTION IN MEXICO USING ONLY MANPOWER

Input	Quantity/ha	kcal/ha
Labor	1,144 hrs	589,160
Ax + Hoe	16,570 kcal	16,570
Seeds	10.4 kg	36,608
Total		642,338
Corn	1,944 kg	6,901,200
Kcal output/kcal input		10.74

Source: Pimentel and Pimentel 1979.

Although fossil energy inputs in mechanized agriculture have vastly improved yields per acre, this is due not to machinery itself but rather to fertilizer and hybrid seed inputs. Overall this system is energetically less efficient than producing corn by hand. Intensive corn production in the United States now returns about 2.4 cal of grain corn per calorie of energy input compared with about 15 for hand-produced corn (Tables 1.1 and 1.2). This is a diminished return in corn calories, compared to yields in 1945 when the return was nearly 4 cal per calorie of input (Pimentel et al. 1973). This trend also tends to confirm Thompson's (1975) analysis that production in the U.S. Corn Belt has reached near maximum yields.

The positive return of 2–3 cal per calorie of input characteristic of most cereal grains and legumes such as soybeans is not typical of most other crops. With fruits and vegetables a return of 1 cal requires about 2 cal invested (Leach 1976; Pimentel and Pimentel 1979; Pimentel et al. 1980B). Most fruits and vegetables are raised not for their food energy but rather because they are excellent sources of vitamins A and C and of minerals.

The energetics of livestock production contrast sharply with those of plant production. Thus, for every calorie of animal protein produced, from 20 to 80 cal are used (Pimentel et al. 1975; Pimentel et al. 1980A). This represents a relatively large investment of fossil energy, one that is needed to supply the animal products consumed in the typical American diet.

If we were faced only with increasing crop yields and did not have to consider energy supplies and cost, the adaptation of our highly mechanized agricultural techniques to world agriculture might hold promise. Unfortunately, this is not an option we have. For example, if we were to feed the current world population of 4 billion a typical U.S. diet, high in calories and protein and produced using U.S. food system technology, the energy requirement would be 5,000 billion liters of fossil fuel each year. Assuming the known petroleum reserves will be used only for food and not for transportation, heating, or cooling, these reserves would feed 4 billion people for only 13 years (Pimentel *et al.* 1975). But by 2000 we will need to supply food for an estimated 6 to 7 billion people and also must find ways to supply the increased energy needs of sectors of the world economy other than those involved with food production.

Because fossil energy costs are even now escalating at an alarming rate, it is obvious we must begin to use energy more efficiently in our agricultural system. There are many indications that this has already started. For example, corn growers in the Midwest used to apply most of their nitrogen fertilizer during the winter months when they had labor and machinery available. Of course, the water-soluble nitrogen fertilizer was leached into the ground water and streams and lakes and was not fully utilized by the corn crop. Today this practice is not so common as it was, and more nitrogen fertilizer is applied during the spring and summer, when the corn crop can use this essential nutrient.

In addition, higher pesticide prices, due to the rising cost of petroleum from which these chemicals are made, are stimulating farmers to look for ways to employ these chemicals more efficiently. One practical way to do this is to employ integrated pest management.

MEETING THE CHALLENGE OF THE FUTURE

The basic goal of a sound agricultural policy for the present and more especially for the future is to find ways to maximize crop yields and provide adequate economic returns to farmers, while considering the needs of society as a whole. This will be a challenge to scientists, farmers, and government policymakers alike.

First, we must recognize that agriculture is only one part of a large, interacting system. For this reason a broad approach, one based on a total systems management, should be developed and used. In the past new technology has been introduced on an *ad hoc* basis. As a result new crop varieties, fertilization practices, and pest control methods each have been developed and used independently, with little consideration of their broader interactions with other parts of the agroecosystem.

Therefore, an important improvement would be to evaluate all new technologies in a broader way, based on a thorough understanding of their effects on the entire crop or livestock system.

Two brief examples illustrate the existing problem and the need for change. Currently, herbicide recommendations for specific crops are based on their effectiveness for weed control, and little or no evaluation is done concerning the indirect effects. Unfortunately, some herbicides, while decreasing or controlling weeds, may also increase insect and disease problems (Pimentel 1971; Oka and Pimentel 1976). Herbicides may also reduce the nutrient quality of the crop (Pimentel 1971). Certainly all such indirect effects should be known and then considered when deciding what weed control practice to use. Augmenting an integrated crop management system would mandate a more extensive assessment of the total weed and crop system.

The recommendation of "no-till" agricultural practice, whereby crop remains are left on the surface of the land also illustrates why a pest management approach is advantageous. No-till has a major advantage, that of significantly reducing soil erosion in crop production (Larson et al. 1978). However, there are several disadvantages that must also be considered. For instance, when crop residues are left on the surface of the land, they provide a ready source of insect and disease pests for the next crops planted. Then, too, the soil covered by vegetation is kept cool and damp, which often results in poor germination of the crop seed the following season. In fact, additional seeds may be required to obtain the desired stand. Frequently, pesticide applications must be increased to deal with the increased pest problems, which may cause associated environmental problems to develop. As a result, no-till crop production may use more total energy than normal cropping systems when all energy inputs including additional pesticides and seeds are tallied. Thus, there are both benefits and costs in using "no-till" culture. A careful analysis may confirm that the benefits of no-till outweigh the costs. We should, however, carry out a complete analysis before making any recommendations.

Because arable land is the prime resource in agriculture, U.S. cropland must be protected from further conversion into highways and urban areas. We can not afford to wait another decade or two for action. An effective land-use policy developed by both federal and state governments is essential if we are to protect our cropland. Each acre of cropland that is taken out of production by highways and urbanization means more energy must be used to intensify production from the remaining land or to drain swamps and obtain land for production. No matter which alternative is selected, both the energy and the environmental costs are high.

Although the need for soil conservation policies that guarantee sound management of the land to control soil erosion is recognized, to date little has been done to reduce effectively the soil erosion problem. This should have high priority in our agricultural plans for the future.

Water use in agriculture must also be improved, because agriculture currently consumes about 83% of the water used in the United States. To reduce competition with other users and gain more benefit from the resources available, a vastly improved water management technology is needed.

Concerning energy use, another essential resource to agriculture, many alternative technologies exist to conserve fuel and substitute nonfuel use technologies for some practices already in use.

Because both machinery and the fuel to run the machinery comprise one of the largest inputs in U.S. crop production, more efficient use of tractors in the acreage served per tractor and use of the appropriately sized tractor would conserve fuel. Substituting diesel motors for gasoline and keeping the engines tuned would also contribute to the reduction of fuel consumption in crop production.

To make most efficient use of commercial fertilizers, we need to know more about methods of application and their timing. A careful analysis is needed to determine the best time to apply nitrogen fertilizer and how it should be distributed in the planted field to be most effective. Certainly, when nitrogen fertilizer is applied during the fall and winter months, a significant amount of nitrogen is lost during the fallow periods.

As well as investigating how fertilizers should be applied, we should determine more accurately the optimum amount needed by a specific crop. The quantity of fertilizer applied can affect the actual growth of the crop, and too much can be applied. Experiments have demonstrated that when more than 250 kg of nitrogen per hectare is applied to corn, the nitrogen may become toxic to the crop, thus reducing yields (Munson and Doll 1959).

Augmenting the use of crop rotations has several advantages to agricultural production. Crop rotations can reduce insect, disease, and weed pests (PSAC 1965). In addition, rotating corn with other crops can significantly reduce the amount of pesticide that is used each year. Rotations also reduce soil erosion and water runoff (Pimentel et al. 1976).

Plant breeding can contribute in important ways to energy conservation. For example, increasing the protein content of corn by even 1% is calculated to reduce the need for soybeans by about 1.8 billion kg annually in the United States (Sprague 1955). Although some increase in nitrogen fertilizer inputs would be needed to produce corn cultivars that had a higher protein level, the benefits would more than offset any of the costs.

Another promising strategy is to breed corn and other cereals for insect, disease, and bird resistance and in this way to reduce the energy inputs associated with pesticide use. Decreased pesticide use also would reduce associated pollution problems. Then, if new crop varieties could be developed that had faster maturity, reduced moisture content, greater water-use efficiency and improved fertilizer response, overall energy inputs in production could be significantly reduced. Obviously much research needs to be done in this area.

Irrigation is another energy-intensive operation. Depending on widespread irrigation to increase the world supply of arable land may be impractical. There are circumstances, however, under which water management for crops can be improved. For example, when appropriate contours in terracing are devised, available water can be conserved for crop use. Also, appropriately designed water catches help to slow the runoff of water and keep it available for crops. Mulches and crop remains also slow runoff (Larson *et al.* 1978).

Labor or manpower is another basic resource that can be used more efficiently in agricultural production. To increase the labor inputs effectively requires careful considerations of both the economic and social aspects of the problem. Corn can be produced primarily by hand and requires about 1,144 hr of manpower per hectare. In contrast, mechanized corn production such as in the United States requires only 12 manpower hr input per hectare. Because a U.S. farmer can manage about 50 times more hectares of corn than a farmer producing corn by hand, he has a higher production rate and a higher income.

Employing manpower, however, does have advantages, especially as large numbers of people are without work. With some aspects of production, manpower based upon a kcal output/input ratio can do the same work but use less energy than machinery. For example, the application of herbicides employing a tractor and sprayer expends about 4.7 liters of petroleum (4,700 kcal/ha) whereas using a hand sprayer expends about 740 kcal/ha (Pimentel *et al.* 1973). Other hand operations either simplify or eliminate many machine operations. If, as anticipated, manpower will be available, we need to make every effort to use it effectively for the welfare of both the individual and society as a whole. One way may be to augment manpower inputs in appropriate agricultural technology as mentioned previously. This would decrease fossil fuel inputs while keeping production levels high.

Many improvements could be made in food processing and packaging to reduce energy expenditures substantially while not decreasing the nutritional value of the food itself. A few specific changes that would eliminate waste include a reduction in the amount of "junk" foods processed and packaged, a reduction in the highly prepared and energy-expensive packaging associated with TV dinners and other "convenience" foods, and reduction in individual-serving packaging. Attention to this segment of the food production system holds great promise for making meaningful reductions in energy use.

One way to reduce the amount of energy expended in marketing food crops is to locate market gardens as close as possible to the northeastern United States. This would decrease the variety of fresh produce available year round. Certainly, when energy supply becomes critical, it will be hard to justify the 1800 kcal fossil energy expended to transport a one-half kg head of lettuce, which has an energy value of 50 kcal, across the country by truck (Pimentel *et al.* 1976).

Perhaps it is not unrealistic to expect that more basic changes will occur in the American food supply as the constraints of the energy supply are felt by the rapidly growing human population. With increased demand or need for foods here and worldwide, the economic value of food will increase. With abundant grain harvests and an increased demand on the world market, we can expect grains to be a profitable export commodity. Even now our grain exports help balance our high imports of oil. If a time comes when our harvests no longer satisfy both the needed volume of exports and the amounts needed for our high animal protein production, less animal protein may be produced (Pimentel *et al.* 1980A). Animal protein products can be expected to be in shorter supply than at the present and be higher priced. The overall effect would be a decrease in the amount of animal protein consumed per capita in the United States. As our per capita consumption of protein is a high 102 g per day, of which about 70 g is animal protein, this reduction will not adversely affect the nutritional status of most Americans. In fact, Dietary Goals for the United States (U.S. Senate 1977) suggests a reduced intake of animal protein.

It should be emphasized, however, that those with low income may not be able to purchase sufficient protein and may have a nutritional risk.

CONCLUSION

With the U.S. population increasing about 22% between now and the year 2000 and the increased need for food exports to pay for rising fossil oil energy imports, much pressure will be put on our agricultural system to increase food production. To meet this increased demand more land, water, fertilizers, energy, labor, and other resources will be needed. These pressures for increased food production undoubtedly will result in increased conflicts between agriculture and the other segments of society that compete for many of these same essential resources.

Thus, during the next 20 years land-use planning and effective soil conservation practices must be implemented as demand for rising food production increases. In the western United States agriculture may well lose some of the water supply needed for irrigation as competition increases among urbanization, industry, and mining in this region. Urbanization, industry, and mining interests are expected to demonstrate greater economic and social justification for water than agriculture.

As a result, energy conservation must increase on farms. The effort should start now. Some of the basic conservation steps are making more effective use of commercial fertilizers and livestock manures and substituting some "green manures" for fertilizers; utilizing tractors, other farm equipment, and fuel more efficiently than presently; and where possible increasing the use of human labor.

In the decades ahead food will become an even more important resource of the United States than it is today, and the proportion of U.S. incomes spent for food will gradually increase. The role of agriculture in our economy and society as a whole will also become increasingly important. As agriculture incomes improve, a larger proportion of the U.S. labor force will be attracted into agricultural production.

As agricultural production rises and production technology intensifies, the problems of environmental pollution can also be expected to intensify. Probably the major agricultural pollutant will be pesticides, closely followed by fertilizers. We hope that the pesticide use problem will encourage researchers to develop effective nonchemical controls that minimize environmental pollution.

Certainly as priority conflicts arise between agriculture and the other sectors of the social and ecological system, a systems approach to environmental management of resources will have to be employed in agriculture. This will help us integrate the various production technologies employed in agriculture. In addition, a broad approach includes a focus on conserving and effectively utilizing natural resources while seeking to reduce pollution and preserve the essential nonrenewable resources for future generations.

REFERENCES

ANDREWS, N.B.   1954.   The Response of Crops and Soils to Fertilizers and Manures, 2nd Edition.   State College, Mississippi.

BEASLEY, R.P.   1972.   Erosion and Sediment Pollution Control.   Iowa State Univ. Press, Ames.

BENNE, E.J., HOGLUND, C.R., LONGNECKER, E.D., and COOK, R.L.   1961. Animal manures: what are they worth today?   Mich. Agr. Exp. Sta. Cir. Bull. No. 231.

BENNETT, H.H.   1939.   Soil Conservation.   McGraw-Hill, New York and London.

BERRY, J.H.   1979.   Pesticides and energy utilization.   In Pesticides: Role in Agriculture, Health and Environment.   T.J. Sheets, and D. Pimentel (Editors).   Humana Press, Clifton, N.J.

BRYSON, R.A.   1974.   A perspective on climatic change.   Science 184, 753–760.

BRYSON, R.A. and WENDLAND, W.M.   1975.   Climatic effects of atmospheric pollution.   pp. 139–147 In The Changing Global Environment.   S.F. Singer, (Editor).   D. Reidel, Dordrecht, Holland.

CEQ.   1979.   The President's Environmental Program 1979.   Council on Environmental Quality, Executive Office of the President, Washington, D.C.

COOK, R.L.   1962.   Soil Management for Conservation and Production.   John Wiley and Sons, Inc., New York.

DYAL, R.S.   1963.   Agricultural value of poultry manure.   In Natl. Symp. on Poultry Ind. Waste Mgt. Nebr. Ctr. for Continuing Ed., Lincoln, Nebraska.

EPA.   1974.   Strategy of the Environmental Protection Agency for Controlling the Adverse Effects of Pesticides.   Environmental Protection Agency, Office of Pesticide Programs, Office of Water and Hazardous Materials, Washington, D.C.

GAO.   1977.   To protect tomorrow's food supply, soil conservation needs priority attention.   Report to the Congress by the Comptroller General of the United States.   General Accounting Office, Washington, D.C.

GEORGHIOU, G.P. and TAYLOR, C.E.   1977.   Pesticide resistance as an evolutionary phenomenon.   pp. 759–785 In Proc. XV Internatl. Congr. Entomol.

GERTEL, K. and WOLLMAN, N.   1960.   Rural-urban competition for water: price and assessment guides to western water allocation.   J. Farm Econ. *42*(5), 1332−44.

HARGROVE, T.R.   1972.   Agricultural Research: Impact on Environment. Spec. Rep. 69, Agric. Home Econ. Exp. Sta., Iowa State University of Science and Technology, Ames, Iowa.

HUBBERT, M.K.   1972.   Man's conquest of energy: its ecological and human consequences.   The environmental and ecological forum 1970−1971.   pp. 1−50.   U.S. Atomic Energy Commission, Office of Information Services. Oak Ridge, Tennessee.

KELLOGG, W.W.   1975.   Climate change and influence of man's activities on the global environment.   pp. 13−23 *In* The Changing Global Environment. Singer, S.F.   (Editor).   D. Reidel, Dordrecht, Holland.

LANDSBERG, H.E.   1970.   Man made climate changes.   Science *170*, 1265−1274.

LARSON, W.E., HOLT, R.F., and CARLSON, C.W.   1978.   Residues for soil conservation.   pp. 1−15   *In* Crop Residue Management Systems.   W.R. Oschwald   (Editor).   Am. Soc. Agron. Spec. Publ. No. 31.   Madison, Wisconsin.

LEACH, G.   1976.   Energy and Food Production.   IPC Science and Technology Press Limited, Guilford, Surrey.

LOCKERETZ, W.   1980.   Energy inputs for nitrogen, phosphorus, and potash fertilizers.   pp. 23−24   *In* Handbook of Energy Utilization in Agriculture, D. Pimentel (Editor).   CRC Press, Boca Raton, Florida.

LOEHR. R.C. and ASCE, M.   1969.   Animal waste—a national problem.   J. San. Eng. Div., Proc. Am. Soc. Civil Eng. *2*, 189−221.

MALONE, T.   1974.   Transcript of National Academy of Sciences Luncheon Meeting.   May 28.   Unpublished.

MANABE, S. and WETHERALD, R.T.   1975.   The effects of doubling the CO_2 concentration on the climate of a general circulation model.   J. Atmos. Sci. *32*, 3−15.

McEACHRON, L.W., ZWERMAN, P.J., KEARL, C.D., and MUSGRAVE, R.B. 1969.   Economic return from various land disposal systems for dairy cattle manure.   pp. 393−400   *In* Animal Waste Management.   Cornell Univ. Conf. Agr. Waste Mgt., Ithaca, New York.

MUNSON, R.D. and DOLL, J.P.   1959.   The economics of fertilizer use in crop production.   pp. 133−169   *In* Advances in Agronomy, Vol. II.   A.G. Norman (Editor).   Academic Press, New York.

MURRAY, C.R. and REEVES, E.B.   1977.   Estimated use of water in the United States in 1975.   Geological Survey Circular 765.   U.S. Dept. Interior, Geol. Surv.

NAS.   1970.   Land Use and Wildlife Resources.   National Academy of Sciences, Washington, D.C.

NOAA.   1968−1975.   Climatological Data.   Vols. 19−26.   National Oceanic and Atmospheric Administration, Environmental Data and Information Service, National Climatic Center, Asheville, N.C.

OKA, I.N. and PIMENTEL, D.   1976.   Herbicide (2,4-D) increases insect and pathogen pests on corn.   Science *193*, 239−240.

PIMENTEL, D.   1971.   Ecological Effects of Pesticides on Non-Target Species.   U.S. Govt. Print. Off., Washington, D.C.
PIMENTEL, D. (Editor) 1981.   Handbook of Pest Management in Agriculture, Vols. 1–3.   CRC Press, Boca Raton, Florida.
PIMENTEL, D. (Editor) 1980.   Handbook of Energy Utilization in Agriculture.   CRC Press, Boca Raton, Florida.
PIMENTEL, D. and GOODMAN, N.   1974.   Environmental impact of pesticides.   pp. 25–52   In Survival in Toxic Environments.   M.A.Q. Khan and J.P. Bederka, Jr. (Editors).   Academic Press, New York.
PIMENTEL, D. and TERHUNE, E.C.   1977.   Energy and food.   Ann. Rev. Energy 2, 171–195.
PIMENTEL, D. and PIMENTEL, M.   1979.   Food, Energy and Society.   Edward Arnold (Publishers) Ltd., London.
PIMENTEL, D., HURD, L.E., BELLOTTI, A.C., FORSTER, M.J., OKA, I.N., SHOLES, O.D., and WHITMAN, R.J.   1973.   Food production and the energy crisis.   Science 182, 443–449.
PIMENTEL, D., DRITSCHILO, W., KRUMMEL, J., and KUTZMAN, J.   1975.   Energy and land constraints in food-protein production.   Science 190, 754–761.
PIMENTEL, D., TERHUNE, E.C., DYSON-HUDSON, R., ROCHEREAU, S., SAMIS, R., SMITH, E., DENMAN, D., REIFSCHNEIDER, D., and SHEPARD, M.   1976.   Land degradation: effects on food and energy resources.   Science 194, 149–155.
PIMENTEL, D., KRUMMEL, J., GALLAHAN, D., HOUGH, J., MERRILL, A., SCHREINER, I., VITTUM, P., KOZIOL, F., BACK, E., YEN, D., and FIANCE, S.   1978.   Benefits and costs of pesticide use in U.S. food production.   BioScience 28, 772, 778–784.
PIMENTEL, D., OLTENACU, P.A., NESHEIM, M.C., KRUMMEL, J., ALLEN, M.S., and CHICK, S.   1980A.   Grass-fed livestock potential: energy and land constraints.   Science 207, 843–848.
PIMENTEL, D., ANDOW, D., GALLAHAN, D., SCHREINER, I., THOMPSON, T., DYSON-HUDSON, R., JACOBSON, S., IRISH M., KROOP, S., MOSS, A., SHEPARD, M., and VINZANT, B.   1980B.   Pesticides: environmental and social costs.   pp. 99–158   In Pest Control: Cultural and Environmental Aspects.   D. Pimentel and J.H. Perkins (Editors).   Westview Press, Boulder, Colorado.
PRB.   1978.   World population data sheet.   Population Reference Bureau, Washington, D.C.
PSAC.   1965.   Restoring the Quality of Our Environment.   Report of Environ. Pollution Panel.   President's Science Advisory Committee, The White House.
PSAC.   1967.   The World Food Problem.   Vols. I, II, III.   Report of Panel on the World Food Supply, President's Science Advisory Committee, The White House.   U.S. Govt. Print Off., Washington, D.C.
ROBERTS, L.W.   1976.   Improving the production and nutritional quality of food legumes.   pp. 309–317   In Nutrition and Agricultural Development.   N.S. Scrimshaw and M. Behar (Editors).   Plenum, New York.

SCHNEIDER, S.H.   1976.   The Genesis Strategy: Climate and Global Survival.   Plenum, New York.
SCHNEIDER, S.H.   1978.   Climatic limits to growth: how soon?   pp. 219–226 *In* Carbon Dioxide, Climate and Society.   J. Williams (Editor).   Pergamon Press, New York.
SCS.   1977.   Cropland erosion.   Soil Conservation Service, U.S. Dept. Agr., Washington, D.C.
SINGER, S.F.   1975.   Environmental effects of energy production.   pp. 25–44   *In* The Changing Global Environment.   S.F. Singer (Editor).   D. Reidel, Dordrecht, Holland.
SLIPHER, J.A.   1945.   Manure: its management in barn and field.   Ohio State Univ. Agr. Ext. Serv. Bull. 262.
SMERDON, E.T.   1974.   Energy Conservation Practices in Irrigated Agriculture.   Sprinkler Irrigation Assn. Ann. Tech. Conf., Denver, Colorado.
SPRAGUE, G.F.   1955.   Corn and Corn Improvement.   Academic Press, New York.
SPRAGUE, H.B.   1936.   The value of winter green manure crops.   N.J. Agr. Exp. Sta. Bull. 609.
SURBROOK, T.C., SHEPPARD, C.C., BOYD, J.S., ZINDEL, H.C., and FLEGAL, C.J.   1971.   Drying poultry waste.   *In* Proc. Int. Symp. Livestock Wastes.   Am. Soc. Agr. Eng., St. Joseph, Mich.
THOMPSON, L.M.   1975.   Weather variability, climatic change and grain production.   Science *188*, 535–541.
TISDALE, S.L. and NELSON, W.L.   1966.   Soil Fertility and Fertilizers, 2nd Edition.   Macmillan Co., New York.
USDA.   1965.   Losses in Agriculture.   U.S. Dept. Agr., Agr. Res. Serv. Handbook No. 291.
USDA.   1967.   Agricultural Statistics 1967.   U.S. Govt. Print. Off., Washington, D.C.
USDA.   1968.   A National Program of Research for Environmental Quality.   Pollution in relation to agriculture and forestry.   A report prepared by a joint task force of USDA and Directors of Agricultural Experiment Stations.   USDA Research Program Development and Evaluation Staff.   Washington, D.C.
USDA.   1971.   Agriculture and the environment.   U.S. Dept. Agr., Econ. Res. Serv. No. 481, July 1971.
USDA.   1974.   Agricultural Statistics 1974.   U.S. Govt. Print. Off., Washington, D.C.
USDA.   1976.   National food situation.   U.S. Dept. Agr., Econ. Res. Serv. NFS-158.
USDA.   1978.   Agricultural Statistics 1978.   U.S. Govt. Print. Off., Washington, D.C.
U.S. SENATE.   1977.   Dietary Goals for the United States.   Select Committee on Nutrition and Human Needs.   U.S. Govt. Print. Off., Washington, D.C.
van den BOSCH, R. and MESSENGER, P.S.   1973.   Biological Control.   Intext Educational Publishers, New York.

WADLEIGH, C.H.   1968.   Wastes in relation to agriculture and forestry. U.S. Dept. Agr., Misc. Publ. 1065.

WAGENER, K.   1977.   Recycling of excess carbon dioxide from fossil energy conversion by plants.   pp. 319–328 *In* Living Systems as Energy Converters.   R. Buvet, M.J. Allen, J.-P. Massué, (Editors).   North–Holland, Amsterdam.

WITTWER, S.H.   1978.   Carbon dioxide fertilization of crop plants.   pp. 310–333   *In* Crop Physiology.   U.S. Gupta (Editor).   Oxford and IBH Publishing, New Delhi.

2

The Potential for a Sustainable Agriculture

Gil Friend

INTRODUCTION

The story is told of the time the first European took plow to the American prairie. As he went about his work, he was watched, from a nearby rise, by a lone Cherokee on horseback. After a time, the farmer stopped to rest, and the Indian rode down for a closer look. He dismounted beside the plow and knelt to examine the furrow, putting his hand into it to gauge its depth, examining the overturned sod, quietly looking. He slowly remounted his horse, turned to the farmer, and said, "Wrong side up," and rode off.

Agriculture today, for all its strengths, is also wrong side up, in more ways than just the manner of working the soil. At its most general level, this has manifested in an almost single-minded devotion to production, but in ways that cannot be sustained and erode the very resource base upon which not only agriculture, but our very prosperity, depend.

The strengths, and the message, of alternative agriculture are that it understands the importance of sustainability—not as a "factor" to be taken into account, but as a central organizing principle of production—and that it has read, studied, and embraced the story told by natural systems.

There is something very telling in the fact that the concept of "sustainability" is increasingly on the lips of resource managers, be they farmers, government officials, or corporate managers. In the period between the appearance of the *Limits to Growth* in 1972 and of the U.S. *Global 2000 Report to the President* (Meadows *et al.* 1976; Barney *et el.* 1980), a message

28

finally seems to be sinking into many minds. The era of incredible promise widely hoped for after World War II—the promise of nuclear energy so cheap it would not be metered, of better living through petrochemistry, of unlimited growth and endlessly rising standards of living—that imagined era is now recognized to have very real limits and previously unsuspected failings. People, governments, and businesses are beginnning, again, to consider the possibility that all the wealth in the world "don't amount to a hill of beans" if it is not sustainable, and certainly not if it consumes its very resource base in the production process.

Unfortunately, this new interest in sustainability has been accompanied by a faddish application of the word to all sorts of concepts, many of which have little to do with the problem. My concern here is with the most fundamental matter of *biological* sustainability—not with the economic survival of the family farm, though that is certainly important; not with the future of pesticide supplies. The real issue is both simple and urgent. Can the living systems upon which our own lives depend continue to remain productive, not just in our lifetimes, or will their productivity remain founded on the erosion, consumption, and deterioration of the finite (however renewable) resource base on which all life depends? The question of sustainability is the question of whether, as we produce our food, we will leave our progeny gardens or deserts. The challenge of a sustainable agriculture is to produce the food and fiber needed by people in a way that preserves or improves fertile soils; that maintains or expands supplies of clean water; that protects or regenerates the biological diversity and health or earth's ecosystems; that supports or enriches vital, coherent human cultures; and that re-members the role of the farmer both as producer of food and fiber and as steward of natural resources (Merrill 1980).

CONTEMPORARY AGRICULTURE

Agriculture has emphasized productivity in the past, with both great success and some narrow-mindedness. The successes are unarguable—significant increases in yields for commodities ranging from maize (with production averaging over 6 metric tons/ha in the United States in 1978, up from 2 metric tons/ha in 1945) to milk (with a good cow in a good herd now producing 6600 kg/year up from 3900 in 1945). (USDA 1958, 1979) Consumers now have access to a much greater variety of food over a much longer portion of the year than ever before.

But failures are evident as well, and all too many of them are inseparable from the successes. Corn yields are up, but the production of a bushel of corn from the heart of the U.S. corn belt "costs" two bushels of topsoil, and soil loss remains as serious a problem in the U.S. today as it was during the Dust Bowl of the 1930s (Comptroller General 1977; Pimentel *et al.* 1976). Pesticide technology has brought farmers seeming relief from the age-old struggle against pests and disease, but has left them on a treadmill of using even more pesticides against increasingly resistant pests. In California, for example, 17 of 25 major pests are now resistant to one or more types of pesticides. (Barney *et al.* 1980) Vast irrigation systems have made it possible to farm lands that were once desert, but the accompanying salination of soils is creating new deserts out of once fertile farmland. Agricultural research brings great leaps in productivity but displaces farmers at a prodigious rate, adding to urban pressures. The list, of course, could go on.

One of the most important weaknesses of contemporary agriculture, from the perspective of the need to feed a hungry world, is that sufficient resources do not exist to support the transfer of Western-style industrial agriculture worldwide. Even at a fraction of the energy intensity we know in North America, extension of comparable practices to the agricultural lands of developing areas would require a vast increase in the world energy budget, for just those agricultural needs. (Alexander 1974; Pimentel *et al.* 1975) Most non-OPEC third-world nations already suffer severe energy shortages. To rest hope for feeding a rising population on future access to such a level of energy availability (given what we have learned about energy, for example, from Lovins (Lovins 1977) and from on-the-ground experience) is at once technically naive and cruelly misleading for the billions of people in the world for whom such questions are matters of life and death, not mere intellectual interest.

An agriculture that is to meet the needs of the world's hungry, then, must be not only productive and sustainable but also extremely conserving of resources. Western agriculture has emphasized labor productivity, and the Japanese land productivity; but over the coming decades, agriculture in North America as well as in the developing world will necessarily emphasize *resource* productivity—producing needed food and fiber while maximally conserving energy, soil, and water resources. Although the necessity of energy conservation has been widely realized, because of the irresistable pressure of rising energy prices, the response has been largely "technical fix," rather than systemic change, and therefore of limited significance. There has been, in response to rising prices, increasing investigation and adoption of specific new *tools*, such as no-till planters and solar grain dryers, and these are certainly valuable contributions to reducing energy use in agriculture. But there is also dramatic potential for changes in technique and approach, as evidenced by the over 60% reduction in on-farm energy use by conventionally organized and equipped farmers who have learned to raise their crops without chemical fertilizers and biocides (Klepper *et al.* 1977). This enormous potential is being steadily developed by farmers themselves and by individual researchers or research groups but has been largely ignored until quite recently by the academic majority.

Such concrete weaknesses are relatively easy to see. Others, though less visible, are equally important. Margalef (1968) has noted that the flow of energy through a system tends to simplify the system. It would seem that not only our practices but also our *thinking* about agriculture has been simplified as well. This has happened in two ways. First, *what* we think is important has been simplified, as evidenced by areas of research that have been relatively neglected for over 30 years. Microbially mediated nutrient transformations are one such area; why be concerned with microorganism mineralization of fixed phosphorus and the impact of organic matter on the activity of those organisms, when it is "cheaper" to just add more super-phosphate (Gerretsen 1948)? Second, *how* we choose to respond to those questions that we identify as worthy of investigation reflects an even more dangerous simplicity of thought. Let me draw an example from a recent California state program to encourage the development of renewable resources in agriculture by funding innovative research. The leading proposal would research genetic engineering to develop crop varieties that could tolerate rising salt levels in Central Valley soils. Not a single proposal out of more than 100 submitted offered to look at ways to modify crop or irrigation or soil management to reduce or eliminate the salinity problem before it became a problem.

It seems much more difficult for the scientific method to accommodate the complexity of the anticipatory research; the band-aid was more tractable. But studying the parts of a system, while it can tell us many things, cannot grasp the whole (Harwood 1980; Rose 1981).

The challenge that we all face today, as scientists, technicians, farmers, policymakers, and people who eat, is to begin to deal with wholes as well as parts and to integrate the two factors of production and sustainability, which are in fact not at all separate in the long term. To do this will require an evolution from the chemical fix permitted by the postwar period of cheap energy to a growing reliance on sophisticated strategies of applied ecology.

Economists in the past may have assessed and debated the balance between capital intensive and labor intensive strategies; these times call for *knowledge* intensive strategies of production, protection, and resource management that will permit understanding and design to substitute for energy intensive inputs or human drudgery. The body of principles and practices known as "ecological agriculture" has already made important contributions to this necessary transition from chemical/industrial to biological/ecological management of agricultural systems and holds important future promise for all agriculturalists.

BIOLOGICAL AGRICULTURE

Ecological agriculture (or organic agriculture as it is often unfortunately called) or biological agriculture, as I prefer to call it, has unfortunately been an emotional issue for far too long. Today's pressing world problems require moving beyond ideological conflict to pragmatic assessment. But what is being assessed?

"Organic farming" has been commonly defined as "the practice of recycling organic matter as fertilizer and minimizing the use of commercial fertilizer and inorganic pesticides" (National Science Council of Taiwan 1980). Such a definition, though, reduces a system of agriculture to a mere collection of techniques (and only some of its techniques, at that). What makes a system a system, and something more than the sum of its parts, are the interactions among those parts. Biological agriculture, in fact, is not a cookbook definition—chemicals or no chemicals, manure or no manure—and thus, much of the past debate has been falsely focused. It is instead a sophisticated systems approach to agriculture that emphasizes *optimization* at the level of the agro-ecosystem rather than maximization of single crops or system components and that places primary emphasis on managing *biotic* interactions in ways that maximize agro-ecosystem stability and minimize demands for human and industrial inputs. Practitioners place great importance on ecosystem balance, especially on the vitality and health of the soil community (Oelhaf 1978; Howard 1947; Walters 1975).

The label "organic agriculture" is useful in one specific sense, for, as Berry (1981B) notes:

An organic farm, properly speaking, is not one that uses certain methods and substances and avoids others; it is a farm whose structure is formed in imitation of the structure of a natural system; it has the integrity, the independence, and the benign dependence of an *organism* [emphasis added]. . . . A farm that imports too much fertility, even as feed or manure, is in this sense as inorganic as a farm that exports too much or that imports chemical fertilizer.

Thus, though conventional farmers and many biological farmers can both be found doing many of the same things, such as spreading manure, the differences are profound. Whereas specific aspects of biological farming practice are being increasingly adopted by conventional growers and research may look more at some of the components of that practice, the components can be temporarily separated for study only at considerable risk of loss of significant information, and wisdom, if the whole is not properly reassembled in the farmer's or researcher's mind.

Biological agriculture is not a return to the past, by any means, though it is often casually characterized as such. This characterization has been easy to make, because biological agriculture draws on many methods that were familiar to agriculture in the past but have been largely abandoned for a generation. Yet they were not abandoned because they did not work or because they were old fashioned. They were abandoned because they were outcompeted economically by cheap energy-intensive inputs and by pesticide technology. As the temporary economic advantage of these technologies fades, the older methods are back in the running.

Biological agriculture at its best represents an integration of many wise traditional techniques in the framework of modern scientific theory and experience (a framework that *conventional* agriculture has been all too able to ignore, again because of an agricultural "chemotherapy" that has masked the reality of a deteriorating resource base) (Barney 1980; Krauss and Allmaras 1982). It does not reject modern advances, but draws upon them selectively, as it finds many of them unnecessary, inefficient, or counterproductive; neither does it unquestioningly embrace the past, but rather utilizes that collected experience selectively. It does not represent helplessness before the struggle with nature, but sophisticated management of biotic systems and biotic interactions.

Biological agriculture has served at least two important functions during the brief cheap-energy era. It has been both an important source of innovation for agriculture in general and a valuable preserve for many traditional techniques that are now returning to favor. Let us examine an example of each.

Limited tillage, which has been increasingly widely adopted in recent years by farmers across the continent (Giere et al. 1980; Phillips et al. 1980) is an innovation that has been practiced for decades by many biological farmers, albeit for different reasons. While the current trend is largely in response to rising energy prices and the increased cost of tillage, biological farmers acted from their concern for the biological and physical status of the soil, feeling that the soil should be disturbed as little as necessary and that crop residues should be left to decompose on or near the soil surface to minimize deleterious population shifts among soil organisms (and the possibly resulting plant stress) (Faulkner 1943). Moreover, these farmers have found ways to practice no-till without recourse to herbicides, in most cases (McLeod and Sweezy 1979). In this instance, as in many others, organic farmers take their lessons from the functioning of natural systems. The forest floor becomes a kind of idealized model—subject, of course, to modifications necessitated by a commercial, exporting system—for sustainable management of soil fertility (Howard 1947).

Legume-based rotations and the use of green manures and cover crops are certainly traditional techniques that have been a key fertility management tool for biological farmers, even through the decades when they were dismissed or deemphasized by mainstream agriculture as "uneconomic" in comparison with fossil-fuel based fertility and pest management strategies. One finds biological farmers using rotations not only to fix nitrogen, control pests and diseases, and build soil organic matter, but also to improve deteriorated land, to translocate minerals from the subsoil to the rooting zone of primary crops, and to make most effective use of soil volume by rotating crops of different rooting, as well as feeding, characteristics. The use of these and other practices are not only energy efficient, they make good sense for soil and water conservation.

The U.S. Department of Agriculture recently observed (USDA 1980) that, however one might feel about "organic agriculture" per se, it was evident that its practitioners were generally using best management practices for soil and water conservation. Many conventional farmers do as well, and hopefully more will as the impact of soil deterioration becomes better understood. But it is probably safe to say that biological farmers have typically been conservation-minded all along. For them, conservation strategies are not something added on to production strategies if possible or affordable; they are, rather, an integral part of the production strategies themselves.

In the area of pest management as well, the innovative role of biological agriculture is apparent, although perhaps less obviously than with the examples just noted. Because of their general reluctance to use toxic chemicals for pest control, biological farmers were early users of beneficial insects as biological control agents. Full-blown integrated pest management (IPM) programs were, of course, beyond the development capability of most individual farmers, but the experience of biological farmers profitably producing respectable yields without use of pesticides has long stood as a major challenge to the once-assumed necessity of pesticide use and as a major argument for IPM strategies that put toxic chemicals in their proper place as tools of last, not first, resort. Integrated pest management is now, by policy, the preferred strategy in California and is being steadily developed as an effective tool in more and more crops. Growers in California are reaping substantial savings by reducing or eliminating expensive chemical applications, yet farmers elsewhere are still told that "pesticides are necessary" for productive agriculture. That is no longer reliable as a general statement.

One of the most interesting contributions of biological agriculture in the area of pest management is also the least understood. Many biological farmers— certainly three-fourths of the sample I interviewed in Western Europe several years ago—maintain that they have few pest problems, yet they take little direct action to control pests (Friend 1978A). At this point, the one common explanation offered by proponents of biological agriculture is the notion that "a healthy soil produces healthy plants" and that pests will selectively graze unhealthy plants, an "old saw" that was never proved and was commonly discounted by agricultural scientists. Recent work by the French parasitologist Chaboussou (1977, 1980) and, more recently, by researchers at the University of California, (Toscano et al. 1982) has begun to identify some of the mechanisms of adverse effects on pest resistance resulting from pesticide and possibly fertilizer use. Toscano et al. (1982), focusing on iceberg lettuce, found that "insurance" treatments with several common classes of pesticides disrupted crop photosynthesis and transpiration, resulting in lower yields. Chaboussou (1977, 1980) found that not only pesticide applications but also nutrient imbalances and various combinations of the two could depress protein synthesis and increase the proportion of less complex "intermediate metabolites," which would, in turn, be more attractive to sucking insects (Ferree 1979). Both reports suggest promising areas of research for the future that may offer some explanation of biological farmers' relative success with pest problems.

Another essential, and more accessible, aspect of crop protection as an emergent property of these agro-ecosystems is the significance of crop ecology on pest susceptibility. It is another underresearched area, yet one of potentially great significance, both for explaining the apparently reduced pest problems of many biological farmers and for suggesting important new strategies for the design of self-regulating agro-ecosystems. A growing body of evidence suggests that the diversity and physical distribution of crop plants may both reduce pest damage and be an economical way to do so. (Root 1973, 1975).

Suggested mechanisms for these interactions include: confusing olfactory and/or visual stimuli from nonhost plants may disrupt pest feeding or breeding behavior; plants may provide shelter or supplemental food sources for beneficial insects; "trap crops" may divert insects from the main crop to secondary plants, where they are easier targets for natural enemies or highly localized pesticide applications. Some plantings serve several of these roles simultaneously (Merrill, 1974; Perrin and Phillips 1978). These general effects have long been recognized by farmers and horticulturalists. The use of multipurpose hedgerows and windbreaks, as well as plantings of flowering plants in or near crops, provide some of these benefits. The "companion planting" lore popular with organic gardeners attempts to apply the same mechanisms, based on generations of observation, however imprecisely synthesized and passed on. Considerable work is yet to be done, however, in identifying the specific species interactions that will enable these principles to mature into working design tools for agriculture.

AGRO-ECOSYSTEM DESIGN

Such interactions have a significance beyond themselves. They point to vast new potentials for conscious ecological design in agriculture. To the extent that agricultural systems have been consciously designed in the past, they have been designed as economic systems that accommodate biological realities only to an extent that was unavoidable. It is time now to consider the potential for designing agricultural systems as stable, self-maintaining ecological systems that would of course have to accommodate economic realities as well; but on the way to a balanced integration of the two perhaps we could afford a pendulum swing, for a time, in the neglected direction.

The generic model for such design strategies must be natural ecosystems, for entirely pragmatic reasons. Natural systems provide the catalog of results from billions of years of trial and error development of complex, stable systems. Natural ecosystems are, granted, not sufficiently productive in the chosen commodities to satisfy our nutritional or economic needs. But they are wholes, not parts, and thus by definition possessors of health of a particular and valuable type. Humans, in turn, have thousands of years of experience managing productive agricultural systems and several decades of experience doing so in a period when we were sufficiently powerful to impose our will, temporarily, on the landscape. It should be possible now to synthesize both those bodies of experience, draw the best from each, and combine productivity with sustainability.

Such an agriculture would, of course, look different in different places, in contrast to the current trend toward uniformity and reduced genetic diversity. It would show great local variation, learning from traditional indigenous knowledge, drawing on dominant local ecotypes as the model for its structure and its specific crops, yet certainly common principles would be evident in each case. It would exhibit high levels of diversity of several types: species diversity, that is, polycultural rather than monocultural plantings; spatial diversity, that is maximizing spatial heterogeneity to the extent feasible given constraints of farm operations; structural and temporal diversity, that is, mixing plants of different stature, from grasses to vegetables to shrubs to trees, and different degrees of permanence; and trophic diversity, that is, complexifying the feeding links among organisms in the ecosystem by, for example, providing habitats for beneficial insects to control selected crop pests. It is the trophic diversity that gives species diversity its significance as a tool of agro-ecosystem design and in large measure determines the contribution of ecosystem stability (Watt 1973).

Such an agriculture would exhibit an economy of design that would emphasize multifunctional relationships in areas of farm enterprise ranging form fertility management to pest control to climate control in buildings. It would exhibit a dynamic structure, moving through stages of development like the successional patterns of natural ecosystems, from simple to complex associations, from pioneer to climax species—a specialized form of rotations, one might say. Most or all stages might be evident simultaneously at any given time on a particular farm, enabling the farmer to benefit from characteristics of both immature and mature ecosystems. These strategies can build stability, resource economy, and integrity into the structure and operation of agricultural units (ASA 1976; Fukuoka 1978; Mouison and Holmgren 1978; Musick 1980; Perrin 1977). Not all biological farmers do all these things, by any means. But many do, and others are closer to doing so, in their approach and their practice, than farmers who rely on industrial inputs to serve many of these biological functions.

In fact, many of these characteristics can be found operating, to varying degrees, in a variety of agro-ecosystems. Market gardens often produce a wide variety of vegetables, occasionally accompanied by flowering ornamentals. Hedgerows and windbreaks can provide, if composed of the proper species, not only erosion control and boundary marking but also habitat for beneficial organisms, forage for stock, biomass for fuel, and other benefits (MacDaniels and Lieberman 1979). Tropical slash-and-burn systems, while often denigrated by Westerners, are quite sophisticated ecologically and are sustainable as long as population levels are suitably low. They provide perhaps the most advanced model of patterning agricultural systems on natural systems that we know of. They are labor-intensive systems, to be sure, but when considered for energy productivity and environmental compatibility they rival any modern practice (Hunter and Kwaku Ntiri 1978; Nye and Greenwald 1960). Surely, though, there are ways to link the ecological sophistication and resource productivity of the shifting cultivation systems with the technical sophistication and labor productivity of modern agriculture to generate agro-ecosystems that are productive, efficient, self-stabilizing, and sustainable, as well as tailored to diverse climates and regions.

Though it may seem that tropical ecosystems have little relevance for North American agriculturalists, they are significant for two reasons.

First, there are more evident and familiar models of what might be called "ecosystem mimicry" based on tropical forests (Gleissman 1981; Hart 1977) than on temperate forests, although the latter do indeed exist, agro-forestry grazing systems being perhaps the best known example (Russell Smith 1929; Sholto–Douglas 1976; Spurgeon 1980). Thus, the traditional polycultural systems can illustrate a point that may be adapted to local needs in diverse biomes. Second, developing countries, which face the greatest resource and population pressures, are the very places where traditional agricultural systems are being displaced in the name of the greater "efficiencies" of Western export agriculture. The bulk of the increases needed in the world food production must come from the developing world and can be met there with much greater resource efficiencies than increasing production in the West, where agriculture has already moved into the zone of diminshing returns of the inputs–productivity curve. Moreover, developing countries must achieve increases in production with much lower levels of inputs than modern agriculture has become accustomed to; the energy, water, and other resources just won't be there for a bigger appetite. Traditional agricultural systems have important contributions to make in feeding these hungry nations and have much to teach temperate-zone agriculture as well. Biological agriculture offers the framework for a "middle way" that links the strengths of highly productive, mechanized, resource-intensive Western agriculture and of stable, labor-intensive, resource-efficient traditional systems. The challenge is to learn enough from traditional systems before they are irretrievably displaced by a "development " process that does not recognize their value (Bishop 1978; Freeman and Fricke 1980; Mollison 1979; Nair 1977).

One of the strengths of biological agriculture is its insistent "whole systems" perspective on agricultural management. Biological agricultural presents, in fact, a wholly different paradigm for agro-ecosystem management than the one modern agriculture has been relying upon—with partial and temporary, albeit impressive, success—and encompass much more than the commonly noted use of organic wastes and avoidance of synthetic chemical inputs.

The following principles outline the framework of biological agriculture practice (Friend 1978; Hodges 1978):

- Management focuses on long-term optimization rather than short-term maximization of the productive capability of the farm system, and,
- On maintaining a diversified agro-ecosystem in which various living components can be stewarded to perform a variety of complementary functions that would otherwise have to be provided by the farmer or the off-farm industrial support system.
- Management concentrates on building up the biological fertility of the soil so that crops can take the nutrients they need from the steady nutrient turnover within the soil, mediated by microorganisms

nourished by soil organic matter; excessive nutrients are not presented to the plant at any time, and there is no great tendency for the loss of nutrients by leaching from the soil.

- Soil is kept under continuous cover, to the extent feasible, and extensive use is made of legume-based rotations, cover crops, and green manures.
- Biological agriculture returns suitable waste products to the soil and augments this by drawing on minerals in the subsoil through deep-rooting plants.
- When loss of nutrients from a farm (e.g., exported in crops) requires use of imported fertilizers, these are usually applied in the form of relatively insoluble compounds, which are slowly broken down by the natural processes within the soil.
- There is an indivisible connection between the health of the soil and that of the crops grown on it and the animals and people who consume those crops.

Within that framework, a variety of approaches may be brought to bear: diversification rather than specialization of the farm unit (which among other benefits, addresses much of the problem of manure transportation logistics between feedlots and feed-producing farms); extensive use of rotations, to provide nitrogen and carbon from their legume hay and grass constituents, and to enable crops with different nutrient requirements to draw down soil nutrients in a more balanced way; deep-rooting crops, to translocate leached and subsoil minerals and to more fully utilize soil volume; undersowing and catch crops to minimize exposure of bare soil; reduced tillage and general avoidance of the moldboard plow, in order to keep decomposing organic matter in the zone of maximum biological activity and to preclude anaerobic fermentation in the soil; reliance on ecosystem stability, crop health, and biological and cultural controls rather than pesticides; and of course, use of manure, compost, mulch, and slow release fertilizers (e.g., rock powder) not only to provide nutrients for crops, but to improve soil structure and resistance to erosion and to feed a balanced soil community (Aubert 1977; Koepff *et al.* 1977; Walters and Fenzau 1979).

None of these practices is unusual; some are traditional and only recently abandoned. In fact, they are found more and more on "conventional" farms around the United States in one form or another. All the more reason—given the apparent productivity and profitability of these enterprises—that the effects of these practices, individually and in concert, should be investigated to determine how soil processes, nutrient balances, and other factors may differ from those of comparable farms under conventional practice.

It is critical to recognize, as Merrill (1981) has noted, that:

many of these alternatives are being researched and practiced *separately* but not *systematically*. For example, the agricultural research establishment continues to plug away at many of these alternatives in isolated stations, cranking out data, suggesting new *tech-*

niques. But nowhere is there an agricultural research station investigating the entire spectrum of these economic and ecological alternatives simultaneously as a holistic unit . . . as a living agro-eco-system.

In part as a response to this void, alternative research and training institutes have appeared across the United States in recent years, and in many other countries as well. Examples of such "alternative" research and extension centers in the United States include the Rodale Research Farm in Pennsylvania, the New England Small Farm Institute and the New Alchemy Institute in Massachusetts, the Rural Education Center in New Hampshire, the Small Farm Energy Project in Nebraska, and the Tilth Research Farm in Washington State.

Many apparent benefits of these techniques require additional verification and evaluation. The most obvious is reduced energy consumption, which researchers found to be only one-third as high on organic farms as on comparable conventional farms in the U.S. Corn Belt, essentially as a result of the non-use of chemical fertilizers and pesticides (Klepper *et al.* 1977); in addition, traction power required can be significantly reduced as tilth is improved (Pimentel *et al.* 1981).

Another benefit is reduced displacement of nutrients from the agro-eco-system into ground and surface waters. Lockeretz *et al.* (1981) estimate soil loss at one-third less on farms in their sample, in large part because of the erosion-reducing effect of rotating meadow. What impact can management practices have on nutrient losses and salinity problems, as well as on erosion? Can reduced soil deterioration, as a result of use of continuous cover and minimal tillage, make possible expansion of agriculture to more sensitive lands without disastrous consequences?

More difficult to document, and already subject to conflicting experimental results, are claimed effects of different management practices on crop quality and animal health. Improved keeping quality of crops is one factor, however, that does seem to turn up in many reports (Pettersson 1977). Effect on animal health is also widely, albeit informally, reported, and is the reason most commonly cited by farmers for their transition to biological methods (Wernick and Lockeretz 1978). Can these effects be confirmed? If so, what are their economic and public health impacts? Further, what mechanisms can explain the differences—reduced reliance on feed concentrates and corn silage in biological husbandry, variations in chemical composition of crops raised on different fertilization programs, or other factors? Research directed at these questions has finally begun in earnest (Vogtmann 1981), but much more will be required to make up for the years when many of these questions were not considered realistic or relevant.

Many of these benefits translate into direct economic advantage for farmers as cash expenditures for fertilizers, pesticides, diesel fuel, and veterinary bills decline. Farmers do not miss the fact that with yields from biological agriculture generally comparable (with some crop by crop variation) with yields from conventional agriculture (Lockeretz *et al.* 1981), these conservation-minded strategies can mean equal or higher net income, even though most biological farmers market through conventional channels at conventional prices. There is also the indirect economic advantage of a halt to soil deterioration, and, in many cases, measurable improvement of farm soils. One might say that, at its best, biological agriculture is as much in the business of managed soil formation as it is in the business of growing food (Friend 1978B; Birdwell and Hole 1965; Albrecht 1956).

In a period when farmers are squeezed between rising input costs and mounting debt, not only can these advantages be significant, they might be the difference between staying in farming or selling out the farm. One might even speculate that the sort of diversification and reorganization of farm systems just discussed might make it possible for farmers to conceive of productive operations at a much lower level of capitalization and debt. As things stand today, industrialized agriculture is not only energy intensive, water intensive, and soil mining, it is "unsustainably overcapitalized" (Lovins and Lovins 1980).

If the comparative benefits of the "biological" approach, or components thereof, continue to be confirmed, as I expect they will, and if energy prices remain high and rise in the future, as I have no doubt they will, biological agriculture will continue to attract the attention of farmers who will incorporate its features into their practices. Some changes will be made relatively easily; others more slowly or with more difficulty. Some changes will be made willingly by farmers; others under some degree of regulatory compulsion (as with controls over "non-point" pollution).

For all of these levels of change, though, farmers need realistic assessments of what they can expect from different practices. That will require both a new level of awareness on the part of extension personnel and new research of a sort which, I suspect, will prove quite a challenge for existing research establishments to provide, as such a drastic reorientation in their thinking is required.

CONCLUSIONS

The summary importance of this array of strategies and techniques just described is their contribution to the stability, resilience, and flexibility of agro-ecosystems. In this unfolding historical period of shifting relative resource prices, shifting political power, shifting weather, and general uncertainty, resilience is a characteristic to be highly prized, whether in our agricultural systems, our energy systems, or our personal approaches to our daily lives. It is a worthwhile exercise to compare the characteristics of consciously designed polycultural systems, and of more conventionally structured biological agriculture units, with "state-of-the-art" modern agricultural units, in terms of Holling's (1978) criteria for system resilience: dispersion; numerical redundancy; functional redundancy; optional interconnection; flexibility; modularity; internal buffering; technical simplicity and forgivingness; easily reproduceable. The advantage society reaps from a more resilient agriculture may begin to be seen in the present but will really come in the future when, it is to be hoped, sustainable agriculture is the only kind practiced.

The key to achieving many of these characteristics, and to the development of the perspectives and strategies previously discussed, may require not only different ways of practicing agriculture but also different ways of thinking about it as well. Western science and technology have been very good at analyzing details of systems in isolation, in studying linear pathways of cause and effect—models that are quite powerful in dealing with physical and mechanical systems. But in biological systems, the linkages of cause and effect, of material and energy exchange, are complex networks; components interact in complex ways; and it can be difficult and even foolish to attempt to isolate single functions as separate from all others. Yet we persist in attempting to do so, and in so doing we remain blind to what Bateson (1979) called the "pattern which connects."

In order to move from modes of thought, and practices, that have given us solutions to problems that either create new problems—such as efficient feedlots that generate massive waste management problems—or that perversely worsen the problems they are meant to solve—such as air conditioners whose exhaust heat warms the city, increasing the need for air conditioners—we will have to move beyond definitions of problems that are so narrow that they are "either false or . . . virtually false" (Berry 1981B.)

Scientists need, then, to develop tools for looking at wholes that are as good as the tools they have had for looking at parts. If scientists are not up to the task—because, for example, some of the relationships that need further understanding do not lend themselves readily to statistical analysis and replication—they at least ought not condemn people who have found other ways to understand, design, and manage whole systems that can attend to quality as well as to quantity (Harwood 1981).

I return to the example of tropical shifting cultivators. Their agriculture is not "scientific," in our terms; but their understanding of the structure and dynamics of their ecosystems surpasses, in many ways, what our science has been able to achieve. Modern agriculture needs to emulate the sensitivity to pattern of such so-called primitive people. Biological agriculture may be as close as we have come, so far. Eventually, we too may learn that "knowledge will never replace respect in man's dealings with ecological systems" (Rappoport 1974).

In relation to the pressing world food situation, touched on earlier, biological agriculture may offer ways to increase food production without worsening environmental degradation—if wise agricultural professionals can persuade developing nations that they need not trade their futures for short-term production. Biological agriculture, because of its resource productivity, can do a better job in this realm than industrialized agriculture, and in a way that is ultimately more sustainable. The introduction of industrialized agriculture typically means the displacement of traditional systems and cultures and the loss of their generations of accumulated experience and wisdom. Biological agriculture, with its whole-systems perspective and inherent sensitivity to natural systems, can be effectively adapted to work with traditional systems. In that way, it becomes a true example of what E.F. Schumacher referred to as an "intermediate technology."

However one accounts for it, the rise of interest in biological agriculture is unmistakable, although not always labelled as such. Biological farmers are rising in numbers and are operating profitably throughout the world. The recent *USDA Report and Recommendations on Organic Farming* (USDA 1980) reversed official U.S. government hostility after USDA scientists took a look at existing organic practice and found it worthy of respect and additional study.

The media, sparked by the federal report, have discovered biological farmers everywhere (Taylor 1981) and found them hard to stereotype: like other farmers they farm large acreages or small, are conservative or liberal, are making good money or hitting hard times, but they are all practical people, who don't do things that don't work, whatever name those things go by.

The rising interest is widespread. In Europe, as well as in some parts of the United States, private farm advisory services have sprung up, and in some cases even small private research institutes, to provide farms with the kind of information they have found so hard to get from governmental and university extension services (Friend 1978A). In Japan, biological farmers nationally have organized sophisticated direct marketing links with urban consumers that conventional as well as biological farmers on this continent would do well to emulate (Forster 1981). A California central valley firm produces compost and supplies soil management advice for tens of thousands of acres of farmland; its clients consider themselves "conventional" farmers, but they are taking what is in fact "organic" advice—because it works (Swift 1980).

The International Federation of Organic Agriculture Movements (IFOAM)[1] has formed as a nongovernmental link among researchers and practitioners, with the goal, among others, of stimulating the research needed to confirm, understand, and advance the practice of biological agriculture.

In Nicaragua, where agriculture is being rebuilt and reorganized after a costly civil war, integrated pest management, biological techniques, and sophisticated polycultures are being looked toward as means of reducing the loss of foreign exchange to the importation of agrochemicals (Sweezy 1981).

The World Bank has also recognized that in many cases biological agriculture is the only practical way of improving the nutritional status of hungry populations in developing countries whose poor infrastructure

---

[1]IFOAM c/o Chateau, F-91730 Chamarande, France.

makes the timely transport and delivery of agricultural supplies impractical (Schumacher 1979).

Throughout the world, biological agriculture is becoming a serious option for the future. For we must recognize, as Breimyer (1977) writes, that "agriculture has an intergenerational dimension. It requires that a moral choice be made between generations—ours, and those of the future."

REFERENCES

ALBRECHT, W.A.   1956.   Physical, chemical, and biochemical changes in the soil community.   In Man's Role in Changing the Face of the Earth.   W.L. Thomas, Jr. (Editor).   University of Chicago Press.

ALEXANDER, M.   1974.   Environmental consequences of rapidly rising food output.   Agro-Ecosystems 1, 249–264.

ASA.   1976.   Multiple Cropping.   ASA Special Publication #27.   American Society of Agronomy.   Madison, Wisonsin.

AUBERT, C.   1977.   L'Agriculture Biologique.   Le Courrier Du Livre, Paris.

BARNEY, G.O.   1980.   The Global 2000 Report to the President: Entering the Twenty-First Century, Vol. 1.   U.S. Government Printing Office, Washington, D.C.

BATESON, G.   1979.   Mind and Nature: A Necessary Unity.   E.P. Dutton, New York.

BERRY, W.   1981A.   The making of a marginal farm.   In Recollected Essays, 1965–1980.   North Point Press, San Francisco.

BERRY, W.   1981B.   Solving for pattern: standards for a durable agriculture.   New Farm 3 (1), 70–72, January 1981.

BIRDWELL, O.W. and HOLE, F.D.   1965.   Man as a factor in soil formation.   Soil Science 99, 65–72.

BISHOP, J.P.   1978.   The development of a sustained yield tropical agroecosystem in the Upper Amazon.   Agro-Ecosystems 4, 459–461.

BREIMYER, H.F.   1977.   Biological man and social organization.   In Farm Policy: 13 Essays.   Iowa State University Press, Ames.

CHABOUSSOU, F.   1977.   Effects of pesticides on the biochemistry and resistance of the plant.   Acad. Agric. Fr. C. R. Seances 63 (5) 369–380.

CHABOUSSOU, F.   1980.   Les Plantes Malades des Pesticides: Bases Nouvelles d'une Prevention Contre Les Maladies et Parasites.   Editions Debard, Paris.

COMPTROLLER GENERAL.   1977.   To Protect Tomorrow's Food Supply, Soil Conservation Needs Priority Attention.   U.S. General Accounting Office report CED-77-30.   Washington, D.C.

FAULKNER, E.H.   1943.   Plowman's Folly.   University of Oklahoma Press, Norman.

FERREE, D.C.   1979.   Influence of pesticides on photosynthesis in crop plants.   In Photosynthesis and Plant Development.   R. Marcelle, H. Eligsters, and M. Van Poucke (Editors).   Dr. W. Junk Publishers, The Hague.

FORSTER, T.   1981.   Personal communication.

FREEMAN, P.H. and FRICKE, T.B.   1980.   Ecologically Oriented Agriculture.   Unpublished manuscript.

FRIEND, G.   1978A.   Biological agriculture in Europe.   CoEvolution Quarterly (17), Spring 1978.

FRIEND, G.   1978B.   Waste management, nutrient cycles, and a sustainable agriculture.   Paper presented at Second International Congress of Ecology, Jerusalem, September 1978.

FUKUOKA, M.   1978.   The One Straw Revolution.   Rodale, Emmaus, Pennsylvania.

GERRETSEN, F.C.   1948.   The influence of microorganisms on the phosphate intake of the plant.   Plant and Soil *1* (1), 51−81.

GIERE, J.P., JOHNSON, K.M., and PERKENS, J.   1980.   A closer look at no-till farming.   Environment *22* (6), 14−41.

GLEISSMAN, S.R.   1981.   The ecological basis for the application of traditional agricultural technology in the management of tropical agroecosystems.   Agro-Ecosystems (in press).

HARWOOD, R.R.   1980.   Organic farming and the scientific method.   New Farm *2* (3), 69−70, March/April 1980.

HARWOOD, R.R.   1981.   Helping researchers connect the pieces.   New Farm *3* (3), 44−45, March/April 1981.

HART, R.D.   1977.   A natural ecosystem analog approach to the design of successional crop systems for tropical forest environments.   Paper presented at AIBS symposium on tropical sucession.   East Lansing, Michigan, August 1977.

HODGES, R.   1978.   The case for biological agriculture.   Ecologist Quarterly.   Summer, pp. 122−143.

HOLLING, C.S.   1978.   Myths of ecological stability: resilience and the problems of failure.   *In* C.F. Smart and W.T. Stanbury (Editors).   Studies on Crisis Management, Butterworth for the Institute for Research on Public Policy, Montreal.

HOWARD, A.   1947.   The Soil and Health: A Study of Organic Farming.   Devin−Adair.   Old Greenwich, Conn.

HUNTER, J.M. and KWAKU NTIRI, G.   1978.   Speculations on the future of shifting agriculture in Africa.   Journal of Developing Areas 12 (2), 183−207.

KLEPPER, R., LOCKERETZ, W., COMMONER, B., GERTLER, M., FAST, J., O'LEARY, D., and BLOBAUM, R.   1977.   Economic performance and energy intensiveness on organic and conventional farms in the Corn Belt: a preliminary comparison.   American Journal of Agricultural Economics *59* (1), 1−12.

KOEPFF, H.H., PETTERSSON, B.D., and SCHAUMANN, W.   1977.   Biodynamic Agriculture.   Anthroposophic Press, Spring Valley, New York.

KRAUSS, H.A. and ALLMARAS, R.R.   1982.   Technology masks the effects of soil erosion on wheat yields: a case study in Whitman County, Washington.   *In* B.A. Schmidt (Editor).   Determinants of Soil Loss Tolerance.   Soil Science Society of America, Madison, Wisconsin.

LOCKERETZ, W., SHEARER, G., and KOHL, D.H.   1981.   Organic farming in the Corn Belt.   Science 211, 540−547.

LOVINS, A.B.   1977.   Soft Energy Paths: Toward a Durable Peace.   Ballinger, Cambridge.

LOVINS, A.B. and LOVINS, L.H.   1980.   If I Had a Hammer: Improving World Energy Productivity and Production.   Unpublished manuscript.

MacDANIELS, L.H. and LIEBERMAN, A.S.   1979.   Tree crops: a neglected source of food and forage from marginal lands.   BioScience 29 (3), 173−175.

MARGALEF, R.   1968.   Perspectives in Ecological Theory.   University of Chicago Press, Chicago.

McLEOD, E.J. and SWEEZY, S.L.   1979.   Survey of Weed Problems and Management Technologies in Organic Agriculture.   Unpublished manuscript.

MEADOWS, D.H., MEADOWS, D.L., RANDERS, J., and BEHRENS, W.L.   1972.   Limits to Growth.   Universe Books, New York.

MERRILL, R.   1974.   Mixed crops and companion planting.   In Energy Primer. Delta, New York.

MERRILL, R.   1980.   Personal communication.

MERRILL, R.   1981.   Some preliminary thoughts on a bioregional food system.   Raise the Stakes 1 (2), 13−14, Winter 1981.

MOLLISON, B.   1979.   Permaculture Two.   Practical Design for Town and Country in Permanent Agriculture.   Tagari, Stanley, Tasmania.

MOLLISON, B. and HOLMGREN, D.   1978.   Permaculture One.   A Perennial Agriculture for Human Settlements.   Transworld, Melbourne.

MUSICK, M.   1980.   Natural Farming—Tools and techniques.   Tilth 6 (3), 12−17, Fall/Winter 1980.

NAIR, P.K.   1977.   Multispecies crop combinations with tree crops for increased productivity in the tropics.   Die Gartenbauwissenschaft 42 (4), 145−150.

NATIONAL SCIENCE COUNCIL OF TAIWAN.   1980.   Science bulletin, October 1, 1979.   Quoted in L.S. Robertson.   A time for building bridges and mending fences.   Crops and Soils.   November 1980.

NYE, P.H. and GREENWALD, D.J.   1960.   The Soil under Shifting Cultivation.   Technical Communication #51.   Commonwealth Bureau of Soils, Henpenden, Farnham Royal, England.

OELHAF, R.   1978.   Organic Agriculture: Economic and Ecological Comparisons with Conventional Methods.   Halsted Press, New York.

PERRIN, R.M.   1977.   Pest management in multiple cropping systems.   Agro-Ecosystems 3 (2), 93−118.

PERRIN, R.M. and PHILLIPS, M.C.   1978.   Some effects of mixed cropping on the population dynamics of insect pests.   Entomologia Experimentalis et Applicata 24 (3), 585−593.

PETTERSSON, B.   1977.   A report on six years' work in Sweden to compare "conventional" and bio-dynamic farming methods by the use of standard

quality parameters on plant products.   IFOAM, Sissach, Switzerland.
PHILLIPS, R.E., BEVINS, R.L., THOMAS, J.W., FRYE, W.W., and PHILLIPS,
S.H.   1980.   No-tillage agriculture.   Science 208, 1108–1113.
PIMENTEL, D., DRITSCHILO, W., KRUMMEL, J., and KUTZMANJ.   1975.
Energy and land constraints in food protein production.   Science *190*, 754–
761.
PIMENTEL, D., TERHUNE, E.C., DYSON–HUDSON, R., ROCHEREAU, S.,
SAMIS, R., SMITH, E., DENMAN, D., REIFSCHNEIDER, D., and SHEP-
ARD, M.   1976.   Land degradation: effects on food and energy resources.
Science *194*, 149–155.
PIMENTEL, D., MORAN, M., FAST, S., WEGG, J., BUKANTES, R., BEL-
LIETT, L., BOVING, P., CLEVELAND, C., HINDMAN, S., and YOUNG, M.
1981. Biomass energy from crop and forest residues.   Science *212*, 1110–
1115.
RAPPOPORT, R.   1974.   Sanctity and adaptation.   CoEvolution Quarterly
(2), Summer 1974.
ROOT, R.B.   1973.   Organization of a plant-arthropod association in simple
and diverse habitats: the fauna of collards (Brassica olerace).   Ecological
Monographs *43*, 95–124.
ROOT, R.B.   1975.   Some consequences of ecosystem texture. S.A. Levin (Edi-
tor).   Ecosystem Analysis and Prediction.   Proceedings of a SIAM-SIMA
Conference, Alta, Utah, July 1–5, 1974.   Society for Industrial and Applied
Mathematics, Philadelphia.
ROSE, D.J.   1981.   Continuity and change: thinking in new ways about large
and persistent problems.   Technology Review 83 (4), 53–67.
RUSSELL SMITH, J.   1929.   Tree Crops—A Permanent Agriculture.   Har-
court Brace, New York.
SCHUMACHER, A.   1979.   Personal communication.
SHOLTO–DOUGLAS, J. and HART, R.A. deJ.   1976.   Forest Farming.   Wat-
kins, London.
SPURGEON, D.   1980.   The promise of agroforestry.   American Forests 85
(10), 20–23.
SWEEZY, S.   1981.   Personal communication.
SWIFT, C.   1980.   Personal communication.
TAYLOR, R.B.   1981.   Are pesticides really necessary?   Los Angeles Times,
26 April 1981,   p. F10.
TOSCANO, N.C., SENCIS, F.V., JOHNSON, M.W., and LaPRE, L.F.   1982.
The effect of various pesticides on lettuce physiology and yield.   Journal
of Economic Entomology.   In press.
USDA.   1958.   Agricultural Statistics.   U.S. Government Printing Office,
Washington, D.C.
USDA.   1979.   Agricultural Statistics.   U.S. Government Printing Office,
Washington, D.C.
USDA.   1980.   Report and Recommendations on Organic Farming.   USDA,
Washington, D.C.
VOGTMANN, H.   1981.   The quality of produce originating from different
systems of cultivation.   Soil Association.

WALTERS, C.   1975.   The Case for Eco-Agriculture.   Acres, USA, Raytown, Missouri.

WALTERS, C. and FENZAU, C.J.   1979.   An Acres USA Primer.   Acres, USA, Raytown, Missouri.

WATT, K.E.F.   1973.   Principles of Environmental Science.   McGraw-Hill, New York.

WERNICK, S., and LOCKERETZ, W.   1978.   Motivations and practices of organic farmers.   Soil Association Quarterly Review 4 (3), 1-6.

3

The New Consumers: Food Habits and the Basis of Choice

Tom R. Watkins

INTRODUCTION

A link between diet and disease has been known for years, and the public seems aware of it. Polls have been conducted by national pollsters, and general news magazines have carried feature stories about Americans' poor eating habits. Many popular books have appeared on bookstall shelves promising better health through diet (Yudkin 1964; Williams 1978; Wade 1978). The consumer has become more aware and interested in the link. Subsequently, the shopper has begun to choose foods at the market that are believed to promote health to a greater extent than foods formerly popular in the market. However, in light of the changes in food consumption patterns in the United States in the past 50 years (Brewster and Jacobson 1978) and concomitant increases in the incidence of debilitating diseases (Senate Select Committee 1974), one can conclude that the consumer might further refine food choices for health.

Changing food intake and its relation to deteriorating health has been brought to public attention by the White House Conference on Food, Nutrition and Health (1968) and the Health and Nutrition Examination Survey (1972). Recently increased incidence of hypertension, cardiovascular disease, obesity, dental caries, and cancer, all of which raise morbidity and lower mortality statistics, were documented. The food intake data reported in these surveys has showed that large numbers of people, irrespective of income group, eat poor diets, that is, diets providing less than two-thirds of the U.S. Recommended Daily Allowances for several nutrients, including iron, ascorbic acid, and vitamin A, based upon the Recommended Dietary Allowances set by the National Academy of Sciences Food and Nutrition Board (NAS 1980A).

Overnutrition has also been documented by these reports, such as overconsumption of calories, fat, saturated fat, salt, and sugar; in fact, overnutrition has been considered a greater health threat to the public than undernutrition. Large changes occurring in the American diet in the past 50 years have been implicated in this overnutrition. It has become high in calories, fat, saturated fat, sugar, salt (sodium), and cholesterol. The percentage of calories supplied by sugar has increased, as starch intake decreased, and the total energy intake has decreased somewhat (Friend 1967). In addition, the proportion of dietary energy from fat has also risen. Consumption of refined foods such as colas, candy, and snack foods—foods typically rich in sugar, fat, and/or salt but generally devoid of other nutrients—has also increased in this period. In the same period, Americans have become exceedingly sedentary, expending less energy (Hegsted 1979). This sort of diet has been associated with increased incidence of obesity, coronary disease, diabetes, and some types of cancer in America and also in Europe, South Africa, and other regions.

DIETARY GOALS AND DIETARY GUIDELINES

In light of increased death rates from these diseases, which have an implicated nutritional etiologic factor, the Senate Select Committee on Nutrition and Human Needs convened to collate the available evidence about the diet–disease relationship and issued the Dietary Goals for the United States (U.S. Senate 1977A). These were first issued in February 1977; later, they were revised and reissued with minor changes in December 1977 (U.S. Senate 1977B). The Committee recommended that Americans:

1. Increase carbohydrate consumption to account for 55 to 60 percent of the energy (caloric) intake.
2. Reduce overall fat consumption from approximately 40 to 30 percent of energy intake.

3. Reduce saturated fat consumption to account for about 10 percent of total energy intake; and balance that with polyunsaturated and mono-unsaturated fats, which should account for about 10 percent of energy intake each.
4. Reduce cholesterol consumption to about 300 mg a day.
5. Reduce sugar consumption by about 40 percent to account for about 15 percent of total energy intake.
6. Reduce salt consumption by about 50 to 85 percent to approximately 3 grams a day.

They suggested the following changes in food selection and preparation:

1. Increase consumption of fruits and vegetables and whole grains.
2. Decrease consumption of meat and increase consumption of poultry and fish.
3. Decrease consumption of foods high in fat and partially substitute polyunsaturated fat for saturated fat.
4. Substitute non-fat milk for whole milk.
5. Decrease consumption of butterfat eggs, and other high cholesterol sources.
6. Decrease consumption of sugar and foods high in sugar content.
7. Decrease consumption of salt and foods high in salt content.

In 1980 the U.S. Department of Agriculture and the U.S. Department of Health and Human Services jointly issued another set of dietary guides, Nutrition and Your Health: Dietary Guidelines for Americans (USDA and HHR 1980), which recommended changes qualitatively similar to the Dietary Goals.

The Dietary Guidelines differ little from the Dietary Goals but are a joint recommendation from USDA and HHS. The Guidelines offer no quantitative advice; each recommendation exhorts one to moderate eating habits for a class of foods in a certain direction, somewhat on the order of the Greeks' "Golden Mean." One point on which the Guidelines contrast with the Goals is the emphasis given to exercise as an adjunct to diet to control weight; another is that the Guidelines specify caloric values for common activities to enable a person to calculate caloric expenditure.

The Dietary Guidelines for Americans can be succinctly stated:

1. Eat a variety of foods.
2. Maintain ideal weight.
3. Avoid too much fat, saturated fat and cholesterol.
4. Eat foods with adequate starch and fiber.
5. Avoid too much sugar.
6. Avoid too much sodium.
7. If you drink alcohol, do so in moderation.

One can see the striking similarity in intent in the two sets of dietary guides. The Dietary Guidelines for Americans, the more recent of the two, has been more widely distributed and is currently used.

NATURAL, ORGANIC, AND HEALTH FOODS

As consumers have tried to find the appropriate foods to promote optimal health, they have sought foods that offer what they believe to be optimal nutrition with greatest safety. Some of these have been labeled natural, organic, and health foods. Unfortunately, these terms have been used in multiple senses, so that considerable confusion clouds their usage (Consumer Reports 1980). Currently, no legal definitions exist, which means that any advertising claims, justified or not, may not be regulated. In an effort to regulate advertising claims, the Federal Trade Commission has issued a definition for *natural* applied to food. However, functional definitions will be presented here. First, *natural* has more than 30 definitions in Webster's Third International Dictionary, several of which apply to food (Webster 1961). *Natural* foods have been described as being foods in the same form as they were harvested, hence they are unprocessed (Leverton 1974). Marshall has defined natural foods and ingredients as those substances made by nature. Although the substance may have been processed, it has not been modified in a chemical sense (Marshall 1974). The natural food ingredient must not have been modified for efficiency of processing. A natural food is one made only from ingredients recognized as foods (FTC 1978). This sense of *natural* conforms with its medieval sense of anything that has not been interfered with, such as wood before it is carved or raw vegetables (Lewis 1967).

The sense of *natural food* in usage in commerce now is recognized to mean a minimally processed food, which processing includes washing, cutting, peeling, grinding, separating, homogenizing, and the like, or one that has been made edible or preserved by baking, canning, bottling, fermenting, or pasteurizing and to which no artificial ingredients have been added (Clancy 1980; FTC 1978). This standard also prohibits claims that natural foods are nutritionally superior to or safer than other foods.

The term *organic* has been widely used in food advertisements having considerable consumer clout, but it has diverse meanings. Organic refers to the method of growing foods. In this case, the IFT Expert Panel on Food Safety and Nutrition has defined organic food as food that has been grown with only animal manure and/or composted materials (Anon. 1974). Leverton (1974) has defined organic food as any food containing carbon, but organically grown food as food that has not been subjected to chemical pesticides or mineral fertilizers and has been grown in soil whose humus has been increased by added organic materials. A comprehensive, recently proposed definition (Knorr 1982) is: food resulting from an agricultural production system (organic farming) that avoids or largely excludes the use of (synthetic) agricultural chemicals and relies on the use of organic matter and biological pest control.

Organic and *natural* have been used somewhat interchangeably, as when university and industry scientists apply the label natural to the method of growing consumable plant crops, to the general confusion of the consumer. This ambiguity has been documented in detail in testimony before the Federal Trade Commission (FTC 1978).

The term *health food* has not been defined adequately either, if indeed it can be reasonably defined. Marshall has defined health foods as those believed to be beneficial in promoting physiological and psychological well-being and insuring resistance to stress, infection, and disease (Marshall

1974). A health food has also been defined as any food that retains all of its nutritionally desirable constituents and has not had added any substance that is harmful (Sinclair 1976). As one would more appropriately speak of healthy diets, one would similarly be on safer ground speaking about health foods, plural. Adequate nutrition depends upon variety in a mix of foods, all taken together promoting health.

The use of these terms in multiple senses has somewhat clouded the issue of why people have chosen to eat these foods. Of the multifarious reasons for choosing to eat specific foods, perhaps the outstanding one has been the implied superior nutritional content. Other consumers choose such foods for reasons of food safety, as pointed out by Bates (1981). In overall terms, consumers perceive natural, organic and health foods as better in some respect than traditional, nonnatural foods (Anon. 1974; Leinen 1978), often stating that good food promotes good health.

THE NEW CONSUMERS AND ALTERNATE MARKETS

Consumers shop in markets other than traditional supermarkets, since these natural, organic and health foods have not been readily available in traditional markets. For some consumers, the alternate market as the retail outlet of choice has been necessitated as part of a spiritual revitalization of total lifestyle, which includes shopping where the so-called vital foods are sold, such as the health food stores. These consumers see a strong diet–disease link and hence wish to buy the proper medicaments, which are sold at the health food stores (Marshall 1974). Other consumers shopping alternate markets feel compelled to seek organic and natural foods because they have been grown without synthetic fertilizers and other energy-intensive processing, additive, and packaging technologies (Pimentel and Pimentel 1979; Null 1978). For such consumers, shopping in the natural/organic food store represents a stand to protect the environment and their bodies from further pollution and also to conserve energy. Still another group of consumers, members of cooperatives and food-buying clubs, may have joined for economic reasons, for fear of loss of nutritional value in traditionally processed foods, as well as a desire to return to a more meaningful, simpler life that is more family oriented (Marshall 1974). For whatever reasons, these consumers shop alternate markets in order to obtain the food quality and safety that they perceive appropriate, and they will pay 10% or more over supermarket prices to receive this food quality, whether the purported differences in safety and nutritional quality can be or have been documented (Oelhaf 1978; Wells 1979; Consumer Reports 1980).

Most consumers, regardless of market type, claim to know enough about food to choose a health-insuring diet. Yet the high incidence of debilitating diseases and associated mortality in the United States compared with other countries suggests that consumers may not know all that they claim to know or that they are not sufficiently motivated to change food habits. In studies undertaken to determine the value of food and nutrient labeling, consumers were unable to define what they claimed to know about food or to relate it to daily needs (Jacoby *et al.* 1977). Further, consumers cannot estimate food portions accurately. In a sample of 26 university students studying food science or nutritional science, in which each was asked to estimate portions of food in common portion (and metric) units, students typically made large errors in portion estimates. Errors ranged to 50% over or under actual values, with the underestimates typically being foods of high caloric density (Watkins and Lea 1980). Because of this and other complications and inaccuracies in 24-hour dietary recall information purported to be quantitative (Beaton *et al.* 1979), consumers responding in this survey were asked to report frequency of food consumption.

The proportion of meals taken away from home has been increasing sharply since 1971, especially the dollars spent in sit-down restaurants. A.C. Nielsen, Inc., analyzed grocery and restaurant business trends, reporting that 40 cents of every food dollar was spent in restaurants in 1977 (Shaw and Pinto 1978). In another study, the increase of business done by smaller stores was also reported (Rinde 1980). In addition to the smaller stores polled in this survey, other small retail outlets included alternate markets, here defined as bantam markets, organic and health food stores, cooperatives, roadside or farmers' markets, and natural food stores. They now claim more than one billion dollars of food market expenditures annually (Eagle 1980), which is 3% of the total retail food expense.

TYPES OF TRADITIONAL AND ALTERNATE MARKETS

In moving from traditional eating habits toward alternate food choices, consumers have opted for other retail outlets and food products. For example, they have begun to shop in cooperative markets that tend to buy more locally produced truck and maintain more stringent inventory control and quality control in terms of freshness. By performing the retail functions of procuring, weighing, packaging, and stocking for sale themselves, they save money on the food bill. Although most of these cooperatives have relatively small membership rosters, numbering in the hundreds, some have grown to the size of independent grocers. By performing the retail function themselves, consumers in 25 New York City buying clubs saved an average of 33% over traditional supermarket prices (transportation and time not calculated) (Gallo 1977).

Another market option has been the natural or health food store, the chief distinguishing feature being its sale of vitamins and minerals, representing as much as 40% of the total revenues (Oelhaf 1978).

Yet another market option has been the roadside stand in which the farmer markets directly to the consumer. This market type has been supported by the U.S. Government with the Farmer-to-Consumer Direct Marketing Act, 1976 (Lindstrom and Henderson 1979), which was designed to support and promote direct marketing of farm products. These markets offer fruits and vegetables as the main products. The total crop moved through this channel represents a small proportion of the total, the most revenue derived in the United States by direct marketing being in New Jersey, where 8% of revenues were generated this way (Lindstrom and Henderson 1979).

Perhaps the simplest alternative to the supermarket has been the home garden. The numbers of gardens in the United States, 25 million in 1971, rose to 32 million in 1978, located on suburban plots, vacant city lots, backyards and apartment balconies. Forty-three percent of all families had some kind of garden; the cultivated land totaled seven million acres (Stokes 1978). A USDA survey reported 44% of the sampled households maintained a garden. From these data, the 1976 garden production estimate was set at 11% of total production, a rather generous number (Kaite 1977). Home gardens were included with the roadside, health food, and cooperatives in the alternate market class in this survey.

Analyses of commodities in these alternate retail food markets and traditional shops showed that the alternates offer foods at considerably higher prices. A survey in the *New York Times* of traditional and health food stores in the city showed that prices differed by 7 to 61% for a 34-item shopping list, compared on a brand basis where possible (Wells 1979). Other reports of higher prices have appeared that attribute higher health food store prices to larger retail markups and gross margins, and not to farm production costs. Gross margins in health food stores averaged 34% in contrast with 21% for supermarkets (Oelhaf 1978). The main reasons cited for the differences were (small) scale economies in processing, transportation, and retailing and brand loyalty or quality differences.

In light of the changing food habits in the last 50 years, and the consumer's search for health-promoting and safe foods—now a chief concern among organic food shoppers (Bates 1981)—one would wish to know how the traditional and alternate shoppers choose food at the market. This would permit eventual comparison of their food choices and the bases for them, which might be useful in educating consumers about food and revealing some salient features about consumers in alternate food stores.

FOOD SURVEY

A market survey was conducted by the author to learn about consumers' food choices (Watkins 1980). Survey results were compared with reference dietary guides such as the Dietary Goals for the United States and the Dietary Guidelines for Americans (USDA and HHS 1980). Consumers were polled about food choice in four different kinds of markets: the traditional supermarket and the alternates: the cooperative market, or food buying club; the natural food store; and the roadside stand, which here included farmers' markets and home gardens. By asking questions about the frequency of intake of groups of foods, rather than foods styled "natural," "organic," or "health" food, the definitional problems associated with these terms could be circumvented. From these data and dietary guides, one can compare the shoppers' food habits in traditional and alternate markets and compare the trends with recommendations in the guides.

THE SAMPLE

This exploratory study was done in five cities in the fall of 1979: Newark, Delaware; Memphis, Tennessee; Phoenix, Arizona; San Jose, California; and Seattle, Washington. These cities were chosen in different regions of the country and ranged in size from 40,000 to 1,000,000 so that the data would be drawn from diverse groups. The 162 respondents answered the survey questions in or near the markets where they shopped, being casually approached by the interviewer at various times of day and on different days of the week. The purpose was to gather some evidence from consumers at the marketplace about that particular type of market. Although these consumers were questioned about their food buying habits in the market-place, they responded to questions about total food purchases, not foods purchased soley at that particular store. Some of the alternate markets sell little or no meat; however, the food intake data included all of their buys, at the market where the poll was conducted and elsewhere. Although the consumers were polled in cities less than and greater than 100,000 and in widely separated geographical regions, no claims are here made that these data clearly reflect regional or city differences.

Some salient features of the sample follow. Four of five consumers polled in supermarkets were female; and three-fourths of the shoppers in alternate markets including farmers' markets, food cooperatives, and natural food stores were women. Most shoppers polled were in the third to fifth decade of life. Twelve percent of the total sample was 12 to 19 years of age. Looking at the shoppers according to age, one sees that 47% of all shoppers were between 20 and 35 years of age; 27% were 36−50 years old. Further, roughly 13−25% of the sampled population for each market type was 50 years of age or older. Supermarket shoppers included 14% in the 12−19 years category, and 13% in the over-50 category. A larger proportion of respondents were young and middle-aged adults polled in the alternate markets; a larger percentage of teenagers was polled in traditional markets.

Over 94% of the sample was Caucasian. The rest were Black, Hispanic, American Indian, or American Oriental.

Education

The shoppers in alternate markets generally had completed about the same number of years of schooling as the traditional shoppers. The distribution of traditional supermarket shoppers by schooling last completed was broad, including 10% who had finished grade school and 28% who had at least four years of college. The typical alternate market shopper polled had completed high school, with most having studied in college for two years. Two-thirds of the supermarket regulars had completed two or more years of college; 57% of alternate shoppers polled had finished two years. However, more of the latter had continued their studies: 43% of the alternates had completed four or more years of college study in contrast with 28% for the supermarket group polled.

Job

On the basis of the differences in the highest level of school completed, one would expect that proportionally more shoppers in supermarkets than alternate shoppers might serve in trade jobs and those involving manual labor, with correspondingly fewer in white collar business and professional work. More than 70% of shoppers in alternate markets were in business or professional work. In contrast, 52% of shoppers in traditional markets worked in business and professional jobs. Ten percent of supermarket shoppers reported holding manual labor jobs or trades work; fewer than 5% of alternate consumers reported so doing. Twenty percent of alternates reported working in the home or being unemployed or retired, twice the proportion of those frequenting traditional markets.

The emphasis on college training by alternate shoppers was also seen in modest differences in the proportion of respondents with household incomes over $16,000 per year: 28% of traditionals versus 36% of alternates. However, cooperative shoppers polled reported lower incomes. Only 12% of cooperative shoppers fell into these upper income classes. Small, but insignificant, differences also existed in the proportion of shoppers in each market type in the less-than-$16,000 classes: 72% of traditional compared with 64% of alternate shoppers.

Meals Away from Home

Shoppers in alternate markets, here including cooperatives, natural food stores, and roadside stands/farmers' markets, tended to eat away from home about as frequently as traditional shoppers. For example, 78% of traditional shoppers reported eating away from home up to three times per week; alternates, 85%. Fifteen percent of traditionals ate away four to six times per week, compared with just 2% of alternates who ate away from home so frequently. Less than 10% reported eating away from home seven or more times per week in either class of market.

Survey of Food Habits

Let us now compare the results of this survey qualitatively with the Dietary Guidelines for the United States in order to compare dietary habits of consumers in different market types with the Goals. Comparisons will be by generic food group such as fruits and vegetables, red meat, fish and fowl, dairy products, bread and cereals, and vitamins. Comparisons will be of the supermarket consumer, the cooperative shopper, the natural food store

customer, and the roadside/farmers' market shopper. Shoppers at food cooperatives, natural food stores, and farmers' markets and those having home
gardens will be classed as alternate shoppers; supermarket shoppers will be
styled traditional shoppers. Food intake has been reported as the number of
times an item is eaten per week, assuming similar portion sizes on the
average.

Fruit and Vegetables.   Alternate market shoppers sampled eat fruits
and vegetables more frequently than traditional shoppers. Two-thirds of
the traditional shoppers at the supermarket reported eating vegetables and
fruit eight or more times per week (Table 3.1). All alternate shoppers
reported more frequent intake of vegetables and fruits: of cooperative
members, 93% eating them eight or more times per week; roadside shoppers, 89%; and natural store customers, 100% (Fig. 3.1). Although 7% of the
supermarket shoppers claimed to eat vegetables only once or twice per
week, none of the alternate shoppers reported such infrequent vegetable
consumption.

Meat.   Traditional shoppers reported consuming meat such as beef,
lamb, pork, veal, and organ meats more frequently than the alternate
shoppers (Table 3.1). Largest differences in frequency of consumption appeared in the groups eating red meat less than three times per week. Thirty
percent of traditional shoppers ate red meat infrequently, whereas about
half (48%) of alternate shoppers polled reported such infrequent red meat
consumption. Within alternate shoppers, 62% of coop and 75% of natural
food store respondents claimed to eat meat so infrequently. A similar trend
was documented for persons eating red meat three to seven times per
week: traditionals, 59%; alternates, 39% (Fig. 3.2).

Red Meat.   An additional question appearing at the end of the questionnaire asked whether or not the respondent consumes red meat; this served
as an internal check on the (earlier) meat question. Responses to this query
corroborated the meat question data. Supermarket customers are predominantly red meat eaters; only 6% reported not eating red meat. In contrast,
26% of alternates reported eating red meat. These data confirmed the

TABLE 3.1.   FOOD CONSUMPTION IN TRADITIONAL AND ALTERNATE MARKETS

Weekly Frequency	Fruit & vegetable (%)	Meat (%)	Bread (%)	Milk (%)	Fowl & fish (%)	Legumes & nuts (%)	Vitamins (%)
	Traditional ($N = 116$)						
3	5.1	29.3	10.3	2.6	37.9	44.8	49.1
3–7	28.4	54.8	34.5	24.1	55.2	37.1	16.4
7+	66.4	12.9	55.2	73.3	6.9	18.1	34.5
	Alternate ($N = 46$)						
3	2.2	47.8	0	8.7	56.5	8.7	28.3
3–7	8.7	39.2	44.4	17.4	43.5	50.0	17.4
7+	89.1	13.0	55.6	73.9	0	41.3	54.3

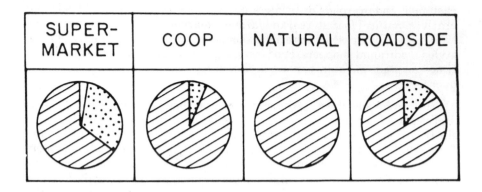

SUPER-MARKET	COOP	NATURAL	ROADSIDE

☐ 1-2   ▦ 3-7   ▨ 8 or more

TIMES EATEN PER WEEK

FIG. 3.1.   FRUIT AND VEGETABLE INTAKE

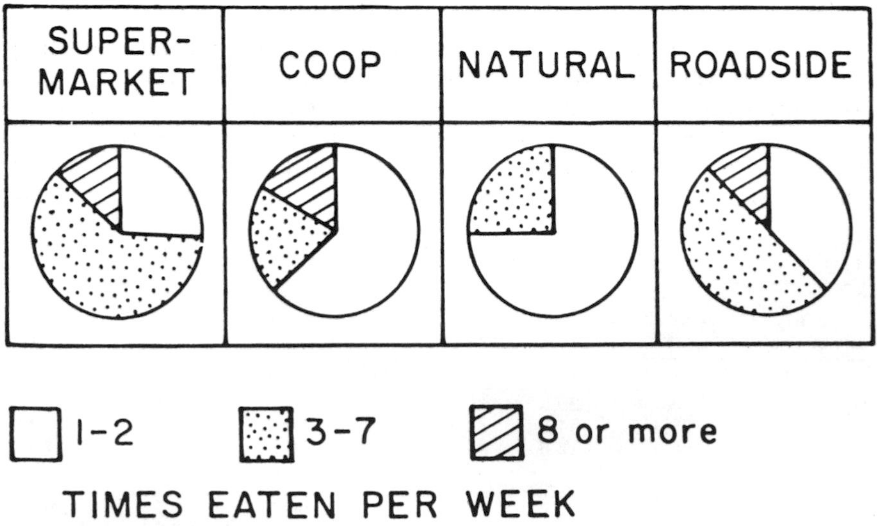

SUPER-MARKET	COOP	NATURAL	ROADSIDE

☐ 1-2   ▦ 3-7   ▨ 8 or more

TIMES EATEN PER WEEK

FIG. 3.2.   RED MEAT INTAKE

responses in general for the frequency of red meat consumption earlier in the questionnaire. Hence, the internal consistency of the data about red meat and meat intake tends to lend credibility to the survey overall.

Fish and Fowl.   In terms of non-red meat consumption, fish and fowl were grouped together. The responses of consumers about poultry and seafood intake showed remarkable differences between shoppers at the four types of markets. In general, the traditional shoppers reported consuming fish and fowl more frequently than customers of alternate markets. For example, the data in Table 3.1 show that 7% of traditional shoppers polled reported eating fowl or fish more than seven times per week; 55%, three to seven times; and 38%, two or fewer times per week. Alternate shoppers reported that they rarely consume fish or fowl daily; fish or fowl do not replace the red meats they do not eat. Fifty-seven percent reported eating fish or fowl less than three times weekly, and 43% three to seven times (see also Fig. 3.3).

Legumes and Nuts.   Besides large differences in frequency of eating meat, fish and fowl, consumers differed in their consumption of legumes, including beans, peas, and nuts (Table 3.1). Much larger proportions of alternate market customers reported regular bean consumption than was the case for supermarket consumers. Legume consumption distinguishes traditional and alternate shoppers perhaps more markedly than other foods. Nearly half of the traditional shoppers (46%) reported eating legumes less than three times per week; 36% eat them three to seven times per week; and 19% reported eating them more often than once daily. Only 9% of

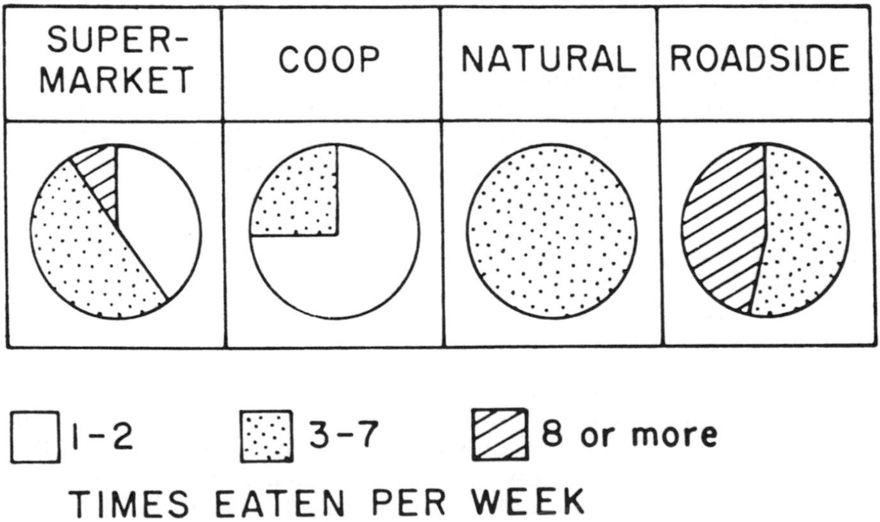

FIG. 3.3.   FISH AND FOWL INTAKE

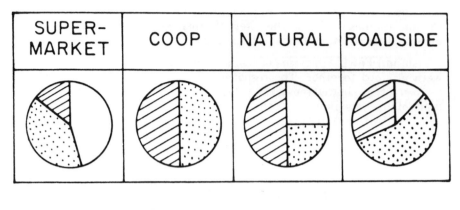

| SUPER-MARKET | COOP | NATURAL | ROADSIDE |

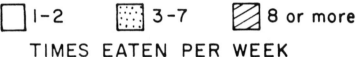

☐ 1-2   ⬚ 3-7   ▨ 8 or more

TIMES EATEN PER WEEK

FIG. 3.4.   BEAN INTAKE

alternate shoppers eat legumes less often than three times per week; half reported eating legumes or nuts every other day; and 41% claimed to eat them daily, twice the proportion of traditionals (see also Fig. 3.4).

Bread, Cereals, and Pastas. Because of the central place of bread in the diet, nearly all polled would be expected to eat bread regularly. The data confirmed this: half of the respondents reported eating bread daily (Table 3.1). When consumer bread consumption frequencies were cross-tabulated with market type, large differences occurred by market type for people who eat bread. Some traditional shoppers reported eating bread only once or twice a week; all alternate shoppers reported eating bread at least three times weekly. More than half of all shoppers polled reported eating bread eight times weekly or more often, in all markets (Fig. 3.5). In the three to seven times per week category, a larger percentage of alternate shoppers responded in this class than the traditional shoppers: 44% of alternates compared with only 34% of traditionals. The general trend of the data shows that the alternate shoppers tended to rely somewhat more upon bread as a mainstay in the diet.

Milk, Cheese, and Yogurt. As in the data about bread consumption, frequency of milk consumption showed smaller overall differences for shoppers classed according to market type than in the cases of fruits, meats, fish and fowl, legumes, and vitamins (Table 3.1). High percentages of all shoppers reported drinking milk daily or more often: 73% of supermarket shoppers and 74% of alternates (Fig. 3.5). Few of the traditional shoppers, 3%,

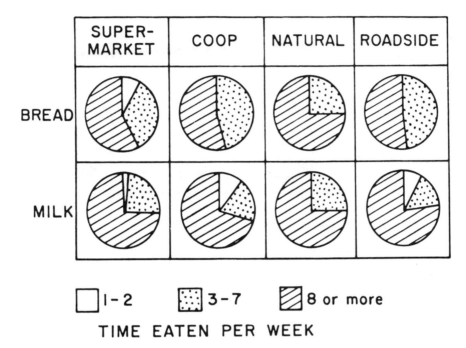

|-2   3-7   8 or more

TIME EATEN PER WEEK

FIG. 3.5.   BREAD AND MILK INTAKE

and a slightly larger proportion, 9%, of the alternate market customers reported drinking milk or eating yogurt or other dairy products less than three times per week. In the three-to-seven-times weekly category, fewer alternate shoppers responded in this class than traditional shoppers' responses: 17% versus 24%, respectively. These data corroborate the typical American's regular consumption of milk products on a daily basis.

Vitamins. The other distinguishing food habit about which these consumers were polled was multiple or single vitamin and mineral usage (Table 3.1). Traditional shoppers use vitamins less than the shoppers at alternate markets. For example, half of them (48%) reported taking pills less than three times per week, 17% three to seven times per week, and 34% daily or more often. In contrast, of the customers polled in the alternate markets, more than half (54%) reported daily vitamin usage, with 17% using supplements on alternate days and just 28% using vitamins less than three times per week. These differences in reported use of vitamins suggest that the alternate shoppers consider vitamins important to health and the diet limited, apparently incomplete, without a daily vitamin supplement. They may consider that a diet of whole food cannot provide for all body nutrient needs. Hence, they consume vitamins in tablet form. Further research should be done to confirm this (see also Fig. 3.6).

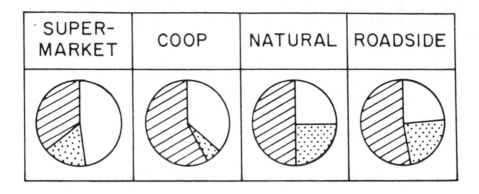

TIMES EATEN PER WEEK

FIG. 3.6.   VITAMIN INTAKE

The increased vitamin usage by alternate shoppers deserves further attention. First, since these consumers have reported more frequent vegetable and fruit intake than the traditional consumer, and fruits and vegetables represent rich sources of many vitamins and minerals, then one might expect less frequent vitamin usage by the alternate shoppers. Further, vitamins represent highly processed foods, in contrast to the trend toward less processed foods by alternates. The reported more-frequent consumption of vegetables represents greater reliance upon minimally processed foods. One may also speculate that this high vegetable diet coupled with non-use of red meat by a larger percentage of alternates suggests a trend toward vegetable-based dietaries. See Fig. 3.7 for a summary of food intake data by market type.

SOURCES OF INFORMATION AFFECTING FOOD CHOICE

Traditional and alternate market shoppers sampled relied upon different sources of information in choosing food. Traditional shoppers reported using various sources of information about food. One-third of them read books about food; 27% obtained guiding advice in school; 17% relied upon friends for nutrition education; about the same proportion, 15%, used news media; 6% took government advice from pamphlets. On the other hand alternate market customers rarely depended upon government, news media, or school sources of information about food: merely 17% reported such sources. Although 83% polled relied upon books and/or friends, only 51% of traditionals did.

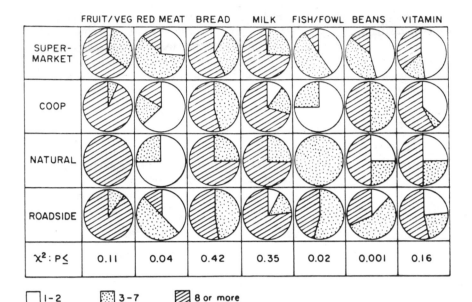

	FRUIT/VEG	RED MEAT	BREAD	MILK	FISH/FOWL	BEANS	VITAMIN
SUPER-MARKET							
COOP							
NATURAL							
ROADSIDE							
$x^2 : p \le$	0.11	0.04	0.42	0.35	0.02	0.001	0.16

□ 1-2   ▦ 3-7   ▨ 8 or more
TIMES EATEN PER WEEK

FIG. 3.7.   FOOD CONSUMPTION BY MARKET TYPE

Few of either the alternate shoppers or traditional market regulars claimed to place much stock in government reports or school-supplied information. Whether this means that these have not been exposed to government literature or will not accept the advice is unclear. However, on the basis of informal interviews with consumers, these shoppers tend to reject government nutrition advice.

The data presented by these shoppers do not reveal whether the information which they used in making food choices was accurate. Yet the food choice patterns above suggest that in terms of general health, the habits of the alternate shoppers may be more salutary than those of the traditional shoppers, using as a reference standard the Dietary Goals or the newer guide, "Nutrition and Your Health: Dietary Guidelines for Americans" (USDA and HHW 1980). A large number of popular nutrition and diet books contain misinformation apparently unrecognized as such by the consumer (Brisset and Lewis 1979).

The precise source of information that compelled the shopper to seek food in alternate shops is not clear. However, whether taught at college or by college-associated stimulation, the alternate shopper had studied food and was more motivated to modify food source adequately and to change markets.

Knowing the trend of food intake patterns at the different types of markets, what might one say about the reasons behind them? An attempt has been made in this study to determine the general bases for food choice by the shopper. The economic exchange between the customer and the seller involves people, and hence the interaction may lend itself to analysis as in the case of other social interactions, whether or not the two parties know each other well personally.

BASIS OF MARKET CHOICE

In describing the interaction between two or more people in a society, Eric Berne in *Games People Play* (1964) has pointed out that the exchange can be classified as characteristic of children, pleasure based; similar to child-parent interaction, authority based; or typical of decision-making, interacting adults, cybernetic based. With this transactional analytic approach, the following paradigm was set up to describe food choice. The questionnaire offered the consumer three responses to justify a food choice: *taste*, a hedonic, pleasure-referenced criterion; *home*-derived input, analogous to an authority-referenced interaction; or *outside*, nonhome information, constraint-based factors more nearly typical of a factually based, decision-weighted operation such as recent information, time, or money constraints. If one could ascertain the mental operational basis of consumer food choices, food choice could be modified, possibly by other techniques that do not rely upon taste alone or upon the standard approach of teaching a list of nutrients in foods; or others might be developed. With this three-step criteria paradigm before them, the consumers explained their food choices.

Fruit and Vegetables.   Palatability plays an important role in the consumers' food choosing habits. Alternate shoppers may have been guided more by other factors than taste. Most consumers relied upon taste in choosing fruits and vegetables (Table 3.2). The percentages in the taste category by market were: supermarket, 52%; alternate, 44%. More super-

TABLE 3.2.   BASIS FOR FOOD CHOICE

Source	Fruit & vegetable (%)	Meat (%)	Bread (%)	Milk (%)	Fowl & fish (%)	Legumes & nuts (%)	Vitamins (%)
	Traditional (N = 116)						
Taste	51.7	49.1	63.5	58.1	49.6	42.2	17.7
Home[1]	35.3	30.4	31.3	27.3	25.6	27.6	31.0
Outside[2] information	12.9	20.5	5.2	14.5	24.8	31.0	51.3
	Alternate (N = 46)						
Taste	44.2	27.3	60.5	55.6	46.7	62.2	8.9
Home	32.6	38.6	9.3	17.8	22.2	13.3	28.8
Outside information	23.3	34.1	30.2	26.7	31.1	24.4	62.2

[1] Home: training learned at home.
[2] Outside information: learning other than home training, or economic, availability, or convenience constraints.

market shoppers used what they had been taught at home, 35%, than reported relying on outside constraints, 11%. Similarly to traditional food shoppers, one-third of the alternates reported using what they had learned at home in selecting food. Nearly twice the share of alternate shoppers as traditionals claimed to use outside-the-home constraints in choosing food, 23% versus 13%.

Red Meat.   The data in Table 3.2 about the basis for choosing red meats reveal that, although half of the traditional shoppers also used taste as chief guide in choosing to eat red meats, nearly a third, 31% used home training and 20% outside (similar to the fruit results), alternate shoppers relied more upon home or outside influences than taste. About half the proportion of alternate shoppers as traditional used taste as the main guide in choosing red meat, 27%, with about the same percentage, 38%, following home training and 34% being influenced by other factors than taste or home training.

Fish and Fowl.   Traditional shoppers ate fish and fowl less often than alternate shoppers. Responses by each of the four types of consumers about fish and fowl choices (Table 3.2) resembled the pattern for fruits and vegetables. Again, all consumers used taste as the chief guide in food choice of fish and fowl in both markets: supermarket, 51%; alternates, 48%. About the same proportions were guided by home training, 26% versus 22%; and other constraints, 25% versus 31%. Here again, somewhat more of the alternate shoppers reported being influenced by other constraints than taste or home training about food.

Legumes and Nuts.   In addition to red meat and fish and fowl, the reported intakes of legumes and nuts differed markedly between traditional and alternate market shoppers (Table 3.1). In this case the reasons behind the choices of traditional shoppers were about equally distributed in each category, with more import given to taste, 44%; home, 29%; and outside influences, 27%. Counter to the trends for choice in the other food groups, alternate shoppers relied primarily on taste in opting for beans and nuts; secondarily, outside-the-home information; and lastly, home. The percentages for each category—taste, home, outside—by market were: traditional, 42%, 28%, and 31%; for alternates, 62%, 13%, and 24%.

Bread and Dairy Products.   All consumers polled in this sample reported eating bread and milk products very frequently. Over half of them in each type of market used taste to choose grain and dairy products (Table 3.2). Nearly one-third of supermarket shoppers, 31% in the case of grain and 27% for milk, based their choice on their home training, compared with only 9% and 18% respectively for the alternate shoppers. In the case of outside factors, 5% of traditionals in the case of breads and 14% in the case of dairy products were influenced by other factors, but of the alternate shoppers 30% relied upon other constraints for cereal products and 27% for milk products. Consumption was justified with different factors in the various markets.

Vitamins.   A majority of alternate and one-third of supermarket shoppers reported daily ingestion of vitamins (Table 3.1). This habit correlated best with outside information; next, home; and least, taste (Table 3.2).

Market Choice.   The home environment affects the shopping site of the typical consumer in a large way. For example, 62% of the supermarket group reported being influenced by home rearing, whereas merely 16% of alternate shoppers reported being so influenced (Watkins 1981, unpublished). Choice of market was affected in the case of one-fifth of traditionals by outside information, but three-fifths of alternates sought supplementary, nonhome information which affected their market selection. Still, about one in five consumers polled in both types of markets claimed to choose the market because of food taste considerations.

In another series of recorded market interviews, alternate shoppers have given several reasons for patronizing those shops, including: availability of some foods, such as various whole grains; the quality of produce available in terms of freshness and variety; and in some fewer cases, health reasons such as allergy (Kumpf and Watkins 1980).

FOOD ADVERTISING APPEALS

Advertisements for food in general appeal to taste without reference to nutrition information. Food advertisements, particularly in the trade magazines, orient consumer appeals chiefly to taste (Table 3.3). According to these data, advertisements in popular lay readership magazines rarely use nutrition information as an appeal. In an advertisement content analysis, nutrition information was used as an appeal in less than 20% of all advertisements; fewer than 30% of the advertisements rested the case for a food on its nutritional merit for any one category of magazine. Most magazines'

TABLE 3.3   USE OF NUTRITIONAL APPEALS IN FOOD ADVERTISEMENTS IN MAGAZINES

Type of magazine	N^1	Nutritional message (% of food ads)	Frequently used appeals
Sports	3	0	Flavor, quality
Business	3	0	Freshness, taste
Glamour, fashion	8	12	Taste, enjoying life personal attractiveness
Culinary	5	2	Quality, cuisine
Homemakers	18	11	Cost, ease of preparation, freshness, family satisfaction, versatility, taste
General Interest	3	33	Taste, quality
Total	40		

Source: C.M. Jackovitz and T.R. Watkins 1979.
[1] Number of magazines analyzed.
[2] Nutritional message is defined as one with reference to nutrients, proximate food parts (e.g., fat, protein, carbohydrate), or a diet-related health issue.

appeals relied upon nutrition only about 10% of the time or less. Culinary, family, and some general news magazines contained nutrition-oriented appeals, but never in more than one-third of the cases sampled. On the basis of this content analysis of food advertisements, taste and flavor tend to receive more prominence for the general consumer in advertisements than nutritional information. These data confirmed what the respondents have reported about the importance of taste in choosing food, and marketing strategists feature taste in advertising appeals.

In the case of red meats only among the food groups does some other influence manifest itself here for the traditional consumer. Home-derived information and nonhome originated influences affect choices, and here nonhome inputs could well be operative. The USDA has reported an 11.1% decline in red meat consumption by the U.S. consumer, the largest drop since 1945, compensated somewhat by pork intake with mild gains in fish and fowl (Moore 1980). These changes were attributed in large part to the rising cost of red meats (Longen and Stucker 1980).

Home training and experience stand second in order after taste as the criterion or influence used to include or exclude foods from a menu. The alternate shopper reported using home training more frequently than other constraints in this survey population. According to Berne's paradigm, this home type of interaction is classed child–parent, being authority referenced.

Third in order of usage and a deciding factor in designing a menu, or deciding how or where to eat, is information garnered from sources or other circumstances, for example economic, convenience, or social considerations. The alternate shoppers here polled reported depending upon this sort of guide in many cases, notably the food groups red meats, milk and dairy, legumes and nuts, and vitamins. The responses about source of information showed that the alternate consumer relied heavily upon friends and self-selected reading materials (in contrast to school books in the case of some traditional shoppers) to set criteria used to choose foods. This sort of seeking, collecting, integrating, and using information as a rule falls in the category of adult–adult interaction in Berne's scheme.

RECENT CHANGES IN FOOD HABITS

In the period 1970 to 1980 these consumers reported shifting their food choices in the following ways. At least half of the consumers at all market types reported increasing their fruit and vegetable consumption, with nearly as many reporting increased legume and nut intake (Table 3.4). More than half of the shoppers at each market type reduced their red meat consumption, although a larger percentage of the alternate shoppers reported eating red meat less often: 74% versus 58%. Nearly half of the shoppers at each type of market also chose to eat less bread and other cereal products, 42% of traditionals versus 49% of alternates; but about the same percentages reported no change. Although 44% of both types of shoppers did

TABLE 3.4.   CHANGES IN FOOD HABITS IN TRADITIONAL AND ALTERNATE FOOD
MARKETS, 1970–1980

Change[1]	Fruits & vegetable (%)	Red meat (%)	Bread & cereals (%)	Dairy (%)	Fish & fowl (%)	Legumes & nuts (%)
	Traditional (N = 116)					
More	64	17	16	39	57	47
Less	9	58	42	17	10	14
No change	27	25	40	44	33	39
	Alternate (N = 46)					
More	72	13	13	38	39	67
Less	2	74	49	18	30	4
No change	26	13	38	44	30	28

[1]Change in food habits in the period 1970–1980 with respect to habits prior to 1970.

not change their milk and dairy usage, well over half of all consumers
polled have changed their dairy intake recently, with more than one-third
of them emphasizing the place of dairy products in the diet. More than 60%
of consumers changed their fish and fowl intakes during the decade, and
most of those changing reported deciding to favor fish and fowl intake in
this sample, 57% of traditional shoppers compared with 39% of alternate
market customers. Two-thirds of the alternate shoppers polled in this
survey reported increasing their bean and nut intakes, compared with
about half of the traditionals (47%). The new consumer may have perceived
the high nutritional value of the legume or may have chosen to eat legumes
more frequently for economic reasons (Watkins 1980).

CONCLUSIONS

The salient differences in eating habits by food group reported in this
survey for consumers by market type concerned fruit and vegetable, red
meat, fish and fowl, and legume and nut consumption, as well as vitamin
usage (Table 3.1). The consumer at the alternate market ate fruit and
vegetables, fish and fowl, and legumes and nuts more frequently than the
traditional shopper, and also used vitamins more regularly. Traditional
shoppers ate bread and other grain products less often than alternate
shoppers, too.

Overall, food habits of customers in the alternate markets more nearly
followed the recommendations issued in the Dietary Goals for the United
States and the Dietary Guidelines, based upon the frequency of consumption data. In adopting the Dietary Guidelines in personal food selection, the
traditional shopper will become more like the profile of the alternate consumer polled in this preliminary study.

Great Waters of France sponsored a survey about Americans athletically
active or inactive and their eating habits called the Perrier Study (1979).
They reported that more of the "High Actives" in the group of 1560 individ-

uals polled ate more fresh vegetables and fruit and drank more water and had slightly larger intakes of milk and cheese and breakfast cereal than the "Actives" (Perrier Study 1979). Little, if any, difference was reported in the red meat, poultry, or fish intake of the two groups, although the "Actives" reported eating less fried food than the public at large or non-actives. The "High Actives" also reported that stepped-up activity had been accompanied by increased intakes of energy, fruit and fruit juices, whole wheat products, fish and poultry, with decreases in red meat and eggs.

The preliminary food intake data released by the USDA from the 1977–1978 Nationwide Food Consumption Survey compared with the 1965–1966 Household Food Consumption Survey indicated that Americans have decreased their daily food intake: men, 35–50 years, 2300 kcal; women, 35–50, 1550 kcal; eat less protein: men, 95 g; women, 60 g; eat less fat: men, 100 g; women, 70 g; less vitamin A: men 5500 I.U.; women, 4200; and more vitamin C: men, 90 mg; women, 80 mg (Pao 1979). No change was reported in calcium intakes: men, 750 mg; women, 550 mg.

These USDA data corroborate the data presented qualitatively, although the vitamin A would be expected to increase in diets with higher vegetable content, as reported here. However, as one-day recall data vary widely for nutrients heterogeneously distributed in food (Hegsted 1975), the one-day household figures may be somewhat unrepresentative of actual individual intakes.

The food intake frequency data in this paper suggest that the alternate shopper has been making reasonable food choices, as the foods selected align well with the Dietary Goals and Guidelines for a Healthy Diet. The majority of a population in traditional and alternate markets apparently wish to use palatability as the chief criterion in selecting a diet, rather than parental or sibling training, or peer or other sort of influence. That this would be expected in an affluent society has been discussed (Yudkin 1964). If this be the case, the future course of food product development ought to include design constraints that rely on the traditional quality criteria, such as taste, color, odor, texture, size, and microbiological safety and stability, in addition to nutritional values of the product such as caloric density, cariogenicity, and the like.

Enrichment or fortification and destruction of antinutritional factors will be given preeminence in future food design along with the widely accepted color, flavor, and texture guides. Hence, taste may not be a completely blind guide, and nutritional excesses and deficiencies—if they exist—would be corrected at the factory for the typical consumer. For those who do not wish blindly to follow the palate, nutrition education may play a role in food choice and menu design.

Trends reported of changes in food habits over the past ten years were qualitatively similar in both market types, differing quantitatively by modest increments. How do these changes compare with the U.S. Dietary Goals of the McGovern Committee and USDA Guidelines? First, the general direction of change for each market type is consistent with the Goals.

That is, most shoppers sampled chose to eat somewhat more fruits and vegetables, fish and fowl, and beans and dairy products and somewhat less red meat in the period 1970 to 1980. The generally decreased bread, pasta, and cereal intake ran counter to the recommendation to emphasize foods in the bread group as one chooses a varied diet. (The remarkable exception appeared to be the reduced fish and fowl intake by cooperative members.) The turn away from red meat toward fruit and vegetables, legumes, and fish and fowl to some extent in the menu was more apparent among the customers of alternate markets in this poll.

A large proportion of people from both types of markets, traditional and alternate, as the data showed, apparently wish to learn about diet and health and are changing their eating styles. Whether this is based primarily upon diet–health knowledge or economic contingencies was not revealed by these data. However, a revival in nutrition education has been reported in medical schools, dental schools, universities, high schools, and grade schools (Darby 1977). Public lectures are sponsored by health organizations, and ethnic cooking clubs offer gourmet approaches to a healthful diet. Diverse sites of the nutrition education may be effective, including the home. Solomon said, "Train the child in the way he should go, and in his older years, he will not depart from it." Habit established in youth may influence food choice somewhat more forcefully than later education. In these data, one-fourth to one-third of consumers polled claimed to base food choice upon home training. Hence nutritionists may wish to use the home and other sites for early food training. Other educational sites could well be child care centers, food clubs, sports clubs, radio shows, newspapers and magazines. Incentives such as reduced health insurance premiums may be an appropriate device to galvanize the consumer to study and change dietary habits.

The health food and natural food market segment of the food industry has been growing at a rapid pace recently, now claiming more than one billion dollars of the market (Eagle 1980). This consumer perceives a need to change diet to protect health as well as for other reasons (Brisset and Lewis 1979). If this market's major consumer appeal rests on home training about food value and safety, then this segment would be expected to grow. If, however, its appeal rests primarily upon the whetted appetite of the consumer for nutrition knowledge—currently self-taught—coupled with the motivation to change eating habits, then the market segment would not be expected to continue its rapid growth, as few consumers would be expected to take the time to do the reading about food and modifying their behavior without economic incentives.

Looking at the prospects for improving the health of most Americans, one would surmise that the general consumer apparently does not perceive the need to change eating habits drastically to avert a health catastrophe. Recent disclosures about the diet and disease link by Olson (1980), and the Food and Nutrition Board (NAS 1980B), as well as others, may result in a blasé attitude in the consumer, such that some care less about food choice and possible future disease. According to Becker's "Health Belief Model" no change in habit or activity can be anticipated unless the subject perceives the need for change and accurately perceives the degree of hazard and consequences of the disease (Becker 1976). Until the representative American consumer appreciates the diet–disease link clearly, no drastic dietary changes will be expected. Until the education level of the general populace rises sufficiently, the onus rests upon the shoulders of food and nutritional scientists to process foodstuffs with appropriate nutritional modifications such as caloric and salt dilution, fiber supplementation, fat modification, fat reduction, and perhaps even vitamin fortification in order to compensate for Americans' excesses at the table.

Food consumption frequency data here presented have been compared with two recommended dietary patterns, the Dietary Goals and the Dietary Guidelines. The reported diet of the alternate market shopper more nearly conformed with the Guidelines than the traditional shopper's diet for this population. In the development of diet-related disease, food intake patterns afford the most sensitive index in predicting likelihood of disease incidence as in the progression: dietary change (excess, deficit) → biochemical lesion →clinical sign → disease → death. With concomitant information about the health status of a survey population, one could identify the eating pattern associated with specific diseases and corrective educational programs planned. The value of conventional classroom education in inducing changes of food choice appears open to question based upon these data. This approach has been considered (Schwerin et al. 1980). Changes in food patterns of shoppers at each of the market types surveyed occurred similarly in the period 1970 to 1980. Many shoppers polled, regardless of market type, reported adopting diets more like the Dietary Goals and Dietary Guidelines than unlike them.

ACKNOWLEDGMENTS

The author wishes to thank G. Singh, H. Watkins, E. and S. Workman, M. Piggott, B. Dugan, B. Workman, and H. Reynolds for help in conducting this survey and to thank D. Mueller, H. Reynolds, and L. Little for valuable criticism.

REFERENCES

ANONYMOUS. 1974. Organic foods. Food Technol. 28, 71.

BATES, R. 1981. The uneasy interface between food technology and "natural" philosophies. Food Technol. 35, 50.

BEATON, G.H., MILNER, J., COREY, P., McGUIRE, V., COUSINS, M., STEWART, E., DeRAMOS, M., HEWITT, D., GRAMBSCH, P.V., KASSIM, N., and LITTLE, J.A. 1979. Sources of variance on one-day recall data. Am. J. Clin. Nut. 32, 2546.

BECKER, M.H., (Editor 1974).   The Health Belief Model, Ch. B. Slack, Thorofare, New Jersey.

BERNE, E.   1964.   Games People Play.   New York, Grove Press.

BREWSTER, L. and JACOBSON, M.F.   1978.   Changing American Diet. Center for Science in the Public Interest, Washington, D.C.

BRISSET, D. and LEWIS, L.S.   1979.   The Natural Health Food Movement: A Study of Revitalization and Conversion.   J. Am. Culture 1,61.

CLANCY, K.   1980.   Regulation of Natural by the FTC.   Inst. Food Technol. 40th Ann. Mtg., New Orleans.

CONSUMER REPORTS.   1980.   It's organic, it's natural, or is it?   45, 410.

DARBY, W.J.   1977.   The renaissance of nutrition education.   Nutr. Rev. 35, 33–38.

DWYER, J.T., MAYER, L.D.V.H., DOWD, K., KANDEL, R.F., and MAYER, J. 1974.   The new vegetarians: the natural high?   J. Am Diet Assoc. 65, 529.

EAGLE, J.   1980.   The Health Food Market.   Inst. Food Technol.   40th Ann. Mtg., New Orleans.

FEDERAL TRADE COMMISSION.   1978.   Proposed Trade Regulation Rule on Food Advertising, 16 C.F.R., Part 437, Phase I, 25 September 1978. Washington, D.C.

FRIEND, B.   1967.   Nutrients in United States food supply: a review of trends 1909–1913 to 1965.   Am. J. Clin. Nutr. 20, 907.

GALLO, A.   1977.   Marketing developments.   National Food Situation. USDA, Economic Research Service, Washington, D.C.

HALL, R.L.   1979.   Food ingredients and additives.   In Food Science and Nutrition, F. Clydesdale, (Editor).   Prentice Hall, Englewood Cliffs, New Jersey.

HEALTH and NUTRITION EXAMINATION SURVEY.   1972.   DHEW, Washington, D.C.

HEGSTED, D.M.   1975.   Dietary standards.   J. Am. Diet Assoc. 66, 12.

HEGSTED, D.M.   1979.   Nationwide Food Consumption Survey—Implications.   Nat. Agric. Outlook Conf. No. 11, G.P.O., Washington, D.C.   6 November 1979.

JACKOVITZ, C.M. and WATKINS, T.   1979.   Nutrition's role in food advertising.   Unpublished data.

JACOBY, J., CHESTNUT, R.W., and SILBERMAN, W.   1977.   Consumer use and comprehension of nutrition.   J. Cons. Res. 4, 119.

KAITE, E. 1977.   National Food Situation.   USDA, Economic Research Service, Washington, D.C.

KNORR, D.   1982.   Natural and organic foods: definitions, quality and problems.   Cereal Foods World, 27, 163.

KUMPF, B. and WATKINS, T.   1980.   Market choice by alternate food shoppers.   Unpublished data.

LEINEN, N.J.   1978.   Survey reports significant jump in "natural is better" consumer attitude.   Food Proc. 39, 28.

LEVERTON, R.   1974.   Organic, Inorganic: What They Mean.   Yearbook of Agriculture.   USDA, Washington, D.C.

LEWIS, C.S.   1967.   Studies in Words, 2nd edition.   Cambridge University Press, Cambridge.

LINDSTROM, H. and HENDERSON, P. 1979.   Farmer-to-consumer marketing.   Nat. Food Rev., USDA, Fall, p. 22.

LONGEN, K. and STUCKER, T.   1980.   More fish, more poultry, less red meat.   Nat. Food Rev., 9, 28.

MARSHALL, W.E.   1974.   Health foods, organic foods, and natural foods—what they are and what makes them attractive to consumers.   Food Tech. 28, 51.

MOORE, P.   1980.   Food Consumption in 1979.   Nat. Food Rev., 9, 26.

NATIONAL ACAD. SCIENCES, FOOD NUTR. BOARD.   1980A.   Recommended Dietary Allowances.   Ninth edition.   Washington, D.C.

NATIONAL ACAD. SCIENCES, FOOD NUTR. BOARD.   1980B.   Toward Healthy Diets.   Washington, D.C.

NEW, P.K.M. and PREIST, R.L.   1967.   Food and thought: a sociologic study of food cultists.   J. Am. Diet. Assoc. 51, 13.

NULL, G.   1978.   The New Vegetarians. Morrow, N.Y.

OELHAF, R.   1978.   Retail markets for organic foods.   In Organic Agriculture. R. Oelhaf (Editor).   Allenheid, Asmun and Co. Montclair, New Jersey.

OLSON, R.E.   1980.   Statement to the House Agriculture Subcommittee on Domestic Marketing, Consumer Relations, and Nutrition.   Nutr. Today. 15, 12.

PAO, E.M.   1979.   Nutrient Consumption Patterns of Individuals in 1977 and 1965.   Consumer and Food Economics.   Institute, Human Nutr. Center, USDA Washington, D.C.

PERRIER STUDY: FITNESS IN AMERICA.   1979.   Great Waters of France, New York.

PIMENTEL, D. and PIMENTEL, M.   1979.   Food, Energy and Society.   John Wiley, New York.

RINDE, R.M.   1980.   Trends in the Food Market.   Seminar at Rutgers University.   A.C. Nielsen, Northbrook, Illinois.

SCHWERIN, H.S., STANTON, J.L., RILEY, A.J. JR., SCHAEFER, A.E. LEVEILLE, G.A., ELLIOTT, J.G., WARWICK, K.M., and BRETT, B.D.   1981.   Food eating patterns and health: a reexamination of the Ten-State and HANES I Surveys.   Am. J. Clin. Nutr. 34: 568.

SHAW, R.E. and PINTO, D.   1978.   Where's Your Next Meal Coming From? A.D. Nielsen, Northbrook, Illinois.

SINCLAIR, H.   1976.   The rationale of health foods.   In Health and Food, G.G. Birch, L.F. Green and L.G. Plashett (Editors).   Applied Science, London.

STOKES, B.   1978.   Small Is Bountiful, Worldwatch Paper 17.   Local Responses to Global Problems—A Key to Meeting Human Needs.   Worldwatch Institute, Washington, D.C.

USDA and HHR.   1980.   Nutrition and Your Health: Dietary Guidelines for Americans.   G.P.O., Washington, D.C.

U.S. SENATE. SELECT COMMITTEE ON NUTRITION AND HUMAN NEEDS. 1977A.   Dietary Goals for the United States.   G.P.O., Washington, D.C.

U.S. SENATE. SELECT COMMITTEE ON NUTRITION AND HUMAN NEEDS. 1977B.   Dietary Goals for the United States, 2nd edition.   G.P.O., Washington, D.C.

U.S. SENATE. SELECT COMMITTEE ON NUTRITION AND HUMAN NEEDS. 1977C.   Diet Related to Killer Diseases, Parts I – V. G.P.O., Washington, D.C.

WADE, C.   1978.   Health Is What You Eat.   Parker Publ. Co., West Nyack, N.Y.

WALKER, R.   1976.   Food additives: benefits/risks.   J. Biosoc. Sci. 8, 211.

WATKINS, T.   1980.   Food Habits in Traditional and Alternate Markets and Dietary Guides.   Inst. Food Technol., 40th Ann. Mtg., New Orleans.

WATKINS, T. and LEA, R.   1980.   Errors in food portion estimation by university students.   Unpublished data.

WEBSTER.   1961.   Webster's Third New International Dictionary of the English Language Unabridged.   Merriam Webster, Springfield, Massachusetts.

WELLS, P.   1979.   Supermarkets versus health shops: prices compared.   New York Times, 6 June 1979.

WHITE HOUSE CONFERENCE ON FOOD, NUTRITION AND HEALTH. 1968.   Washington, D.C.

WILLIAMS, R.J.   1978.   Nutrition Against Disease.   Bantam Books, New York.

YUDKIN, J.   1964.   Changing Food Habits.   Macgibbon and Kee, London.

Part II

Agricultural Production

4

Energy in U.S. Agricultural Production

William Lockeretz

INTRODUCTION: THE PERVASIVE ROLE OF ENERGY

The sharply deteriorating energy situation of the early 1970s stimulated a flurry of interest in the use of energy in agriculture. Largely ignored less than a decade ago, this topic is now an important concern of farmers, extension workers, and researchers in fields like agricultural economics, agronomy, and agricultural engineering. Indeed it concerns people working in just about every aspect of agricultural production. One obvious result of this development has been that we now have much more factual information on the topic than we had even a few years ago. But another consequence has been that the interpretation of these facts has become a subject of considerable controversy. Perhaps this is an understandable result of how suddenly attention has been focused on the subject, and undoubtedly some of the controversy will be resolved in the next few years as the field matures. But some of the disagreements involve fundamental questions of values and attitudes and cannot be resolved by purely objective analysis.

In fact, discussion of what agriculture should do to adjust to recent energy problems sometimes serves as a jumping-off point for a much deeper look at basic features of our agricultural system. Perhaps the most positive result of energy problems in agriculture will be that they force a reexamination of some of the uncritically accepted assumptions underlying agricultural development in the United States for the past few decades. As every aspect of that development has had some energy implications, so, in trying to decide what to do about energy, we must also think about what we want to do about agriculture in general. Given the demonstrated ability of U.S. agriculture to produce an enormous quantity of food at relatively low cost, people who are concerned about more subtle secondary aspects of the system often find it is hard to get their views across. But a crisis, whether real or perceived, can be an effective way of reopening the debate on questions that previously were considered closed.

The prominent place of energy problems in the consciousness of farmers and the public in general may be very advantageous to people working to change the future direction of U.S. agriculture. Reduced tillage methods that can go a long way to control the serious and chronic problem of excessive soil erosion, but which still are not used everywhere they are suitable, have received an added boost because they also require less fuel than conventional tillage. The cost of energy for pumping may turn out to be what finally ends the wasteful and inefficient use of water that too often has characterized irrigated agriculture in the United States, especially where the water has been "free," that is, provided at public expense or simply there for the taking. The long-term health and environmental effects of using certain pesticides might not become apparent except after long and careful study, but the heavy dependence of our current pest control strategies on petroleum is quite easily grasped. The energy required to manufacture inorganic fertilizers provides an additional argument against the disposal, rather than the land application, of livestock manures and other organic wastes, a practice that turns such materials into pollutants instead of valuable sources of plant nutrients and organic matter.

Many more examples could be offered. In short, to analyze how energy is used in agriculture is to analyze agriculture itself. To keep the following discussion to a reasonable length, the primary emphasis will be on energy as such. It should be kept in mind, however, that isolating energy this way is really just a matter of convenience and that this separation is not a very accurate reflection of the true relation between energy and other agricultural issues.

Most of this chapter is concerned with conservation methods and alternative energy sources that can reduce the dependence of agriculture on fossil fuels. Although it might seem that no one could seriously doubt that such a goal is desirable, in fact the whole issue is a subject of considerable contention. To place the remaining material in a proper framework, therefore, it first is necessary to examine some broad features of the use of energy in agriculture and to discuss some of the controversy surrounding this issue.

AN OVERVIEW OF ENERGY INPUTS IN U.S. AGRICULTURE

In contrast to the situation of a few years ago, there now is an abundance of detailed and fairly systematic data on how much energy is used in agricultural production and in the food system as a whole. In fact, there is almost an embarrassment of riches. For the data to be a means toward a more interesting end, it is necessary to select intelligently the most relevant pieces and to analyze them in a way that is appropriate for the particular question being answered. Otherwise, the result at best is a meaningless academic exercise, and at worst gives a misleading appearance of supporting whatever point the author wishes to make.

For example, some people have argued that energy consumption in agricultural production is not a significant issue and that concern should be focused instead on the remainder of the food system (processing, distribution, etc.), which consumes about five times as much energy. This argument is valid if the topic under discussion is reducing national energy consumption, for example. But if the issue is how energy prices affect farm income, then energy consumed after the food leaves the farm is quite irrelevant. Farmer energy bills could still be a serious problem even if food processors use more energy than do farmers.

The data given in this section, which represent only a small fraction of the total available in the cited sources, were chosen primarily to illustrate the various ways the use of energy for agriculture can be presented. The order is from the more general to the more specific: the entire food system, agricultural production as a whole, and then specific crops and specific locations within the agricultural sector.

The Overall Food System

From the viewpoint of the consumer and of the national energy picture as a whole, agricultural production should be regarded as just the first stage in a larger food system that includes processing, distribution, marketing, and home preparation. This food system consumed about 12×10^{18} joules (J) of energy (fossil, nuclear, and hydro) in 1977, or a little less than one-sixth of the national total of 79×10^{18} J (Van Arsdall and Devlin 1978) (10^{18} J = 9.48×10^{14} BTU = 0.948 quads; 1055 joules = 1 BTU). Only one-eighth of this amount (1.6×10^{18} J) actually went into production of food for U.S. consumption (Table 4.1). Processing and home preparation each consumed more than twice as much energy as production, with away-from-home meals and marketing and distribution also making important contributions. The $24 billion spent on energy from the farm to the store or restaurant amounted to about 12% of the retail value of food. Energy for home storage and cooking in effect adds another 6% to the retail cost of food, almost as much as the energy used in growing and processing it.

Energy Embodied in Production Inputs and Energy Used on the Farm

From the viewpoint of the farmer, the relevant data on energy consumption are those dealing with what happens until the product leaves the farm,

TABLE 4.1.   ENERGY CONSUMPTION IN THE U.S. FOOD SYSTEM, 1977.

Sector	Energy	
	Quantity (10^{18} J)	Cost (10^9 $)
Production[1]	1.6	4.1
Processing	3.8	8.1
Marketing and distribution	1.3	4.6
Away-from-home meals	2.2	7.1
Home preparation	3.4	11.5
Total	12.3	34.4

Based on Van Arsdall and Devlin (1978).
[1]Production of food for domestic consumption. Production of agricultural exports and nonfood items adds an additional 6×10^{17} J, so that the total for all agricultural production is 2.2×10^{18} J.

as the farmer has no control over energy used in subsequent stages of the food system unless he takes over some processing or marketing functions in addition to production. Of the total of 2.2×10^{18} J used in agricultural production in 1977, about one-third (8×10^{17} J) was embodied in purchased fertilizers and pesticides, most of which are made with natural gas, petroleum, or electricity (Van Arsdall and Devlin 1978). In fact, fertilizers are the largest single consumer of energy in agricultural production. Nitrogen fertilizer, which requires 5.1×10^7 J per kilogram of nitrogen, mostly in the form of natural gas, accounts for over four-fifths of the energy consumed in fertilizer manufacture (Davis and Blouin 1977).

Along with this embodied energy, an additional 1.4×10^{18} J is used directly on farms. This overall figure represents a complex mix of different forms of energy used for a variety of functions to produce many different products, with the further complication that each of these factors also varies geographically. As shown in Table 4.2, the biggest on-farm uses (exceeded only by fertilizers, for which the energy is consumed before the product reaches the farm) are field machinery and transportation, both of which require liquid fuels. Not surprisingly, then, about two-thirds of on-farm energy use is in the form of gasoline and diesel fuel. The remaining energy is in the form of natural gas, electricity, and LPG, which perform functions such as water pumping, grain drying, and livestock shelter heating and lighting. (Very detailed data on the forms of energy and the functions of each are given in FEA/USDA).

Comparing the Energy Intensiveness of Various Agricultural Products

About nine-tenths of the energy used in agricultural production goes to raise crops, with the remainder used in livestock operations (Table 4.2). Of course, the overwhelming proportion of crop output is used to feed livestock, so that from the viewpoint of total energy use, livestock ultimately are considerably more energy intensive than crops (Lockeretz 1975).

Table 4.3 illustrates the energy consumption of a range of crops. Corn and

TABLE 4.2.   ENERGY USED IN U.S. AGRICULTURAL
PRODUCTION, BY FUNCTION, 1977

Function	Energy Quantity (10^{18} J)	Energy Percentage
On-farm		
Field machinery	0.41	18
Transportation	0.33	15
Irrigation	0.27	12
Livestock	0.23	10
Crop drying	0.11	5
Miscellaneous	0.06	3
Subtotal	1.43[1]	64[1]
Embodied		
Fertilizers	0.70	31
Pesticides	0.11	5
Total	2.24	100

Based on Van Arsdall and Devlin (1978).
[1]Does not equal total because of rounding.

soybeans were selected because they are the two leading crops in terms of total value; alfalfa is a major forage crop; citrus and fresh vegetables are two important classes of nonfield crops; flue-cured tobacco was included because it has an exceptionally high value per unit of area and is produced with unusually intensive management methods.

The data in Table 4.3 have been presented in several ways. Because there are different reasons to compare different crops, there are different bases on which comparison should be made. For example, if we wish to reduce agricultural energy consumption as much as possible, then the energy used by the entire crop might be a relevant way of choosing crops to concentrate our efforts on. If we are analyzing how rising energy prices will affect the overall mix of agricultural products, then energy per unit value would be more relevant. This would also be relevant to a farmer making plans concerning future production. However, if energy supplies become very tight, so that price is not the only consideration, energy per unit area might be more relevant. Of course, in the case of an individual farmer, the range of choices is much narrower than is shown in Table 4.3, where the various crops were deliberately chosen to cover a broad spectrum.

Table 4.3 shows that comparative energy consumption depends strongly on which measure is used. Corn, soybeans, and alfalfa are less energy intensive than the others per unit area, but use more energy as a whole because they are such important crops. It is not coincidental that crops that are very energy intensive per unit area tend to be low in consumption for the entire crop, as intensively managed crops generally are raised on small areas. Note that energy per unit of value varies by considerably less than energy per unit area, since intensively managed crops are high-value crops as well. Thus, though tobacco is almost eight times as energy intensive as corn on an area basis, it requires only about one-fifth more energy per unit value.

TABLE 4.3. COMPARATIVE ENERGY CONSUMPTION OF SELECTED CROPS, 1974

				Energy Consumption		
Crop	Harvested area (10^6 ha)	Total value (10^6 \$)	Value per unit area (\$/ha)	Total crop (10^{15} J)	Per unit area (10^9 J/ha)	Per unit value (10^6 J/\$)
Corn	26.39	16,328	618	527	20	32
Soybeans	21.79	9,480	437	134	6	14
Alfalfa	10.78	3,654	339	128	12	35
Citrus	0.49	925	1888	57	118	62
Vegetables (fresh)	0.63	1,858	2957	24	39	13
Flue-cured tobacco	0.25	991	3966	39	155	39

Source: FEA/USDA 1976. All figures are national averages. Energy consumption in crop production varies widely with location, growing conditions, and production methods.

Geographic Variation in Energy Intensiveness of Crop Production

The preceding figures are national averages that do not reflect the considerable regional variation in energy intensiveness. Table 4.4 shows the energy consumption of crop production in selected states characterized by very different farming systems. The low energy input per unit area in South Dakota is characteristic of extensive small grain and hay production. Illinois is about equal to the national average, as it is dominated by the nation's two leading crops, corn and soybeans. California is almost twice the national average because of irrigation and because of intensively managed crops like fruits and vegetables. New Mexico is an extreme example because most of its crop production is irrigated and because the water often is pumped from very deep aquifers. Irrigation accounts for over four-fifths of the energy used in crop production in New Mexico.

As with the comparisons of different crops shown earlier, comparisons of different states present a very different picture when they are based on energy per unit value rather than per unit area. In fact, the first three states shown are very close to each other and to the national average in energy per unit value, even though they differ by more than a factor of five in energy per unit area. Once again, this is because intensively managed crops with high energy inputs per unit area also are high-value crops. New Mexico is an interesting exception. Because it is dominated by irrigated field crops, rather than fruits and vegetables, its high energy input per unit area is not offset by a high value of production.

Economic Significance of Energy Used in Agricultural Production

In examining the economic impact of energy use, perhaps the most relevant measure is the value of energy consumed per unit value of product. At 1977 energy prices, the 2.2×10^{18} J consumed in agricultural production had a value of about $7.2 billion. This corresponds to about 7% of the value of farm sales ($96 billion), 8% of total production costs ($88 billion), and 12% of current operating expenses ($61 billion) (USDA 1978). These percentages

TABLE 4.4.   ENERGY CONSUMPTION OF CROP PRODUCTION IN SELECTED STATES, 1974

	Value per unit area ($/ha)	Energy consumption	
		Per unit area (10^9 J/ha)	Per unit value (10^6 J/$)
South Dakota	185	5	28
Illinois	555	13	23
California	1394	27	19
New Mexico	352	57	161
National average	450	14	30

Source: FEA/USDA 1976.

may seem rather small, in view of the sharp increases in energy prices that had already occurred by 1977. The explanation is that all farm production costs were increasing during the same period, some even faster than energy prices, even though those increases did not receive the same degree of publicity among the nonfarm public. Likewise, farm prices rose sharply during the same period, although not steadily (Fig. 4.1).

CONTROVERSIES CONCERNING THE ROLE OF ENERGY IN AGRICULTURE

Net Energy Analysis

The previous discussion offered several different measures of the quantity of energy used in agriculture. Each has a certain validity, provided it is used only for those questions for which it is appropriate. In most cases, the appropriate choice should be fairly obvious and should not arouse much controversy unless someone is deliberately trying to be misleading. But there is another commonly used measure of energy intensiveness that is

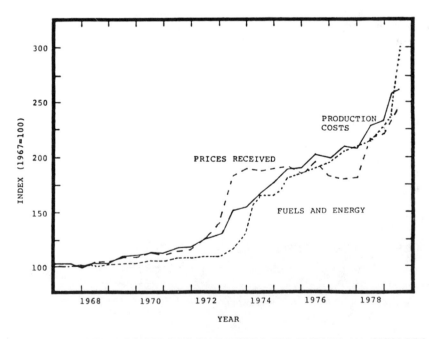

FIG. 4.1. CHANGES IN PRICES PAID BY FARMERS FOR ENERGY, ALL FARM PRO-DUCTION COSTS, AND PRICES RECEIVED BY FARMERS, 1967–1979. DATA FROM USDA 1979.

very controversial, with the controversy related to some fundamental questions regarding agricultural goals, policies, and strategies. Consequently, it deserves to be singled out for special attention.

This controversial measure is the energy input/output ratio. Expressed this way, the energy intensiveness of corn production is 0.36, i.e., 0.36 units of fossil energy are consumed to produce one unit of food energy in corn (Pimentel et al. 1973). For all of U.S. agriculture, however, the ratio is about 2, primarily because most corn and other major crops are consumed by livestock, with corresponding loss of food energy.

This measure of energy intensiveness is an example of energy accounting analysis, which makes energy the primary basis for analyzing production and consumption processes, just as money is the basis of conventional economic analysis. Among its other attractive features, this measure is a pure efficiency ratio. That is, it is a "pure" dimensionless number (although this advantage is usually obscured by using redundant units in the numerator and denominator and expressing the results as kcal/kcal, or even worse, BTU/kcal). This type of physical efficiency ratio would be appropriate for a process that simply converted energy from one form to another of equivalent usefulness. But its application to agriculture, while fairly common, has come under strong criticism for two main reasons (Connor 1977; Pasour and Bullock 1977). One is that energy is but one of many inputs to agricultural production and should not be singled out for special consideration. Thus the fact that the energy efficiency of crop production could be improved somewhat if hand weeding were substituted for petroleum-based herbicides is just one of many factors that should be considered in evaluating such a change.

Another important criticism is that while fossil energy and food energy are both measured in energy units, they are very different in every other respect. Thus their ratio only appears to be a true measure of efficiency, so that the fact that agriculture is a net energy consumer is not nearly so damaging a criticism as might be thought. Quite apart from the fact that food has many values besides energy (in fact, for an overweight person the energy content of food is a disadvantage), food energy and fossil energy are so different in their usefulness that a straight numerical comparison is pointless. Most production processes other than agriculture also are net energy consumers. The difference is that as their output usually cannot be measured in terms of energy, an "energy efficiency" computation is not even mathematically possible. The one case where an energy input/output ratio is meaningful in agriculture is when the crop is raised to produce a substitute for fossil fuel, such as corn grain used as feedstock to produce alcohol for use as a motor fuel.

But even if there are convincing arguments against the extreme proposal of totally replacing conventional economic analysis by net energy analysis, recent energy problems have certainly called attention to the shortcomings of conventional economics. Kelso (1977) has pointed out that the tradition in which most agricultural economists work takes no account of the fact that natural resources can be irreversibly depleted. This results in sharp discrepancies between short-term private well-being and long-term social well-being. Calling for a reconciliation between natural resource economics and conventional economics, Kelso anticipates that the latter will have to adjust to the former.

Alternative Views Concerning Adjustments to Energy Problems

All of this is more than mere academic quibbling over formal subtleties. Proponents and critics of net energy analysis frequently differ in their views as to what farmers should do about the energy situation (with these views sometimes put in the form of a prediction of what farmers *will* do). Thus Pasour and Bullock (1977), defending conventional economic analysis, state that "It is neither reasonable nor realistic to expect rapid shifts in energy use merely because of increased social concern about the adequacy of energy resources. . . . Becoming energy efficient as measured by these types of input-output ratios is not a reasonable policy goal." Perelman (1973), in contrast, in his analysis of the energy input/output ratio of agriculture, says that the energy situation "will require that agriculture undergo a drastic reorganization" and concludes that "highly mechanized technology currently used in the U.S. may be inappropriate."

A third energy future frequently proposed is simply to give agriculture a preferred, protected status. Unlike the view that agriculture should adjust only to the extent dictated by economic conditions or that a reduction in energy use should be a high priority objective, this view does not have any particular theoretical underpinning and is basically an *ad hoc* argument. Thus Stout (1974) states that "American agriculture will have to be given priorities that will assure adequate fuel supplies during the critical years that lie ahead," and calls on his fellow agricultural professionals to "assume active roles in earmarking nonfarm energy resources for future agriculture use because modern agriculture has become thoroughly dependent upon the availability of nonrenewable fossil fuels."

This argument has considerable appeal. Those who make it correctly note that agriculture uses only a small part of the total national energy budget, in return for which we receive a very valuable product. But like any of the very simple solutions to the energy situation in agriculture, it has drawbacks. As Doering (1977) pointed out, it takes away farmers' motivation to do anything constructive about energy problems. Also, it could generate a backlash against agriculture, something that farmers can hardly afford. Stout (1974) was sensitive to this point, noting that his proposal for top priority for agriculture was being made at a time "when everyone else in the nation is being asked to cut back on energy use," and further observing that "the farming community, being such a small segment of the population, often faces difficulties in gaining either sympathy or understanding from the citizenry at large." He proposed fuel priority not only for farmers but also for all those involved in getting food to the consumer. Ironically, he included truckers. During the fuel shortages in the summer of 1979, truckers demanded, and got, top priority in obtaining diesel fuel. They achieved this at the expense of farmers, whose previous priority was taken away. The summer of 1979 was the first time that farmers really needed their fuel priority. Thus the true complexity of an apparently simple solution became apparent only when the question of priorities became a practical matter, not just an abstraction.

Conceivably, a suitable compromise could reconcile these conflicting views as to the appropriate energy strategy for agriculture. Conventional economic analysis seems like a good starting point. Even without expecting an individual farmer to sacrifice for the common good, however, the net energy view could modify the resulting individual strategy (and most certainly could affect the choice of public policies). Long-range decisions being made now are based on assumptions concerning the future. The fact that fossil resources are depletable and therefore will become much more expensive argues for energy costs to be given at least somewhat more weight than in a conventional economic analysis. Likewise, conventional analysis assumes that inputs such as energy will always be available when needed; the only variable is price. But we no longer can make this assumption, an important consideration in view of how much can be lost if energy is not available to perform certain agricultural operations at just the right time. This does not mean that we have to give agriculture a preferred status regarding energy supplies. Rather, it suggests that some investment in conservation or alternative energy sources beyond the conventionally calculated economic "optimum" may still be justified even from the farmer's narrow private viewpoint, as well as on the basis of society's interest in having an assured food supply (Lockeretz 1979). Just how much weight to give to these various considerations is impossible to say. Simple solutions based on dogmatism are inadequate for this complicated problem. On the individual level, the best answer must be worked out by each farmer; on the societal level, the divergent views must be reconciled as they would be with any public policy issue.

ENERGY CONSERVATION

Despite the controversies just discussed, everyone agrees that agriculture should strive to reduce its energy consumption at least to the extent that this can be done without appreciable added costs or loss of production and without conflicting with other constraints, such as availability of capital or labor. Fortunately, even with these restrictions, the potential for energy conservation is considerable. Some conservation techniques represent the fruits of recent research and development efforts undertaken specifically in response to the changing energy situation. Others, however, have been known for a long time but were not used to the fullest extent because energy was sufficiently cheap and its supply sufficiently reliable that conservation was not worth the bother.

Because the products of U.S. agriculture are so varied and because the techniques for producing a particular product vary so strongly with the region, the type and size of farm and growing conditions, nothing even approaching a comprehensive analysis of the various energy conservation possibilities can be undertaken within the scope of this chapter. Fortunately, a growing body of technical and semitechnical material is available, summarized, for example, in Benson (1977), Frank (1977), Van Arsdall (1977), and Wynn (1977). The following discussion is therefore intended as a very brief overview of some of the most important areas.

Reduced Tillage

One of the most significant changes in crop production techniques in recent years has been the tendency toward reduced tillage, that is, alternatives to the moldboard plow, which since the nineteenth century has been the dominant implement for primary tillage. In contrast to the moldboard plow, which buries all crop residues by inverting the top 10 to 20 cm (the "plow layer"), reduced tillage methods such as chisel plowing or discing leave some or all of the residue on the surface. In extreme cases, the so-called no-till or slot-plant systems, the seed is placed in a slit cut into otherwise undisturbed soil. Initially, interest in reduced tillage arose because of concern over erosion, because leaving crop residues on the surface greatly decreases runoff and soil loss (Laflen *et al.* 1978). In fact, reduced tillage is frequently called "conservation tillage." More recently, energy problems have generated even more interest in the topic. About 17% of the energy used on-farm in crop production is used in tillage and cultivation, so that taken together they are second only to irrigation (FEA/USDA 1976).

An example of the energy saving possible with reduced tillage is given by Wittmuss *et al.* (1975). For the case of dryland corn grain production in Nebraska, the fuel required for field operations except harvesting for four different systems varied from 10 liters of diesel fuel equivalent per hectare for slot-plant to 38 liters/ha for conventional tillage. Because labor and machinery depreciation and repairs are roughly proportional to fuel use for a given size of machinery, these numbers also indicate qualitatively the range in the monetary cost of these tillage systems.

Reduced tillage illustrates three principles that characterize many important energy conservation strategies in agriculture. First, the value of energy conservation depends on whether one cares about the quantity of energy used or the reliability of supply. Because tillage and cultivation represent just a portion of energy use, the total energy requirements of the four systems examined by Wittmuss *et al.* (1975) differ by only 8%. But fuel for tillage operations is a sharply peaked demand, placing heavy pressure on the fuel supply system in early spring. As Wittmuss *et al.* (1975) note, if farmers adopted reduced tillage, this pressure would be alleviated, and farmers would be more likely to get the fuel they needed when they needed it.

The second point is that reduced tillage has significant environmental implications. The reduction of erosion, and consequently of the associated problem of sedimentation, has been amply demonstrated. But a significant reduction in tillage is generally regarded as requiring additional applications of pesticides (USDA/ERS 1975). This is because reduced tillage implements do not tear up weeds so effectively as does a moldboard plow; in the case of no-till, weeds are not torn up at all. Moreover, the residues remaining on the surface provide an environment for the spread of insects and diseases. It is worth noting that organic farmers using no herbicides or insecticides tend to prefer reduced tillage methods (Lockeretz et al. 1978). However, in their case this generally means chisel plowing, which is only a partial reduction in tillage. The association of more thorough-going tillage reductions with greater pesticide use undoubtedly is still valid. Whether the benefit of reduced erosion outweighs the detrimental environmental impact of increased pesticide use is beside the point. The important principle exemplified by reduced tillage is that energy-conserving techniques can have environmental effects, effects that could be good or bad, depending on the particular system being considered and on the particular conditions under which it is being applied.

Third, and perhaps most important, reduced tillage to some extent represents replacement of fossil energy by management ability (but not, as noted above, by labor, a tradeoff sometimes assumed to characterize all energy conservation strategies). The moldboard plow is a "brute force" tillage method that manipulates the soil quite vigorously to put it into the desired condition. In contrast, reduced tillage, and especially no-till, is a "gentler" approach that may leave the field more vulnerable to insect, weed, and disease problems. Also, tillage methods affect soil temperature and soil moisture and consequently affect the optimum planting date and other practices. For all these reasons, a farmer using reduced tillage or no-till must pay more attention to the condition of his fields at various stages in the growing season and adjust his practices accordingly, and in fact must make an intelligent decision as to whether these methods are desirable at all under his particular conditions.

In short, reduced tillage requires flexibility, judgment, and monitoring, which is also true of several other energy conservation methods to be discussed later. For example, careful irrigation management, which means taking account of the soil moisture profile, weather, and the condition of the crop, can reduce considerably the energy consumed in irrigation, as well as the water requirement, compared to the simple approach of automatically putting down the same amount every year. Pest control methods that are based on monitoring the actual pest levels and current weather conditions can cut the use of petroleum-based pesticides by a very substantial amount compared to the "insurance" strategy of applying a given amount whether or not it is actually needed. Similarly, by combining precise information on soil nutrient status with intelligent timing of fertilizer applications and careful use of nutrient-conserving manure storage and handling methods, a farmer can reduce the need for purchased energy-intensive fertilizer, especially in comparison to the common alternative of simply using whatever amount the fertilizer dealer recommends.

Thus it would be a serious mistake to assume that the only alternative to the current level of energy is a return to tedious, backbreaking hand labor. Nor is it true, as some advertisements in farm magazines appear to suggest, that use of energy-intensive technology is an inherent requirement of sophisticated, "top management" farming. In fact, in many cases, increased energy use has been substituted for sophisticated techniques, and in the years ahead the "top manager" may be the one who knows how to get high production with minimal use of energy.

Irrigation

Irrigation is the single largest on-farm consumer of energy, accounting for about one-fourth of the energy used on-farm in crop production, or about one-eighth of the total energy used in agricultural production (FEA/USDA 1976). But because irrigation is important only in certain regions, these national figures understate its contribution to the energy requirements of crop production where irrigation is used. Thus, in the 17 Western states, which account for more than nine-tenths of the total energy used in irrigation (Sloggett 1977), irrigation accounts for almost half of the energy used on-farm for crop production, double the national average. On the level of the individual farm, its importance can be still greater. To take an extreme example, Larson and Fangmeier (1978) calculated that with sprinkler irrigation from groundwater, irrigation accounts for 96% of the total energy required to produce alfalfa in Arizona.

But as with reduced tillage, the real motivation for reducing irrigation energy requirements may lie not in the total energy saving that could result, but in the fact that irrigation places a highly peaked demand on the energy supply and distribution system, especially for electricity. Summer peak load problems are exacerbated by the fact that the peak demands for irrigation and air conditioning coincide. Nebraska has had to curtail new electrical irrigation hook-ups (Sanghi and Johnson 1978), and sporadic brown-outs have occurred. As with tillage and many other agricultural energy uses, timeliness in irrigation is critical. For a particular case in Nebraska, Sanghi and Klepper (1977) showed that a 20% reduction in irrigation energy during July and August would reduce the net returns to corn production by 38% (1975 prices). By contrast, energy prices would have had to go up by more than three-fold to have the same effect.

Energy-intensive irrigation development in Nebraska and other parts of the Great Plains provides another example of why energy use cannot be analyzed separately from other resource and environmental questions. Serious groundwater depletion problems are anticipated, and degradation of groundwater quality and excessive erosion have already occurred (Aucoin 1979).

Fortunately, many techniques are available to reduce irrigation energy requirements without loss of production. Many of these really involve reducing the water requirements, so that two resources are saved. The optimal amount of irrigation water is variable, depending on rainfall, other weather conditions, and soil moisture profile. Because of recent research on the detailed water requirements of various crops at various points in the growing season, it is possible for irrigators to apply just the amount that the crop actually needs. In some areas, professional assistance is available to enable them to do so (Splinter 1976). Another approach is to increase water use efficiency, that is, the fraction of the water pumped that is actually delivered to the crop. For example, either a sprinkler irrigation system or a surface system with runoff reuse will save appreciable amounts of water—and energy, when the water is pumped from an appreciable depth—compared to conventional surface irrigation. Finally, irrigation pumps and engines are often not maintained in proper adjustment, and considerable energy saving results simply by bringing them up to performance standards. Gilley and Watts (1977) estimate that by combining all these approaches, energy savings of 35–45% are "realistic and attainable."

Reduction in Agricultural Chemical Use

As noted earlier (Table 4.2), the energy used to make fertilizers and pesticides is the single biggest contributor to the energy requirement of agricultural production, accounting for about one-third of the total. Although these materials are generally credited with a major portion of the increase in total U.S. agricultural output during the past several decades, at the same time there are ways to reduce appreciably the quantities used without sacrificing output. Traditionally, agricultural experts have emphasized the need to increase the use of these "underused" inputs, which were quite cheap relative to the value of the increased production they yielded. More recently, however, a growing recognition of the potential health and environmental hazards they entail, concern over their energy requirements, and increases in their cost relative to crop prices that were, in part, but only in part, a result of energy price increases have stimulated interest in using them more efficiently and prudently. It must be understood, however, that a reduction in agricultural chemical use would require a reversal of one of the most significant trends in the nation's agricultural development. The use of chemicals is now almost eight times the 1945 level, having risen almost four times as rapidly as any other input category (Durost and Black 1978).

A very small minority of U.S. farmers have reduced their use of fossil fuel-derived agricultural chemicals to a drastic degree by not using any conventional modern fertilizers (inorganic nitrogen, urea, acidified phosphates, or muriate of potash) or any synthetic herbicides or insecticides. As this approach—variously called "organic farming," "biological agriculture" or "eco-agriculture"—is discussed in more detail in another chapter, only its energy implications will be considered here (see "The Economic Feasibility of Widespread Adoption of Organic Farming" by R.C. Oelhaf).

For mixed grain/livestock farming in the Midwest, which is one of the major farming systems in the country and the one for which the most data on organic farming are available, organic agriculture is only about two-fifths as energy intensive as conventional methods (Lockeretz et al. 1978). The single most important contribution to this difference comes from the difference in energy inputs for producing corn, which is the leading crop in both systems and which receives the most fertilizers and pesticides on the conventional farms (Lockeretz 1982). However, the fact that organic farmers are more likely to raise other, less energy-intensive crops in rotation with corn also is important. Of course, there are so many points of difference between the two systems—yields, crop mix and environmental impact, for example—that energy alone is not an adequate basis for choosing one over the other. In fact, organic farmers themselves, in contrast perhaps to nonfarmer supporters of organic methods, do not seem to place energy considerations very high among the advantages of organic methods (Wernick and Lockeretz 1977).

Most farmers regard organic methods as an extreme alternative. Those who wish to reduce pesticide use while retaining fertilizers can do so by using a mix of practices usually described under the general label of "integrated pest management." This topic is also discussed in other chapters (see "Role of Stress Tolerance in Integrated Pest Management" and "Design of Small-scale Food Production Systems and Pest Control"). It should be noted that because pesticides account for only about 5% of the total energy used in agricultural production (Table 4.2), the potential energy saving is not very great. But here too, other considerations—especially effectiveness, costs, environmental impacts, development of resistant pest strains, and effects on natural control mechanisms—all should govern the choice of pest control systems, with energy being a small additional consideration.

Several approaches are available to farmers wishing to reduce fertilizer use while staying generally within conventional practices. Various organic wastes—sewage sludge, food processing wastes, and wastes from packing houses, for example—can be used as low-analysis fertilizers and also may improve the physical characteristics of the soil because of their organic matter content. Nationally, the supply of such materials is not adequate to replace more than a fraction of fertilizer use. Further, the sources often are very distant from the land to which they might be applied. However, there are many areas where organic wastes can be an important supplement to conventional fertilizers, assuming they are used intelligently. For example, Blobaum et al. (1979) showed how the wastes from the Omaha metropolitan area could replace a significant amount of fertilizer in an environmentally sound way and with an overall cost saving, provided adequate attention is given to soil characteristics and appropriate adjustments are made in crop rotations and field operations.

Livestock manure is another organic fertilizer material, of course. In contrast to the ones just mentioned, it is in common use, and has been for centuries. But a large portion of the fertilizer value of manure is lost before it is applied to the field, especially if farmers treat application as merely a way of disposing of it and therefore handle it in whatever way happens to be most convenient. In contrast, taking extra steps such as composting it, storing it in a place where leaching will be minimized, and incorporating it into the soil right after spreading will retain a much larger fraction of the nutrients.

Another feasible approach—one that in fact is used by many farmers—is to grow nitrogen-fixing legume forages such as alfalfa in rotation with crops with heavy nitrogen fertilizer requirements, such as corn. Legume forages once were the principle source of nitrogen in U.S. agriculture, but gradually they were supplanted by purchased inorganic fertilizers such as anhydrous ammonia. Nevertheless, they still are important crops in many parts of the country. In much of the Corn Belt, for example, rotations such as corn/corn/oats/hay/hay are fairly common, with the hay consisting of either a pure legume stand or a grass/legume mixture. About four-fifths of all hay is consumed on the farm on which it was raised. As it substitutes for corn silage and to a more limited degree with corn grain as a cattle feed, farmers with mixed crop/livestock operations can readily switch to more hay and less corn if nitrogen fertilizer prices rise rapidly compared to other costs. It should be clearly understood that legume forages are raised primarily as feeds, with their nitrogen value a secondary benefit. Moreover, it is conceivable that even cash grain farmers may be motivated to make such a change. It is interesting to note that in the past few years, the ratio of the price of hay to that of corn has risen by about 20% compared to its level in the 1960s, having more than recovered from a decline during the early and mid-1970s when the price of corn rose sharply. Moreover, great advances in harvesting of hay, so that an increased future role for hay is not as unthinkable as it would have been only a few years ago.

A final area for possible savings in fertilizer is more careful choice of application rates, such as through more frequent testing to determine available soil nutrient levels. Unfortunately, in the case of nitrogen, which is the leading energy-consuming fertilizer, availability is not easily measured, and the optimum application rate can be determined only if one knows the yield response curve under the particular conditions of interest. An alternative is to analyze plant tissue early in the season. Yield response to nitrogen varies appreciably with soil type, growing conditions, and management practices. It is possible that a farmer will overfertilize if his impression of yield response is based largely on results from experiment stations. There is some evidence (Taylor and Swanson 1973) that yield response under realistic, on-farm conditions is lower than on experiment stations, where there is more careful control of other factors that might limit yields, such as weeds, moisture, and plant density. Further research on the extent to which this is true might result in significant savings in nitrogen fertilizer with no loss of yield and without requiring any other modifications in production methods.

Energy Conservation in Livestock Production

The biggest energy user in livestock production is growing the feeds. Consequently, different feeding practices, such as the change to more hay and less corn just discussed, are an important area for energy conservation. Livestock operations apart from feed production account for about one-tenth of agriculture's energy requirement. Nationally, therefore, the potential energy saving is not very great. However, as agricultural production is very heterogonous, energy used in livestock production is still important for those farms which have major livestock enterprises. Because of the great variety of livestock facilities and production methods, many different conservation techniques are possible, only two examples of which will be mentioned here: waste heat recovery for dairy water heating and reduction in the heating load of poultry houses. These two areas account for 15% of the total energy used in livestock operations, and are the two leading uses other than those involving vehicles (FEA/USDA 1976), a topic that will be discussed later.

Heating water for cleaning milking equipment and for preparing the cow requires about one-fifth of the total energy used in dairying (FEA/USDA 1976). The bulk tank compressor used to cool the milk is a convenient nearby source of low temperature heat, releasing almost as much heat as is required for water heating. Commercially available units can recover about half of this heat for preheating the water supply, thereby reducing fossil energy use by about one-half. While the exact saving depends on the quantity and temperature of the water and the type and price of fuel used, in most situations this technique will be very economical, paying for itself in a few years. Interestingly, such units were available in the 1950s but were not widely adopted because water heating was such a small portion of dairy farmers' costs. In the 1970s, however, they began to catch on in a substantial way.

Poultry brooding, especially for broilers, accounts for over half of the total energy consumed in poultry production (FEA/USDA 1976). Among the most straightforward conservation techniques are several that are basically the same as for any heated building. Substantial savings are possible by keeping burners in proper working order, adding insulation, and cutting down on infiltration losses (Benson 1977). A more far-reaching change is to modify the heating and ventilation schedules. Conventional brooding practices evolved to provide optimal growing conditions (temperature, relative humidity, and removal of ammonia) that maximize feed conversion efficiency and minimize mortality. Increased fuel prices have led to reconsideration of the standard formulas, however, and substantial energy savings are possible with little or no loss of production (Collins and Walpole 1977). However, because of the potential for disease problems, this approach requires more careful attention to the condition of the flock. Poultry brooding therefore provides a good illustration of a point made earlier, namely, that the key to energy conservation in agriculture frequently is a higher level of management, not necessarily an increase in hand labor.

ALTERNATIVE SOURCES OF ENERGY

The techniques just described constitute one important way of reducing fossil fuel use, namely, by reducing the total amount of energy required. The other approach is to use the same total amount of energy, but to obtain some of it from renewable rather than fossil sources. The many alternative energy systems that in principle could be used by farmers range from some that once were in common use (windmills) to others that are commercially available (solar collectors), to still others that are technically feasible but that essentially are still at the do-it-yourself stage (methane from livestock manures). In all cases, however, the number of such systems in actual use is negligible in comparison to their potential applicability.

From a purely technical viewpoint, renewable energy theoretically could replace all fossil fuel use on farms. Whether such a change is practical or desirable, however, is quite another matter. Realistically, the two particular examples discussed next—solar energy and alcohol from farm products—should be looked at as no more than partial substitutes for current energy use. Alcohol is the strongest candidate for a renewable alternative to liquid petroleum fuels, which, as noted earlier, account for about two-thirds of on-farm energy use. The potential role of solar thermal energy is much more limited. However, it is the most technically feasible renewable energy source, and the one that is most likely to be adopted in the near to mid-term future.

Solar Thermal Energy

Despite the important role now played by fossil energy, photosynthetically fixed sunlight is still by far the largest single energy input in U.S. agriculture, a fact that is sometimes often overlooked because energy input/output balances do not deal with it explicitly. This is why agricultural production systems may be shown as net energy producers. In contrast, nonphotosynthetic uses of sunlight, such as solar thermal energy, traditionally have been of little importance, which may be about to change.

Because solar energy is relatively diffuse, it is best suited for low-temperature applications, rather than higher temperature uses that require elaborate concentrating mechanisms. Fortunately, almost all the heat used in agricultural production is at a low temperature. Sometimes, as with grain drying, a few degrees temperature rise above ambient can be useful, but in any case, the required temperature is well below 100°C. The major low temperature heat uses—crop drying, livestock shelter heating, poultry brooding, and dairy water heating—together represent about 7% of the fossil energy consumed in agricultural production (FEA/USDA 1976).

The basic principles and equipment for using solar energy for agricultural applications are essentially the same as for the corresponding domestic applications. The same kinds of flat plate collectors, both air and water types, have been used. Some storage medium—such as rocks, water, or a eutectic salt solution—is needed for times when there is no sunlight. Because of occasional extended periods of cloudy weather, storage and collectors large enough to meet the entire load would be prohibitively expensive, and a conventional backup system is a practical necessity. As with the typical residential case, a reasonably sized space heating or water heating system will usually supply about half of the total energy required, although the fraction varies with location. For many applications, passive technologies such as those that do not require a heat transfer fluid that is pumped between the collecting surface, storage, and the point of use can be used instead of, or in addition to, an active system. Grain drying, which constitutes about two-thirds of all low temperature heat use, offers additional flexibility, especially as the grain can serve as its own heat storage medium. Examples of several grain drying systems that certainly are technically feasible and that are economically promising are given in Hartsock (1978) and Heid (1978). The economic competitiveness of other solar applications is less clear, although more will be said on this topic later.

Alcohol for Fuel

In contrast to low temperature heat, which is a relatively low-grade form of energy, mobile engines require a very high-grade source. In addition to providing the high temperatures necessary for efficient conversion to mechanical work, the energy source must be sufficiently concentrated to be carried by the vehicle. At present, the most practical way that farmers could meet these requirements with renewable sources would be with alcohol, particularly grain alcohol, or ethanol. Methanol can be produced from crop residues, but at present this is not being done. Methane, because it can not be liquified, is relatively inconvenient for mobile engines.

Even though the idea of using ethanol as a motor fuel is as old as the internal combustion engine, it was not seriously pursued because petroleum-derived gasoline was cheaper. The idea was taken up again in the 1930s mainly as a way of using up price-depressing grain surpluses. Once again economic conditions proved unfavorable, but recent energy price increases have revived interest in the idea. During the late 1970s there was an enormous increase in research and development efforts and in federal and state programs in this area. These mainly concern "gasohol," which is usually defined as a blend of 10% (by volume) agriculturally derived ethanol and 90% unleaded gasoline. Gasohol is highly controversial from the viewpoint of economic competitiveness, net energy production, and effects on the prices and supplies of agricultural commodities. Scheller and Mohr (1977), Kendrick and Murray (1978), Litterman *et al.* (1978), DOE 1979, and Weisz and Marshall (1979) are a sample of the great many reports and articles on these questions that have appeared in the past few years.

Regardless of the advantages or disadvantages of a major national gasohol program, such a program is a separate matter from alcohol as a renewable fuel source for farmers. In a national gasohol program, farmers would sell a crop, most commonly corn grain, to alcohol producers, who in turn would sell alcohol through the national fuel market to the general driving public. An alternative but less ambitious approach is for farmers to process the grain into alcohol themselves for use in their own tractors, trucks, and cars or to have it processed by a local cooperative that returns the alcohol to them.

As noted earlier, diesel and gasoline account for about two-thirds of on-farm energy use, so that alcohol would have to play an important part in any scheme to increase substantially the energy self-sufficiency of U.S. agriculture. For gasoline engines, using ethanol is no problem. With at most minor adjustments, it can be blended with gasoline in any proportion, or can even be used by itself. However, there has been a strong trend toward diesel field equipment because of its considerably greater fuel efficiency. Beyond about 10% ethanol content, diesel–ethanol mixtures perform poorly in unmodified engines (Strait *et al.* 1978), but there are anecdotal reports of farmer-modified diesel tractors that successfully burn up to 50% ethanol (SFEP 1979A).

In recent years, there has been a tremendous burst of farmer interest in alcohol fuels, an interest that has just begun to be reflected in a corresponding research and development effort. Until some of these projects have been underway for a reasonable time, there will be many unknowns concerning the overall energy and economic balance of producing and consuming ethanol on farms. What is clear, however, is that the potential role of ethanol is very significant.

Energy Conservation in Comparison to Alternative Sources

Alternative energy sources often overlap, to a greater or lesser degree, with several of the conservation techniques discussed earlier. To take a simple example, both a solar water heater and a waste heat recovery unit reduce the fossil energy needed to provide dairy hot water; the dairy farmer uses that water in the same way, regardless of how it was heated. Comparing alcohol and reduced tillage is more complicated; both cut down on fossil fuel requirements for field operations, but in the latter case, pest control and other practices frequently have to be modified as well. In a few areas, there is no overlap at all; for example, no on-farm energy source substitutes for insecticide use.

When there is overlap, a farmer interested in reducing fossil fuel consumption has to make choices as to the most suitable approach. On the level of the individual farm, no firm rules can be stated because the choices depend on so many factors, such as the existing buildings and equipment, the farmer's credit and cash flow situation, the availability of labor, and personal tastes and preferences, the last still a valid consideration even though it frequently is ignored in formal analyses. Despite these complexities, there are a few points that seem reasonably valid as generalizations, even if they are too broad to determine completely a detailed program of action for an individual farmer.

Quite clearly, the "housekeeping" type of conservation methods should be done first. There is little reason to produce alcohol as a gasoline extender for use in an engine that wastes fuel because of poor maintenance, and it makes no sense to install a solar broiler house heater before tightening up windows and other sources of leaks.

Among the more thorough-going conservation methods, several appear to be simpler and more economical than the corresponding renewable energy alternatives. More insulation for poultry houses seems to be economical (Collins and Walpole 1977), whereas a solar heating system is marginal at best (Cain and Van Dyne 1977); waste heat recovery seems to be a considerably cheaper way of reducing dairy fuel requirements than a solar water heater. In still other areas, no simple economic comparison is possible, since factors besides cost, such as required management ability, also must be taken into account.

But despite the general principle of "conservation first," there still are two important roles for certain renewable energy sources. One, obviously, is to reduce a farm's energy requirements by more than is possible even with an aggressive conservation program. Usually, conservation and alternative sources can play complementary roles, rather than mutually exclusive ones, although the saving from the combination may be less than the sum of the separate savings. For example, solar will contribute less when used together with waste heat recovery, as it is harder for a relatively low-temperature heat source like a solar collector to transfer heat into water that has already been warmed.

Renewable energy can also become an important strategy if its costs are kept very low. The usual economic calculations assume that a solar energy system, for example, is bought off-the-shelf from commercial suppliers and is priced accordingly. But although this may be an appropriate assumption for most residential buyers, it neglects the fact that many farmers can do most of the installation work themselves and, moreover, that they often can use secondhand or scavenged materials. See, for example, SFEP (1979B) for a series of case histories of simple but effective and economical farmer-built renewable energy systems. Unfortunately, the price of some commercial renewable energy systems has been rising about as rapidly as that of fossil fuels, so that one cannot automatically assume that it is simply a question of waiting for energy prices to increase enough for such systems to become competitive. Despite this problem, however, most research and development efforts in renewable energy for farms still are continuing to concentrate on systems that may offer only slightly greater performance or convenience, but at a much greater price, compared to what a farmer could do himself if given appropriate technical advice and guidance.

CONCLUDING COMMENTS: ENERGY PROBLEMS AND AGRICULTURAL PROGRESS

A common thread running through the great variety of changes that U.S. agriculture has undergone in the past several decades has been the tendency toward reduced self-sufficiency, that is, a greater reliance on inputs brought in from off the farm. Thus from 1914 to 1977, when total inputs in agriculture rose by only 12%, purchased inputs rose almost three-fold (Durost and Black 1978). Total nonpurchased inputs, such as operator and family labor, fell by almost half in the same period. Greater use of fossil energy has been a key factor in many of the changes in this direction: purchased fuels for purchased tractors, instead of farm-raised feeds for farm-raised draft animals; purchased energy-intensive fertilizers instead of farm-produced manures; petroleum-powered combine harvesters instead of hand picking of corn by the farm family. Thus a shift toward eliminating current reliance on external fuel supplies could have far-reaching implications for some basic features of our agricultural system, a point discussed in the introduction. This does not mean, however, that energy self-sufficient farming necessarily means a return to old-fashioned farming.

Until a few years ago, there was little reason for a farmer to be concerned about a farm's heavy reliance on outside energy sources. Those who strove to be self-sufficient in energy, or in other inputs for that matter, did so primarily because of personal values and beliefs, the Amish offering a well-known example. Whether these values are right or wrong is immaterial, and in fact is intrinsically unanswerable. The point is that they were values that the majority of farmers apparently did not share.

Now, however, there are purely pragmatic reasons—anticipated price increases and possible shortages—for reconsidering whether a greater degree of energy self-sufficiency would not be desirable. Most of this paper has focused on relatively modest steps in that direction, steps that many people could agree with despite differences in personal values. But recent energy developments have helped to stimulate a new interest in farm energy self-sufficiency as an end in itself, that is, for reasons other than any possible economic saving.

This idea is a highly controversial one, and its advocates constitute a very small minority. Many people doubt that it is desirable or even feasible to eliminate most of the current dependence on external energy supplies, correctly pointing out that this could entail considerable expense, loss of production, or excessive demands on a farmer's labor and management. But it is much harder to understand the views of those who equate greater energy self-sufficiency with a return to farming methods of several decades ago, presumably reasoning that since we were energy self-sufficient when we farmed that way, therefore we must farm that way to be energy self-sufficient. A further basis of this "all-or-nothing" view may be the belief that a farmer is either completely "progressive" or completely "old fashioned." That is, anyone who rejects the progressive tendency toward greater reliance on fossil energy automatically must be someone who rejects all modern developments. Such a person, therefore, not only would have to go back to old methods to be able to achieve self-sufficiency, but actually would want to do so anyway. This point is discussed in more detail for the case of organic farming by Lockeretz and Wernick (1980). Gavett (1975), discussing possible responses to energy problems, presented a detailed analysis of why 1918 farming methods could not be adopted again without, however, actually citing anyone who argued that we should try to do it. White–Stevens (1977) claimed that abandoning just one modern energy-intensive input (fertilizers) would mean a "retreat to the way of life of a century ago," requiring 20 million workers to return to the "toil of the soil" and leaving 100 million Americans without food.

The "all-or-nothing" view ignores that fact that farmers could still get modern grain yields without purchasing fertilizers if they used modern equipment to handle and apply organic wastes and to grow forage legumes in rotation with grains and that they could still run that equipment without petroleum if they used some of their grain to produce alcohol (not to feed horses) and that they could use modern drying and storage methods for the rest of the grain without burning LPG if they used a solar grain dryer.

Certainly there are problems and limitations associated with all of these approaches. What is needed, therefore, is further objective analysis of the potential benefits and drawbacks, together with a greater effort devoted to new farming methods appropriate to new energy conditions. Preferably such an effort would be on a scale that at least begins to approach the one that produced our current energy-dependent methods. This undertaking will certainly not be helped by more comparisons of current practices to the worst possible low-energy alternatives or by more attempts to associate low-energy farming with obsolete and extremely labor-intensive farming or with the specter of famine. What will help is an open-minded approach that creatively and imaginatively takes the best new ideas and modern, improved versions of older ideas, combining them in whatever way is appropriate, without any regard to whether someone chooses to label the result as "old-fashioned."

REFERENCES

AUCOIN, J. 1979. The irrigation revolution and its environmental consequences. Environment 21 (8), 17–20, 38–40.

BENSON, V.W. 1977. A Guide to Energy Savings for the Poultry Producer. USDA and Federal Energy Administration, Washington, D.C.

BLOBAUM, R., FAST, S., HOLCOMB, L., and SWANSON, L. 1979. An Assessment of the Potential for Applying Urban Wastes to Agricultural Lands. Roger Blobaum & Associates, West Des Moines, Iowa.

CAIN, J.L. and VAN DYNE, D.L. 1977. Economic Feasibility of Heating Maryland Broiler Houses with Solar Energy. MP 898. Maryland Agricultural Experiment Station, College Park.

COLLINS, N.E. and WALPOLE, E.W. 1977. Computer evaluation of alternative broiler production programs for energy conservation potential. pp. 431–444. *In* Agriculture and Energy. W. Lockeretz (Editor). Academic Press, New York.

CONNOR, L.J. 1977. Agricultural policy implications of changing energy prices and supplies. pp. 669–681. *In* Agriculture and Energy. W. Lockeretz (Editor). Academic Press, New York.

DAVIS, C.H. and BLOUIN, G.M. 1977. Energy Consumption in the U.S. Chemical Fertilizer System from the Ground to the Ground. pp. 315–331. *In* Agriculture and Energy. W. Lockeretz (Editor). Academic Press, New York.

DOE. 1979. The Report of the Alcohol Fuels Policy Review. DOE/PE-0012. U.S. Department of Energy, Washington, D.C.

DOERING, O.C., III. 1977. Agriculture and energy use in the year 2000. Am. J. Agric. Econ. *59*, 1066–1070.

DUROST, D.D. and BLACK, E.T. 1978. Changes in Farm Production and Efficiency, 1977. Statistical Bulletin No. 612. Economics, Statistics, and Cooperatives Service, USDA, Washington, D.C.

FEA/USDA 1976. Energy and U.S. Agriculture: 1974 Data Base. Vol. 1. Federal Energy Administration and USDA, Washington, D.C.

FRANK, G.G. 1977. A Guide to Energy Savings for the Dairy Farmer. USDA and Federal Energy Administration, Washington, D.C.

GAVETT, E.E. 1975. Can yesterday's farming feed today's people? Farm Index *14* (8), 10–13.

GILLEY, J.R. and WATTS, D.G. 1977. Energy reduction through improved irrigation practices. pp. 187–203. *In* Agriculture and Energy. W. Lockeretz (Editor). Academic Press, New York.

HARTSOCK, J.G. (Editor). 1978. Solar Grain Drying Conference Proceedings. Jointly sponsored by Purdue University, U.S. Department of Energy and USDA, West Lafayette, Indiana.

HEID, W.G. JR. 1978. The Performance and Economic Feasibility of Solar Grain Drying Systems. Agricultural Economic Report No. 396. U.S. Department of Agriculture, Washington, D.C.

KELSO, M.M. 1977. Natural resource economics: the upsetting discipline. Am. J. Agric. Econ. *59*, 814–823.

KENDRICK, J.G. and MURRAY, P.J. 1978. Grain Alcohol in Motor Fuels: An Evaluation. Report No. 81. The Agricultural Experiment Station, University of Nebraska, Lincoln.

LAFLEN, J.M., BAKER, J.L., HARTWIG, R.O., BUCHELE, W.G., and JOHNSON, H.P. 1978. Soil and water loss from conservation tillage systems. Trans. ASAE *21* (5), 881–885.

LARSON, D.L. and FANGMEIER, D.D. 1978. Energy in irrigated crop production. Trans. ASAE *21* (6); 1075–1080.

LITTERMAN, M., EIDMAN, V., and JENSEN, H. 1978. Economics of Gasohol. Economic Report ER 78-10. Department of Agricultural and Applied Economics, University of Minnesota, St. Paul.

LOCKERETZ, W. 1975. Consumption of agricultural resources in the production of fat cattle and food grains. J. Soil Water Conser. *30* (6); 268–271.

LOCKERETZ, W. 1979. Energy Use in Northeast Agriculture and the Potential Role of Renewable Sources. NESEC-4. Northeast Solar Energy Center, Cambridge, Massachusetts.

LOCKERETZ, W. 1982. Comparison of the energy consumption of crop production on organic and conventional farms in the midwestern United States. *In* Basic Techniques in Ecological Farming. S. Hill (Editor). Birkhäuser, Basel, Switzerland.

LOCKERETZ, W. and WERNICK, S. 1980. Organic farming: a step towards closed nutrient cycles. Compost Science/Land Utilization *21* (2), 40–46.

LOCKERETZ, W., SHEARER, G., KLEPPER, R., and SWEENEY, S. 1978. Field crop production on organic farms in the midwest. J. Soil Water Conser. *33* (3); 130–134.

PASOUR, E.C. JR. and BULLOCK, J.B. 1977. Energy and agriculture: some economic issues. pp. 683–693. *In* Agriculture and Energy. W. Lockeretz (Editor). Academic Press, New York.

PERELMAN, M. 1973. Mechanization and the division of labor in agriculture. Am. J. Agric. Econ. *55*, 523–526.

PIMENTEL, D., HURD, L.E., BELLOTTI, A.C., FORSTER, M.J., OKA, I.N., SHOLES, O.D., and WHITMAN, R.J. 1973. Food production and the energy crisis. Science *182*, 443–449.

SANGHI, A.K. and JOHNSON, D. 1978. The Ground Water and Energy Supply Situation for Great Plains Irrigation. CBNS-AE-10. Center for the Biology of Natural Systems, Washington University, St. Louis, Missouri.

SANGHI, A.K. and KLEPPER, R. 1977. Economic impact of diminishing groundwater reserves on corn production under center pivot irrigation. J. Soil Water Conser. *32* (6); 282–285.

SCHELLER, W.A. and MOHR, B.J. 1977. Gasoline does, too, mix with alcohol. Chemtech (Oct.), 616–623.

SFEP. 1979A. Alcohol Fuel Production for the Farm. *Small Farm Energy Project Newsletter* (January). Hartington, Nebraska.

SFEP. 1979B. *Small Farm Energy Project Newsletter* (various issues). Hartington, Nebraska.

SLOGGETT, G. 1977. Energy and U.S. Agriculture: Irrigation Pumping, 1974. Agricultural Economic Report No. 376. Economic Research Service, USDA, Washington, D.C.

SPLINTER, W.E. 1976. Center-pivot irrigation. Scientific American (June); 90–99.

STOUT, P.R. 1974. Agriculture's energy requirements. pp. 13–22. *In* A New Look at Energy Sources. ASA Special Publication Number 22. American Society of Agronomy, Madison, Wisconsin.

STRAIT, J., BOEDICKER, J.J., and JOHANSEN, K.C. 1978. Diesel oil and ethanol mixtures for diesel-powered farm tractors. Agricultural Engineering Department, University of Minnesota, St. Paul, Minnesota.

TAYLOR, C.R. and SWANSON, E.R.   1973.   Experimental nitrogen response functions, actual farm experience and policy analysis.   Illinois Agric. Econ. *13* (2), 26–32.

USDA.   1979.   *Agricultural Prices*, Annual Summary, 1978 and various months. Economics, Statistics and Cooperatives Service, USDA, Washington, D.C.

USDA/ERS.   1975.   Minimum Tillage: A Preliminary Technology Assessment, USDA, Economic Research Office, Office of Planning and Evaluation.   Prepared for the Committee on Agriculture and Forestry, U.S. Senate.   Committee Print, 94th Congress, 1st Session.

VAN ARSDALL, R.T.   1977.   A Guide to Energy Savings for the Livestock Producer.   USDA and Federal Energy Administration, Washington, D.C.

VAN ARSDALL, R.T., and DEVLIN, P.J.   1978.   Energy Policies: Price Impacts on the U.S. Food System.   Agricultural Economic Report No. 407. Economics, Statistics, and Cooperatives Service, USDA, Washington, D.C.

WEISZ, P.B. and MARSHALL, J.F.   1979.   High-grade fuels from biomass farming: potentials and constraints.   Science *206*, 24–29.

WERNICK, S. and LOCKERETZ, W.   1977.   Motivations and practices of organic farmers.   Compost Science *18* (6); 20–24.

WHITE–STEVENS, R.   1977.   Perspectives on fertilizer use, residue utilization and food production.   *In* Fertilizer and Agricultural Residues. R. C. Loehr (Editor).   Ann Arbor Science, Ann Arbor.

WITTMUSS, H., OLSON, L., and LANE, D.   1975.   Energy requirements for conventional versus minimum tillage.   J. Soil Water Conser. *30* (2), 72–75.

WYNN, N.A.   1977.   A Guide to Energy Savings for the Field Crops Producer. USDA and Federal Energy Administration, Washington, D.C.

5

Energy and Agricultural Production in Europe and in the Third World

Yves Le Pape and Jean-Roger Mercier

Introduction
Energy and Agricultural Production in Europe
Energy and Food Production in the Third World
Conclusions
References

INTRODUCTION

To deal with the present topic appropriately within the limits of this short chapter requires that two drastically different problems be considered. First, in Europe, agriculture is an economic activity closely integrated into the general socioeconomic system of each nation of the European Community. In that sense, it must observe the general rules of financial profitability. In France, for instance, agricultural production is regarded by the government as a source of sufficient foreign currency earnings to more than cover increasing oil imports. In addition, farmers are responsible for supplying food to urban areas at prices sufficiently low to keep wages as low as possible. In the past, farmers were called upon to leave their land and make their labor available to industry. The recent trend is to ask them to stay on their farm in order not to aggravate the general unemployment situation. Alternatively, they are also asked to be the "housekeepers" or "gardeners" of rural areas, which more and more are being dedicated to the leisure of city dwellers. The ultimate aims of Western agriculture thus are defined in sociopolitical terms. Strictly speaking, the food production process is but one component of agriculture and is more or less important depending on the country.

Second, in the countries conventionally referred to as the "Third World," we have a totally different problem. Agriculture provides the material basis of survival and food supply for the vast majority of the population. In some countries another constraint is that cash crops have to be grown for export (e.g., coffee, cocoa, cotton, groundnuts). In any case, the cost of production must be low enough to avoid severe competition from grains produced in Asia and in North America.

ENERGY AND AGRICULTURAL PRODUCTION IN EUROPE

Review of the Literature

Since 1974, numerous articles, books and reports have been devoted to the study of the relationship between energy and food production in France and other European countries, following the articles by Pimentel et al. (1973) and Pimentel and Pimentel (1977) in the U.S. Most of the French studies try, with more or less success, to relate energy analysis to technical and socioeconomic trends in agriculture. In France, historically, the first study published was that of Carillon (1975), which was updated recently (Carillon 1979). The decrease in energy efficiency, as pointed out by the author, is due to the elimination of cultivation with animals and also to the increasing consumption of animal products. This analysis leads to a vigorous plea in favor of agricultural mechanization with the conclusion that agriculture as an economic sector has to be protected by being given high priority in the event of energy rationing. Only a few marginal improvements can be made, but these do not question the basic trends of the past few decades. An entirely different conclusion was reached by Mercier (1978), who, in contrast, advocated a complete reorientation of agricultural practices in the direction of an ecological type of farming, based on previously established results of organic farming and new agricultural research prospects. These objectives are the results of an analysis that is based on an energy appraisal of the agricultural predictions of French planners, among other things.

The INRA / IREP group (Institut National de la Recherche Agronomique / Institut de Recherche sur l'Economie et la Planification) more recently conducted a methodological study (Bel et al. 1978) on the potential and limitations of energy analysis applied to agricultural production (Table 5.1). Some computations have been made to test this type of analysis both nationally (French agriculture in 1961 and 1972) and for several French districts ("departments"), each typical of a conventional agricultural system. Examples include grain production in Eure-et-Loir (West) and livestock and milk production in Jura (East). These computations show that the energy efficiency of French agricultural production decreased over the last decade. This drop is more dramatic in places where an intensive livestock industry or vegetable and fruit production dominate than in regions where mixed farming is still practiced. Only the grain producing areas can compensate for the intensification of their practices by increasing their specialization in highly energy efficient production.

TABLE 5.1.   ENERGY BALANCE IN FRENCH AGRICULTURE

| | Energy balance | |
	1961 (10^{12}kcal)	1972 (10^{12}kcal)
Inputs:		
Fuels	15.4	63.4
Fertilization	15.4	37.6
Electricity	1.8	5.6
Machinery	5.7	13.4
Animal feed	2.1	8.5
Total	40.4	128.5
Outputs:		
Crops	44.9	98.3
Animal products	22.4	27.4
Total	67.3	125.7

Source: INRA/IREP (Bel *et al.* 1978).

Jean-Claude Tirel, head of the economics department at INRA, published a report (Tirel 1978) in which he tried to demonstrate how energy analysis could be applied to agriculture. With various reference prices for fossil fuels, he used a linear programming model that evaluated how several price levels, or alternatively a rationing of fossil energy sources, would affect the intensive livestock production in competition with crop production and extensive livestock production. It gives trends that can be understood only within a given social framework and with little or no change of consumption patterns. However, such changes should also be considered.

In Belgium, Jean-Pierre Le Bailly at the Science Department of the Agricultural University of Gembloux has begun a thesis (Le Bailly 1979) devoted to energy analysis of food production and distribution. A completed thesis by Jean-Marie Bellostas (1978) gives reference data on the agriculture of the Mediterranean Basin. Other publications in International Federation for Organic Agriculture Movements from Northern Europe (Germany, Netherlands, Sweden) gave a broad picture of this phenomenon for all of Europe (IFOAM 1977).

In France, two approaches different from the ones above have been taken by agronomists who have shown the original contributions they can make to the solution of the energy problem.

Analysing at the level of experimental plots, Hutter (1978) at INRA Toulouse showed that differences could occur among crops, notably between grasslands and grains, and among alternative rotations. His results are that from the viewpoint of the input/output ratio at the plot level, grasslands have a less favorable energy ratio than grains. Thus the level of intensification of fossil energy inputs can be less important than the choice of crops.

The work done by ITCF (Institut Technique des Cereales et des Fourrages) at Boigneville (Paris 1979) give interesting results on the variable efficiency of farms specializing in grain production. Although this study only takes account of some inputs (seeds, pesticides, fertilizers) and does not consider agricultural mechanization, it clearly shows that, of a sample of 20 farms in the "Bassin Parisien," the best results were obtained by farms that used few inputs, as well as by two farms that were very close to the average in terms of energy inputs. Of the last two, one is the largest pesticide consumer in the sample. This clearly shows that the energy analysis can not be taken as the only criterion, or even the most significant ecological criterion, for decision making or planning in agriculture. It is very important to put energy consumption analysis in its proper place with regard to other analyses that use monetary indicators or labor force accounting. This is also true for agricultural policy options and social choices in general.

In spite of very different points of view, and even sharp disputes, some common conclusions can be drawn from this literature overview.

First, in Europe the direct consumption of energy in agriculture is a minor part of the overall energy consumption of each country. In France, agriculture consumes only 3% of total energy consumption. If indirect energy consumption in the form of machinery, fertilizers, and chemicals is added, this share increases to 6–8%, depending on the source. This is a very low figure compared to other sectors, such as transportation, especially private cars.

Second, energy efficiency decreased continuously between World War II and the present because of several factors, mainly intensification of agricultural practices, regional crop specialization, and increasing consumption of meat products. In France, for instance, if the objectives of the Seventh Five Year Plan are reached (Mercier 1978), agriculture will need more fossil energy inputs than it will produce in the form of food for people (Table 5.2). Agriculture is increasingly becoming a poor transformer of energy, whereas it used to be the only activity capable of producing more energy than it consumed, thanks to photosynthesis.

Third, the increasing importance of the livestock industry has played a crucial part in the decrease in efficiency (Bel *et al.* 1978). This obviously is more important in the case of intensive livestock production, which has grown in Europe in recent decades. It is generally estimated that 8 to 10 kcal of energy inputs are used to produce 1 kcal as meat. Energy efficiency also is a problem for less intensive forms of animal husbandry. In mixed farming systems and biological agriculture where animal production is important, its low energy efficiency tends to decrease overall efficiency even though waste products are put to good use as organic fertilizers.

Fourth, energy analysis is closely correlated with regional specialization, particularly in France. Migrations from rural to urban areas also play an important part in this phenomenon. In some places, agricultural labor is so scarce that even extensive production activities are questionable. At least two million hectares (ha) presently lie idle in France. The imbalance created by this labor-land relationship partly explains the continuing trend toward increasing installed mechanical power, which might seem surprising in view of the energy crisis (Reboul 1978).

TABLE 5.2.   ENERGY BALANCE IN FRENCH
AGRICULTURE AS PROJECTED BY ENERGY
PLANNERS, (SEVENTH FIVE-YEAR PLAN)[1]

	Energy balance (10^{12}kcal)
Inputs:	
Fuels	74.2
Fertilization	73.6
Electricity	30.6
Machinery [2]	22.5
Animal feed	10.6
Miscellaneous	22.7
Total	234.2
Outputs:	
Grains	180.0
Beets	11.4
Oil crops	9.9
Milk	10.6
Cattle	3.8
Pork	5.6
Broilers	1.1
Eggs	1.2
Total	223.6

Source: J.R. Mercier (1978).
[1] Reference year 1980.
[2] Including buildings.

Fifth, the decrease in energy efficiency is linked to that of agricultural income, at least for those farmers who stay out of commercial agriculture. Similarly, indebtedness has increased and largely offsets net income. These conditions together explain the increasing vulnerability of a large number of farms that have become more and more marginal under the pressures of the economic system. It justifies paying attention to even minor items like energy. Such attention perhaps can ensure the survival, even if only short-lived, of a large number of farms.

Energy and New Agricultural Options

Energy analysis can be used for the design of new agricultural options that are bound to be considered in view of increasing energy costs. Some people believe that we must approach an ecological type of farming. Such an approach can be described as ideally producing little or no negative impact on the environment, high-quality products, an increase in farmers' decision-making power, and generation of satisfactory agricultural income. Clearly, a system fulfilling all of these criteria does not presently exist. But some experiments, marginal so far, show the possible "alternative paths."

Biological farming, such as the systems described by Aubert (1977), must be analysed, with energy analysis as one criterion. The few available data suggest that it can be more profitable than conventional farming. Of course, comparable farming systems must be used in the comparison. Otherwise, it is obvious that a mixed biological farm will have lower energy efficiency

than a conventional grain producer, even if the latter uses intensive practices. In one particular case, namely vegetable production, Anne Froment
showed that in the southwest of France efficiency with organic practices
was twice as high as with conventional ones (Froment 1978).

One of the major advantages of organic farming lies in fertilization
methods. The energy consumed in producing chemical fertilizers—computed by the ecology team at the University of Paris VII (Deleage *et al.*
1977) among others—is so high that organic fertilization has a clear advantage. Of course, organic matter must be in abundant supply. Some specialized organic farms have to import manure or straw. This is possible only
because the neighboring coventional farms have an excess of organic materials or do not recycle it themselves. If organic farming is to be extended to
sizeable amounts of land, the availability of organic matter becomes a
problem. Some organic farms might have difficulties getting enough, although at present this is not a problem. In some regions conventional
farming produces such large amounts of animal wastes that not enough
agricultural land is available to spread it without hazards for the environment. This is mainly a problem in regions where intensive livestock industry dominates, like those studied by Professor Noirfalise for the European
Economic Communities (EEC) (Noirfalise 1974). In mountainous areas, it
is increasingly apparent that conventional farming systems cannot be
extended on a large scale. According to official studies and statements of
government agencies, the emphasis should be on new development models
that stress decreases in production costs, improvement of the quality of the
produce, and even substitution of labor for capital and energy. Unfortunately, the means made available to carry out these ideas are not adequate to
solve the enormous problems found in regions that increasingly are becoming marginal and that more and more frequently are turning into deserts.
In this regard, also, energy analysis can be used to estimate the opportunities for reorienting production systems in such regions (Derreumeaux
1978).

Finally, it is well known that in addition to the traditional use of solar
energy for photosynthesis, agriculture can make a direct use of solar energy
for its own productive uses. For stationary equipment, as well as for thermal
needs, Jean-Francois Miquel (1978) demonstrated that various solar arrays
could help increase the energy self-sufficiency of the farm, at least in
principle. A well-integrated solar greenhouse is capable of heating the
house in winter, increasing food production, and drying grains and forages
in summer. Farmers may well go faster than official research in areas such
as biogas. Anaerobic digestion of organic matter with reasonably high
carbon content gives a mixture of methane, carbon dioxide, and traces of
other gases. Many machines were built to use biogas during World War
II—some tens of thousands according to various sources—a few of which
survived during the cheap oil period of the 1950s.

A new factor is that in addition to an increase in energy demand, there is
also a trend toward using manures of various origins (from cattle to rab-

bits). Indeed, some industrial groups, including some large ones, have financial interests in developing biogas generation. One notable approach is that taken by the FIAT company, which developed a system called TOTEM (Total Energy Module). This uses a simple car engine to generate power and heat from biogas. The manufacturer has made interesting claims concerning efficiency: 25% for power, plus 65% for heat.

Now that there have been several years of experiment on full-scale equipment (mainly in Switzerland), the energy/financial results of TOTEM should be assessed. As opposed to this simple application, those which require gas separation, purification, and compression seem to be financially profitable only in the very long run.

The direct utilization of solar energy—apart from solar cells, which will have rapidly decreasing costs in the near future—can be valid only in the following cases: space heating on farms in winter, water heating for barns year round, barn heating in winter, grains and forage drying in summer and autumn, and solar greenhouses in winter.

In the last application, "solar greenhouse" might be a misleading term. There is no need to add solar collectors in front of a greenhouse. Rather, from the beginning, the greenhouse should be designed to collect and store solar heat as well as possible. Preferably it will not be completely glazed, which leads to a waste of energy when the sun does not shine after the greenhouse has overheated in the daytime. But south-glazed and well-insulated greenhouses can save up to 70% of the average fuel consumption of conventional greenhouses. (40 liters of oil per m^2 per year). This is at least the preliminary estimate for the passive solar greenhouse being built in the southwest of France, a test that is unique in Europe.

Finally, in the field of renewable energy sources, biomas utilization seems to be very promising. Wood, sugar surpluses, and various kinds of vegetable matter can be used to produce ethanol or methanol, very valuable alternative fuels. This at least is what the North American promoters of "gasohol" think. In France, in spite of traditional factors that are favorable, such as long experience with alcohol as an automotive fuel in the 1920s, widespread production of sugarbeets, and large amounts of surplus fruits and vegetables, the official research is very skeptical and consequently very little valid information exists.

The potential is very high for renewable energy sources in agriculture. Some authors even are of the opinion that agriculture could produce enough energy for its own self-sufficiency, mainly out of biomass. But what would the cost of that challenge?

What are the major arguments concerning agricultural use of energy? Cost is the major argument of those in favor of conventional systems. They estimate that the changes forced upon agriculture by the energy crisis can only be marginal as regards the existing technologies. True enough, the tuning of tractor carburetors can produce energy savings up to 10%, and moreover can be implemented immediately. However, these improvements are limited. Another argument given by some official sources is that nothing should be said about energy and agriculture, as any dispute strengthens those who want to curtail the supply of oil to agriculture in favor of other sectors. This type of argument simply leads to acceptance of the present misleading policies while refusing to question a very fragile balance.

Finally, there is a need to declare openly that there are alternative approaches to agriculture and energy. The president of the Republic of France emphasized repeatedly during 1979 that "agriculture should be the green petroleum of the nation." The Centre National d'Etudes et d'Experimentation du Machinisme Agricole (CNEEMA) studied the possible contribution of biomass to the overall energy balance of agriculture. But agriculture, as the major potential producer of liquid fuel, will be under heavy pressure from other economic sectors, notably transportation. The question then is: will agriculture have to produce energy on the same basis as it produces food? In other words, won't agricultural net income be fixed low enough that industrial profits can be saved? An affirmative answer to this question is very likely. When do we then expect the Organization of Peasants Exporting Biomass (OPEB) to be created?

This is a valid concern, which distinguishes between the technocrats who think of energy as something agriculture should supply to the rest of the nation and those who think of energy as an expense for farmers, an expense that should be avoided as much as possible to leave farmers with decent incomes.

Conclusion

The use of energy in agriculture has many different aspects. Although some authors consider it in purely technical ways, it has many social and political implications as well. There is a need for political interpretation of energy in agriculture. Energy problems now compel us to look for new development paths for Western agriculture. No legitimacy should be given to the contention of those who want agriculture to be treated as a protected sector, with no restrictions applied in case of national supply shortage.

It is our view that many farmers, primarily those who did not embark upon intensive schemes, can benefit from the new options in production practices and techniques. These options can permit energy conservation or even energy production to increase their independence with respect to the non-agricultural sectors (specifically the agro-industries), who presently dictate their choices.

But these new options should also serve larger purposes than those of the farmers themselves. This is especially true at the regional level, particularly in regions where there is underdevelopment, with its questionable benefits of overexploitation by tourism, as around the Mediterranean Sea. It is, however, very clear that the development of renewable energy sources in these regions can only be made in the framework of a national, or even better, a European energy policy. Contradictions and conflicts already exist. A typical example is the development of the sheep industry. The latter is probably the most suitable way to take advantage of the available resources in the Mediterranean area. Ongoing research has shown that more productive practices could be implemented to use the extensive grasslands better. However such practices can be developed only if there is a decision not to locate sheep production only in New Zealand.

At the national level, not all European governments agree that it is in their interest to go to a more self-sufficient and energy-conserving type of agriculture. The extreme dependence on American soybeans as a cattle feed is not being opposed to the same extent by every European government. A uniform policy at the European level thus depends on individual political choices in each of the member nations of the Community.

There is an urgent need for present experiments on alternative agricultural methods to go from the marginal stage to widespread development. The purely demonstrative effect will not be sufficient, however, and many administrative, social, and political bottlenecks must be overcome. These present considerable handicaps, but recent trends among some institutions that usually call for more intensive agriculture, notably INRA, show that something is changing.

In the face of these changes, one can clearly perceive a defensive posture on the part of some advocates of organic farming in Europe who feel threatened in their present positions and as a result turn in on themselves and their own prospects. This is all the more absurd because organic farming as it is presently practiced by a few thousand farmers in Europe (possibly 10,000) cannot by itself constitute an alternative agricultural policy that could solve the entire problem, particularly regarding energy. Many research activities are needed to take full advantage of the experience of these pioneers. But starting from this sound basis, other paths can be tried if we want to design technical solutions that could be integrated into an agricultural policy meeting the needs of threatened farmers who see their region becoming a desert.That agricultural policy could also respond to the wishes of all those who want an energy future other than nuclear development and who hope for an alternative political future to the one presently being developed in Europe.

ENERGY AND FOOD PRODUCTION IN THE THIRD WORLD

Energy Consumption: Recent Trends

While energy conservation has already become a major goal in most of the industrialized countries, the problem of controlling energy consumption at the world level is frequently seen as amounting to oppressing the poor countries. These countries claim that their demand for more energy is directly related to an increase in their standards of living. Nuclear advocates in France, using this legitimate objective for their own propaganda, go as far as justifying their heavy nuclear program by the fact that more

TABLE 5.3.   COMMERCIAL ENERGY
CONSUMPTION IN 1976

Country	Coal equivalents per capita per year (kg)
Upper Volta	13
Nigeria	94
Senegal	120
Ghana	200
Ivory Coast	370
India (1975)	375
United States	10,805

Source: Asian Development Bank 1977.

petroleum would supposedly be at the disposal of Third World countries if nuclear power generation were developed quicker in the rich countries.

The basic argument is that Western countries, which have an energy consumption level of over 5 tons of coal equivalent per capita per year (Table 5.3), are so accustomed to waste that it might be possible to stabilize energy consumption without reducing the standard of living. Moreover, their slow population increase means that zero energy growth could well be the rule in these nations. In contrast, in the Third World, socioeconomic factors tend to lead to the opposite conclusions: population growth is large, current energy consumption is low, and economic development is changing toward a more diversified pattern. The result of all this should be a large increase in energy demand. In that respect, seeking zero growth in energy consumption in the Third World would again mean frustrating these nations and playing the part of the bad guy.

Indeed, the growth in energy consumption worldwide mainly results from that of the Third World. This is seen from the fact that studies estimate that the Third World, which had 50% of the population in 1975 but consumed only 15% of the world's energy, by 2020 will have 65% of the population and 23% of the world's energy consumption. If no severe control of this growth is practiced, then 25% would represent 16 billions of coal equivalent, or nearly twice the present world consumption.

The thesis developed in the rest of this chapter is that it should be possible to control energy growth and develop renewable energy sources while increasing the standard of living of the majority of the population. The need for achieving this stems from the following factors.

Part of the energy consumed is not recorded in the official statistics, especially fuel wood and crop/animal residues. Makhijani (1976) estimates that this type of energy accounts for much more than conventional commercial energy sources. Depending on the particular case, the ratio of noncommercial to commercial energy consumption is estimated to be between 5 and 20. However, because of the lack of statistical information estimates of growth are very inaccurate. In any case, utilization of noncommercial energy sources has very dramatic ecological consequences on soil fertility (no recycling of organic matter) as well as on climate (increased desertification). This type of energy consumption pattern is not sustainable.

Population control is gradually becoming a must in the long run for all the nations of the Third World. Growth rates like these of the past—3 to 3.5% per annum—are no longer likely.

There is no obvious reason why Third World nations should necessarily follow what is being done in the industrialized countries. Placed at a decisive point of their history, with a recent record of poverty and starvation behind them and a future largely determined by a crisis of the industrialized countries, they are still in a position to choose a different path. They might embark on a development pattern that gives priority to fulfilling the basic needs of their people. One typical example is food. A famous article in CERES, an FAO sponsored newspaper (Borgstrom 1974), explained that because of the predominance of meat consumption, the overall energy content of the average American diet was 6 to 7 times greater than that of the predominantly vegetarian Indian diet, considering both the primary energy content of the crops fed to animals and the grains and legumes directly eaten by humans.

The energy consumption is clearly much higher, without any corresponding advantage from the dietetic point of view. In view of this, Third World people could decide to remain on a vegetarian diet, as some well-off people in the industrialized countries are now doing.

Energy and Food Production

The most important work done on Third World policy is that of Makhijani (1976, 1977). It is the starting point for much more thorough research, which unfortunately has not been yet carried out so extensively as it has been for Western agriculture. Makhijani develops his thesis around the idea of substituting a rational and long-term development based on renewable energy instead of the present plundering of noncommercial energy sources. There is obviously an argument about the "renewability" of a particular good. Wood and crop residues are renewable in their very nature, but only if the rate of utilization is not excessive.

The description of village-level organization is very interesting, but the actual decision-making processes are totally overlooked because of a lack of macroeconomic thinking. However, a fundamental question is addressed: how to collectively manage the village and regional resources to fulfill the needs of the community.

Numerous academic and official publications have been issued on the topic, one of the better known being the collective book edited by Bill Stout (1978) on which FAO and the French CNEEMA cooperated.

The University of Paris VII (Applied ecology) produced a few studies on the relationship between energy and agriculture, particularly in the Sahelian countries. CIRED (Centre International pour la Recherche sur l'Ecologie et le Development) edited "Nourrir en harmonie aver l'environment," a good review of the existing literature. One original approach, mixing action and information, is that of the GRET (Groupe de Recherche et d'Echangers Technologiques). It has created a network of subscribers and distributes practical bulletins on renewable energy sources and appropriate technology, as well as dealing with subscribers' questions and problems. Such a model, which is largely based on the U.S. VITA, has given good publicity to the concept of renewable energy sources, such as at the 1979 U.N. Conference on Science and Technology for Development in Vienna. Application de Recherches sur l'Energie et la Societé (ARES) is presently editing a collective book, "Technology and Rural Development," summarizing recent French experience in the connection between technological choices and rural development policies, with an emphasis on the utilization of local and renewable resources.

Energy in Third World Food Production[1]

The majority of non-wage-earning family farmers in a given region practice a homogeneous cropping pattern, such as millets and sorghum in the Sahelian countries, tubers in coastal areas of West Africa, or paddy rice in Madagascar. The present technologies reflect historical experience, practices imposed by the colonial authorities and their successors, and limits in ability to invest. Someone unfamiliar with Third World farming might find it hard to accept this argument; however, a net cash income of approximately $200 U.S. per year, typical of Upper Volta, does not permit heavy savings.

The prevailing techniques are based on human and animal labor, metal or wood implements, and limited use of modern inputs like chemical fertilizers and biocides. These present practices are not by themselves efficient enough to produce the food required for a reasonable standard of living for Third World people, nor can they keep up with the population growth rate and the resulting increase in food consumption.

The signs of this failure are there: chronic malnutrition, particularly among children, and periodic occurrence of uncontrolled famines requiring emergency external assistance, which may turn out to be as humiliating as it is harmful.

Something has to be changed. To limit ourselves to strictly technico-economic matters, one can try to improve three types of agricultural budgets: the protein budget, the fertilization budget, and the energy budget. "Budget" is defined here as production less consumption. In the case of protein, livestock have an important role. In Third World countries, animal husbandry is heavily connected with daily life or, alternatively, makes use of nonproductive lands. It does not entail the same waste as it does in Western countries.

The search for an improved *protein budget* has far-reaching consequences and raises questions regarding the objectives of the production system itself. For example, we have calculated that, in Senegal, peanuts—a crop

---

[1] The obvious limitations of this section mean that it doesn't replace a comprehensive analysis of a specific problem in the Third World. What follows applies mostly to farmers in West and Central Africa, Latin America, and South Asia.

highly promoted by the colonial authorities—would be sufficient to meet 80% of the protein requirements of the population, provided this commodity is not exported to Europe to provide super profits to peanut oil companies. Similarly, research activities in the field of high-protein crops have hardly been encouraged by the foreign research centers established in Africa. The difficulties of introducing soybeans in West Africa are well known. The U.S. National Academy of Sciences boldly contributed to the information struggle by publishing several books on the subject (e.g., the winged bean) (National Academy of Sciences 1975A,B).

The *fertilization budget* is of particular importance, but it has hardly been addressed in the past, except for transferring the solutions applied in Western agriculture, despite obvious differences. Agronomists in Western countries claim that organic nitrogen mineralization is slow and that productivity is high enough to lead to a large production of residues that can be plowed back into the soil. In the Third World, the situation is altogether different: on the one hand, nitrogen mineralization is very quick and, on the other hand, *competition is very high between alternative uses of the limited amount of organic matter available.*

Here again, there is no unique or obvious solution. Several sources of fertilization will have to be combined:

—Atmospheric nitrogen fixation by legumes (and later by grain crops)
—Combining fertilizer/energy production using methane generation
—Complementing organic fertilization with a minimum level of chemical fertilization (preferably from local resources)

The *energy budget* in Third World agriculture is yet another issue:

—As it now stands it gives a very satisfactory energy out/in ratio much more favorable (for a given crop) than in Western agriculture (Lockeretz 1977; for sorghum in France, Hutter 1978).
For instance:

Crop	Third World		Western Countries	
Wheat	6.25	(India)	2	(U.S.)
Rice	7.7	(Philippines)	1.35	(U.S.)
Corn	16.67	(Mexico)	2.7	(U.S.)
Sorghum	20	(Sudan)	3.1	(France)

—The energy consumption pattern will have to be adapted to the technologies needed to feed people adequately in a latter development stage.
—The reasonable optimism of promoters of renewable energy sources, who can produce tables showing how resources and utilization match perfectly (as in Table 5.4, which was abstracted from a workshop in Tanzania) is partly cancelled by the crying lack of actual technologies.
—Finally, mechanization, which ultimately will be needed in most cases (if

TABLE 5.4. SOLAR ENERGY APPLICABILITY MATRIX.[2]

Solar technology	Energy use							Heating						
	Water pumping	Light-ing	Cool-ing	Com-muni-cations	Water desalt-ing	Spin-ning	Saw-ing	Cook-ing	Space	Domes-tic water	Grind-ing	Dry-ing	Trans-port	Fertil-izing
Solar cells	+	+	+	++	–	+	–	–	–	–	+	–	–	–
Flat-plate collectors*	++	–	++	–	++	–	–	+	++	++	–	++	–	–
Concentrating thermal collectors	+	+	+	+	+	–	–	+	–	–	–	–	–	–
Solar, Stirling (small scale)	+	+	+	+	–	+	+	–	–	–	+	–	–	–
Solar, rankine	+	+	+	–	–	+	+	–	–	–	+	–	–	–
Wind (mechanical)	++	–	–	–	–	+	+	–	–	–	++	–	–	–
Wind generator	++	++	++	++	–	+	+	–	–	–	++	–	–	–
Water (mechanical)	++	–	–	–	–	++	++	–	–	–	++	–	–	–
Hydroelectric	++	++	++	++	–	++	++	–	–	–	++	–	–	–
Bioconversion wood/charcoal	–	+	–	–	–	–	–	++	.++	++	–	++	–	+
Biogas	+	++	+	–	–	–	–	++	–	++	–	+	+	++
Draft animals	++	–	–	–	–	–	–	+	–	+	++	–	++	++

Source: Workshop on Solar Energy for the Villages of Tanzania (Tanzania National Scientific Research Council 1977).
[1] Animals included as solar technology (based on photosynthesis).
[2] Includes solar stills.
Note: Symbols: ++, applicable; +, potentially applicable; –, not applicable.

only for irrigation and some seasonal agricutural work), not only raises questions concerning the supply of fuels but even more importantly involves issues of professional skills and logistics (spare parts).

In a first stage, it could be adequate to concentrate primarily on improving the efficiency of existing processes, instead of using limited research resources solely to investigate new energy sources. One typical example is that of domestic cooking. Although solar cooking seems to make good sense in places with abundant sun, unfortunately it is not attractive at present. The fact that only one of the seven main types of solar cookers identified and analyzed by the Georgia Institute of Technology (Bomar *et al.* 1978) led to some commercial development does not merely reflect a lack of interest on the part of governments and private companies. It also is a consequence of the inadequacy of the technology—*at present*—both financially and technically. However, the efficiency of wood burning could easily be increased in the very short run from the present 5% (open fire) to 15% with very cheap, long-lasting stoves. Similarly, any cheap improvement that increases the efficiency of draft animal cultivation should be encouraged.

However, in the short run these improvements will provide only marginal changes in the economic systems of the Third World. The real technological revolution to be sought is that of a 100% renewable society. This is by no means a "back to autonomy" claim, but rather a hope for regionally autonomous communities. Njieunde (1976) has clearly shown that total self-sufficiency was a dream of the past. But experiences like these of the New Alchemy Institute in the United States demonstrate that some type of convergence between the most advanced scientists and grass-root agricultural development in the Third World could be accomplished during the twenty-first century.

Renewable Energy Sources in Rural Areas

Two reference books exist on the subject (Ministere de la Cooperation 1977; National Academy of Sciences 1976). Unless unprecedented efforts are made, both financially and from the human point of view, development of renewable energy sources in the Third World will have to be a long-run matter. Research has been so poor and so obviously dominated by foreign countries that no base exists for the immediate development of renewable energy sources in the Third World. However, there are surprising figures that give a clue to the potential development of these energy sources. There regularly falls on each m^2 of a Sahelian country (Table 5.5) a minimum of 1,500,000 kcal per annum or 0.15 tons of oil equivalent in solar energy, roughly the energy requirement of one individual for one year. Besides, population density is generally so low in these countries (selected here because they are among the poorest in the world) that each inhabitant has at his disposal 5 ha, or 50,000 m^2, or 50,000 times the area theoretically needed to meet his energy needs with 100% efficiency. This is probably what makes some French "experts" say that at the gathering stage, Africa can

TABLE 5.5   RANGE OF SOLAR RADIATION IN SAHELIAN
COUNTRIES

	Solar radiation (1000 kcal/m²/day)	
	Minimum	Maximum
Niamey (Niger)	4.7	6.0
Abidjan (Ivory Coast)	3.4	4.6

Source: Mercier 1978.

easily feed its own population. The only trouble is this statement is not true. People are not getting enough food; and among the technologies using renewable energy sources, one could even say that the one that commercially is the most advanced—solar pumps—has not convinced either the skeptics or the supporters of solar energy.[2]

The Tanzanian seminar called in 1977 (Tanzania National Scientific Research Council 1977) concluded that the technologies to be developed in the short run were electricity generation by photovoltaic cells, biomethane generation, electricity generation by small-scale hydraulic systems, solar refrigeration, and solar drying of agricultural produce. Nothing in this could significantly change the development pattern of the rural areas in the Third World.

However, the same seminar describes the list of research activities needed to bring the development of renewable energy sources from the stage of marginal but highly suggestive demonstrations to eventual full reliance on renewable energy sources as described qualitatively in Table 5.4. The surprising fact is that no major technological breakthrough is needed to accomplish that stage, except gains in manufacturing productivity and a rise in the cost of conventional fuels, which cannot but happen.

In the meantime, apart from exploiting the sound idea of developing profitable techniques immediately instead of wrongly trying to address fundamental problems, the question arises of who is going to invent, test, and develop the basic technique for a "100% renewable" society.

Some elements of the answer are in the following statements.

Choosing a technology policy is clearly a political matter. The most outstanding proof of this was given by a World Bank official, V.V. Bhatt (1978), who showed how large industrially based development is directly correlated with one particular type of agricultural development and with the choice of a very centralized political structure. In his comparison between Ghandi's Sarvodaya and Nehru's socialist approaches to development, there is a clear parallel between, on one hand, small-scale, cottage-based political power utilizing appropriate technologies and the resources of craftsmanship and, on the other, centralized power utilizing large, imported technologies and hired

---

[2]The capital cost of a solar pump in Mali was estimated recently at $36,000 U.S. for a nominal power output between 1.5 and 2kW.

labor. Coming back to our original purpose, this clearly establishes that no hope can be placed in political structures heavily dominated by foreign interests, whether from the West or from the East. It is significant that Tanzania, one of the most independent nations of Central Africa, was the one to organize an international seminar on solar energy with operational applications.

Likewise, little hope should be placed in the existing research centers, particularly the old French research centers in Africa. Even if some individuals tried to promote innovative research topics, the machinery has its own momentum and goes on copying the Western model. One possible solution, given this deficiency and also the lack of interest on the part of local governments, could be the creation of small funds aimed at financing innovation, financed through external grants for unallocated purposes and capable of helping original projects. This approach could help make the activities of groups working on community development compatible with the ideas of certain groups in international financial organizations. It might prove more efficient than the billions poured into traditional projects like building huge dams, which impose monolithic technological choices.

In fact, the technological alternative often exists, and an ability to observe may be all that is needed to notice it. In a notable multidisciplinary study, Michailof *et al.* (1975) showed that, in building a sugar factory, one could choose from several possible technologies and that size alone was not the only variable in an investment decision. The technology itself can be a decision, for instance, between the large "modern" factories presently being developed in the Ivory Coast and the intermediate "khandsari" industry in India. The former usually is very capital intensive, generates little employment, and dissipates foreign currency. Instead of giant 50,000-ton per year sugar factories, a balanced network of 5,000-ton khandsari factories could help promote a sounder, more autonomous regional development. What is true in the sugar industry could be true for other economic activities as well, such as agricultural mechanization.

CONCLUSIONS

This section has tried, in a short space, to deal with an enormous problem, namely the basis of a rural organization in the Third World that can survive the energy crisis. What remains is to try to give the outlines of a program of research-action to be implemented immediately. Probably the most qualified groups are those who participated in the 1979 U.N. Conference on Science and Technology for Development in Vienna. They called for more resources allocated to research programs in their own home countries. The required means are out of proportion with the present budgets. Reminding the assembly of the past famous scientists living at the time in what is presently called the Third World, Abdus Salam, 1979 Nobel Prize winner, estimated that the budgets for science and technology in the poor nations should be multiplied by ten, reaching a minimum level of $20 billion U.S. This effort should preferably be carried out in the home countries with national research institutes.

Under these conditions, a new development of science and technology would be possible, and the fame of once-famous centers like Samarkand, Jaipur, or Baghdad could be reborn.

REFERENCES

ASIAN DEVELOPMENT BANK. 1977. Annual Report.

AUBERT, C. 1977. L'agriculture biologique. Le Courrier du Livre, Paris.

BEL, F., LE PAPE, Y., and Mollard, A. 1978. Analyse énergétique de la production agricole. Concepts et méthodes. INRA, Grenoble.

BELLOSTAS, J.H. 1978. Stuctures énergétiques des pays de la facade nord-méditerranéenne. Analyse de la consommation agricole. Thèsis Faculté de Droit et des Sciences économiques. Université de Montpellier, France.

BOMAR, S.H. Jr., et al. 1978. A state of the art survey of solar powered irrigation pumps, solar cookers and wood burning stoves for use in sub-Sahara Africa. Georgia Institute of Technology, Atlanta, Georgia.

BORGSTROM, L. 1974. Le coût d'un tracteur—CERES. November–December, FAO Rome.

CARILLON, R. 1975. Essais de réflexion sur l'énergie en agriculture. Etudes n° 404 and 408. Centre National d'Etudes et d'Experimentation du Machinisme Agricole (CNEEMA) Paris.

CARILLON, R. 1979. Actualisation de l'estimation de la consommation annuel le d'énergie directe de l'agriculture pour la production agricole. Bulletin d'Information du CNEEMA No. 258, 27.

DELEAGE, J.P., SAUGET-NAUDIN, N., and SOUCHON, C. 1977. Analyse éco-énergétique du système agricole français en 1970. Laboratoire d'Ecologie Générale et Appliquée. Université de Paris, Paris.

DERREUMEAUX, J.D. 1978. Analyse énergétique d'un groupe d'exploitations des Alpes du Sud. Centre d'Aide Aux Technologies Appropies Dans Les Alpes du Sud. France.

FROMENT, A. 1978. Comparaison de la consommation d'énergie en culture légumiere conventionnelle et biologique. Mémoire de fin d'études. Ecole Nationale des Ingénieurs des Techniques Horticoles d'Angers. France.

IFOAM. 1977. Towards a sustainable agriculture. Proceedings International Conference. Sissach. Wirz Verlag, Aarau, Switzerland.

LE BAILLY, J.P. 1979. Analyse énergétique de la production agricole belge. Faculte agronomique de Gembloux. Belgique.

MAKHIJANI, A. 1976. Agriculture and Energy in the Third World. Ballinger press. New York.

MAKHIJANI, A. 1977. Energy Policy for the Rural Third World. International Institute for Environment and Development. Washington, D.C.

MERCIER, J.R.   1978.   Energie et agriculture: le choix écologique.   Debard, Paris.

MICHAILOF, S., GUERIN, B. and ARMAINGAUD, J.   1975.   Technologie appropriée étude de cas de l'industrie sucrière de khandsari.   Delegation Générale á la Recherche Scientifique et Technique.   Paris.

MINISTERE DE LA COOPERATION.   1977.   Evaluation des énergies nouvelles poulre développement des Etats africains.   Paris.

MIQUEL, J.F.   1978.   L'énergie solaire en zone agricole.   Centre National de la Recherche Scientifique.   THIAIS.   France.

NATIONAL ACADEMY OF SCIENCES.   1975A.   Underexploited tropical plants with promising economic value.   National Academy of Sciences.   Washington, D.C.

NATIONAL ACADEMY OF SCIENCES.   1975B.   The winged bean: Protein crop for the tropics.   National Academy of Sciences.   Washington, D.C.

NATIONAL ACADEMY OF SCIENCES.   1976.   Energy for rural development.   Washington, D.C.

NJIEUNDE, G.   1976.   Les vertus de l'auto-consommation.   CERES, September/ October.   FAO, Rome.

NOIRFALISE, C.   1974.   Consèquences écologiques de l'application des techniques modernes de production en agriculture.   Informàtiones internes sur l'agriculture.   No. 137.   European Economic Communities.

PIMENTEL, D. and PIMENTEL, M.   1977.   Compter les calories.   CÉRÈS.   September/October, 17–21.

PIMENTEL, D., HURD, L.E., BELLOTTI, A.C., FORSTER, M.J., OKA, I.N., SHOLES, O.D., and WHITMAN, R.J.   1973.   Food production and the energy crisis.   Science 182, 443–449.

PARIS, C.   1979.   Analyse énergétique d'exploitations céréalières du Bassin Parisien.   Institut Technique des Céréales et des Fourrages.   Boigneville.   France.

STOUT, B.   1978.   Energy for worldwide agriculture.   University of Michigan, East Lansing.

TANZANIA NATIONAL SCIENTIFIC RESEARCH COUNCIL.   1977.   Workshop on solar energy for the villages of Tanzania.   Dar es Salaam.   August 10–19.

TIREL, J.C.   1978.   Comment valoriser les résultats de l'analyse énergétique en agriculture?   Quelques réflexions méthodologiques.   INRA.   Département d'Economie et de Socologie Rurales.   Paris.

FURTHER READING

ANTAGANA, H.   1977.   The Energy Crisis.   Afriscope.   Yaounde–Cameroons.

BAKER, R.C.   1977.   The Sahel: An Information Crisis.   Pergamon Press.   New York.

BHATT, V.V.   1978.   Development problem: Strategy and technology choice: Sarvodaya and socialist approaches in India.   World Bank, Washington, D.C.

BROWN, N. and HOWE, J.   1978.   Solar energy for village development. Science *199*, 651–657.

CROSSON, P.   1978.   Report to the USAID on applications of science and technology to rural development in India.   Resources for the Future.   U.S. Agency for Intern.   Development, Washington, D.C.

DALAI, V.   1976.   Energy strategies for India: An assessment of new energy technologies.   Publication.   Princeton Univ., Princeton, N.J.

FAO.   1976A.   The state of food and agriculture: Energy and agriculture. FAO, Rome.

FAO.   1976B.   L'énergie au service de l'agriculture dans les pays en développement.   Bulletin mensuel économie et statistique agricoles 25, No.2.   FAO, Rome.

HOWE, J.   1977.   Energy for Villages of Africa.   Overseas Development Council.   Washington, D.C.

HUTTER, W.   1978.   Efficience de l'énergie consommée par les travaux culturaux.   Bulletin Technique d'Information.   Paris.

LOCKERETZ, W. (Editor).   1977.   Agriculture and Energy.   Academic Press, New York.

MOUTTAPA, F.   1978.   Natural resources management for food and agriculture production through self-sustaining agriculture in developing countries. FAO, Rome.

REBOUL, C.   1978.   Déterminants économiques de la mécanisation agricole L'accroissement du parc des tracteurs de grande puissance.   Département d'Economie et de Sociologie Rurales, Paris.   Institut National de la Recherche Agronomique.

6

Role of Stress Tolerance in Integrated Pest Management

Eliot W. Coleman and Richard L. Ridgway

Introduction
Historical Perspective
Defining the Concept
Factors Affecting Stress Tolerance
Discussion
Conclusions
References

INTRODUCTION

Modern production technology, which has been developed and put into use in the United States over the past fifty years, has resulted in great increases in yields from crops and livestock. For instance, since the mid-1940s, increased use of improved varieties, fertilizers, irrigation, and pesticides have resulted in three-fold increases in yields of corn and potatoes and two-fold increases in yields of wheat (USDA 1979A). During this same period, use of synthetic organic pesticides (insecticides, herbicides, fungicides, nematicides, etc.) has increased from less than 23,000 kg per year to a current annual use of over 450 million kg (Ridgway *et al.* 1978). These pesticides have been used primarily to combat such pests as insects, weeds, plant diseases,and nematodes. The current use of large quantities of pesticides, while producing substantial real or perceived benefits, is creating increasing concerns. Specifically, these concerns include pesticide toxicity to both human and wildlife populations, pest resistance to chemicals, pesticide destruction of beneficial populations, and increasing pesticide costs to farmers (Anon. 1979). These concerns have resulted in placing more emphasis on integrated pest management, i.e., the selection, integration, and use of methods of pest control on the basis of anticipated economic, ecological, and sociological consequences (USDA 1977). A wide range of methods of pest control, in addition to conventional pesticides, is available for possible use. These include cultural controls, host resistance, biological agents (parasites, predators, and microbial agents), genetic controls, attractants and repellents, and growth regulators. These various methods of pest suppression, together with loss thresholds and survey and prediction techniques, comprise components of integrated pest management systems. The selection and integration of the most appropriate methods and techniques for use to manage a pest complex then forms an integrated pest management system (USDA 1979B). A number of comprehensive reviews are available that deal with the general field of pest management (NAS Vol. I−V 1975; Metcalf and Luckmann 1975; Apple and Smith 1976; OTA 1979). Other reviews deal with control of certain types of pests such as weeds (Anderson 1977; Crafts 1975; Rice 1974; Shaw 1974) and plant diseases (Horsfall and Cowling 1977), while still others emphasize different methods of pest control such as host plant resistance (Maxwell and Jennings 1979), parasites and predators (Huffaker and Messenger 1976; Ridgway and Vinson 1977), microbial agents (Baker and Cook 1974; Burges and Hussey 1971; Huffaker and Messenger 1976), attractants and repellents (Beroza 1976; Shorey and McKelvey 1977), insecticides (Metcalf and McKelvey 1976) and herbicides (Andus 1976).

Protection of crops from pest attack and subsequent loss of production is an essential part of modern food production. This protection can best be achieved through the use of integrated pest management. However, considerable information is already available on integrated pest management and many of its commonly recognizable components. Therefore, in this chapter, only the potential for reducing pest losses to crops through manipulation of the nongenetically controlled physiological state of plants, thus reducing susceptibility of plants to attack by insects and plant diseases, will be considered. This particular area of emphasis has been selected because it previously has received less attention than it would seem to deserve in light of the available evidence (El-Tigani 1962; Krauss 1969; Trolldenier 1969; Leath and Ratcliffe 1974; Perrenoud 1977). Although this topic often has been referred to as plant health, the term "stress tolerance" has been chosen for use in this chapter. However, the term "plant health" may be preferred where that usage is more likely to convey the meaning of the concept.

The concept of stress tolerance to pest attack is presented here from the point of view of the agriculturist rather than the specialist. In using this approach, no attempt has been made to review all the relevant literature. Rather, emphasis is placed on developing the concept from a broad perspective in an attempt to emphasize its potential application in food production.

HISTORICAL PERSPECTIVE

Perhaps the earliest reference to the role of stress tolerance in the susceptibility of plants to pests is a statement by Erasmus Darwin (1800), the grandfather of Charles Darwin. In his treatise on agriculture and gardening, he referred to the condition of fruit tree leaves damaged by insects. He related the opinion of "some observers" that the affected leaves were "previously out of health which occasioned them to supply a proper situation for those insects which molest them."

Kirby and Spence (1867) recognized the same concept, but they were more philosophical. They considered the total balance of the natural system and the place in that balance of plants and insects. They felt that the role of insects as a countercheck to the "hurtful luxurience" of plants was of utmost importance in promoting the general welfare of the natural system: "It is a wise provision that there should exist a race of beings empowered to remove all her superfluous productions from the face of nature; and in effecting this, whatever individual harm may arise, insects must be deemed general benefactors."

The beginnings of a more scientifically based expression of the importance of stress tolerance must be credited to Ward (1890), a leading proponent of what was at that time referred to as the "predisposition theory." Ward (1890) expressed the basic concepts of the predisposition theory as follows:

I hope to show in the course of this lecture, how the modern study of the pathology of plants differs in methods from that of our predecessors, especially in this very particular—the recognition of the reactions of the host to its living and non-living environment, as opposed to the reactions of the parasite to its living and non-living environment, and, further, of the truth that disease is the outcome of a want of balance in the struggle for existence just as truly as normal life is the result of a different positing of the factors of existence. . . . it is evident that a plant may vary within very wide limits of the condition we term health. . . . in some of its deviations from the normal the plant offers conditions to an attacking parasite which may be at one time favorable, at another not. . . . Under certain circumstances, the parenchymatous tissues of the living plant may be in a peculiarly tender, watery condition, where the cell walls are thinner and softer, the protoplasm is more permeable and less resistant, and the cell sap contains a larger proportion of organic acids, glucose, and soluble nitrogenous materials than usual. When the external conditions become more favorable . . . increased transpiration and respiration lead to more normal metabolic activity.

Lees (1926) wrote that resistance to pests seems to be variable according to the condition of the plant and that cultural practices such as irrigation and manuring can cause internal changes in the plant that will have an influence on the attacking pests. Lees viewed these processes as a two-way street. Because the intervention of man in the natural system could modify host resistance in a negative direction, it would seem logical that contrary treatment might have a positive effect on host resistance. He concluded by suggesting that "perhaps, in the future more reliance will be put on correct cultural conditions than on spraying and the conditions of the host plant be more closely watched than the presence of the insect parasite."

Felt and Bromley (1931) were also in accord with the preceding. In a discussion of the potential for developing resistance in trees against pest attack they contended that trees grown under stressful conditions are less vigorous and more prone to insect problems. They suggested that since the physical condition of the tree is a key to the severity of the insect attack the aim of the grower should be to upgrade that resistance through proper cultural practices. Thiem (1938) contended that such agricultural practices as monoculture, often considered a causative factor of insect multiplication, present no problem if other cultural practices succeed in assuring resistance. He suggests that much more research is required on the mechanisms for altering the physiological state of the plant through cultural practices: "That far reaching changes in the condition of plants exist beyond differences in individual hereditary inclination, can be considered proven . . . what we lack is the precise physiological expressions for these changes."

Johnson (1968), in an extensive review of the relation of insect attack to the physiological condition of the host, concurs. He states that there is no doubt that a principal component affecting the multiplication of feeding insects on a plant is the condition of the plant as influenced by nutrient or moisture stress. He further noted that even though the evidence is abundant to document the influence of plant physiological condition on insect numbers, there is no correspondingly detailed evidence to quantify the insect–plant relationship. Such information would aid in predicting the impact on pest population changes and the subsequent need for additional control measures.

Baker and Cook (1974), nearly 85 years after Ward (1890), quoted before, described the concept in almost identical terms: "The occurrence of a plant disease thus indicates that some aspect of the biological balance is not in equilibrium."

The general concept that the condition of the plant has substantial influence on its susceptibility to pests such as insects and plant diseases has been recognized for nearly two centuries. However, to understand the concept of stress tolerance so that it can be carefully studied and used in practical food production, additional elaboration is needed.

DEFINING THE CONCEPT

The concept of stress tolerance to pests can perhaps best be defined within the context of resistance of plants to pest attack. However, in defining stress tolerance, it is important to remember that we are not dealing with genetically influenced plant resistance, but rather with an induced resistance dependent on environmental factors. There is no doubt that genetics plays a very important part in determining the susceptibility of different varieties to pests. However, plants influenced by environmental factors to be stress tolerant is a separate phenomenon and one that only a limited number of researchers have tried to define.

McColloch (1924) recognized two types of resistance, which he called natural and artificial. He defined natural resistance as that which is shown by native plants or acquired by cultivated ones, while he defined artificial resistance as that which is developed in cultivated plants by selections, crossing, breeding, and stimulation by means of alterations in cultural or other practices. He further divided artificial resistance into two types: first, the breeding of resistant plants and, second, the development of non-inherited or temporary resistance in plants that can be induced by proper fertilizer application.

Mumford (1931) proposed the term epiphylaxis for external protective mechanisms and the term endophylaxis for the internal protection afforded by "biochemical qualities." As examples of epiphylaxis he cited thickness of the epidermis, external hairs, and maturity date. Under endophylaxis he gave examples of the effects of differing fertilizer regimes on plant resistance. He further speculated on the correlation between the physicochemical properties of the cell sap and resistance or susceptibility of plants to sap-feeding insects.

Thiem (1938) referred to both an absolute and a relative immunity against pests. The former he called genetic immunity and the latter pheno-immunity. He considered plants to be genetically immune when their resistance was such that a specific pest would never reproduce on them. He defined pheno-immune plants as those whose degree of resistance is such that they will be susceptible or resistant depending upon outside influences. He then concluded that if the resistance of a pheno-immune plant is to be adequately maintained, cultural conditions such as soil type, fertilization, moisture, and so forth must be carefully considered.

Yarwood (1959) defined predisposition as "the tendency of non-genetic conditions, acting before infection, to affect the susceptibility of plants to disease." This definition thus has to do with internal resistance of susceptibility resulting from external causes.

Van Emden (1966) began his discussion of environmentally induced plant resistance with the suggestion that he was going to express a totally inverted view of the subject of plant resistance to insects. This inverted view holds that plant resistance is the norm and that plant susceptibility is the unusual phenomenon. In the course of his paper, he presented considerable evidence to support this inverted view. He suggested that man had modified the plant environment in ways detrimental to the plant vis-à-vis its insect enemies, that is, monoculture, fertilization for maximum yield, and abiotic stress. Many of our standard agricultural practices have worked to undermine the natural resistance of the plant. Considering the accumulated evidence, he suggested that "environmental modification of the plant provides scope for producing a plant with sufficient resistance to pest attack to be valuable in the field, where restraint by natural enemies is also operative."

Singh (1970) referred to natural as opposed to artificial influences on the nutrition and consequent chemical composition of plants. Under natural factors he listed: plant variety, part, age and maturity, water stress, osmotic pressure, and growth conditions and environmental factors such as light, temperature, humidity, and wind. He defined the artificial factors as fertilizers, insecticides, fungicides, herbicides, hormones, and minerals. He made the general statement based on his review and abstracting of 127 studies that the chemical composition of a plant can indeed be altered sufficiently to restrict the feeding of insects and that "this nutritional principal can be manipulated to our advantage for pest control."

Chaboussou (1976) defined the factors that can influence the physiology of the plant as intrinsic factors and extrinsic factors. Among intrinsic factors he included genetic character, plant or tissue age, and rootstock. He considered extrinsic factors to be both climatic and cultural, including soil structure, soil chemical composition, the use of fertilizers, and pesticide treatments that can cause adverse side effects in the plant.

Thus, numerous writings provide a wide range of terms and their definitions useful in describing the concept of stress tolerance. The terms used by various authors such as non-inherited resistance, endophylaxis, phenoimmunity, artificial factors, and extrinsic factors are all helpful in describing the concept of stress tolerance. However, for the purpose of this paper, stress tolerance will be defined as the reduced susceptibility of plants to pests due to the manipulation of non-genetically controlled physiological properties of the plant.

FACTORS AFFECTING STRESS TOLERANCE

Stevens (1960) in his review of the value of cultural practices for disease control in plants made a number of observations useful in establishing some general categories of environmental factors that can be manipulated to affect stress tolerance: (1) application of fertilizers and other soil amendments, (2) soil factors governing the availability of nutrients, (3) balance between nutrients, (4) form in which nutrients or other substances are applied to the soil, and (5) other environmental factors. These categories provide a useful framework for further discussion.

Fertilizers

The conventional reason for fertilizer use is to improve plant growth and increase yields, but fertilizers also have been shown to produce significant effects on the susceptibility of plants to both insects and plant diseases. However, because there has been less emphasis in previous reviews on insects as compared to plant diseases, a series of insect-related examples has been selected for illustrative purposes.

Andrews (1921) found that he could induce almost total resistance in tea plants to a plant feeding bug by the addition of soluble potash to the soil. He determined that the increased ration of potash to phosphoric acid in the leaf in turn increased the resistance of the plant to insect attack; Davidson (1925) noted significant differences in aphid infestations, which he attributed to variations in the feeding value of the sap caused by different fertilizer treatments.

Wittwer and Haseman (1945) observed in greenhouse trials a "striking relationship" between levels of soil nitrogen and calcium available to New Zealand spinach plants and their resistance to attack by common greenhouse thrips. They stated that the nutrient content of the plant may be extensively altered by soil fertility and that the potential exists for manipulating soil fertility to produce "plants resistant to or unsuitable as food for insect pests." They theorized that "the ever greater and more destructive ravages of insect pests is aggravated by the gradual but general decline in soil fertility from year to year."

Dahms (1947) demonstrated a correlation between nutrient level and multiplication of chinch bugs; numbers of chinch bugs on milo and sorghum were significantly higher under conditions of high nitrogen and low phosphorus and chlorine. Garmand and Kennedy (1949) showed that the variable vigor of bean plants and the level of mite populations fluctuated according to heavy or light fertilization.

Rodriguez (1958) determined that increasing nitrogen caused significant increases in two mite species on apple trees. Increased phosphorus supply counteracted the greater susceptibility induced by the nitrogen. In a subsequent review, Rodriguez (1960) cited Russian research indicating that high rates of fertilizer increase the osmotic pressure of the plant sap to 2 to 3 times the normal pressure. There was a concurrent increase in mite populations to notably higher numbers.

Kononova (1964) found that an improvement in plant condition due to proper fertilization and irrigation increased resistance to leaf-devouring insects. She also reported that when the plant condition deteriorated, larval survival increased correspondingly.

Wooldridge and Harrison (1968) found that, by varying the amount of fertilizer applied to tobacco, they were able to demonstrate a positive correlation between amount of fertilizer and the number of aphids on tobacco. Van Emden and Bashford (1969) found that both increased levels of nitrogen fertilization and low potassium (at high nitrogen levels) increased the soluble nitrogen in the plant leaf. The increased soluble nitrogen was directly related to increased fecundity of aphids.

In a study of rice crops from 970 sites in Brazil, Primavesi et al. (1972) stressed the importance of minor element nutrition in protecting paddy rice from rice blast. From field experiments they determined that even when they grew a susceptible variety on unsuitable soil using infected seed and heavy N fertilization, rice blast did not occur if there were sufficiently high levels of Mn and Cu despite climatic conditions favorable to the fungus.

Bussler (1974) also emphasized that trace elements may be even more important contributing factors to stress tolerance than the major elements. He described three successive phases in the development of mineral deficiencies in plants with each successive phase being included in the previous one. First, metabolic changes occur that are not visually detectable but can be determined analytically. For instance, changes in the pattern of organic constituents may take place because of a shift in the pattern of mineral ions inside the plant cells. Second, histological changes may result from mineral deficiencies because "certain structures are not built up any more or are changed in their organization or destroyed." In the third stage, as a result of continuing nutritive disturbance, visible symptoms of mineral deficiencies become apparent. However, long before the visual symptoms appear, the plant has become less resistant. From the moment of the initial metabolic changes in the plant's component substances, there is a higher susceptibility to insects. Bussler (1974) noted that the intentional manipulation of plants to increase stress tolerance is a complicated affair, however. "The recognition of these relations is made difficult through the diverse effects of nutrients and also through their regular behavior of plant species."

Leath and Ratcliffe (1974) investigated the influence of inorganic fertilizers on disease and insect resistance of forage crops. Although they made no general recommendations applicable to all crops, pests, and conditions, they felt that "the provision of a desirable pH with an optimum, well balanced nutrient supply for the crop will usually result in the best and most forage and the least loss from diseases and insects."

Brader (1976) reviewed the literature relating cotton fertilization to stress tolerance. He determined from the available evidence that there is a direct effect (either negative or positive) of various fertilizers on numerous pest species. He concluded: "It would certainly be of considerable interest to extend this type of research with a direct view to decreasing the impact of pest attack on crop production."

Cooke (1976) concluded from long-term experiments at Rothamstead in England that wheat fertilized with adequate phosphorus showed much less infection with a fungus. He did not report in what manner the infection was lessened, but he did observe that understanding of the nature of the effects will probably have to wait for developments in the biochemistry of the mechanism of fungal infections, which will be related to changes in the concentrations of ions in cell contents caused by fertilizers.

Because of the many complex factors involved, the mechanism by which fertilizers influence the susceptibility of plants to pests is not well understood. But the evidence that an important relationship exists is so great that the role of fertilization in pest management must be critically examined.

Soil Factors

The influence of different soil factors and soil types on relative plant composition has been commonly accepted for many years. Ross and Mehring (1938) in the USDA Yearbook "Soils and Men" emphasize the influence of distinct soil types. "It is well known that crops grown on different soils differ greatly not only in yields but also in quality, appearance, and resistance to spoilage. . . . The view has been advanced that highly fertile soils may differ from those that are less productive in that they contain the proper balance of all the essential plant-food elements for maximum growth without any excess or deficiency of any mineral constituent." Thiem (1938), who seems to have been exceptionally perceptive on its subject, emphasized that such diverse soil conditions as drought and stagnant water were as important as fertilizer use in affecting susceptibility of plants to pests. He also noted that the influence of soil conditions (he refers to "resistant" soils and "susceptible" soils) is not permanent. "Susceptible" soils can be improved through improving aeration, creating crumb structure, and rectifying soil compaction. "Resistant" soils can become susceptible when conditions deteriorate.

Sheldon et al. (1948) stated that the importance of soil influence in controlling plant metabolism is far more significant than normally recognized. They demonstrated that wide variations in amino acid concentration of lespedeza hay were a result of the inherent fertility of the soil. In a later study, Sheldon et al. (1951) stressed the important connection between the soil type and the resultant organic chemical pattern of the crop. Various soil may not deliver adequate supplies of the inorganic nutrient elements. They showed that the amount of the amino acid, tryptophane, varied widely in alfalfa, soybean, and red top hays depending upon the inorganic composition of the substrate upon which the plants were grown. Amino acid production was adversely affected by low levels of magnesium, boron, manganese, iron, and calcium.

Lebanaskas et al. (1972) determined that poorly aerated soil had a detrimental affect on citrus. The leaves of plants grown under such conditions contained more nonprotein amino acids and less protein amino acids than normal leaves. This increase in soluble nitrogenous compounds tended to increase the susceptibility of plants to insects.

Baker and Cook (1974) related soil factors more directly to susceptibility. They stated that the ability of plants to resist pathogens is dependent on normal respiration and growth of roots and that soil conditions unfavorable to respiration and root growth are detrimental to overall plant health.

Chaboussou (1976) stressed the influence of aeration and soil temperature on the synthesis of plant components by the roots. He quoted Dufrenoy (1936) in reference to soil conditions: "Every circumstance which is unfavorable to the formation of new cytoplasm tends to cause the accumulation in the cell vacuole of useless soluble compounds such as sugars and amino acids; this accumulation of soluble compounds appears to favor the nutrition of parasitic micro-organisms and thus to lessen the resistance of the plant to parasitic diseases." Chaboussou (1976) expressed the opinion that the same applies to the susceptibility of plants to insects.

The Balance of Nutrients

Not only is the quantity of elements used as fertilizer important in affecting the plant, but possibly the relative balance between elements is of even greater significance. Rodriguez (1960) stated that since the well-being of the pest is influenced by the abnormal chemical make-up of the plant, the fertilizer program should be conservative and not overbalanced toward any one element. He specifically mentions certain phytophagous pests known to benefit either directly or indirectly from an overbalance of nitrogen fertilization.

Thomas and Mac (1941) investigated the significance of the balance of nutrients on disease of greenhouse tomatoes under various levels of nutrition. They found streak disease to vary from severe on plants fertilized with only sodium nitrate to negligible on plants growing in plots fertilized with rotted manure and complete commercial fertilizer. They plotted the equilibrium in trilinear coordinates between the N, P, and K percentages of the leaves as determined by foliar diagnosis. They concluded that "the infection of the virus was associated with a type of nutrition having quantitatively a lower intensity with respect to the plastic elements, and qualitatively with a disequilibrium with respect to these elements, characterized predominantly by higher values for N and much lower values for K in the composition of the NPK unit of the susceptible compared with resistant plants."

Grainer (1956) speaks of the "disease potential" of the host plant in relation to plant nutrition; he defined potential as "the relative physiological ability of a host crop or plant to contract disease at different stages of its life history." He found that periods of low disease potential correspond to a low percentage of total carbohydrate in the whole plant. In an attempt to quantify this situation, Grainer (1956) formulated a hypothesis relating resistance to carbohydrate content. He used the ratio Cp/Rs. Cp denotes the carbohydrate content of the whole plant and Rs denotes the residual dry weight (dry weight less weight of carbohydrate). His studies showed that the higher the ratio the more rapidly the disease developed and the more damage it did. He demonstrated that it is possible to control the Cp/Rs ratio. He recommended using cultural practices that maintain the ratio below 0.5 for as long as possible during the growing season; these ratios apparently were modified only by externally induced physiological changes and were not related to inherent varietal susceptibility.

Benepal and Hall (1976A) found that the nutrient balance affected the free amino acid concentration of the plant and its response to insects. They observed a significant feeding preference of squash bugs on summer squash to be correlated with an increase in plant content of total free amino acids. Plants grown in cultures deficient in P, K, and S showed increased free amino acid concentration compared with plants in the complete solution. The insect feeding increased progessively when P, K, and S, in turn, were excluded from the growing medium. They found that varietal (genetic) resistance and the nutrient effects were independent of each other.

In a related study of cabbage varieties resistant to the cabbage looper, Benepal and Hall (1976B) found that the total free amino acid content was naturally higher in susceptible varieties than in resistant ones when both were grown on a controlled medium. This suggests that one possible effect of correct cultural manipulation of the soil may be to create resistant qualities in otherwise susceptible cultivars.

Bussler (1974) offered extensive documentation to demonstrate the relationship between fertilizing methods and the mineral nutrient content of plants. He linked the most desirable development of plants, that is to say, high yields and optimum quality, to the total balanced nutrition of the plant. He objected to the simple criterion of yields to determine the optimum fertilizer application because, he contended, the quality of the produce often suffers in the process. Bussler (1974) stressed, first, that all nutrients (including micronutrients) must be supplied and, second, that they should be supplied in an optimal proportion to each other. He cited the work of Homes (1963) as the basis on which his concept of balance is postulated.

Perrenoud (1977) stressed the importance of a balance between nitrogen and potassium. He declared that the balance between the nutrients is as important as their total amounts in determining the physiological status of the plant and that "relative nitrogen excess or relative potassium deficiency generally have the same effect in decreasing crop resistance."

Zannini and Frilli (1977) contend that there are "ample records" to substantiate how nutritional imbalance, either an excess or a deficiency of an element, can cause functional disorders in the plant that favor heavier insect infestation.

The Form in Which a Nutrient Is Applied

The merits of the application of nutrients in organic versus inorganic forms have been discussed by numerous writers (Chesters and Street 1948; Haworth and Cleaver 1963; Brady 1974; Cooke 1977). These writers emphasize the value of organic sources of nutrients in terms of more desirable rates of release of nutrients, improved soil structure and water-holding capacity, and the availability of growth-promoting substances. Most of these studies deal more with plant growth and vigor than with susceptibility to pests. However, there are examples where susceptibility to pests is reduced when organic sources of nutrients are used.

Van der Lann (1956) carried out trials on the specific influence of organic manuring on a nematode. The nematode population was significantly lower on the organic manure series. He accounts for this difference as follows: (1) Organic matter improved soil structure and moisture-holding capacity, and many parasites are known to cause less damage in improved soil. (2) Organic matter increased soil microorganisms, and the nematodes may have been killed by their natural enemies. (3) Organic manuring is known to effect the morphological structure of the plants and their roots, and these changes may have made the plant more resistant to the nematode. (4) Physiological changes also occurred that added to the resistance of the plant. Also, nematodes that did manage to penetrate the roots of the plants treated with organic matter developed significantly more slowly than did nematodes in plants fertilized artificially or in the control.

The important role of organic fertilizers in inhibiting diseases and pests due to physical and chemical changes of soil qualities and microbiological balance was also noted by Fuchs and Grossman (1972). They postulated that stress tolerance in plants may be increased by substances present in organic matter that are toxic to diseases and insects that are absorbed by the plant. Likewise, Krassilnikow (1956) reported that sap of manure-fertilized plants is more bactericidal than that from plants not fertilized with manure.

Baker and Cook (1974) reviewed a wide range of studies that documented how management of soil organic matter can be used to reduce the incidence of soil-borne diseases. The concept of stress tolerance was not considered per se, but some of the effects on the susceptibility of the plant could be interpreted in this sense.

Zannini and Frilli (1977) stated that the humification process of organic substances in the soil induces greater plant resistance to parasitic attacks. They ascribed this result to the stimulation of plant metabolic activity by the physiologically active substances in humus. They contended that these humic acids and growth substances are absorbed into the plant tissue through the roots, resulting in increased formation of protein by influencing the synthesis of enzymes and enzymatic action, and that these processes contribute to increasing the vigor and insect resistance of the plant.

Other Environmental Factors

There are numerous other external factors that logically have some effects on stress tolerance. Although the mechanisms are sometimes difficult to define precisely, crop rotations often provide a means of increasing yields and reducing pests, and some of these effects are likely to be related to stress tolerance (Ripley 1941; Odland and Smith 1948; Agerberg and Bjorklund 1963; Toderi 1975). Other effects of biochemical interactions among plants (allelopathy) could also be significant in this regard. The use of allelopathic relationships can be considered a manipulation of the soil environment (Rice 1974; Putnum and Duke 1978). Also, certain pesticides, even when used conservatively, can have effects on the chemical composition of a plant that can be detrimental to its physiological state vis-à-vis insects (Yarwood 1959; Rodriguez 1960; Chaboussou 1976).

DISCUSSION

The idea of enhancing stress tolerance undoubtedly has considerably broader potential than is currently being recognized. However, there are situations where application of the concept may be limited. The most obvious of these situations arises when a new plant species or a new pest is imported into an environment so that the relationship between plant and pest is a recent phenomenon.

This problem is encountered with insects and plant diseases. If a new pathogen appears against which the host has no evolved tolerance, the ensuing epidemic may be far more serious because of this one factor. The American chestnut blight and the Dutch elm disease are two examples of such situations. In lieu of other solutions, one must hope that in these cases for the chance existence of a resistant gene in a few individuals of the species so that in years to come their descendants may once again grace the landscape.

In light of the hypothesis advanced in this paper, the chestnuts or the elms do not possess a satisfactory level of stress tolerance. Our understanding of the evolutionary relationship between external factors and stress tolerance initially presupposes a longstanding association between host and pest in which the effect of certain beneficial cultural practices used by the farmer is to tip the biological balance in favor of the plant. A new pathogen invalidates this natural evolutionary balance. If a new balance is not soon effected, the pathogen perseveres. In the case of a newly established host–parasite relationship, the effect of external factors is no longer predictable or predetermined.

A similar situation exists with regard to insects where new pests are accidently imported into a new environment where plants have not been previously exposed to the pest. Fortunately, in many instances, the importation of natural enemies from the same geographical origin as the pest can correct the problem (Huffaker and Messenger 1976).

Another example of an introduction in which the stress tolerance concept may have limited application can be found in the introduction of the potato into the western United States, where the Colorado potato beetle was a relatively unknown insect feeding on wild host plants. As noted by Smith (1909) in reference to the Colorado potato beetle, "the species that had been so rare that it had practically no specific natural enemies, found conditions so materially changed in its favor that it increased by leaps and bounds." Rarely is an insect so marvelously favored by the changed conditions produced by man. In the case of the beetle–potato relationship, it is yet to be determined whether adequate levels of resistance can be induced by manipulating the nutritional and cultural inputs of the potato plant. The longstanding evolutionary balance most favorable to application of the stress tolerance concept does not exist under these conditions.

Haseman (1946) explored the influence of mineral nutrition through the soil on the activity of the potato beetle and found the beetle–potato relationship only minimally affected in his trials. He postulated that when the Colorado potato beetle changed from its wild host to the potato plant, it found an extremely favorable combination of plant nutrients that aided its rapid development from obscure insect to widespread agricultural pest. However, the stress tolerance concept to plant protection is not totally without application in such a situation. For instance, the efficacy of nongenetic factors in increasing tolerance to pests may depend on the influence of these factors on the interior physiological modifications of the nitrogen content of the plant, amino acid relationship, carbohydrate content, secondary substances, and the like, which duplicate the physiological conditions naturally present in varieties known to be genetically resistant. An analysis of potato cultivars resistant to the Colorado potato beetle might indicate genetically determined conditions capable of being duplicated in susceptible varieties by cultural manipulations of the soil environment.

CONCLUSIONS

The concept of stress tolerance, that is, the reduced susceptibility of plants to pests by manipulation of the nongenetically influenced physiological properties of the plant, can contribute substantially to the improvement of integrated pest management. Such factors as rates of fertilizer, source and balance of nutrients, soil properties, water management, crop rotations, and pesticide applications all may influence the susceptibility of plants to pests. The possiblity of manipulating these factors within the context of producing adequate yields in an economically viable production system should receive additional attention. There is a need to determine how each of the factors affect tolerance, so that their influence on pest losses and yields can be more accurately quantified. Brader (1976) effectively summarized this topic:

Full consideration should be given to those practices (fertilization included) that interact in some way with the development of the pest species concerned. It is well known that small changes in the reproduction rate of insect or mite species may have considerable consequences in determining the overall population levels and thus on the amount of damage caused. And this will, in turn, command the intensity of pest control needed. . . . For a pest control strategy, we need more information on the numerical response of pests to fertilizer application and on the population dynamics of the various species. Only then will we be able to fully evaluate the significance of fertilizers on plant health.

However, perhaps the major impediment to more definitive work in the field of pest-related stress tolerance is the interdisciplinary nature of the subject. Such a wide-ranging approach to pest control requires the input of entomologists, plant pathologists, plant physiologists, soil chemists, soil microbiologists, and agronomists. The mechanisms by which nutrition affects the susceptibility of plants to pests range across the subject matter of all these disciplines. It is hoped that the necessary collaboration will be forthcoming. There is a strong need for such interdisciplinary efforts if the eventual beneficiaries of agricultural research, the farmers, are to be enabled to successfully integrate the many components into an economically viable and environmentally sound pest control system.

REFERENCES

AGERBERG, L.S., and BJORKLUND, C.M.   1963.   Effect of preceding crops in rotations on subsequent crops, in the light of results from Swedish field trials. Lantbrukshaegsk. Husdjursfoerooeksanst. Medd. 6A: 1−27.

ANDERSON, W.P.   1977.   Weed Science Principles.   West Publishing Co., New York.

ANDREWS, E.A.   1921.   Some notes on attempts to produce immunity from insect attack on tea.   Proc. 4th Entomol. Mtg., Pusa.

APPLE, J.L. and SMITH, R.F. (Editors).   1976.   Integrated Pest Management. Plenum Press, New York.

ANDUS, L.J. (Editor).   1976.   Herbicide Physiology, Biochemistry, and Ecology.   Academic Press, New York.

ANON.   1979.   Report of the National Research and Extension Users Advisory Board. USDA, Washington, D.C.

BAKER, K.F. and COOK, R.J.   1974.   Biological Control of Plant Pathogens. W.H. Freeman and Co., San Francisco, California.

BENEPAL, P.S. and HALL, C.V. 1976A. The influence of mineral nutrition of varieties of *Cucurbita pepo* L. on the feeding response of squash bug *Anasa tristis* De Geer. Am. Soc. Hortic. Sci. *90*, 304–12.

BENEPAL, P.S. and HALL, C.V. 1976B. Biochemical composition of host plants of *Brassica oleracea* var. *capitata* L. as related to resistance to *Tricho-plusia ni* (Hubner) and *Pieris rapae* Linne.   Am. Soc. Hort. Sci *91*, 325–30.

BEROZA, M. (Editor).   1976.   Pest management with insect sex attractants. ACS Symp. Ser. 23.

BRADER, 1976. Fertilizers in regard to plant resistance to pests: their role in FAO's integrated pest control programme.   pp. 307–16. *In* Fertilizer Use and Plant Health.   Proc. 12th Colloquium of the International Potash Insti-tute, Worblaufen–Bern, Switzerland.

BRADY, N.C. 1974. The Nature and Properties of Soils. McMillan Pub-lishing Co., New York.

BURGES, H.D. and HUSSEY, N.W. (Editors). 1971. Microbial Control of Insects and Mites. Academic Press, New York.

BUSSLER, W. 1974. The importance of "balanced fertilizers" with 12 min-eral nutrients for higher yields and adequate quality. *In* Fertilizers, Crop Quality and Economy.   V.H. Fernandez (Editor).   Elsevier, Amsterdam and New York.

CHABOUSSOU, F. 1976. Cultural factors and the resistance of citrus plants to scale insects and mites.   pp. 259–80. *In* Fertilizer Use and Plant Health. Proc. 12th Colloquim of the International Potash Institute, Worblaufen– Bern, Switzerland.

CHESTERS, C.G. and STREET, H.E. 1948. The effect of some organic sup-plements on the growth of lettuce in sand culture. Ann. Appl. Biol. *35*, 443–459.

COOKE, G.W. 1976. Contribution to the discussion on the effects of fertiliz-ers on the infection of the roots of crops by fungi. pp. 183–185. *In* Fertilizer Use and Plant Health. Proc. 12th Colloquium of the International Potash Institute, Worblaufen–Bern, Switzerland.

COOKE, G.W. 1977. The roles of organic matter in managing soils for higher crop yields. Proc. International Seminar on Soil Environment and Fertility Management in Intensive Agriculture, Tokyo, Japan.

CRAFTS, A.S. 1975. Modern Weed Control. University of California Press. Berkeley, California.

DAHMS, R.G. 1947. Oviposition and longevity of chinch bugs on seedlings growing in nutrient solutions. J. Econ. Entomol. *40* (6), 841–845.

DARWIN, E. 1800. Philosophy of Agriculture and Gardening. J. Johnson, London, England.

DAVIDSON, J. 1925. Biological studies of *Aphis rumicus* Linn; factors af-fecting the infestations of *Vicia faba* with *Aphis rumicis*. Ann. Appl. Biol *12* (4), 472–506.

DUFRENOY, J. 1936. Le traitement du sol, desinfection, amendment, fumure, en vue de combattre chez les plantes agricoles de grande culture les affections parasitaires et les maladies de carence.   Ann. Agron. Suisse *37*, 669−728.

EL-TIGANI, M.E.   1962.   De Einfluss der Mineraldüngung der Pflanzen auf Entwicklung und Vermehrung von Blattäusen.   Wiss. Z. University Rostock 11, 307−324.

FELT, E.P. and BRONLEY, S.W.   1931.   Developing resistance or tolerance to insect attack.   J. Econ. Entomol. 24, 437−443.

FUCHS, W.H. and GROSSMAN, F.   1972.   Ernährung und Resistenz von Kulturpflanzen gegenüber Krankheitserregern und Schädlingen.   pp. 1006−1107.   *In* Handbuch der Pflanzenernährung und Duengung, Linser, H. (Editor). Springer-Verlag, Wien.

GARMAN, P. and KENNEDY, B.H.   1949.   Effect of soil fertilization on the rate of reproduction of the two-spotted spider mite.   J. Econ. Entomol. *42*, 157−158.

GRAINER, J.   1956.   Host nutrition and attack by fungal parasites.   Phytopathology *46*, 445−456.

HASEMAN, L.   1946.   Influence of soil minerals on insects.   J. Econ. Entomol. *39*, 8−11.

HAWORTH, W. and CLEAVER,   J.   1963.   Soil potassium and the growth of vegetable seedlings.   J. Sci. Food and Agr. *14*, 264−268.

HOMES, M.V.   1963.   The method of systemic variations.   Soil Sci. *96* (61), 380−386.

HORSFALL, J.G. and COWLING, E.B. (Editors).   1977.   Plant Disease: An Advanced Treatise.   Vol. 1, How Disease Is Managed.   Academic Press, New York.

HUFFAKER, C.B. and MESSENGER, P.S.   (Editors).   1976.   Theory and Practice of Biological Control.   Academic Press, New York.

JOHNSON, N.E.   1968.   Insect attack in relationship to the physiological condition of the host tree.   N.Y. State Agric. Exp. Stn., Cornell University, Ithaca, N.Y.

KIRBY, W. and SPENCE, W.   1867.   An Introduction to Entomology.   Longman, Green, and Co., London, England.

KONONOVA, N.E.   1964.   Survival of leaf devouring insects in relation to the condition of the plant.   Zool. Z. Moskva. *43* (1), 37−43.

KRASSILNIKOW, N.A.   1956.   Cited in W.H. Fuchs and F. Grossmann, 1972.

KRAUSS, A.   1969.   Einfluss der Ernaehrung der Pflanzen mit Mineralstoffen auf den Befall mit parasitaeren Krankheiten und Schaedlingen. Pflanzenernaehr.   Bodenkd. *124* (2), 129−47.

LEATH, K.T. and RATCLIFFE, R.H.   1974.   The effect of fertilization on disease and insect resistance.   pp. 481−503.   *In* Forage Fertilization.   D.A. Mays. (Editor).   Am. Society of Agronomy, Crop Science Society of America and Soil Science Society of America, Madison, WI.

LEBANASKAS, C.K., STOLZY, L.H., and HANDY, M.E.   1972.   Protein and nonprotein amino acids in citrus leaves as affected by *Photophthora* spp., root infestation, and soil oxygen contents.   J. Am. Soc. Hort. Sci. *97* (4), 433−436.

LEES, A.H.   1926.   Insect attack and the internal condition of the plant. Ann. Biol. 13, 506–515.

MAXWELL, F. G. and JENNINGS, P.R. (Editors).   1979.   Breeding Plants Resistant to Insects.   John Wiley & Sons, Inc., New York.

McCOLLOCH, J.W.   1924.   The resistance of plants to insect injury.   Kansas State Hortic. Soc. 37: 196–208.

METCALF, R.L. and LUCKMANN, W.H.   1975.   Introduction to Insect Pest Management.   John Wiley & Sons, Inc., New York.

METCALF, R. L. and McKELVEY, J.J. (Editors).   1976.   The Future for Insecticides, Needs and Prospects.   John Wiley & Sons, Inc., N.Y.

MUMFORD, E.P.   1931.   Studies in certain factors affecting the resistance of plants to insect pests.   Science 73 (18), 49–50.

NAS. 1975.   Pest control: an assessment of present and alternative technologies. Vol. 1, Contemporary Pest Control Practices and Prospects.   Report of the Executive Committee.   National Academy of Sciences, Washington, D.C.

NAS.   1975.   Pest control: an assessment of present and alternative technologies.   Vol. II, Corn / Soybean Pest Control.   National Academy of Sciences, Washington, D.C.

NAS.   1975.   Pest control: an assessment of present and alternative technologies.   Vol. III, Cotton Pest Control.   National Academy of Sciences, Washington, D.C.

NAS.   1975.   Pest control: an assessment of present and alternative technologies.   Vol. IV, Forest Pest Control.   National Academy of Sciences, Washington, D.C.

NAS.   1975.   Pest control: an assessment of present and alternative technologies.   Vol. V, Pest Control and Public Health.   National Academy of Sciences, Washington D.C.

ODLAND, T.E. and SMITH, J.B.   1948.   Further studies on the effects of certain crops on succeeding crops.   J. Am. Soc. Agron. 40, 99–107.

OTA.   1979.   Pest Management Strategies in Crop Protection.   Office of Technology Assessment.   Vol. 1. U.S. Government Printing Office, Washington, D.C.

PERRENOUD, S.   1977.   Potassium and plant health.   International Potash Institute, Worblaufen–Bern, Switzerland.

PRIMAVESI, A.M., PRIMAVESI, A., and VEIGA, C.   1972.   Influence of nutritional balances of paddy rice on resistance to blast.   Agrochimica 16 (4–5), 459–472.

PRISTUPA, S.A.   1978.   Amino acid composition of pea seeds as a function of fertilizer.   Translation from Russian.   Agrokhimiya 11, 79–82.

PUTNUM, A.R. and DUKE, W.B.   1978.   Allelopathy in agroecosystems. Annu. Rev. Phytopathol. 16, 431–451.

RICE, E.L.   1974.   Allelopathy.   Academic Press, New York.

RIDGWAY, R.L. and VINSON, S.B. (Editors).   1977.   Biological Control by Augmentation of Natural Enemies: Insect and Mite Control with Parasites and Predators.   Plenum Press, New York.

RIDGWAY, R.L., TINNEY, J.C., MACGREGOR, J.T., and STARLER, N.H. 1978. Pesticide use in agriculture. Environ. Health Perspectives 27, 103– 112.

RIPLEY, P.Q. 1941. The influence of crops upon those which follow. Sci. Agri. 121, 522–583.

RODRIGUEZ, J.G. 1958. The comparative NPK nutrition of Panonychus ulmi and Tetranychus telarius on apple trees. J. Econ. Entomol. 51 (3), 369–373.

RODRIGUEZ, J.G. 1960. Nutrition of the host and reaction to pests. In Biological and Chemical Control of Plant and Animal Pests. L.P. Reitz, (Editor). Am. Assoc. Adv. Sci. Publ. 61, 149–167.

ROSS, W.H. and MEHRLING, A.L. 1938. Mixed fertilizers. In Soils and Men Agric. Yearbook 1938. USDA, Washington, D.C.

SHAW, W.C. 1974. Weed science—revolution in agricultural technology. Weeds 12, 153–162.

SHELDON, V.I., BLUE W.G., and ALBRECHT, W.A. 1948. Diversity of amino acids in legumes according to soil fertility. Science 108, 426–428.

SHELDON, V.I., BLUE W.G., and ALBRECHT, W.A. 1951. Biosynthesis of amino acids according to soil fertility. Plant Soil 3, (1) 33–40.

SHOREY, H.H. and McKELVEY, J.J. 1977. Chemical Control of Insect Behavior; Theory and Application. John Wiley & Sons, Inc., New York.

SINGH, P. 1970. Host plant nutrition and composition: effects on agricultural pests. Can. Dept. Agric. Res. Inst. Bull. 6.

SMITH, J.B. 1909. Our Insect Friends and Enemies. J.B. Lippincott Co., Philadelphia, Pennsylvania.

STEVENS, R.B. 1960. Cultural practices in disease control. In Plant Pathology, J.H. Horsfall, and A.E. Diamond, (Editors), Vol. 3, 357–429.

THIEM, VON H. 1938. Uber bedingungen der massenvermehrung von insekten. Abr. Physiol. Angew. Entomol. Berlin–Dahlem 5 (3), 229–255.

THOMAS, W. and MAC, W.B. 1941. Susceptibility to disease in relation to plant nutrition. Science 93 (240), 188–189.

TODERI, G. 1975. Bibliorafia sull 'avvicendamento delle colture. Riv. Agron. 9, 434–468.

TROLLDENIER, G. 1969. Cereal Diseases and Plant Nutrition. Potash Rev. 23 (34).

USDA. 1977. USDA Policy on Management of Pest Problems. Secretary's Memo. No. 1929. USDA, Washington, D.C.

USDA. 1979A. Agricultural Statistics. USDA, Washington, D.C.

USDA. 1979B. Integrated pest management programs. Science and Education Adminis., USDA., Washington, D.C. Unpublished report.

VAN EMDEN, H.F. 1966. Plant resistance to insects induced by environment. Sci. Hortic. 18, 91–102.

VAN EMDEN, H.F. and BASHFORD, M.A. 1969. A comparison of the reproduction of Brevicoryne brassicae and Myzus persicae in relation to soluble nitrogen concentration and the leaf age in the brussels sprout plant. Entomol. Exp. Appl. 12, 351–364.

VAN DER LANN, P.A.   1956.   The influence of organic manuring on the development of the potato root eelworm, *Heterodera* rostochiensis.   Nematology *1*, 113–125.

WARD, H.M.   1890.   On some relations between host and parasite in certain diseases of plants.   Croonian Lecture.   Proc. R. Soc., London, pp. 393–443.

WITTWER, S.H. and HASEMAN, L.   1945.   Soil nitrogen and thrips injury on spinach.   J. Econ. Entomol. *38* (5), 615–617.

WOOLDRIGE, A.W. and HARRISON, P.P.   1968.   Effects of soil fertility on abundance of green peach aphids on Maryland tobacco.   J. Econ. Entomol. *61* (2), 387–391.

YARDWOOD, C.E.   1959.   Predisposition.   pp. 521–562.   *In* Plant Pathology.   J.H. Horsfall, and A.E. Diamond, (Editors).   Vol. 1.

ZANNINI, E. and FRILLI, F.   1977.   Field use of natural products for pest control in relation to environmental protection and productivity.   *In* Natural Products and the Protection Plants.   G.B. Marini–Bettolo, (Editor).   Elsevier, New York.

7

Design of Small-Scale Food Production Systems and Pest Control

Helga Olkowski and William Olkowski

INTRODUCTION

Pest control is a management practice that is ultimately a function of the design of the ecosystem in question. By design we mean the selection of the components of the ecosystem, the methods used to maintain these components, and the practices used to "control" the organisms that arise from the interaction of the desired and the undesired organisms. Control in this context means suppressions of the pest population—in contrast to the usual meaning of elimination, which is seldom if ever achieved in any case. This chapter explores a series of considerations toward the development of a design concept that could be useful for small-scale food producers in designing and altering the design of their nutrient-producing ecosystems. In two previous books (Olkowski and Olkowski 1975; Olkowski *et al.* 1979) we have presented a basic framework for small-scale pest management, called integrated pest management (IPM), and an assortment of specific management techniques.

THE IMPORTANCE OF THE THINKING MODEL

Human-designed food production systems are greatly simplified in terms of species number and arrangement in comparison with the complexity present in most undisturbed natural environments. Ecologists may debate the extent to which species diversity contributes to ecosystem stability in a variety of specific settings (Van Dobben and Lowe–McConnell 1975). However, the fact is that young, simplified agroecosystems appear to lack some important homeostatic mechanisms that provide a kind of elasticity to more mature and complex vegetation systems. Thus, they seem less protected from external perturbations and more subject to the wide fluctuations in pest and pathogen numbers we have come to expect of the cultivated plot.

We are pest managers who have long been active in encouraging the growth of urban food gardens and other small-scale agricultural activities (Olkowski and Olkowski 1975). As such, we are impressed with the degree to which the design and maintenance of such areas are adversely affected by uncritically assuming oversimplified models of biophysical realities. One of the most misleading assumptions is that a "healthy" productive garden consists of a specific number of specimens of identifiable, desirable species of plants and animals. This notion, focused on individual organisms recognized as desirable, for example, a cabbage plant, a honeybee, or a ladybug, leads inevitably to the assumption that all others are therefore undesirable and should be excluded. These other organisms are considered pests and as a consequence efforts are expended to continuously eliminate them, in most cases without adequate observation and analysis to show that they deserve this fate.

In reality, organisms live in communities. It is the complex interactions in these communities that provide the most reliable mechanisms for stability. It is not the presence or absence of a pest insect or plant pathogen alone that will determine the human food yield. Rather, it is the composition of the communities of these organisms, with all the communities of organisms that feed upon and compete with them and each other, that ultimately determines the season's harvest. These communities are found in the air surrounding the plants, covering all the surfaces of the plants, above and below ground, sometimes with intimate internal associations—root-mycorrheal and nitrogen-fixing relationships are examples—as well as in the soil (Baker and Cook 1974; Russell 1961). A myriad of life forms, the greater number too small to be noticed or seen with the naked eye and most without common names and frequently difficult to identify, make up the actual plant and garden environment (Burges and Raw 1967; UNESCO 1969). Any thinking model that does not recognize this dooms the manager to an endless battle against one plague after another without the strategy options that an ecosystem view reveals.

In contrast, a more complex model, or ecosystem perspective, encourages a different approach to both garden design and its consequent maintenance. It may also evoke a stimulating curiosity about and respect for any life form encountered in the garden that may be new to the observer but is nevertheless assumed to have its rightful place in the infinite scheme of things.

This belief, or faith if you will, is by no means solely the newly arrived revelation of the ecologists. It is the commonplace intuition of numerous so-called primitive agricultures and a basic tenet of the modern-day organic or biological agriculture movement in the industrialized societies (Oelhaf 1978). Unfortunately the recognition of this basic tenet in no way lessens the infuriated disdain with which the latter movement has been regarded until recently by scientific agronomists.

The implication of this thinking model for design of food-processing systems is significant. Picture rows of vegetables spaced neatly apart in bare earth containing little organic matter, a thin veneer of regular preventative sprays ensuring perfect foliage, and a near-total absence of creepy-crawlies or nasty weeds—in short, the vision of a 1960 USDA Home and Garden pamphlet. In contrast, envision the native Latin American dump heap gardens (Anderson 1971), the densely planted beds of much publicized European or Asian intensive agricultural systems, or the heavily mulched low-maintenance plots of the U.S. organic garden literature. Without benefit of much specific research, these gardeners have intuitively understood the importance of several basic assumptions that flow from an ecosystem perspective. Among these are the following:

a. Bare soils are more subject to erosion from wind and water, extreme temperature fluctuations, rapid reduction in organic matter due to exposure to the sun, and susceptibility to compaction from rainfall. Little habitat is provided for a variety of permanently or periodically ground-dwelling predators of plant pests. The response to this perception has been the use of mulches, plant spacing, cover cropping, interplanting, and multiple cropping that result in shading the soil surface during much of the growing period.

b. A variety of desirable macro- and microorganisms live in the soil. These decompose organic matter providing plant nutrients in the form of relatively stable compounds (Dickinson and Pugh 1974). They also compete with or actively destroy potentially destructive inhabitants of the soil and root surfaces (Hacskaylo 1971). The response to this assumption is the incorporation of large amounts of organic matter into the soil and the provision of a residue of organic matter at the soil surface to feed and provide habitat for these complex communities.

c. Plants influence each other in the garden. This may be through the production of substances that specifically inhibit (Grime 1979) or enhance the growth of others, through the provision of alternative food sources or habitat for beneficial insects and other organisms, or through their ability to discourage the build-up of undesired organisms. This latter might be accomplished either through reducing the attraction for certain pests or by repelling them. The response to this understanding has been the search for companion plants, a tolerance for adjacent weed or wild plant associations, and the widespread use of a variety of homemade sprays derived primarily from garden sources (e.g., garlic, pepper, and others).

d. Diversity is to be encouraged. The response is to introduce flowering plants into the food garden in hopes that they will feed beneficial insects or birds (see Williamson 1979), to import predatory or entomaphagous insects encountered by chance outside the garden or purchased from commercial sources to protect and encourage a variety of recognizable garden wildlife, (e.g., lacewings, toads, frogs, spiders, and snakes), to avoid the use of biocides (botanical or synthetic chemical) whenever possible for fear of killing off or reducing valuable communities of organisms, seen and unseen, that are assumed to be keeping the environment "in balance" and preventing a catastrophic rise in numbers of the potentially injurious ones.

The purpose of using flowering plants as a pest control technique is to make available a nectar and/or pollen source for beneficial insects. Insufficient research has been done on this subject, and there are no lists of recommended species. In lieu of a specific set of plants for a certain area, however, one can make observations at particular times, learn what flowers support which natural enemy species, and make efforts to plant them whenever possible. The horticultural aesthetic that encourages planting a series of blooming flower crops to provide a continuous presence of flowers throughout the season also has pest management merits.

In our area we have been impressed with a hoverfly feeding on catnip *(Nepeta cataria)* and English lavender *(Lavandula officinalis)*. Hoverflies, members of the fly family Syrphidae, are excellent aphid predators in the larval stages; the adults look like bees and need pollen sources to lay eggs. Apparent flower feeding on English lavender and Finocchio *(Foeniculum vulgare azoricum)* by certain paper wasps *(Polistes* sp.) that are important general predators suggests these plants could become part of the flower crop that can provide aids to pest control. All observant gardeners could learn to make similar practical plant-beneficial insect choices with a little training in the recognition of common parasitic and predatory insects controlling pest insects in their area (Swan and Papp 1972).

e. Some pest damage is desirable. The attitude that some losses are acceptable encourages the build-up of natural enemies of the "pest," which in turn, by reducing pest populations, assures that the damage is tolerable. This is one of the most important considerations in pest control, as there can be no natural enemy populations without their pests being present in some numbers. The most critical time for the novice gardener is when the plot is first established. Here, when the pest first occurs, it is an invader without any natural enemies present and as a consequence is more damaging. In the San Francisco Bay Area a good example of this situation is the earwig *(Forficula auricula)*, which seems to be more damaging with new gardens.

The preceding list by no means exhausts the principles that might be expected to underlie this thinking model. Yet it provides an ample research agenda for the new agriculture and a description of food production design principles that, interpreted locally in endless variation, have provided food gardeners across this nation with satisfying yields and horticultural experience.

THE CONSTRAINTS AND ADVANTAGES OF SMALL SCALE

The basic biophysical constraints of small-scale agriculture, particularly in urban settings, are those of space, light, time, and competition with adjacent land use. The amount of available light is among the factors influencing the occurrence of disease and thus is an important consideration in plant species and variety selection. Adjacent vegetation may also strongly affect a small urban plot, for example, through competition from tree roots. Rural gardens set in open agricultural environments may also be affected by adjacent uses, for example, through heavy routine use of agricultural chemicals on adjacent fields or orchards. These may leach or drift across the area, affecting pest problems within the plot. Adjacent structures that shade or act as windbreaks may similarly provide constraints. A detailed discussion of these, and those of time, both the managers' and seasonal or climatic dictates, is not possible here. The reader is referred to a more thorough discussion (Olkowski and Olkowski 1975; Olkowski et al. 1979). Perhaps the most important limitation to overall food production is that imposed by small size, as this factor limits the amount of plant material available to fix sunlight and absorb nutrients from the soil. Yet, the small scale in turn provides certain advantages through the gardener's more intensive observations, which encourage the discovery of innovative solutions to problems encountered, and through the labor-intensive implementation made possible by the smaller scale.

In a small area the very structure of the soil may be changed through additions of large amounts of organic material or even imported clay or sand. The soil or foundation may be ignored entirely and planting take place in large containers or raised beds filled with a deliberately composed growing medium. Such considerations are virtually impossible when the scale is increased even in a minor way.

In addition, because of the labor-intensive orientation of the manager of the small-scale ecosystem, a variety of physical, cultural, and biological methods of pest control become feasible. Among these tactics are hand-collecting and destruction of pests (e.g., the brown garden snail, *Helix aspera*), selective roguing (removal and destruction) of infested or diseased plants or parts of plants, the invention and use of many kinds of ingenious barriers and traps, adjustments of watering, pruning, and fertilizing to suit the requirements of single specimens of small groups of plants, interplanting species, and enhancement of biological controls through conservation, augmentation, and inoculation of beneficial organisms.

Gardens nationwide have proved the success of these methods in providing nontoxic pest and disease management and yield satisfaction. The greatest limitation on their wider adoption would seem to be the personal, psychological, educational, and cultural constraints of the small-scale growers themselves. The small-scale food producer is surrounded by mass media messages that encourage substitution of the convenience of all-purpose pesticides for the more time-consuming in-depth observation, understanding, and manipulations of the garden environment. Furthermore, there are few authoritative voices in either academia or government that encourage an ecosystem perspective or offer a critique of an oversimplified management approach that focuses more on the products of industry rather than on information. Lacking the necessary background in biology or horticulture, the lay gardener is easy prey for those who would reinforce phobias regarding unfamiliar organisms and a view of nature as basically messy and threatening. Thus, education in basic biogeophysical processes (e.g., the cycling of nutrients, the evolution and nature of soils, population ecology) may be as important for the development of small-scale agriculture as the endless demonstrations of planting, grafting, pruning, and other horticultural techniques ubiquitous in the gardening literature.

THE ROLE OF HORTICULTURAL PRACTICES IN PEST MANAGEMENT

The science of using horticultural techniques as pest management alternatives to reliance on synthetic pesticides is in its infancy. It has not begun to approach the art of the experienced gardeners who have fine-tuned their efforts to meet the requirements of their own individual plots through years of observation, trial and error. Consequently there are few generalizations available to feed those hungry for recipes that confidently claim, "if you do thus and so, then the results will be such." One sees the growth of gardening cults in which mysticism obscures failures and magic substitutes for causality or, on the other hand, a gardening ethic that tries to over-manage, using solely synthetic chemicals and fertilizers amidst a low tolerance level for plant damage.

In our opinion, the solution lies once again in education. Gardeners must be provided with the basic tools needed to observe and analyze their own garden settings. They need exposure to the fundamental concept that everything is really connected to everything else. Therein lies the basis for broadening the focus from the plant and its pests, or the plant and its pathogen, to a consideration of all the other components in the system. In turn, this broadened focus should encourage an appreciation of the many pest management options available in addition to pesticide use.

Gardeners need the sympathetic support of horticultural extension personnel in their search for cause and effect and novel solutions to pest problems in small-scale settings. Above all they need the serious commitment of the scientific community, not just in investigating alternative techniques suitable to such venture, but also in translating the results of research (often a by-product of large-scale agricultural efforts) into appropriate-scaled technologies in the field that are applicable.

APPLYING PRINCIPLES OF IPM
IN SMALL-SCALE AGRICULTURE

The backbone of an integrated pest management (IPM) program is a monitoring system. Traditionally, in large-scale agricultural systems such as cotton, this has meant a focus on arthropod pest populations and their natural enemies. The objective is to arrive at an estimate of the pest population size likely to result in economic injury to the grower. This is referred to as the "injury level," and all management strategies are directed to suppressing pest populations below that level.

Crucial to the manager is the determination of an "action" level, the level at which the pest population reaches the size that warrants treatment and, if left untreated, would rise to the injury level. The action level is determined by factoring in the size of the natural enemy populations, weather, the plant's physiological state, and the expected growth in the pest population.

For the small-scale agriculturalist it is essential to expand the monitoring activities to include observations of the effect of horticultural activities upon pest populations as well as the factors already indicated. In addition, because of the intimate association between the manager and the garden, levels of damage that have no economic (i.e., yield) implications but are aesthetically unacceptable become as important as they are in ornamental horticulture.

To successfully develop a monitoring program for the small-scale cropping system or garden requires information on the potential pests and natural enemies, their biologies, including life cycles and habitat requirements, and familiarity with the damage symptoms associated with various types of pest activity. Obviously, also desirable is the ability to recognize symptoms of plant disease associated with pathogens, nutrient deficiencies, and air pollution.

Is the acquisition of that basic information beyond the interest and capabilities of the small-scale gardener? Probably not, especially if one focuses on the few key pest problems likely to be encountered in any one locale in specific years and the amount of frustration experienced by many gardeners in searching for nontoxic pest control methods that work. A limited amount of information about pest insects is widely available and assimilated by home gardeners already, judging from our experience. What is lacking is equal entry to the world of parasites and predators and the basic ecosystem concepts upon which a successful IPM program can be developed for a specific site.

Timing of horticultural and direct pest management techniques and spot treatment are two additional components of a traditional agricultural pest management program that can be profitably adapted to the small scale. It is important to understand that there are times in their life cycles when either pests or natural enemies may be more or less susceptible to manipulations. Confining specific treatment activities to just those areas where pest populations may exceed injury levels is easily appreciated by an ecosystem-oriented manager whose basic axiom is "don't disturb the natural enemies of pest organisms if you can possibly avoid it."

It is in the selection of treatment tactics that the small-scale, labor-intensive agriculturalist has the greatest range of options and opportunity for innovation. IPM programs have traditionally been described as incorporating physical, cultural, biological, and chemical strategies. Informational or educational strategies should be added to this list. However, it is essential that these not be regarded as equally desirable components of a stew, to be thrown together into the pot and stirred impartially into the finished concoction. To encourage a diverse garden environment that offers the maximum help from natural controls as a buffer against potential pest population invasions and fluctuations, it is essential to consider a prioritized list of tactics in developing a treatment program.

Most of these basic strategies and many of the specific tactics already have been mentioned. However, it may be useful to summarize them here in the order in which they should be considered in approaching a pest control situation.

Plant Selection

The selection of species and varieties will ultimately indicate which pest problems will occur. Many resistant varieties of different plants are known but are frequently avoided or not selected because they are not available at local sources of plant materials or because the manager does not know they exist. Cherry tomatoes in our area, for example, are resistant to a number of pests and pathogens, are continuous producers, and seed themselves in each year but are frequently passed over because "the gardener aesthetic" dictates the production of the big juicy tomatoes produced from special hybrids. With careful reading of seed catalogs and selection of known resistant varieties (e.g., for *Verticillium* wilt) and actual experience, one can frequently have the ideal with no, few, or tolerable pest problems.

As we have previously indicated, selection of other vegetation (e.g., flower beds, border plantings, windbreaks, etc.), also has pest control aspects, although this is seldom appreciated and has not been the subject of intensive study.

Planting Methods

For vegetable gardeners the usual procedure is to use purchased seed and follow the directions on the package, planting all the seeds in designated rows. The frequent consequence is huge losses of seeds and seedlings to cutworms, snails, birds, or other "pests." Loss of seed leaves and even the first true leaves usually means the loss of the plant. For many years we have used transplanting as a successful technique. Here the plant is container-raised indoors or in a protected and warmer environment, hardened off by placing it outdoors for 1 to 3 days after the first true leaves appear, and then transplanted according to usual practice. The overall principle behind use of this technique is to raise the plant in a protected environment past the most susceptible stage before placing it in the site where it will be subject to possible damage. Thereafter it can recover from damage that it would not be able to withstand at an earlier stage.

We have been particularly excited by the application of a transplanting scheme to moderate-sized farm systems (1 to 20 acres). Here we are referring to the system distributed by Jetspeed Industries (Wendfell Farm, Banks, Oregon 97106). This system uses special flats for growing seedlings and a mechanized water jet planter to open holes into which the seedlings are placed. The seedlings are at such a state of maturity that they begin growing rapidly and are planted at such a density that they can out-compete weeds and thus eliminate the need for herbicides. In the plots we have learned about, no adequate research on this system has yet been produced. As more people learn about this process, it will probably be thoroughly studied.

Management of Garden Debris

When the gardener uses garden debris to make compost, a valuable source of plant nutrients is created. However, if this material is composted the slow way—merely by creating a pile in a convenient place—when it is returned to the soil, weed seeds or weed material can frequently be distributed throughout the garden and as a consequence produce, encourage, or create more pest problems. If a hot composting system is used, where temperatures reach 70°C, then the weed seed or weed plant parts are killed and no additional work is created (Olkowski and Olkowski 1975; Olkowski et al. 1979).

Using Compost

How compost is applied to the garden can either create more pest problems or aid in reducing pests. If compost is dug into the garden, the likelihood of bringing weed seed to the surface where exposure to light will bring about germination is increased. In contrast, if compost is placed on the surface and used as a mulch without soil disturbance, no such weed germination is encouraged and weed seed already present at the soil surface is shaded, and as a consequence much does not germinate. Further, it is our observation that if the compost is weed-free as a result of hot processing, it operates as an active medium for a whole decomposer food chain that includes organisms like centipedes, ground beetles, mites and others, which can further reduce pest organisms.

Habitat Management

This was mentioned earlier in terms of overall garden design. The meaning must be broadened to include creating habitats that are most favorable to the natural enemies of the potential pests and least encouraging to the pest organisms themselves. Though some of these manipulations may involve building or installing structures (e.g., fences, paths, windbreaks, birdhouses, trellises, drainage tiles, etc.), most fall into the category of horticultural activities or cultural controls.

Cultural Controls

Varying watering, pruning, fertilizing, and soil management techniques all should be considered from the perspective of how they may affect pest problems.

Physical Controls

Handpicking and use of barriers and traps are the most commonly used successful tactics here. On a small scale these can be extremely effective. Once the initial investment is made in materials and construction, traps and barriers can often be used year after year when the appropriate season comes around.

Biological Controls

There are at least four aspects to the use of biological control in managing pests.

Conservation.   Conservation means preserving the many biological controls already operating to suppress pest and potential pest populations in the area under management. The most obvious tactic here is to avoid the use of synthetic commercial pesticides as much as possible, using them only as a last resort when all other tactics have failed. In choosing pesticide materials, one should consider not only the least toxic to humans but also the most specific in their effects on other organisms. Some commercially available bacterial or microbial insect pathogens have these characteristics, e.g., *Bacillus thuringiensis (B. popillae)*. In many cases conservation may mean protecting the area from vertebrate predators, for example, feral cats or humans that may capture important rodent predators such as snakes or hawks.

The most difficult concept to convey to both small- and large-scale agriculturalists is that most of the potential pests of their crops, whether insects, weeds, or plant pathogens, are under good biological control most of the time by virtue of being part of diverse communities of organisms that keep each other in check through predation and competition. Of course, weather, soil pH, and other abiotic factors have an influence, too. Thus, the cardinal principle of all pest management must be to disturb the natural control of crop pests as little as possible. In an important sense these natural controls are operating for free, day and night, without requiring energy or resource inputs from the human manager of the system.

Augmentation.   Augmentation means using a variety of methods to enhance or increase biological control already present. Using Wheast[R] as a food spray for lacewings and ladybird beetles or using nest boxes to encourage wasps that are caterpillar predators or insectivorous birds would be examples of augmenting biological control. Wheast[R] is a commercially available power, a by-product of cheesemaking, that operates as an attractant to certain predators and parasites. It is a food substitute for naturally occurring honeydew produced by many pest insects.

Other tactics should also be explored, for example, the use of nursery crops, "weeds," hedgerows, and the like to provide necessary food and/or habitat for the natural enemies of crop pests. This is a variation on the theme of companion planting mentioned earlier.

Inoculation.   Releasing lacewing eggs or larvae is an example of using inoculation techniques. Here, living material is being used like a biological insecticide, the result being a short-term suppressive effect upon the pest population.

Periodic releases of mite predators against pest mites in outdoor crops or greenhouses, or fly predators to suppress fly population in the poultry yard or rabbitry, also fall into this category. However, in some situations, particularly in protected settings indoors or where climate and perennial vegetation encourages the presence of low-level pest populations year round, the inoculated biological controls may become established as permanent populations. This is the aim in the following category.

Classic Biological Controls.   Particularly in those cases where the pest organism has invaded from another area and left its natural enemies behind, efforts may be made to seek out and import those that are specific to the pest. Though most frequently used to suppress insect pests, this technique is increasingly showing its value in the control of invaded weeds and plant pathogens.

Such importation efforts should not be undertaken by the small-scale agriculturalist, because they require some extended research and the use of quarantine protocols to locate the right organism and ensure that no undesired species are accidentally imported. However, the successful establishment of such imported natural enemies of pests depends on their finding hospitable, protected environments in which to multiply. The well-designed, diverse small food-producing plot interspersed with flowering ornamentals bordered with permanent vegetation can provide just such a favorable environment for the establishment of imported biological controls. A recent text (Huffaker and Messenger 1976) reviews the field of biological control and provides an analysis of previous cases and the ecological theory upon which the science is constructed. Another recent volume, (Bartlett *et al.* 1978), documents the history of parasite and predator importations throughout the world against arthropod pests and weeds.

CONCLUSION

There are great advantages to producing food in small-scale systems. By making feasible labor-intensive horticultural methods and recycling of wastes, both energy and resources can be conserved. Not the least of the advantages of a small-scale system is the wide range of environmentally benign pest management options that it provides. It is through the design of a biologically complex environment and the adoption of an ecosystem perspective that the small-scale food producer can maximize the operation of the natural controls to suppress potential pests of the crop and discover appropriate least-toxic methods of managing the few problems that do arise.

REFERENCES

ANDERSON, E. 1971. Plants, Man and Life. University of California Press, Berkeley, California.

BAKER, K.F. and COOK, R.J. 1974. Biological Control of Plant Pathogens. W.H. Freeman and Company, San Francisco, California.

BARTLETT, B.R., CLAUSEN, C.P., DeBACH, P., GOEDEN, R.D., LEGNER, E.F., McMURTRY, J.A., OATMAN, E.R., BAY, E.C., and ROSEN, D. 1978. Introduced Parasites and Predators of Arthropod Pests and Weeds: A World Review. C.P. Clausen (Editor). Agricultural Research Service, USDA, Agriculture Handbook No. 480, Washington, D.C.

BURGES, A., and RAW, F., (Editors). 1967. Soil Biology. Academic Press, New York.

DICKINSON, C.H. and PUGH, G.J.G. 1974. Biology of Plant Litter Decomposition. Vols. 1 and 2. Academic Press, London.

GRIME, J.P. 1979. Plant Strategies and Vegetation Processes. John Wiley and Sons, New York.

HACSKAYLO, E. 1971. Mycorrhizae: Proceedings of the First North American Conference on Mycorrhizae, April 1969. Misc. Publication 1189, USDA, Forest Service. Washington, D.C.

HUFFAKER, C.B. and MESSENGER, P.S. 1976. Theory and Practice of Biological Control. Academic Press, New York.

OELHAF, R.C. 1978. Organic Agriculture. John Wiley and Sons, New York.

OLKOWSKI, W. and OLKOWSKI, H. 1975. The City People's Book of Raising Food. Rodale Press, Emmaus, Pennsylvania.

OLKOWSKI, H., OLKOWSKI, W., and JAVITS, T. 1979. The Integral Urban House. Sierra Club Books, San Francisco.

RUSSELL, E.W. 1961. Soil Conditions and Plant Growth, 9th edition. John Wiley and Sons, New York.

SWAN, L.A., and PAPP, C.S. 1972. Common Insects of North America. Harper and Row, New York.

UNESCO. 1969. Soil Biology. UNESCO, Paris.

VAN DOBBEN, W.H. and LOWE–McCONNELL, R.H.   1975.   Unifying
Concepts in Ecology.   (Report of the plenary sessions of the First International Congress of Ecology, The Hague, The Netherlands, September 8–14,
1974).   Centre for Agricultural Publishing and Documentation, Wageningen, The Netherlands.
WILLIAMSON, J.   1979.   The New Western Garden Book.   Lane Publishing Co., Menlo Park, California.

8

The Economic Feasibility of Widespread Adoption of Organic Farming

Robert C. Oelhaf

INTRODUCTION

Organic farming comprises a group of systems of agriculture that avoid chemical pesticides and fertilizers, the elements of conventional agriculture that are most damaging to the environment and pose the most risk to human health. In its developed forms, organic farming is not a throwback to previous eras, but an alternative modern system of production that attempts to rely on biological processes, primarily in the soil, to realize yields and quality often comparable to those achieved with conventional techniques. To a large extent, conventional and organic farming are distinct production systems. Thus production costs of organic systems cannot be found by looking at simple modifications of the conventional system, such as elimination of pesticides.

A changeover to organic farming on a large scale would solve many of the health and environmental problems at times associated with conventional agriculture, particularly those associated with the use of pesticides and chemical fertilizers. Pesticide activity in plants is complex and generally poorly understood.

Pesticide use can lead to off-flavor (Lichtenstein 1973) and to changes in the biological activity of plants (Galston 1976). Residues in food or acciden-

tal contact during spraying may contribute to genetic damage, birth defects, or cancer. Environmental damage resulting from fertilizer use can
include poisoning of streams and wells and loss of the protective ozone layer
in the upper atmosphere. Pesticide runoff may be contributing to a decrease
in ocean life. The oceans contribute 90% of the annual oxygen production of
the earth. Chemical fertilizer use has been linked to lower nutritional
quality, including sterility in the consuming animals (Aehnelt and Hahn
1978). For a general survey of side-effects from the use of agricultural
chemicals, see Oelhaf (1978).

Organic farming systems often consume less energy than conventional
systems (Lockeretz et al. 1976). Conventional agriculture uses more energy
now than is optimal, for many reasons. Production systems now in place
were developed and adopted during a period of low energy prices. With high
costs of energy, conventional farmers are adopting energy-saving methods
such as no-till, which relies on intensive herbicide use. Chemical fertilizers
are being used more judiciously. The high energy use of conventional
agriculture has resulted in great saving in land and labor. One of the
reasons that American agriculture is so energy intensive is the crop mix:
we raise far more vegetables and fruit than other nations, and these crops
are far more energy-intensive than grains and beans (Heichel 1976). One
may argue persuasively, to be sure, that a small fraction of the world's
population should not deplete the world's nonrenewable energy resources.
Still, agriculture makes better use of the energy it gets than many other
sectors of the economy, such as transportation. As high energy prices
become an accepted factor in the American economy, farmers will adopt
conservation measures, including some organic farming methods. Energy
use will certainly continue to play a large role in public policy debates, but it
cannot be the deciding factor for those committed to biological agriculture.
The reasons one chooses to raise or to eat organic food have to do with food
and environmental quality, not with energy use.

Most people would agree that organic farming is better for the environment and for human health. The controversy is over how much health
would be purchased at what cost in lost production efficiency. The remainder of this paper presents results of an investigation into comparative costs
of raising organic and conventional food. But first I will explain some of the
mistakes that can lead to the common view that organic food costs far more
to raise than conventional food.

ESTIMATING ORGANIC FOOD PRODUCTION COSTS

Three methods have commonly been suggested for estimating production
costs under a system of organic agriculture. These are retail food price
comparisons of organic and conventional food, national production in earlier eras, and agricultural experiment station plot data. The problems
inherent in these methods will be explained briefly (Oelhaf 1978).

Retail prices of organic food are often far higher than prices of comparable conventional food, frequently 50 or even 100% higher. These price differences are not primarily a reflection of higher production costs, however. Rather, the high consumer prices of organic food are a result of higher transportation, processing, and retailing costs, plus some brand loyalty. These higher costs mainly stem from the increased costs of handling the small quantities of food that have characterized the poorly developed and highly fragmented "health-food" and "natural food" markets.

Conventional agriculture has posted impressive yield increases when compared with production in the 1930s and earlier. Though production techniques in earlier eras were to a large extent "organic" in the sense of using few chemical fertilizers and pesticides, yields in the 1930s can in no way be taken as an indication of the yield potential of organic farming in the 1970s. Although some organic farming is highly compatible with simpler technologies, and some advocates have attempted to "turn back the clock" and return to the horse and buggy era, this is not the way of modern organic farming in general. Organic farmers today make use of modern ecological and biological knowledge, much of it acquired or applied since the 1930s. Much of the other new technology, including machinery and new varieties developed for use by conventional agriculture, can be appropriated by organic farmers as well.

Experiment station studies also give us little guidance on estimating organic food production costs. Despite the extensive research of agricultural experiment stations, experimental tests of organic farming systems have not been done in a sufficiently controlled and unbiased manner as to allow generalization to farm-scale conditions. It is even questionable whether such experiments are possible, although some carefully designed studies have been begun recently in this country and some completed in Europe (Dlouhý 1977; Pettersson 1977). The bias in most previous studies comes through clearly in reports of "organic" plots that were not weeded or were not treated to any of the modern organic methods of pest protection, such as foliar feeding with kelp. Organic farming research is multifaceted, complex, does not lend itself to quick results, and may depend on the personal involvement of the researcher. Even if valid experimental data were available, the application to working farms is never simple. In particular, experiments may deal with higher pest infestations than normally experienced in the field. There may be externalities between plots, such as pests being chased away from sprayed plots to unsprayed plots. As some time is generally necessary to establish favorable environmental conditions for organic farming, one-year trials can give misleading information.

Because of the general analytical inadequacy of these three common past approaches, other methods for cost estimation are necessary. These include (1) direct examination of functioning organic farms and use of their financial and production records to make estimates of production costs and technical relationships, and (2) mathematical programming and partial and complete budgeting techniques. I will now present the results of some farm price comparisons and input cost analyses.

ESTIMATING PRODUCTION COSTS OF ORGANIC FOOD FROM FARM PRICES

Price differences between organic food and conventional food may be used to estimate production cost differences if these differences are measured at the farm level. Such differences must be adjusted, however, to account for the presence of any excess (or deficiency of) profits over the long-run value of the resources employed. Such excess profits may arise because of strong brand loyalty, a temporary excess demand in an expanding sector, and barriers to enter an expanding sector. The most likely divergences from competitive market structure will tend to overstate the additional cost of producing organic food.

Because agricultural commodity prices became largely free from price supports in the mid-1970s and also receded from the levels achieved during the period of temporary excess demand of the early 1970s, we may take average 1975–1976 prices as relatively good approximations to long-run average production costs for most commodities. *Differences* between costs of organic and conventional food rather than *absolute* levels of costs are the real concern. Thus this assumption is not critical, but rather mainly a convenience.

For many organic crops there are only a few producers in a region or even in the whole nation, if we count only major suppliers. Still, effective collusion to set prices would appear unlikely. There are enough producers or potential producers in most markets to provide some competitive pressures. A sense of fairness in alternative food communities, among producers, merchants and customers, argues for a fairly good approximation of prices to resource cost.

Some brand loyalty has been established at the farm level by organic producers, but, as with conventional foods, the primary effect of brand loyalty on prices is felt at other stages of the health food industry. We assume that excess profits from brand loyalty at the farm stage are negligible. To the extent that this is not true, our estimates of organic food production costs would be biased upwards.

Some increase in organic food prices has occurred because of temporary excess demand, due to the rapid increase in consumer demand in recent years. As it takes a few years to complete a changeover to organic farming, it is reasonable to ask whether there may be unsatisfied demand at long-run equilibrium prices, causing temporary excess profits for those fortunate enough to have converted earlier. Excess profits are probably less a factor at the farm level than at retail. Many farmers already use largely organic techniques but sell their crops on conventional markets because they have no reasonably priced alternative. According to buyers, there is still a reservoir of farmers ready to change over if the market were there. There has been much confusion over the definition of organic food, and much food has been sold as organic food that was not in fact raised that way at all. In the absence of enforced standards in the industry, with consumers unable generally to tell the difference, fraud has been able to satisfy any temporary excess demand to a large extent. The effect of excess demand will be neglected. This neglect could only bias estimates of production cost of organic food upwards.

For price comparisons to be valid, quality must be comparable. In the United States, grains and beans are graded according to United States Department of Agriculture standards. Fruit and vegetables are more difficult to compare. Organically grown citrus may have discolored skin and be downright ugly. Inside, however, the quality is generally as good as that found in supermarket products. Production cost comparisons will be made here on the basis of internal quality. This is of course somewhat unfair to conventional growers, because customers presently demand aesthetically pleasing produce. Internal quality differences (Pettersson 1977) are discussed in detail elsewhere in this book (see chapters by J.A. Maga and by D. Knorr and H. Vogtmann).

From my experience observing produce in supermarkets and in natural food stores that handle fresh produce on a regular basis, my impression is that the overall quality is at least as good in the natural food stores on the average as in the supermarket. Organic food is often fresher, but there are sometimes signs of insect infestation or decay. The damage is generally superficial on outer leaves that are discarded from supermarket produce. Decay from storage is more a result of lack of preservation than production method. When similarly treated, organic food may actually store better (Pettersson 1977; Senn et al. 1972).

Barriers to Entry in Organic Farming

If we can take farm prices as fair measures of the relative average total cost of producing organic and conventional food, then we can estimate the difference in production costs from a comparison of farm prices. However, the measured difference must be adjusted for any barriers to entry.

While land resources can move freely from organic farming to conventional farming, they do not move freely in the reverse direction. In changing over to organic farming, an initial crop loss generally occurs, particularly if the change is made quickly. Soil life needs to be built up. Biological controls may have been weakened or destroyed by chemicals. It may take up to three or four years for residues to lose their effect (DeBach 1974). Crop production fluctuates until production levels have reached their equilibrium levels under organic husbandry. The organic levels may be lower than under the previous regime, but not necessarily. Because maximum availability of nutrients from organic fertilizers does not occur until the second year following application, it is reasonable to expect fertility loss for at least two years (Thompson and Troeh 1973). This loss can be at least partially overcome by using compost.

Whether done quickly or gradually, there is generally a cost of changing over from conventional to organic production. This cost must be paid for eventually by consumers, or producers will be reluctant to convert to organic production. This cost recovery can make farm commodity prices for organic food higher than long-run average total production costs when demand is expanding or steady after an expansion. Some estimates from current costs of changeover, assuming an interest rate of 10% indicate that these barriers are on the order of 5 to 10% of farm price for grains and beans, and 20% or more for deciduous fruit (Oelhaf 1978).

Even if higher prices are in the offing, farmers may not be able to finance the changeover or may be fearful of entering a new market without government support. Chemical fertilizer programs have received federal support; organic farmers have not been so blessed. Price supports give no premium for organic food. Markets for organic food are poorly organized. Such uncertainty and risk raise additional barriers, and to the extent that they influence farmers' decisions on whether or not to enter the organic food market, estimates of production costs will be overstated. On the other hand, some farmers raise organic food for nonfinancial reasons and are willing to trade off income for psychic rewards. How these factors may balance out is hard to say.

Survey of Organic and Conventional Food Prices

Prices of conventional food are available from U.S. Department of Agriculture publications. Prices of organically grown food were obtained from the major wholesalers and grain companies dealing in this food. Detailed price information was obtained from four firms on the basis of personal interviews or questionnaires. When possible, information on markups was obtained so that responses could be compared with wholesale prices adjusted back to the farm. These checks confirmed the farm price information received. (For more details, see Oelhaf (1978), from which the results in this section are drawn.)

All of the prices collected from grain and bean wholesalers point to an average 10% premium for organically raised field crops. If a 5% deduction is made for changeover cost barriers, this leaves a premium of about 5% for these crops. One exception is rice, where organic prices averaged about 35% higher than conventional. The flooded conditions of rice production may make weed control more difficult. Also some of the price differential may derive from market power of the few growers who supply the small national organic rice market or from the small quantities involved. In times of oversupply in conventional markets, organic prices may run comparatively high, due to a desire to keep prices closer to what is felt to be a fair (parity) price.

The most highly developed markets for organic fruit and vegetables in this country are in California. Fresh organic produce is shipped regularly from California, where there are only a few large organic wholesalers. Price information was requested of two of the largest. Both generally pay prices that are closely tied to commercial wholesale prices. Sometimes a premium of 10% is paid for organic produce, however.

An analysis of price information from one large wholesaler indicated that the differences between organic and conventional prices were quite small, and often favored the organic. Average organic vegetable prices were about 7% higher than conventional, after adjustment for seasonal fluctuations. This difference was mainly due to a 40% difference in onion price, which appears an anomaly, and to higher lettuce prices for the organic. Differences in citrus fruit prices averaged out to about zero. Some organic fruit had markedly lower prices, but this may reflect seasonal variability or actual quality differences.

Smaller organic dealers, in closer contact with growers, tend to quote higher premiums than the large wholesalers. Organic produce obtained at little or no markup over conventional food may be organic by default in a saturated market, such as apples from neglected orchards. For top quality organic produce, where careful attention is given to soil building and hand weeding is the norm, the markup may be as high as 50%.

In eastern organic produce markets, premiums have often been higher than in California for regular organic production. For example, in 1977, the premium (markup) for carrots was 35% and that for onions and potatoes, 60%. Eastern growers may receive these higher premiums because of their proximity to the large eastern market, as well as because of greater difficulty in growing.

Price differences between organic and conventional crops tend to be smaller in America than in Europe (Oelhaf 1978; Aubert 1972; FFBDW 1972). For example, cereal and grain premiums run about 20% in Europe compared to 10% in the United States. These higher premiums reflect better natural soil fertility in this country, better climate for some crops, and the more intensive crop cultivation and generally higher yields in Europe.

ORGANIC FARMING INPUT REQUIREMENTS

Estimates of the increased cost of producing organic food can also be made from analyses of input cost structures of organic and conventional farms. For most inputs, organic and conventional farmers have essentially identical costs (Klepper et al. 1977). The major differences come in the use of labor, pesticides, and fertilizers and in associated expenses of application.

A detailed survey of Midwest livestock farms was carried out by Lockeretz et al. (1976) and Klepper et al. (1977). In my survey (Oelhaf 1978), I sought out producers of the major vegetable and fruit crops and nonlivestock field crop producers. Though many people today practice organic gardening, commercial-scale organic farms are rare. I obtained the names of reputable organic farmers from state organic farmer organizations, extension agents, and organic food dealers. Approximately 60 farmers were contacted, with usable data received from 22.

In recent years, well-known organic farmers have been inundated with long forms asking details of every aspect of their operation. To increase farmer cooperation and maximize useful data, I restricted my questions to those parameters and operations for which major differences between organic and conventional farmers were known or suspected to exist. A previous investigation (Lockeretz *et al.* 1976) had verified that investment in equipment and buildings is not significantly different between conventional and comparable organic farms. This was also the almost universal opinion of the farmers I contacted. For nonlivestock farms, fertilizer and pesticide total expenses also appear to be comparable for organic and conventional farms. Recent increases in chemical prices have for the most part eliminated the past large advantage of conventional farmers in this area.

Initial contact with farmers was made by phone and/or by letter, followed by a one-page questionnaire and data sheet. Farmers were asked to compare their operations with those of neighbors and to estimate differences in costs and yields. Though this method is less than ideal, many farmers have a good idea of what they spend and what their yields are. Farmers who expressed uncertainty in this regard were dropped from the survey. Because we are interested in *differences* between operations, there should not be large systematic errors in our estimates, assuming we have isolated the major differences. Incentives present to shade the figures would tend to balance each other out. On the one hand, organic farmers would like to give the impression that they are successful and so might tend to overstate yield and understate cost. Balancing this is the desire to justify the higher price that they usually are able to obtain in organic channels. Organic farmers are generally extremely idealistic, which would encourage honesty. Because of the small sample size, conventional statistical analysis is impracticable.

Field Grains

Five organic farmers reported corn yields ranging from 33% below average for their region to 7% above average, with an average of 15% less. This would mean increasing land required for corn production by about 17%. Yields of other grains are typically slightly higher, compared to conventional farmers. Farmers in Minnesota and New York reported better than state average for rye and oats. Wheat farmers generally report a yield loss less than that for corn, although one large organic wheat farmer in Montana reported 25% lower yields than neighbors. This difference may reflect dryland farming conditions in Montana and also the special care taken with a product sold nationwide under the farmer's own brand. Organic farmers often follow the Biblical practice of leaving land fallow every seven years, which lowers the net yield by about 14%. Thus soybean yields of a large organic producer in Michigan were really 22 to 27% below his neighbors, though he reported yields at 10 to 15% lower. Farmers following a rotation planting generally had soybean yield comparisons that were better than corn.

Vegetables

Four farmers in our survey reported raising potatoes, two in Pennsylvania and one each in New York and Ohio. State average data for 1972 to 1974 for New York State were 340 hectoliters per hectare (ha) for Upstate New York and 245 per ha for Ohio (USDA 1975). No data were reported separately for Pennsylvania. The four organic farms reported yields averaging 230 hectoliters per ha, 33% below the New York State average and 8% below the Ohio average. The Ohio organic farmer reported potato yields about 20% below neighbors, the only crop for which he had a significant yield loss. The New York farmer estimated his yields at 50% of his neighbor's. Recent Swedish plot studies also reveal significant yield losses for organically grown potatoes. The Swedish study reported that potato quality was significantly higher under organic production methods, however. While the organic potatoes suffered a 12% yield loss, they more than made this up by lower grading and storage losses (12.5% versus 30.2% for the conventional) (Pettersson 1977; Dlouhý 1977). In general, yield losses for vegetable crops under organic husbandry are partially compensated for by measurable quality increases (Schuphan 1976).

Yields for other vegetables vary greatly between organic growers. For example, a major producer of organic sweet corn in Ohio reported yields comparable to the state average (6.7 metric tons/ha) over twice the yield of a large Pennsylvania organic producer. These differences reflect soil conditions and management practices, which do vary greatly between growers. The Ohio grower, on naturally fertile soil, makes liberal use of seaweed for fertilization and pest control and fertilizes with a blend of compost, seaweed, bacteria, and rock phosphate. Pennsylvania and New York farmers, with a more traditional organic approach and poorer soil, did not do so well in gross yield.

Carrot production illustrates the spectrum of practices that may be considered "organic" by growers and consumers. Though it is perhaps an extreme case, the reasoning that goes into production decisions is shown. Commercial carrot production requires about 42 manhours per ha in the eastern United States (Snyder 1975). Organic labor requirements depend on the level of purity desired. We may distinguish three levels. The cheapest would use the approved oil herbicide for weed control and have roughly the same labor requirements as the commercial. A small addition of 2 hours for manure of compost handling would increase labor requirements about 12%. A large Ohio organic farm uses a herbicide only early in the season, the most difficult time for carrot growers. Fields must then be weeded twice by hand at an additional labor cost of about 124 man-hours per hectare, making labor requirements about three times or 200% more than commercial. With labor costing $2.30 per hour, the cost of carrots is up $284 per ha or about 1.1¢ per kg (5 to 6%). If no herbicides were used, this farmer estimated that weeding costs might triple to about $865 per ha, a 15 to 20%

increase in carrot cost. This figure is comparable to the increased cost experienced at a large Pennsylvania farm where no herbicides are used at all. One hand weeding of about 100 hours costs $250 (in 1976). But five cultivations are necessary, perhaps two more times through the field than for commercial production. Pure organic production requires about six times the labor of conventional production.

Apples

Tree fruit production technology is rapidly changing, becoming far more mechanized. Because establishment of an orchard is a long-term investment, adoption of mechanization by conventional growers is only in its infancy. Taking the cost structure of the modern commercial apple orchard, I obtained estimates of increased organic production costs by imposing the organic constraints (Oelhaf 1978).

Most apple data are for Delicious and McIntosh, the top varieties (Childers 1975). I obtained data for three commercial organic orchards in New York, Virginia, and Ontario. These orchardists have been in the business for over 30 years each and have orchards of mixed apple varieties covering about 16 ha. They have experimented with fertilization and weed and pest control and have developed systems that produce high quality apples with virtually no use of conventional agricultural chemicals. An occasional pesticide may be used in situations for which no other means of control has been discovered. The main differences between their systems and those of conventional growers are increased site-preparation cost, machine mowing instead of herbicides, biological control of insects, and hand thinning.

Conventional orchards are moving toward hedgerow plantings, rather than the traditional equal spacing of trees. Weed control under young trees in hedgerows almost dictates herbicides. Hedgerows are more efficient for machine operations, commonly used for chemical application and harvesting. As organic growers make less use of machines, they are not excessively inconvenienced by avoidance of herbicides. Also apples do well when surrounded by a mulch of hay or other organic material, which decreases the need for other weed control.

The major operating cost differences between conventional and organic growers come from hand thinning and harvest instead of chemical thinning and mechanical harvest. For chemical thinning (required to produce fewer, larger fruit of higher quality), labor costs per hectare are cut by 25–90% or more.

Hand harvest of fruit trees is still common for apples, but machine harvesting is already satisfactory for the processing market and appears only a matter of time for the fresh market. For other fruit, machine harvesting is already common practice, including some fresh fruit, such as cherries. Organic growers are generally restricted from using machine harvest because they must avoid the chemical sprays required to loosen the grip of the stems on the branches. Mechanical harvesting of apples uses from one-eighth to one-tenth the labor of hand harvesting, a saving of almost $1.40/1000 liters in labor costs in the early 1970s (Childers 1975), about 10% of the sales price. Based on experience with cherries, hand-harvested trees do have about twice the useful life of machine-harvested trees, however, thus lowering the initial investment per ha to bring a ha of trees to bearing age and allowing more of the orchard to be productive at any one time.

Yields for organic orchards, in the range of 210–280 hectoliters for semi-dwarf, are comparable to those found in typical low-density commercial orchards, from 180 to 350 hectoliters per ha. According to growers, quality is also comparable, by United States grade standards. (Organic growers, to be sure, reject these standards.) The Ontario grower averages 80% fancy grade, the northeast United States average (Podany et al. 1973). His culls (fruit of quality so low that packing is not justified) run only about 2%, however, well below the average of 7%. Chemical sprays can lower loss from preharvest fruit-drop from perhaps 20% to only 5% of the crop.

The success of organic fruit production depends greatly on climate; producers not so well located may suffer as high as 50% culls, which have to be used for cider or juice. Assuming good climate and other conditions, under current conditions of hand-harvest, organic production has about 10% higher production costs because of needing about 25% more labor, primarily in hand thinning. If there is a general shift to machine harvest that cannot be followed by organic growers, 40% higher costs would be incurred, again, due to higher labor requirements, this time some five times greater than the (projected) conventional requirements.

BARRIERS TO EXPANSION OF ORGANIC FOOD PRODUCTION

In recent years, organic food consumers have often had difficulty finding sufficient products to fill demand. Yet many producers have had difficulty marketing their high-quality production. While some of these kinks are being worked out, much remains that inhibits increased production and consumption of organic food. Two general areas are of interest here. First, there are barriers inhibiting individual farmers from changing over to organic methods. We have previously discussed some of the production cost barriers. Second, possible resource constraints could limit large-scale conversion of a significant portion of our farmland to organic methods.

Barriers to Entry

It is difficult for anyone to enter farming today, organic or not. The cost is prohibitive, with land prices beyond the means of most aspirants. Many potential organic farmers are unlanded, presenting quite a barrier to them in particular. Legislation that would limit farm prices and ownership could be especially beneficial to organic farming. When large corporations and the rich are the only ones who can afford to buy land, farming is bound to suffer. Some states have moved in this direction, limiting the acreage of one owner and imposing residence requirements on owners. Land trusts and the sale of development rights are also helpful.

The potential organic farmer faces additional financial barriers beyond those discussed earlier. Conversion generally involves some initial investment of either a cash outlay or a crop loss or both. In either event, the farmer must be carried through this initial period with borrowed funds or his own reserves. It is only fair that the farmer recoup this investment, primarily through higher prices. But a government subsidy could make such a price increase unnecessary and allow expansion to proceed more rapidly.

Beyond quantifiable financial costs of changeover, the potential organic farmer faces a variety of risks and uncertainties. Organic farmers must still to a large extent rely upon their own experiments and hearsay. There is much talk about healthy soil driving away bugs, but in practice serious pest problems may occur. Good advice is usually hard to come by. Successful organic farmers often have many years of experimentation behind them, including some wasted money on various special products marketed to organic farmers. The individual farmer has to sift out the sham from the truth in claims of suppliers, advisors, and university extension agents. The conventional farmer has this work done for him by the state experiment stations. The more we can strengthen advisory services, the easier for the farmer to convert. We need skilled, trained, active advisors, along the lines developed in some European countries—associated with processors, consumer-producer groups, or government.

Marketing has been a problem for organic farmers. There is "many a slip 'tween the cup and the lip." Much organic food is grown that never reaches the organic consumer. Much food is purchased as "organic" that was simply picked up at the nearest commercial wholesale market. This process of "filling in" is justified, say some wholesalers, because retailers and consumers demand external appearance and year-around availability. Unfortunately, organic consumers are often little different from the conventional in this respect. Considerable reeducation is required for consumers here. They must realize that when it is melon season, they should eat melons; when broccoli season, broccoli. Organic consumers are often wasting their money and deluding themselves because they cannot break away from old consumption patterns. Beyond that, the demand for real organic food evaporates. Clearly it is not sufficient only to certify producers. Wholesaler also must be scrutinized.

In some states, organic producers face specific marketing difficulties in the form of State Marketing Orders. The federal government allows growers' associations in states to establish regulations on processing and external appearance, such as color and size, which may be imposed (by a 50% vote) upon all producers in the state. As organic producers may not use chemical fungicides, coloring agents, lye, necessary pesticides, and the like, they may be effectively prohibited from marketing their crop commercially.

Resource Constraints

If consumer awareness developed into a broad demand for organic food or if farmers sought to change over on a broad front, could the needed resources be found at reasonable prices? Or would resource constraints drive prices up? The main factors of interest are land, labor, and fertilizer.

Organic farming does require more labor than conventional farming, and the quality of the labor force needed is different. At present, many organic farmers have little difficulty finding the necessary labor. Students and others seeking to learn organic farming or to go back to the land are often eager to accept traineeships at minimal pay. If organic farming were to expand rapidly, it seems certain that this supply of cheap labor would dry up quickly. Still, with some 4 million unemployed in the United States, we have some reservoir of potential farm labor. Whether these people would want to work on farms or even be useful on organic farms is another matter.

A change in attitude seems necessary to induce much voluntary return to the farm labor force. We could, of course, allow immigration to fill the gap. But beyond numbers, organic farming requires certain characteristics in farmer and farmhand that may be scarce. Organic farming takes humility, a willingness to work with nature rather than trying to overpower her, and some sophistication in understanding ecology.

On a more positive note, we may hope that any large increase in demand for organic food would carry with it an associated appreciation for an organic way of life on the land and thus provide at the same time people who desire to participate in that type of life. Such has in fact been the case in recent years.

Organic farming often experiences lower yields than conventional, which would appear to mean more land required for organic production. For some of the major crops, such as hay and some small grains, no yield loss may be experienced. Corn yields may fall as much as 20%, however. It appears that perhaps 10% more land could be required to achieve the same bulk production under organic management (Oelhaf 1978). This is an area comparable to that set aside in the United States during times of excess production. Such gross calculations neglect the quality advantage of organic food. Lower yields of organic food are compensated to a large extent by higher nutritive value (Balfour 1975; Pettersson 1977; Aehnelt and Hahn 1977). It would appear that gross acreage need not be increased greatly after all. Nevertheless, increased organic food production would place some strains on land of certain characteristics. For many crops, such as citrus, apples, grapes, and cotton, pest infestation can be avoided by suitable choice of geographical location. Irrigated production in California allows easier control of weeds, which is more difficult in regions depending on natural rainfall. Regions naturally hospitable to organic farming are limited in area; increased difficulty, and thus cost, is bound to accompany large increases in production for this reason.

Fertilizer availability is often considered a major factor by opponents of organic farming. Adequate supplies of soil amendments and kelp do appear to be available (Oelhaf 1978), and organic farmers can get by with less potash and phosphate than conventional farmers need. But what about nitrogen? The amount of chemical nitrogen currently used in the United States, a little over 10 million tons a year, is roughly equal to the amount of nitrogen available annually from human and animal wastes. Much chemical nitrogen is lost before the plants can use it, so actually a good bit less than 10 million tons is really needed. Thus it would appear that gross nutrients are available from organic sources, at least in the United States. The problem of heavy metals, particularly copper and zinc, which enter the waste from water pipes, has yet to be solved for long-term application to food crops. Much sludge can be used for several decades under present guidelines. Progress in biological nitrogen fixation could make the foregoing considerations superfluous, however.

CONCLUSION

The most important economic barriers to increased organic food production are inadequate and ill-informed consumer demand, marketing difficulties, and, for large-scale expansion, financing and staffing new farm enterprises. Cost increases in farm food production might average 10% for widespread changeover to organic farming, but the actual increases would depend greatly on the crop and region. Such an increase would translate into about a 4% increase at retail and about 1% of total consumer expenditures. It remains a national policy question whether the environmental and food quality benefits outweigh this modest cost increase. Shifting the balance in agricultural research and extension service more toward biological systems and away from chemicals will make the organic farmers more competitive. Some change in research priorities in the U.S. Department of Agriculture has appeared in the last few years, but the payoffs are many years down the road. In the meantime, policy makers desperately need more food quality research, especially studies of the effects on consumers. Certainly no economic study would be complete without a call for further economic research. Detailed studies by crop and region are needed if more precise estimates of organic food production costs are to be made.

REFERENCES

AEHNELT, E. and HAHN, J.   1978.   Animal fertility: a possibility for biological quality-assay of fodder and feeds?   Bio-Dynamics *125* (Winter), 36–46.

AUBERT, CLAUDE.   1972.   Basic techniques of biological agricultural and its application in France.   AS/Agr (24) 7 Or. Fr. Strasbourg, France: Council of Europe.

BALFOUR, E.B.   1975.   The Living Soil and the Haughley Experiment.   Faber and Faber, London.

CHILDERS, N.F.   1975.   Modern Fruit Science, 6th edition.   Horticultural
Publications, Rutgers University, New Brunswick, New Jersey.
DeBACH, P.   1974.   Biological Control by Natural Enemies.   Cambridge
University Press, London.
DLOUCHÝ, J.   1977.   Vaxtprodukters kvalitet vid Konventionell och bio-
dynamisk odling.   Lantbrukshogskolans Meddelanden.   Reports of the Agri-
cultural College of Sweden, Series A, Nr. 272.   Uppsala, Sweden.
FFBDW.   1972.   Bio-ecological approach to the cultivation of fruit, vegetables
and other farm produce-present position and prospects in Germany.   Pre-
pared by the Forschungsring fur Biologisch-Dynamische Wirtschaftsweise.
AS/Agr (24) 5 Or. German.   Strasbourg, France: Council of Europe.
GALSTON, A.W.   1976.   How safe should safe be?   Natural History 85, 32–
35.
HEICHEL, G.H.   1976.   Agricultural production and energy resources, Amer-
ican Scientist 64, 64–72.
KLEPPER, R., LOCKERETZ, W., COMMONER, B., GERTLER, M., FAST, J.,
O'LEARY, D., and BLOBAUM, R.   1977.   Economic performance and energy
intensiveness on organic and conventional farms in the corn belt: A pre-
liminary comparison.   Am. J. Agr. Econ. 59, 1–12.
LICHTENSTEIN, E.P.   1973.   Environmental factors affecting penetration
and translocation of insecticides from soils into crops.   Qual. Plant—Pl. Fds.
Hum. Nutr. 23, 113–118.
LOCKERETZ, W., KLEPPER, R., COMMONER, B., GERTLER, M. FAST, S.,
and O'LEARY, D.   1976.   Organic and Conventional Crop Production in
the Corn Belt: A Comparison of Economic Performance and Energy Use for
Selected Farms.   CBNS-AE-7.   NSF/RA-760084.   Center for the Biology
of Natural Systems, Washington University, St. Louis, Missouri.
OELHAF, R.C.   1978.   Organic Agriculture: An Economic and Ecological
Comparison with Conventional Methods.   Alanheld, Osmun, Montclair,
New Jersey.
PETTERSSON, B.D.   1977.   A comparison between conventional and bio-
dynamic farming systems as indicated by yields and quality.   Bio-dynamics,
No. 124, 19–27.
PODANY, J.C., BOHALL, R.W. and PEARROW, J.   1973.   Harvesting, stor-
ing and packing apples for the fresh market: regional practices and costs.
Marketing Research Report No. 1009, Economic Research Service, U.S. De-
partment of Agriculture, Washington, D.C.
SCHUPHAN, W.   1976.   Mensch und Nahrungspflanze.   W. Junk, The
Hague.
SENN, T.L., SKELTON, B.J., MARTIN, J.A., and JEN, J.J.   1972.   Seaweed
research at Clemson University 1961–1971.   Research Series No. 141.
South Carolina Agricultural Experiment Station, Clemson University, Clem-
son, South Carolina.
SNYDER, D.P.   1975.   Fruit and vegetable crops costs and returns, from
farm cost accounts, 37 farms—1974.   A.E. Res. 75–27.   Department of
Agricultural Economics and Cornell University Agricultural Experiment

Station, Cornell University, Ithaca, New York.

THOMPSON, L.M. and TROEH, F.R.   1973.   Soils and Soil Fertility. McGraw-Hill, New York.

USDA.   1975.   Agricultural Statistics 1975.   U.S. Department of Agriculture, Government Printing Office, Washington, D.C.

Part III

Food Processing and Distribution

9

Appropriate Food Technology

Robert P. Bates

INTRODUCTION

The role and scope of Appropriate Food Technology (AFT) was well spelled out by Bourne (1978) as "the *best* technology for a given market . . . after taking into account the constraints . . . it considers the complete food production-marketing system and optimizes the total system rather than just the technical components. . . ." His pipeline analogy (Fig. 9.1) is a cogent argument for the balanced or appropriate application of technology to agricultural development. AFT was defined similarly by Caurie (1978) as "the application of modern science and engineering ideas to upgrade traditional or simplify sophisticated food processes and machines in a way compatible with educational, economic, cultural and social needs of less developed countries (LDC)."

A good overview of AFT problems in LDC's was outlined in a U.S. government publication (NAS 1974). Although the term AFT was not in use at the time, out of 42 topics covered, over 35 were directly or indirectly related to appropriate technology (Table 9.1). Like many AT's, AFT is far from new, having evolved over the centuries in response to the demands for a stable, reliable food supply.

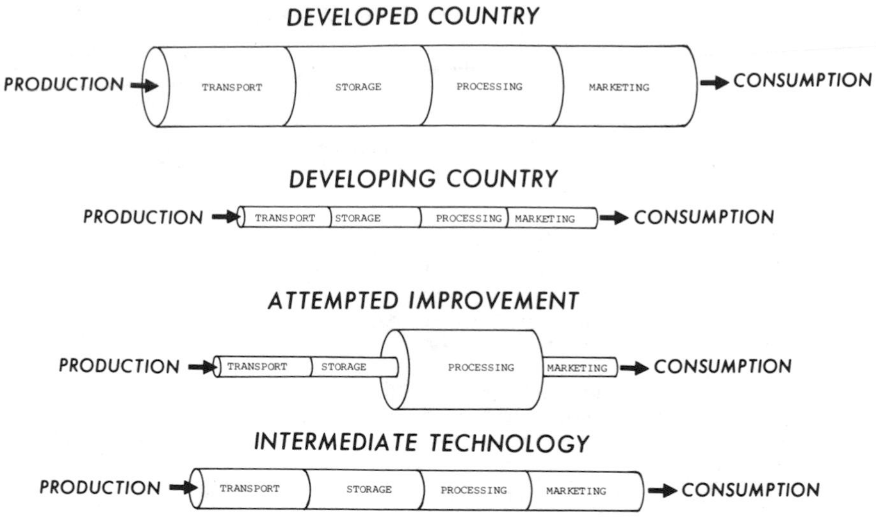

DEVELOPED COUNTRY

PRODUCTION → | TRANSPORT | STORAGE | PROCESSING | MARKETING | → CONSUMPTION

DEVELOPING COUNTRY

PRODUCTION → | TRANSPORT | STORAGE | PROCESSING | MARKETING | → CONSUMPTION

ATTEMPTED IMPROVEMENT

PRODUCTION → | TRANSPORT | STORAGE | PROCESSING | MARKETING | → CONSUMPTION

INTERMEDIATE TECHNOLOGY

PRODUCTION → | TRANSPORT | STORAGE | PROCESSING | MARKETING | → CONSUMPTION

FIG. 9.1.   THE FOOD PIPELINE. COURTESY OF M.C. BOURNE (1978).

Intermediate is synonymous with appropriate in the context of this chapter, because the level of technology under consideration is above primitive but below industrial in capital expenditure, throughput, and technical sophistication. Hence, some of the more elegant food processes will not be mentioned, although there are circumstances where they may be appropriate. The scale of operations range from family food preparation to small "village" industry. Emphasis will be placed on the lower level, as this is where the disparity between the need for increased self-sufficiency and the lack of technological alternatives or their dissemination is greatest (Reusse 1976).

One constituency that benefits greatly from AFT is women. The strenuous, time-consuming nature of many daily tasks—farming, food collection and preparation, water and fuel collection, petty trading, and other domestic and occupational duties—can compete seriously with essential child-care requirements (O'Kelly 1977; Carr 1978).

Important Prerequisites

For appropriate food technology to function, four components must exist and interact. These are knowledge, methods, tools, and philosophy.

Knowledge.   Food Science is a complex and growing field involving the fundamental properties of foods and the multiplicity of reactions between and among foods, the environment, and the human body. Despite the incomplete nature of scientific understanding, enough is known so that considerable though far-from-complete control over food changes can be

TABLE 9.1.   A SELECTION OF UNSOLVED PROBLEMS RELEVANT TO APPROPRIATE
FOOD TECHNOLOGY

Field	Type[1]
New Foods:	
Aquatic weeds as a food resource	*
Use of cake from traditional oil-extraction processes	*
Agronomy of leaf-protein production	*
Potatoes in the lowland tropics	*
Soy-protein-based milk with cow or buffalo milk flavor	*
Milk preserves for hot, humid areas	*
Introducing qualities of ewe's milk cheese into pasteurized cow's milk cheese	*
Raised breads without wheat	*
Flat breads without wheat	*
Upgrading unused oilseed cakes	*
Local low-cost weaning foods	*
Food Processing:	
High cost of packaging thermally processed food	*
Indigenous sources of enzymes for more rapid fermentation of fish	*
Cooking quality of stored beans	*
Storage for food products of plant origin	*
Processing fermented fish products	*
Separating coconut oil and protein by fermentation	*
Keeping qualities of buffalo milk and its processed products	*
Salt for preservation purposes	*
Milling quinua seeds	*
Aging of starchy products	*
Increased use of red palm oil	*
Food Composition:	
Factors governing texture and softness of fermented foods in India	*
Evaluating useful properties of proteins, polysaccharides, and lipids of cereals and legumes	*
Fat composition of fried foods in India	*
Trace elements in animal feeds	*
Biochemical factors limiting the use of legume grains	*
Nutrition and Health:	
Favism	*
Lactose intolerance	**
Malnutrition: A sociological maladjustment syndrome?	**
Vitamin-A fortification of tea	*
Iron fortification of salt	*
Systems approach to food and nutrition policies	**
Factual knowledge of food-consumption patterns	*
Microbiological monitoring kit for small food plants	*
Spoilage of tropical fish	*
Evaluating spoilage of foods of animal origin	*
Influence of germination on digestibility of proteins in pulses	*
Survey of *Clostridium botulinum* in tropical fishing grounds	*
Nutritional factors in endemic dental and skeletal fluorosis	*
Food-science training	**
Mycotoxicosis in humans	*

Source: NAS 1974.
[1] Symbols: *Direct, **Indirect

affected. As the quest for knowledge is continuous, ongoing basic research
will be required to fuel future technological innovation.

Methods.   Food Technology is the state of the art that permits foods to
be manipulated to better serve human needs. These methods are not strictly
new, but neither are they "off the shelf" or readily transferrable from one

culture to another. Hence, the terms "adaptive" to describe appropriate technology has relevance.

Tools.   In the broadest sense, tools are the raw materials, equipment, facilities, utilities, ingredients, and supplies required to acquire knowledge and apply methods. The lack of this "hardware" can be a major disincentive to AFT and can best be overcome by local AT efforts.

Philosophy.   The human factor, that nontechnical component, is philosophy. A main theme here is the attitude that improvement in human well-being is both desirable and possible. Even those in the poorest circumstances have the capability to help and be helped to achieve greater self-sufficiency and dignity. Without attributes such as perseverance, patience, dedication, confidence, optimism, humility, and empathy, tempered by realism and logic, the most potent combination of knowledge, methods, and tools can accomplish little. On the other hand, with a healthy philosophy many material deficiencies can be at least partially overcome. Philosophy incorporates the "software" of AT (Hammond 1976) and emphasizes management skills as well as other desirable traits.

Food Spoilage

A major aspect of AFT is food spoilage reduction. Foodstuffs vary widely in their susceptibility to deterioration and may be classified into three broad categories—durables, semiperishables, and perishables.

Durables.   Durables include dried grains and legumes, nuts, and oilseeds that by virtue of their low moisture contents have a relatively high degree of stability. This ranges from weeks to years, provided that dry harvest conditions prevail and protection from insects and pests is maintained. Unseasonable rains or inadvertent postharvest dampness to above about 15% moisture (depending upon crop and environment) can turn a bountiful harvest into a mold-infested disaster in a few days (Lindblad and Druben 1976). Durables represent by far the largest volume of food staples consumed worldwide (Pekkarinen 1973).

Semiperishables.   Semiperishables are crops such as roots, tubers, and some immature horticultural products, which can have storage lives of weeks to months. These crops are preserved, not by drying, but by protection from physical injury and maintenance of a low, balanced respiration rate, promoted by low temperature, moderate humidity, or sometimes controlled ventilation. When imbalanced respiration, microbial infection, or pest infestation occur, prodigious crop losses result. Due to their ease of cultivation and semiperishable nature, these crops also make a major contribution to world food staples (FAO 1977).

Perishables.   Perishables can be defined loosely as foods with a postharvest life of less than a week at ambient temperature, about 25°C. Many ripe fruits and vegetables are in this category, as are freshly slaughtered or caught animals or fish. Of course, maintaining them in the live state until complete consumption or utilization can be assured is a valuable storage practice. Because of the rapid physiological, biochemical, and microbial changes induced by maturation or death, these perishables must be handled rapidly to avoid almost complete loss, and are more costly and regionally or seasonably scarce (NAS 1978). A major accomplishment of "prescientific" food technology (up to about 1800) was the development and employment of storage and preservation methods that overcame the inherent perishability of these foods. Many still have AFT relevance.

An Inventory of Food Technology

The range and scope of operations (methods) that make up the field are listed in Table 9.2. There are four broad, overlapping categories: refining, preservation, formulation, and consumption.

Refining.   Refining operations are the initial or secondary food recovery steps associated with harvesting and may take place before or after post-harvest storage. These steps can render food either more stable or more susceptible to spoilage, depending upon the removal of more perishable constituents or vectors of spoilage or exposing hitherto protected ingredients to the environment.

TABLE 9.2.   AN INVENTORY OF POTENTIAL APPROPRIATE FOOD TECHNOLOGY OPERATIONS

Refine—Separate edible components, eliminate inedible or contaminating substances.

Clean	Degerm	Crush	Digest
Wash	Screen	Grind	Precipitate
Thresh	Mill	Grate	Scale
Dehull	Peel	Press	Pluck
Shell	Deseed	Expel	Skin
Dehusk	Core	Extract	Eviscerate
Winnow	Slice	Solubilize	Debone

Preserve—Protect from intrinsic spoilage or hostile environments.

Dehydrate	Smoke	Ferment	Refrigerate
Concentrate	Pasteurize	Pickle	Freeze
Salt	Sterilize	Stabilize	Package
Sugar	Irradiate	chemically	Store
		Cool	

Formulate—Combine ingredients, modify structure.

Mix	Homogenize	Puff	Enrobe
Blend	Emulsify	Compact	Wrap
Knead	Extrude	Coagulate	Sprout

Consume—Prepare in convenient, ingestible form.

Proportion	Cook	Bake	Roast
Soak	Reconstitute	Warm	Pan Fry
Precook	Boil	Fat Fry	

Preservation.   Preservation insures that the food material in the crude form or in various stages of refinement does not spoil. The food is protected from intrinsic spoilage or hostile conditions for days to years, depending upon process, commodity, and environment. Preservation techniques are a major aspect of AFT.

Formulation.   Formulation processes, often performed during refining or preservation, to a large extent dictate the physical form and condition of food ingredients and combinations. These operations can have a dramatic effect upon the economics, stability, utility, and acceptability of foodstuffs.

Consumption.   Consumption is the final critical step and involves food preparation on an individual or group basis. The product is transformed into an ingestible, palatable form. In urban circumstances consumption may be the only step under consumer control and their principle interaction with their food supply, whereas in rural areas the consumer may also be the producer, processor, and distributor.

PRODUCTION AGRICULTURE

Although the subject is dealt with elsewhere in this book, it is worthwhile to stress its importance and the often overlooked interdependence between food production and utilization. Without a reasonably economical, reliable food supply, AFT can at best be a stopgap measure. On the other hand, without the capability to stabilize, store, and market foods, even the most abundant harvest is unlikely to fulfill year-round food requirements or smooth out seasonal fluctuations in supply or price. In the absense of AFT, there is little incentive to produce beyond a minimum, that which can reasonably be absorbed by the fresh market, often far below the production potential. Production/utilization balance is especially important for perishables that are highly dependent upon some form of preservation.

POSTHARVEST TECHNOLOGY

It is in conjunction with or after harvest that AFT is first involved. The global magnitude of postharvest losses has prompted a concerted international effort to reduce this waste, which ranges up to 50% of some crops (NAS 1978). There are two major loss reduction goals, (1) to recover efficiently and economically the greatest quantity of edible food from a given durable crop (perishables, semiperishables, and durables will be mentioned later) and (2) to protect this harvest from spoilage throughout the food chain.

1. A number of preliminary refining operations such as cleaning, dehulling, shelling, peeling, and grinding are required. Traditional ways of performing these tasks are often slow, tedious, labor intensive, unsanitary, or wasteful. Figures 9.2 and 9.3 demonstrate some common African and Asian practices.

In contrast, industrial refining operations are rapid, efficient, sanitary, high yielding and labor sparing. However, they are also large-scale, capital

FIG. 9.2.   MILLET MILLING IN ZAMBIA. COURTESY OF A. HANSEN.

FIG. 9.3.   RICE POLISHING IN THAILAND. COURTESY OF H.L. POPENOE.

and energy intensive, and often highly inappropriate logistically. The mechanical principles employed in flaying, manual hull rubbing, and wind winnowing have been improved upon by cracking and rubbing rolls, shaker screens, and blower winnowing. Intermediate-scale devices exist or can be developed based upon these principles, and the AT literature has many useful examples (CFTRI 1979; Harriss 1976; Clarke 1978; Brace 1976).

A major contribution to AFT are designs and operating experience with simple, inexpensive devices for improving refining yields and reducing tedium (Makanjuola 1974). An excellent example of such a device is the Tropical Product Institute's (TPI) hand-held corn sheller. This item is deceptively simple yet highly effective (Pinson 1977). By its use, human labor is made more efficient, and the device can be fabricated readily whenever needed. A village technology unit developed by UNICEF in Kenya has a range of AT systems, including many of AFT relevance, in operation under realistic field conditions (McDowell 1976).

2. Crop protection is difficult to accomplish, as most postharvest losses are attributable to microbial, insect, or pest predation (Bourne 1977). The crop should be reasonably free from contamination and maintained in that state by providing the proper storage environment. Although microorganisms cannot be physically excluded (beyond good sanitation practices), the maintenance of low moisture content is a practical control measure. Pests and insects, along with moisture pick-up from heavy wind-driven rains or flooding can be minimized by well-designed and constructed storage silos. In nonindustrialized circumstances the use of indigenous materials such as bamboo, leaves, plant fibers, wood, mud, straw, and ceramics for granaries has been promoted by practical low-cost construction techniques (Fig. 9.4). With a greater resource base, more substantial material such as metal, masonry, or ferrocement offer enhanced durability (NAS 1973; Lindblad and Druben 1976). Under any circumstance, moisture, insect, and pest control is a matter of continual vigilance from harvest to consumption. Along with the operations to be discussed, there are a number of methods for extending the postharvest life of crops that take advantage of natural or readily obtainable resources. Some are: cassava roots packed in cassava leaves (Aiyer et al. 1978), legumes coated with vegetable oil (LIFE 1979), and acid treatment of moist grains (Rao et al. 1978).

FOOD PRESERVATION

The majority of AFT techniques involve preservation as the key step in preventing food losses. Just as there are numerous pathways to spoilage, the counter measures are manyfold, limited only by scientific knowledge, logistics, economics or imagination. There are introductory texts that deal with food preservation methods (Stewart and Amerine 1973; Desrosier and Desrosier 1977). The principles are well explained, but the practices are industrial situations, without appreciable attention to the resource or cost limitations that characterize LDC's. The few relevant examples of AFT are usually cited in connection with AT agriculture or home food preservation

FIG. 9.4.   STORAGE AND CASSAVA DOUGH DRYING IN ZAMBIA. COURTESY OF A. HANSEN.

(Darrow and Pam 1976; FAO 1976). The following section will stress preservation methods with AFT components.

Dry Preservation

The importance of dry storage of durables has been noted. Solar drying as manifested by dry weather during and subsequent to harvest is an essential farm management system reflected in planting and harvest schedules. To compensate for the vagaries of weather, supplemental crop drying by either solar or other energy sources is a valuable capability. Techniques vary from open sun drying to forced convection of petroleum-generated heat. A considerable choice of designs and descriptions are available (Darrow and Pam 1976; von Oppen 1977; Converse et al. 1978). A major barrier is, again, cost and availability of industrial materials such as metal sheets, screening, plastic, and ventilation fans. Without such items, it takes much greater ingenuity to utilize ambient sunshine effectively.

Semiperishable and perishable food dehydration is more difficult, as the initial moisture content is higher and particle size is larger, thus speeding up deterioration and requiring longer drying times. When drying weather is unreliable, the humidity high, or foods are exposed to a rapacious insect and pest population, solar dehydration becomes quite a challenge, particularly when resources are limited. Some encouraging work with primitive construction materials and plastic has been effective in fish and vegetable drying (Doe *et al.* 1977; Clark 1976).

As it is often impractical to rely solely upon the sun, other energy sources must provide back-up. Where reliable waste heat is available—from power generation, refrigeration condensers, or process cooling streams—direct or indirect use of this heat may be affected, depending upon form, temperature, humidity, and volume.

Rice paddy drying can be accomplished by contact with warm, dry earth (Srinivas *et al.* 1976) and osmotic dehydration can be applied to fruits (Ponting 1973). The ease of handling and regenerating an inert drying medium compared with a perishable food has technological appeal. Inexpensive heat exchangers are the key for both waste heat utilization and solar energy storage. In some agricultural processes the fibrous by-products can be burned to provide energy for drying or water heating. Sugar cane bagasse, cereal grain hulls, nut husks, fruit seeds, and the like so used eliminate a waste problem while producing energy. Crop refuse capable of being converted into alcohol or methane also represents a source of energy (Detroy and Hesseltine 1978).

Wet Preservation

Where water removal is neither desirable nor practical, a number of food preservation techniques become applicable.

Thermal processing or canning.   Food may be effectively preserved by applying heat to destroy microorganisms and inactivate enzymes, provided that it is protected from recontamination and not subjected to temperature extremes. A major safety aspect of thermal processing is pH control. Acid foods (pH < 4.5) only require processing temperatures around 100°C to drastically reduce the microbial load. The low pH enhances the destructive effect of heat and inhibits the germination of surviving bacterial spores. In contrast, low acid foods (pH > 4.5) require an elevated processing temperature obtained only under pressure (generally 10 psi (0.7 at), 240°F (116°C) or above) for the time necessary to achieve adequate heat penetration and spore destruction. If low acid foods are subjected to a low temperature or less time, spoilage is likely, with botulism representing the most critical health hazard. The distinction between high and low acid foods and the relative dangers involved in canning are critical (Worgan 1977).

In the United States there is a long, successful tradition of small-scale canning in both the home kitchen and community canning centers (CCC's) (USDA 1977; Jackson and Mehrer 1978). These operations are economical, versatile means of preserving small quantities of food. Aside from container logistics, equipment needs are as simple as a pot on a stove (acid foods) or a home pressure cooker. CCC's utilize small retorts, steam kettles, and auxiliary processing equipment, as required by the food supply (Figs. 9.5 and 9.6). The CCC concept is attractive, particularly when operated in conjunction with community gardens or farmer's markets, thereby providing both

FIG. 9.5.   A COMMUNITY CANNING CENTER IN OPERATION. COURTESY OF BALL
CORPORATION.

production and preservation capabilities. Although container and equipment availability and costs are severe constraints, canning once revolutionized U.S. food consumption patterns and has a place in LDC's.

Chemical stabilization.   There are a number of chemical substances
that can make food preservation easier and more economical, usually
in combination with some other processing method. The most common
example is acid. Naturally present organic acids are responsible for the ease
of canning low pH foods. The addition of acids to low acid foods permit a less
severe thermal process, pickling (Hertzberg *et al.* 1975).

Another useful adjunct is salt, which reduces the drying requirements
and/or increases the stability of perishable foods. Salt, despite its ubiquitous nature, can be a scarce ingredient. It is either not available at some
inland locations, except at excessive prices, or available in a crude form as
sea salt, requiring further refinement for food use (NAS 1974; Multhauf
1978). In view of the importance of salt as a functional ingredient in many
food systems, simple salt recovery and refining processes are a high AFT
priority.

A number of other chemicals have useful preservative properties. Sulfur
dioxide (Green 1976), nitrate (Dempster 1973), organic acids (Sauer 1977),

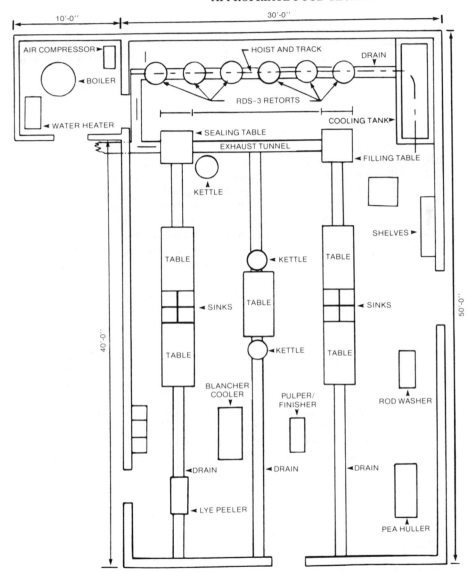

FIG. 9.6. COMMUNITY CANNING CENTER FLOOR PLAN. COURTESY OF DIXIE CAN-
NER EQUIPMENT COMPANY.

and spices and smoke compounds (Daun 1979) together with less well-
recognized natural plant materials can be of practical value when thoroughly evaluated and used prudently. Anand (1975) reported year-long
stability of fresh peas when subjected to a combination of salt, acetic acid,
and metabisulfite, without the need for heat, hermetic packaging, or low
temperature storage. Rice simply soaked and cooked in vinegar has ex-

tended storage life when properly packaged (Mitsuda and Nakajima 1977). The danger of abuse must be recognized, but properly used chemical agents are far less dangerous than the spoilage and economic losses they can prevent.

Fermentation.   A particularly intriguing case of chemical stabilization is demonstrated by a variety of natural fermentations. Under many circumstances these reactions and their end products represent undesirable spoilage. However, by proper adjustment of the environment, in combination with naturally present or added microorganisms, foods can be dramatically altered in susceptibility to spoilage, nutritional value, and acceptability (Whitaker 1978). The manufacture of pickles from cucumbers, sauerkraut from cabbage, cheese from milk, and tempeh from soybeans are common examples. These fermentations have been refined and applied to other food systems with some success (Robinson and Kao 1977).

Less well known, but of great nutritional significance, is fish fermentation as practiced in parts of the Orient (Burkholder *et al.* 1968). In the presence of high salt and low oxygen content, which inhibit microbial spoilage, the digestive enzymes of fish slowly autolyze much of the carcass. The flesh is thereby reduced to a paste that can be easily separated from the skeletal mass to produce a stable, highly flavored, nutritious condiment. Means of improving the speed and efficiency of the digestion are suggested by the use of bacterial or plant enzymes to supplement those naturally present (NAS 1974). Reluctance to develop and popularize these products outside the Orient is probably due to the strong salty flavor, which is foreign to Western tastes. However, when added to the scarce, bland, monotonous, single-staple diet of the poor, fish paste might be viewed as a welcome supplement and practical alternative to fish spoilage. Such fermentations have proved their worth in some regions and need to be extended to other food systems and adapted to other cultures (Weisberg 1973).

The most popular and controversial fermentation is alcoholic. There are few societies that have not developed or adapted an indigenous, traditional alcoholic beverage. These products exist with or without government encouragement and often represent a reliable outlet for agricultural crops. Unfortunately, in the case of beer ingredients and many finished beverages, it is the importer and developed-country agriculture that benefits most (Keddie and Cleghorn 1977). Although the development of a local alcoholic beverage industry based upon indigenous raw materials may introduce social problems (increased alcoholism), the ingenuity necessary and skills developed in carbohydrate conversion, enzyme technology, and distillation engineering can be put to good use. Local talent directed to other food resources and fermentation pathways (i.e., the conversion of by-product carbohydrate to fermentable sugars and then to food, feed, fuel alcohol, and industrial uses) can be a valuable technology.

The subsequent fermentation of alcohol to acetic acid (vinegar) by bacteria is a relatively simple procedure that can be performed at the kitchen level with minimum effort and high yield (Adams 1978). In fact, when alcoholic beverages inadvertently spoil oxidatively, vinegar results. This can be accomplished from practically any raw material capable of first being converted to alcohol, and the resulting acid has important food flavoring and preservation applications (Conner 1976).

In a similar sense, the lactic spoilage reactions of fermentable carbohydrates, when properly induced and controlled, have preservation value. Salt and anaerobic conditions set the stage for the production of lactic acid and the development of desirable pickled and cured meat products (Pederson 1971). A partial lactic fermentation of some staples imparts a desirable flavor and has preservation value, by reducing the pH.

Where time or resources do not permit these natural fermentations, quick pickling can be accomplished by the direct addition of salt, vinegar, or lactic acid juices derived from other fermentation sources. Subsequent thermal processing of these low pH foods and short equilibration produces stable pickled products (Hertzberg et al. 1975).

Molds also contribute to the upgrading of foods. Certain strains, again, under carefully controlled environmental conditions, can impart texture and enhance stability and nutritive value. Steinkraus (1978) describes the improvement of traditional soybean tempeh fermentation by increased understanding of the process and incorporation of technological and sanitary modifications. Although traditionally conducted with soybean and rice a number of other substrates can serve to broaden the utility and appeal of mold fermentations (Beuchat 1978). Some of these foods are becoming popular in vegetarian diets in the United States and should enhance the status of fermented foods globally.

It is not just microbial action or fish digestive enzymes that affect these desirable changes. The vegetable analog is the sprouting process by which the nutritional value and palatability of seeds can be enhanced (Fordham et al. 1975). The durable dormant seed is converted to the easily consumed but perishable sprout. It is, of course, necessary to maintain high seed viability by low temperature and humidity storage of carefully selected seeds and to germinate in a sanitary, physiologically suitable environment (Zamora and Fields 1978). Sprouting has the additional value in producing enzyme systems capable of acting upon other refractory foods to enhance their functionality. For example barley malt exerts amylytic and proteolytic activity upon starch adjuncts such as rice, corn, and wheat during the brewing process. Where barley is not available, other malted cereal grains may perform a similar function to produce a variety of useful food products.

Depending upon available resources, fermentations can range from the highly sophisticated to methods as simple as letting nature take its course (with some assistance from knowledgeable practitioners of AFT). The remarkable chemical processing factory inherent in even the simplest cell is just beginning to be appreciated and tapped to benefit humanity.

Irradiation.   Food irradiation, once optimistically forecast to have a bright future, has fallen on hard times as a consequence of public reaction to nuclear safety and a lack of appreciation of the value of the process (Vas 1977). Although high-energy radiation as emitted from radioactive sources originates in high technology and can be a very dangerous phenomenon, the value of radiation to penetrate matter and interact with biological compounds is underexploited.

Natural radioactive decay can function quite effectively to inhibit or induce physiological changes in plant maturation, destroy insects and their larvae (fumigate), and pasteurize and sterilize foods (Urbain 1978). Once a source is operational there is little additional input except careful radiation monitoring and adjustment of the dose rate as the source decays. Irradiation could be a lot more applicable and more environmentally benign than massive doses of chemicals, energy-intensive preservation methods, or the consequences of rampant physiological, microbial, insect, or vermin activity in a scarce food staple.

Intermediate Moisture Foods

There is a useful preservation category between wet and dry termed intermediate moisture (IM). Foods so preserved are moister than crisp-dry, yet reduced in moisture content to possess the stabilization benefits of dehydration (Gee *et al.* 1977). Raisins, prunes, and other dried fruits usually consumed without rehydration are examples in which the high sugar content obtained by partial drying reduces the water activity (chemical availability) of the remaining moisture to below that required for microbial growth. The concentrated natural fruit acids and sulfur dioxide usually added also serve in preservation.

Substances that possess water-activity-reducing properties are sugars, salts (sodium chloride and other), glycerol, and a number of sugar alcohols (polyols). Honey, molasses, jams, jellies, high sugar confections, heavily salted fish, some cheeses, and comminuted, cured meats rely on IM for their stability, often in synergistic combination with other inhibitory substances such as acids, nitrate, sulfur dioxide, spices, fatty acids, mild heat, and/or refrigeration (Van Arsdel *et al.* 1973). In fact, some traditional fermented milk products that were mixed with dried grains or allowed to partially dehydrate to form cheeses are a worthwhile example of IM foods (Kosikowski 1977; Lang and Lang 1973).

Since many IM foods can be eaten directly, they are a convenient ration ingredient. The most difficult to remove moisture (requiring more energy and drying time) is left, so the process is more efficient and economical than low moisture drying. A major drawback to greater popularization of IM foods is that, except for salt and sugar, the water-activity-reducing substances of greatest value—hydrolyzed starch syrups, glycerol, polyalcohols, and other palatable humectants—are industrial products, unavailable or too costly where needed most. Therefore, simple substitutes and improved IM techniques are badly needed to extend the utility of this process.

Excessive salt has been used to promote dehydration of minced fish cakes.

Water leaching reduces the salt to a tolerable level prior to consumption (Mendelsohn 1974). The use of fats and oils as heat transfer, pasteurization, and water removal and replacement media in cookery merits further investigation. By this manner, palatable IM products with an extended shelf life (limited primarily by lipid stability) could be developed without undue reliance upon industrial ingredients. Although IM technology requires the application of sophisticated physical chemistry, there are probably AFT substitutes for industrial humectants awaiting development, most likely as synergistic combinations of indigenous ingredients, supplemented by proper storage conditions.

Smoking

The process of smoking developed as the initial response to inadequate solar drying conditions (Gilbert and Knowles 1975). Perishable foods (primarily animal and fish) were suspended indoors in the smoke stream from cooking/heating fires. The combined effect of flue heat, dehydration, smoke compounds deposited on the flesh, salt, and curing compounds (if added) effectively preserved the products. The smoke also served to discourage insect and pest attack and contribute a desirable smoke flavor. Although smoke compounds possess measurable antioxidant and antimicrobial activity, the principle long-term preservative effect is dehydration or a combination of heat, partial dehydration, and curing agents, as in intermediate moisture foods. Therefore, the lightly or "cold"-smoked products commonly consumed in the West require additional protection such as refrigeration, freezing, or canning. This is an important distinction. Only properly dried or cured smoked foods can be stored without further processing, and then only if protected from moisture pick-up, surface contamination, insects, and vermin.

Recent AFT smoker designs conserve fuel by improved food exposure geometry, heating, and smoke generation efficiency and reduce human exposure to fumes (Watanabe 1975). Except where heavily smoked dry products are traditionally preferred, it is likely that smoking will be an adjunct process in combination with a variety of wet and IM preservation techniques.

Cold Preservation

The removal of heat from foods followed by refrigerated or frozen storage is taken for granted in the United States. Unfortunately, the energy and capital costs of mechanical refrigeration presently preclude such methods in most tropical LDC's, where, paradoxically, high ambient temperatures accelerate food deterioration. Nevertheless, much more productive use can be made of natural cooling offered by high elevation, glacial run-off and cool ground, aquifers, and deep water. Undersea and underground storage of rice is practiced in Japan (Mitsuda et al. 1972), and scaled-down systems appropriate to tropical locations adjacent to cool water or ground merit investigation.

Where humidity is low and water supply not limiting, evaporative cooling can reduce stored food to near the wet bulb temperature in simply designed porous ceramic or cloth systems (VITA 1970). Lacking these resources, some protection from high ambient temperature can be afforded by storing food in the shade (natural or constructed), taking advantage of breezes and air circulation, and timing harvests to coincide with the coolest part of the day or nighttime temperature drops. Several degrees decrease in temperature may seem marginal, but many food deteriorations have a Q_{10} of around 2 (doubling of the reaction rate for each 10C° temperature rise). Thus, significant storage increases can be affected by common-sense application of the cooling resources available. The ultimate answer, cheap solar refrigeration, is some ways off from becoming a reality.

Packaging

No matter how elegant or ingenious a food preservation technique, unless the product can be protected from the environment and effectively distributed, the process is incomplete. Packaging has been recognized as one of the most serious constraints to achieving adequate food supplies in LDC's (LIFE 1970; NAS 1974).

The rigid, hermetically sealable can and jar of commerce are virtually unavailable in most LDC's (Mahdeviah 1970). Even though the containers may be manufactured locally or imported, they are too expensive for widespread use, except for specialty foods or under conditions of reuse. Even in the United States the expense of cans has prompted an increase in the use of reusable glass jars in home and community canning, and sporadic seasonal shortages of jars and lids occur.

One possible solution is container reuse, a simple matter with canning jars, provided that they are available initially and fresh or reusable lids can be obtained. The situation with cans is more complex. Some older manual can sealers came equipped with a seam-cutting roll and reflanger (Fig. 9.7). Cans could then be reused twice (providing that the tin plate or enamel were sound), until cut down to the side seam hook. With 2-piece cans lacking a side seam, multiple reuse might be possible, if the aluminum seal can be evenly cut and the body reflanged. U.S. manufacturers no longer supply the necessary can sealer parts and the "stackable" geometry of 2-piece cans is different; but with container costs rising, reuse should be a simple alternative worth implementing in the United States and overseas.

With advances in packaging technology, containers need not be rigid. The flexible, retortable aluminum laminate pouch is gaining industrial acceptance (Mermelstein 1978; Lampi 1977). It possesses many of the advantages of the can but may be fabricated in place from roll stock by simple heat-sealing devices. Currently the retortable pouch is almost as expensive as the can it replaces. Expanding markets and improvements in technology

FIG. 9.7. MANUAL CAN SEALER /OPENER/REFLANGER WITH CUTTING ROLL IN PLACE, CIRCA 1930.

should favor the pouch where can fabrication and transportation are limitations. It is the high cost and low throughput of pouch filling, sealing, and processing systems that represent the most serious barriers to increased commercial applications. However, the substitution of labor for such machinery at well-designed pouch filling/sealing stations in operations where low volume production is desirable could have practical implications in LDC's or community canning centers.

For food in which thermal stress resistance or long-term protection from oxygen are not required, simpler pouch material have utility and convenience. Even single-ply transparent pouches were reportedly effective for sauerkraut (Stamer and Stoyla 1978). Hence, acid food thermal processing may eventually be practical in pouches, and a high oxygen-barrier transparent plastic could become analogous to the glass jar.

The packaging requirements for some wet preserved (not requiring high temperature in-package treatments), dry, and intermediate moisture foods are simpler, provided that excessive oxidation, insect infestation, and pest predation can be avoided. In regions where plastics are logistically impractical, discarded industrial containers and indigenous materials—such as plant fibers, leaves, bamboo, wood, husks, mud, ceramics—can function to varying degrees. The natural package provided by the outer husks of nuts, the skins of fruits and vegetables, and the hides and organs of animals are fairly effective, within the storage and environmental constraints of the food systems.

Packaging serves primarily to protect and secondarily for convenience and marketing. It strongly influences the stability, utility, and economy of foodstuffs and is vital even to subsistence cultures and an outward sign of affluence in developed countries. All the previously discussed refining and preservation operations and the formulation ones that follow are dependent upon some form of protective packaging, often the most essential and costly system component and a critical AFT challenge.

FORMULATION

These important food technology operations serve to put food in more convenient forms for subsequent refining, preservation, or consumption.

Extraction

Oil recovery from oil-bearing foods and stabilization for local consumption is an excellent means of increasing the energy density of poor diets. Clearly, local means of extracting and refining vegetable oils are a valuable AFT intervention. Mechanical pressing, the traditional method, is comparatively inefficient in both yield and effort, requiring crushing and preconditioning to affect reasonable yields (Am. Oil Chem. Soc. 1976). Pressing evolved to continuous screw expellers with higher efficiencies, throughputs, and costs and then to prepress or direct solvent extraction systems. These are dependent upon the recovery and reuse of expensive, hazardous organic solvents and extensive pretreatment of the oil-bearing plant material. The extracted oil, in turn, is crude, off-flavored, and susceptible to hydrolytic and oxidative rancidity. The refining and stabilization steps are not easily affected without access to specialized equipment and chemical techniques. There are few examples of simple oil extraction/refining processes appropriate to small-scale, intermittent operations (Donkor 1979).

The extraction and refinement of protein is another high priority AFT need. A considerable global research effort has been underway for the last two decades with a variety of foods and by-products—oilseeds, cereals, legumes, animal and fish, green leaves, and single-cell organisms (IFT 1977). However, economics of scale and production logistics do not favor small processes. Notable exceptions are soybean product manufacture as practiced in the Orient. These procedures or recent refinements (Siegel and Fawcett 1976) should have similar utility and appeal when applied to other food resources. The primary step is a simple water extraction of soybean to produce soymilk (Nelson et al. 1978). The soymilk can be subjected to salt or acid coagulation to produce the curd, tofu (Pontecorvo and Bourne 1978), or heated to produce a surface film, yuba (Wu and Bates 1975). Additional purification steps to concentrate soy and other protein or remove various undesirable substances may be too complicated and/or expensive for small-scale operations, although such steps are standard industrial practices in protein ingredient manufacture (Amer. Oil Chem. Soc. 1979).

Extrusion

One of the more recent food processing innovations is thermoplastic extrusion (Harper 1979). Mechanical energy is transformed into heat under confinement in a barrel where the food is continuously cooked and conditioned under high screw pressure prior to being extruded to the atmosphere. Extrusion has the important advantage of cooking foods with little, if any, added moisture and produces a fairly dry, thermally stable extrudate, often possessing a puffed texture and toasted flavor. A low-cost extruder, developed for on-farm whole soybean cooking for animal feed, has been adapted to instantized flours, cereal blends, and nutritious multimixes. A small batch cooker-puffer developed in Korea and refined in the United States approximates the extrusion process (Sterner et al. 1978). Prototype costs are somewhat high for family use but could probably be reduced by further design refinement.

Texturization

A number of texturization processes have already been mentioned: milk to cheese; soybean to curd, film, or tempeh; flour or whole grain to extruded or puffed products. Additional formulations involving baking can enhance food convenience and acceptability: corn to tortilla, wheat to bread or chapatties, and other grains to textured bake products.

In fact, wheat-based bakery products have been too successful in some applications. When imported wheat replaces indigenous crops in regions where wheat cultivation is impractical or inferior to a native cereal, production incentives for alternate crops may be reduced and scarce foreign exchange expended. This undesirable shift from local staples is due to wheat gluten's superior functional properties and wheat's image of affluence. There have been concerted efforts to partially replace wheat flour while maintaining or even improving the acceptability and nutritional properties of these formulations (Milner 1969).

Complementation

There is a critical need for cereal blends that can replace or at least supplement imported food ingredients or those of questionable economic or cultivation value. The traditional corn tortilla is a much more appropriate food than a slice of bread from imported flour, particularly if the tortilla is complemented nutritionally by legumes or local foods that render the meal more complete nutritionally (Wadsworth et al. 1979). The combination of

foods into mixtures that complement each other nutritionally and functionally is a sound self-sufficiency development strategy. The extent to which
local staples are converted into commercial palatable foods in Nigeria is a
fascinating study of village food processing (Simmons 1975). Formulations
that simplify and encourage such practices are highly desirable (Rajalakshmi and Ramakrishnan 1977; Pellett and Mamarbachi 1979).

CONSUMPTION

No matter what steps precede, unless foods are consumed and metabolized efficiently, their ultimate value is lost. Efficient consumption operations are the vital last step in the food chain. The physical, chemical, and
biological nature of some raw foodstuffs that provides resistance to spoilage
must now be overcome, if maximum food value is to be obtained. Cooking
accomplishes this by rendering refractory components—indigestible cells,
tough tissues, undenatured starch, and protein—more susceptible to digestion and assimilation. In addition, cooking reduces microbial contaminants,
destroys heat labile antimetabolites, and vastly improves the palatability
of many foods. It is during consumption practices that AFT relates most
directly to the individual or family in several important ways: energy and
time conservation, nutrient retention/enhancement, and food acceptability.

In much of the developing world where cooking is fueled by firewood, an
increasingly scarce resource in cost, collection time, and environmental
damage, fuel-efficient systems are a high priority (Hall 1979). A mud stove
has recently been developed that obtains about twice the usable cooking
energy from firewood while also heating water for general use and reducing
smoke pollution (Evans and Wharton 1977). This and other devices that
utilize combustible residues such as sawdust (Simon and Solis 1977), rice
hulls, dried plants, and biogas and replace the inefficient, dangerous 3-
stone fireplace can have immense social and environmental value.

A number of solar cooking systems are being developed. These range
from simple insulated hot boxes to sun-tracking parabolic focusing devices (Darrow and Pam 1976). It will take particular ingenuity to harness
solar energy for cooking purposes capable of functioning during inclement
weather or where local tradition calls for an evening meal prepared after
sundown.

Parallel with and complementary to fuel conservation are methods of
minimum cooking—low water cooking (which also retains nutrients), slow
(low temperature) residual heat cooking, and special soaking solutions or
regimes to reduce cooking time for dried legumes and other foods requiring
extended cooking (Dovlo et al. 1976; Narasunha and Desikacher 1978;
Rockland et al. 1979). A simple salt soaking solution can reduce bean
cooking time by up to 300% and the use of a pressure cooker employing
121°C instead of atmospheric cooking (100°C at sea level and down to 90°C
at 3,000 m elevations) can affect a seven-fold reduction in cooking time
(Silva et al. 1981). Increased use should also be made of plant, animal, and

microbial enzyme systems capable of reducing food toughness prior to or during the application of heat.

Baking as a means of texturization, preservation (pasteurization, partial dehydration), and nutritional complementation is an especially ingenious approach developed centuries ago and still subject to innovation (Milner 1969). Fat frying has similar benefits. In replacing food moisture with lipid, the energy density is increased and the water is driven off at pasteurization temperatures.

MATERIALS AND FABRICATION

Local resources and fabrication techniques must receive high priority with substantial efforts devoted to adaptation and improvision. Tool building from industrial scrap or starting from available resources are necessary AT activities (Darrow and Pam 1976). Some examples of the ingenious use of local raw materials to replace hardware are: stone or wood grinding surfaces in lieu of metal, wood/bamboo frames for angle iron, fiber attachment to replace metal fastenings, textiles for screening, hardwood for bearings and gears, mud/adobe for concrete, ceramics for glass. Local craft industries capable of such fabrications can contribute much toward self-sufficiency in the mechanical arts. The imagination employed in all LDC's to keep worn-out or obsolete industrial equipment and motor vehicles functioning in the absence of replacement parts, proper machine tools, or instruction manuals is a strong testimonial to the competence of local artisans. This talent is urgently needed in AFT applications.

ENERGY

Energy is an even more severe constraint. A simple electric or gasoline powered mill may effectively serve a community, but what happens when the power or fuel is unavailable for an extended period? Animal and human power can be an alternate, reliable energy source in many applications. The bicycle pedal principle is an effective use of muscle power for transportation and machine operation (McCullagh 1977; Ghosh 1978). Hand-cranked devices are often all that are needed to affect a significant improvement over traditional manual, nonmechanized methods in time and labor saving (Figs. 9.8 and 9.9). There is presently an explosive interest in alternate energy systems, as discussed elsewhere in this book. Practical innovations will surely make a positive contribution to AFT.

Resources

A strong feature of AT is that it helps individuals to partially, if not completely, overcome the severe constraints imposed by limited resources and lack of access to high technology. The connotation "appropriate" encourages the AT practitioner to adjust the scale of operation and level of technology to the available resources, natural and human. For example,

FIG. 9.8.   CAST-IRON CEREAL MILL.

clear plastic sheeting greatly simplifies solar dehydration design and operation under conditions of intermittent rainfall. However, lacking covers, manual methods for providing rain protection are less convenient, but possible. Abundant clean water greatly facilitates food preparation and sanitation, but dry cleaning methods combined with water conservation and reuse can be developed. Although these and other cited alternatives are additional AFT complications, they represent steps toward greater self-sufficiency and are distinctly preferable to apathy—the "it won't work here" philosophy.

Equipment/Supply Sources

There are a number of valuable publications identifying and pricing many of the components necessary to put together functioning AFT systems. Some items exist in home, laboratory, and small industry appliance catalogs or as design sketches in the AT literature (Darrow and Pam 1976; VITA 1970; Clarke 1978; Brace 1976). Several recent publications have made a special effort to characterize by operation and manufacturer available AT equipment, many items of which are related to AFT (Boyd 1976;

FIG. 9.9.   SEED CLEANER/SEPARATOR WITH ELECTRIC AND MANUAL CAPABIL-
ITIES.

Branch 1978; O'Kelly 1977). These descriptions are an inventory of commercial and homemade equipment, a guide for development needs (when a
key item does not exist) and a source of design and fabrication ideas. Useful
features sometimes included are a summary of testing experiences, mechanical durability, and cost estimates. Therefore, the AFT practitioner has
many sources to draw upon in developing appropriate responses to food
problems. A much rarer feature is that all-important evaluation of the
intervention under actual operating conditions. Despite the location or
culture-specific nature of AFT applications, there is much to be learned
from the experience of others, both positive and negative. Only by constant
feedback from the field and interactions between innovator, practitioner,
and user can AFT best serve the global community (Dahl 1979).

   Problems with the catalog approach are equipment cost, spare parts and
auxiliary equipment availability (including power, utilities, tools), and
inappropriate scale—units too large or too small for the intended application. Many items are manufactured in developed countries or more industrialized regions of LDC's, with difficulties in importation, transportation,
and access to repair, not to mention the trade-off of importation versus local
manufacture. A similar situation exists for packaging materials, sanitary
supplies, and functional food ingredients. Fortunately, there is usually

opportunity for a mix of indigenous and imported technology, as long as national self-sufficiency is best served (UNIDO 1978).

AFT ORGANIZATIONS AND ACTIVITIES

During the 1970s, in response to underdevelopment and human suffering, there has been a remarkable proliferation of organizations addressing the various components of AT. These organizations evolved in both developed and developing countries and consist of private voluntary organizations, private industry, religious orders, educational institutions, research centers, government bureaus, international agencies, and various alliances among these groups. Some are region-specific while others are global in scope involving bilateral and multilateral interdisciplinary cooperative arrangements. The entire political spectrum (most evident when the philosophical basis of AT is discussed) is represented by their membership, support base, and clientele. However, there is a commendable degree of objectivity regarding social needs and technological measures required.

Accompanying the growth of these AT organizations are a number of newsletters devoted to AT and related subjects (Table 9.3). These publications form an indispensable communications network and source of information on meetings, publications, new developments and programs, research projects and reports, training opportunities, new AT organizations, support sources, and even critiques of these activities. This informational AT network is a valuable source of technical and operational information on AFT. The greatest potential of these newsletters is in promoting meaningful dialogue between and among innovators and users of AT and making the world community aware of the commonality of development problems being faced.

CAVEATS

Food Safety

Foods are complicated biological systems and their interactions with the human body are even more complex. Although AFT operations must be designed for the lay public in LDC's and eventually function routinely without the hands-on assistance of experts, there are certain safety features to be emphasized and manipulations that must be performed very carefully to avoid serious health hazards.

Microorganisms represent the greatest and most immediate threat. Food and waterborne illnesses due to unsanitary conditions or improper food handling can rapidly turn an effective AFT intervention into a calamity and completely negate any positive contribution. Unfortunately, unsanitary conditions are usually a fact of life where poverty is rampant.

Resources such as running potable water, sewage disposal, insect and

TABLE 9.3.   NEWSLETTERS WITH APPROPRIATE FOOD TECHNOLOGY RELEVANCE[1]

Title	Frequency	Publisher
The ADAB News		79 Road 11/A DHANMONDI Dacca 9 Bangladesh
Cassava Newsletter		Centro Internacional de Agricultura, Tropical, Cali, Colombia
Intermediate Technology News	Monthly	*in* Appropriate Technology, Intermediate Technology Publ. Ltd., 9 King St., London WC2E 8HN, England
LIFE Newsletter	Monthly	League for International Food Education, 1126 16th St., N.W., Washington, D.C. 20036, U.S.
The Lund Letter	6–8/yr	Research Policy Institute, University of Lund MAGISTRATVAGEN 15N, S-222 44, Lund, Sweden
Rural Development Network Bulletin	2–3/yr	Overseas Liaison Committee, American Council on Education, 11 Dupont Circle, Washington, D.C. 20036, U.S.
Small Industry Development Network, Quarterly Newsletter	4/yr	Office of International Programs, Engineering Experiment Station, Georgia Institute of Technology, Atlanta, GA 30332, U.S.
TAICH News	4/yr	Technical Assistance Information Clearing House, 200 Park Ave., N.Y., N.Y. 10003
TPI Newsletter	2–4/yr	Tropical Products Institute, 56/62 Gray's Inn Road, London WC1X8LV, England
TRANET Newsletter-Directory	4/yr	Transnational Network for Appropriate/Alternate Technology, P.O. Box 567, Rangely, ME 04970, U.S.
UNICEF News	4/yr	United Nations Children's Fund, United Nations, N.Y. 10017, U.S.
UNU Newsletter	4–6/yr	The United Nations University, Toho Seimi Bldg., 15-1, Shibuya 2-chome, Shibuya-Ku, Tokyo 150, Japan
VITA News	2–4/yr	Volunteers in Technical Assistance, 3706 Rhode Island Avenue, Mt. Rainier, MD 20822, U.S.

[1] A small but typical sampling and source of many others.

vermin-proof construction, and clean-up facilities are scarce or nonexistent. Their development is in the realm of other AT's that interact significantly with AFT and cannot be ignored. Maintenance of food sanitation throughout the food chain is an important prerequisite and an extremely difficult task under primitive conditions. Physical exclusion of potential contaminants and thorough clean-up procedures should be part of any food handling operation. While the rigorous sanitary codes of developed countries are not practical under the economic and logistic constraints of LDC's, the application of common-sense "good manufacturing practices" must continually be stressed (Anon. 1976).

Under the best of sanitary conditions ubiquitous microorganisms can gain a foothold, if proper food handling/processing procedures are not followed. While the consequences of food spoilage are severe, those of food poisoning are even worse. Even in the United States, the home canning practice of subjecting low acid foods to an acid food process (water bath instead of pressure) is still prevalent (Walsh and Bates 1978). The consequences are widespread incidents of post-process spoilage and a few cases of botulism (several annual fatalities). Durables also are subject to hazardous contamination in the form of mold-produced mycotoxins (Rodricks 1978; Foster 1978). Thus, the importance of quantifying and controlling pH, process time, temperature, water activity, oxygen tension, salt content, and a host of factors affecting the efficacy of the various food preservation techniques must be recognized by all AFT practitioners. These parameters, although of vital concern to the food technologist, may be only vague qualitative concepts to the layman and a point of misunderstanding unless thoroughly stressed.

Another safety hazard involves the inadvertent or uncontrolled use of industrial chemicals. These innocuous-looking unlabeled "white powders," similar in appearance to cereal flour, salt, sugar, or ground food ingredients, may be lethal pesticides, cleaning powders, or agricultural chemicals. There are tragic cases of such mistaken identity in food formulations (Munro and Charbonneau 1978). Such compounds clearly have a legitimate place, but not in close proximity to foods, food handling/serving environs, and workers, except under very carefully controlled circumstances.

Physical Safety

Food-processing operations employing high pressure and temperature, moving machinery, sharp cutting edges, fast-moving particles, heavy load movement, electricity, combustion exhaust or flammable materials represent obvious danger to operators. In the design and application of AFT devices, consideration must be given to potential mechanical hazards. Safeguards are particularly important where the users of such equipment possess no prior experience with mechanics. Although AFT tools and techniques must be simple and cheap, safety features are justifiable design criteria and worthwhile investments in worker health.

THE FUTURE OF APPROPRIATE FOOD TECHNOLOGY

The future of AFT is bright but threatened. Never in history has so much talent been directed to the task of helping people help themselves through Appropriate Technology. But never before have the problems associated with human development been so severe—poverty, expanding population, diminishing natural resources, environmental constraints, and political strife.

Technology has received increased notoriety, and AT is no exception (Kassapu 1979; Harrison. 1976). As it promises so much for so many and has such a potentially broad global constituency, the opportunities for mistakes are numerous. The apparent simplicity of AFT belies the complexity of dealing with human behavior under the constraints of poverty and underdevelopment. Food technologists recognize how critical it is to attend to all details in developing a food process. To do otherwise would permit or even encourage spoilage. In an analogous sense, to unwittingly tamper with foreign (or ethnically distinct) food patterns or socioeconomic relationships without a thorough study of the consequences as well as the benefits can result in just as dramatic a spoilage, with the important difference that food is a more expendable resource than the good will of people or their social values. However, the AFT component of AT has immense global potential, if the proper balance of knowledge, tools, techniques, and philosophy is applied by dedicated practitioners. This is slow, hard work, but just as great a challenge as any other facing the food technologist today.

REFERENCES

ADAMS, M.R.   1978.   Small-scale vinegar production from bananas.   Trop. Sci. *20*, 11–19.

AIYER, R.S., NAIR, P.G., and PREMA, L.   1978.   No-cost method for preserving fresh cassava roots.   Cassava Newsletter, No. 4, pp. 8, 9.   Centro Internacional de Agricultura Tropical, Cali, Colombia.

AMER. OIL CHEM. SOC.   1976.   World conference on oilseed and vegetable oil processing technology.   J. Am. Oil Chem. Soc. *53*(6), 224–461.

AMER. OIL CHEM. SOC.   1979.   Proceedings world conference on vegetable food proteins.   J. Am. Oil Chem. Soc. *56*(3), 99–483.

ANAND, J.C.   1975.   Development of appropriate technology for a breakthrough in fruit and vegetable processing industry.   Ind. Food Packer 29(6), 31–35.

ANON.   1976.   Sanitary design principles. Food Proc. *37*(10), 166–170.

BEUCHAT, L.R.   1978.   Microbial alterations of grains, legumes and oilseeds. Food Technol. *32*(5), 193–198.

BOURNE, M.C.   1977.   Post harvest food losses—The neglected dimension in increasing the world food supply.   Cornell International Agricultural Mimeograph 53.   N.Y. State Agric. Expt. Sta., Geneva, New York.

BOURNE, M.C.   1978.   What is appropriate/intermediate food technology? Food Technol. *32*(4), 77–78, 80.

BOYD, J.   1976.   Tools For Agriculture: A buyer's guide to low-cost agricultural implements.   Intermediate Technology Publ. Ltd.

BRACE, F.   1976.   A Handbook on Appropriate Technology.   Brace Research Institute, McGill University, Ottawa, Canada.

BRANCH, D.S.   1978.   Tools for Homesteaders, Gardeners and Small-Scale Farmers.   Rodale Press, Emmaus, Pennsylvania.

BURKHOLDER, L., BURKHOLDER, P.R., CHU, A., KOSTYK, N., and ROELS, O.A.   1968.   Fish fermentation.   Food Technol. *22*, 1278–1284.

CARR, M.   1978.   Appropriate technology for women.   Approp. Technol. 5(1), 4–6.

CAURIE, M.   1978.   Appropriate/intermediate food technology—how not to do it: a view from the third world.   Food Technol. 32(4), 87–88.

CFTRI.   1979.   Grain legumes: Processing and storage problems.   Food and Nutr. Bull. 1(2), 1–7.   U.N. University.

CLARK, C.S.   1976.   Village food technology: solar drying of vegetables.   LIFE Newsletter, April, pp. 1–3.

CLARKE, P.A.   1978.   Rice processing: a check list of commercially available machinery.   Rept. G114.   Trop. Prod. Inst. London.

CONNER, H.A.   1976.   Vinegar: Its history and development.   Adv. Appl. Micro. 20, 81–133.

CONVERSE, H.H., FOSTER, G.H., and SAUER, D.B.   1978.   Low temperature grain drying with solar heat.   Trans. Am. Soc. Agric. Eng. 21, 170–175.

DAHL, H.A.   1979.   Commentary: Factors involved in the development, marketing and financing of appropriate technology in developing countries.   Ecol. Food Nutr. 7, 257–260.

DARROW, K. and PAM, R.   1976.   Appropriate Technology Sourcebook.   Volunteers in Asia, Stanford, California.

DAUN, H.   1979.   Interaction of wood smoke components and foods.   Food Technol. 33(5), 66–71, 83.

DEMPSTER, J.F.   1973.   Curing meat products.   Proc. Biochem. 8(3), 25–27, 30.

DESROSIER, N.W. and DESROSIER, J.N.   1977.   The Technology of Food Preservation, 4th Edition.   AVI Publishing Co. Westport, Connecticut.

DETROY, R.W. and HESSELTINE, C.W.   1978.   Availability and utilization of agricultural and agro-industrial waste.   Proc. Biochem. 13(9), 2–8, 31.

DOE, P.E., AHMED, M., MUSLEMIDDIN, M., and SACHITNANANTHAN, K.   1977.   A polyethylene tent drier for improved sun drying of fish.   Food Technol. Aust. 29, 437–441.

DONKOR, P.   1979.   A hand-operated screw press for extracting palm oil.   Approp. Technol. 5(4), 18–20.

DOVLO, F.E., WILLIAMS, C.E., and ZOAKA, L.   1976.   Cowpeas: Home preparation and use in West Africa.   International Development Research Center, Ottawa, Canada.

EVANS, I. and WHARTON, D.   1977.   The Lorena mudstove: a wood-conserving cookstove.   Approp. Technol. 4(2), 8–10.

FAO 1976.   Rural home techniques, Series 1, Food Preparation, Series 3, Food Preservation.   Food Agric. Organ., United Nations, Rome.

FAO 1977.   1976 FAO Production Yearbook, Vol. 30.   Food Agric. Organ., United Nations, Rome.

FORDHAM, J.R., WELLS, C.E., and CHEN, L.H.   1975.   Sprouting of seeds and nutrient composition of seeds and sprouts.   J. Food Sci. 40, 552–556.

FOSTER, E.M.   1978.   Foodborne hazards of microbial origin.   Fed. Proc. 37, 2577–2581.

GEE, M., FARKAS, D., and RAHMAN, A.R.   1977.   Some concepts for the development of intermediate moisture foods.   Food Technol. *31*(4), 58−64.

GHOSH, B.N.   1978.   A bicycle-operated PTO unit for small-scale farm jobs. W. Crops. *30*, 222−224.

GILBERT, J. and KNOWLES, M.E., 1975.   The chemistry of smoked foods: A review.   J. Food Technol. *10*, 245−261.

GREEN, L.F.   1976.   Sulphur dioxide and food preservation—A review. Food Chem. 1, 103−124.

HALL, D.O.   1979.   Plants as an energy source.   Nature *278*, 114−117.

HAMMOND, R.W.   1976.   The software side of appropriate technology.   Small Industry Development Network, Quarterly Newsletter *2*(3), 2.

HARPER, J.M.   1979.   Food Extrusion.   Crit. Rev.   Food Sci. Nutr. *11*, 155−215.

HARRISON, P.   1976.   Inappropriate technology.   New Scientist. *71*, 236, 237.

HARRISS, B.   1976.   Paddy processing in India and Sri Lanka: A review of the case for technological innovation.   Trop. Sci. *18*, 161−186.

HERTZBERG, R., VAUGHAN, B., and GREENE, J.   1975.   Putting Food By. The Stephen Greene Press, Brattleboro, Vermont.

IFT 1977.   Overview: Unconventional Proteins.   Food Technol. *31*(5), 175−195.

JACKSON, J. and MEHRER, M.   1978.   The food preservation center: An exercise in appropriate technology.   Food Technol. *32*(4), 83−86.

KASSAPU, S.   1979.   The impact of alien technology.   Ceres *12*(1), 29−33.

KEDDIE, J. and CLEGHORN, W.   1977.   Corn beer.   An alternative to lager. Approp. Technol. *3*(4), 13−15.

KOSIKOWSKI, F.V.   1977.   Cheese and Fermented Milk Foods.   Edwards Bros., Inc., Ann Arbor, Michigan.

LAMPI, R.A.   1977.   Flexible packaging for thermoprocessed foods.   Adv. Food Res. *23*, 305−428.

LANG, F. and LANG, A.   1973.   Cultured milk products.   Food Mfg. *48*(2), 23−28.

LIFE.   1970.   Meeting food packaging needs in developing countries: Report of a workshop.   League for International Food Education, Washington, D.C.

LIFE.   1979.   A practical method for bean storage.   LIFE Newsletter, May, pp. 3−4.

LINDBLAD, C. and DRUBEN, L.   1976.   Small Farm Grain Storage.   Action/ Peace Corps, Program and Training Journal, Manual Series No. 2. VITA Publications.

MAHDEVIAH, M.   1970.   The alternatives to sanitary tin can for packing food products.   J. Food Sci. Technol. 7, 3−7.

MAKANJUOLA, G.A.   1974.   A machine for preparing pounded yam and similar foods in Nigeria.   Approp. Technol. *1*(4), 9, 10.

McCULLAGH, J.C.   1977.   Pedal power.   Rodale Press, Emmaus, Pennsylvania.

McDOWELL, J. (Editor).   1976.   Village Technology in Eastern Africa.   UNICEF, Eastern Africa Regional Office, P.O. Box 44145, Nairobi, Kenya.

MENDELSOHN, J.M.   1974.   Rapid techniques for salt-curing fish: A review. J. Food Sci. *39*, 125–127.

MERMELSTEIN, N.H.   1978.   Retort pouch earns.   1978 IFT Food Technology Industrial Achievement Award.   Food Technol. *32*(6), 22–32.

MILNER, M.   1969.   Protein Enriched Cereal Foods for World Needs.   Amer. Assoc. Cereal Chem., St. Paul, Minnesota.

MITSUDA, H., KAWAI, F., and YAMAMOTO, A.   1972.   Underwater and underground storage of cereal grains.   Food Technol. *26*(3), 50–56.

MITSUDA, H. and NAKAJIMA, K.   1977.   Storage of cooked rice.   J. Food Sci. *42*, 1439–1443.

MULTHAUF, R.P.   1978.   Neptune's Gift.   A History of Common Salt.   Johns Hopkins Univ. Press, Baltimore, Maryland.

MUNRO, I.C. and CHARBONNEAU, S.M.   1978.   Environmental contaminants.   Fed. Proc. *37*, 2582–2586.

NARASUNHA, H.V. and DESIKACHAR, H.R.S.   1978.   Simple procedures for reducing the cooking time of split red gram (Cajanus Cajan)   J. Food Sci. technol. *15*, 149–152.

NAS 1973.   Ferrocement: Applications in Developing Countries.   Nat. Acad. Sci., Washington, D.C.

NAS 1974.   Food Science in Developing Countries: A Selection of Unsolved Problems.   Nat. Acad. Sci., Washington, D.C.

NAS 1978.   Postharvest Food Losses in Developing Countries.   Nat. Acad. Sci., Washington, D.C.

NELSON, A.I., STEINBERG, M.P., and WEI, L.S.   1978.   Whole soybean foods for home and village use.   International Agricultural Publ.   INTSOY Series No. 14, Univ. Illinois.

O'KELLY, E.   1977.   Simple technologies for rural women in Bangladesh.   UNICEF/Dacca, Women's Development Program.   United Nations, New York.

PEDERSON, C.S.   1971.   Microbiology of Food Fermentations.   AVI Publ. Co., Westport, Connecticut.

PEKKARINEN, M.   1973.   World Food Consumption Patterns.   *In* Man, Food and Nutrition.   CRC Press, W. Palm Beach, Florida.

PELLETT, P.L. and MAMARBACHI, D.   1979.   Recommended proportions of foods in home-made feeding mixtures.   Ecol. Food Nutr. *7*, 219–228.

PINSON, G.S., 1977.   A wooden hand-held maize sheller.   Rural Technology Guide No. 1.   Trop. Prod. Inst. London.

PONTECORVO, A.J. and BOURNE, M.C.   1978.   Simple methods for extending the shelf life of soy curd (tofu) in tropical areas.   J. Food Sci. *43*, 969–972.

PONTING, J.D.   1973.   Osmotic dehydration of fruits—Recent modifications and applications.   Proc. Biochem. *8*(12), 18–20.

RAJALAKSHMI, R. and RAMAKRISHNAN, C.V.   1977.   Formulation and evaluation of meals based on locally available foods for young children. W. Rev. Nutr. Diet. *27*, 34–104.

RAO, C.S., DEYOE, C.W., and PARRISH, D.B.   1978.   Biochemical and nutritional properties of organic acid-treated high-moisture sorghum grain.   J. Stored Prod. Res. *14*, 95–102.

REUSSE, E.   1976.   Economic and marketing aspects of post-harvest systems in small farm economies.   FAO Mo. Bull. Agric. Econ. Stat. 25(9), 1–7 and 25(10), 8–17.

ROBINSON, R.J. and KAO, C.   1977.   Tempeh and miso from chickpea, horse bean and soybean.   Cer. Chem. 54, 1192–1197.

ROCKLAND, L.B., ZARAGOSA, E.M., and ORACCA-TETTEH, R.   1979.   Quick-cooking winged beans (Psophocarpus tetragonolobus) J. Food Sci. 44, 1004–1007.

RODRICKS, J.V.   1978.   Food hazards of natural origin.   Fed. Proc. 37, 2587–2593.

SAUER, F.   1977.   Control of yeasts and molds with preservatives.   Food Technol. 31(2), 66, 67.

SIEGEL, A. and FAWCETT, R.   1976.   Food Legume Processing and Utilization.   International Development Research Center, Ottawa, Canada.

SILVA, C.A.B., BATES, R.P., and DENG, J.C.   1981.   Influence of presoaking on black bean cooking kinetics.   J. Food Sci. 46, 1721–1725.

SIMMONS, E.B.   1975.   The small-scale rural food-processing industry in Northern Nigeria.   Food Res. Inst. Studies 14, 147–161.

SIMON, E. and SOLIS, P.   1977.   Economic stove that burns sawdust as fuel.   Approp. Technol. 4(1), 23, 24.

SRINIVAS, K., RAGHAVENDRA, RAO, S.N., BHASHYAM, M.K., and DESI-KACHAR, H.S.R.   1976.   Studies on the use of dry earth as a contact medium for absorbing moisture from paddy.   J. Food Sci. Technol. 13, 142–145.

STAMER, J.R. and STOYLA, R.O.   1978.   Stability of sauerkraut packaged in plastic bags.   J. Food Prot. 41, 525–529.

STEINKRAUS, K.H.   1978.   Tempeh—an Asian example of appropriate/intermediate food technology.   Food Technol. 32(4), 79–80.

STERNER, M.H., STERNER, M.M., and ZEIDLER, G.   1978.   The hand texturizer—A high protein, quick cooking food producer.   Approp. Technol. 4(4), 20–22.

STEWART, G.F. and AMERINE, M.A.   1973.   Introduction to Food Science and Technology.   Academic Press, New York.

UNIDO.   1978.   Technologies from developing countries.   UNIDO Development and Transfer of Technology Series No. 7.   United Nations, Rome.

URBAIN, W.M.   1978.   Food irradiation.   Adv. Food Res. 24, 155–227.

USDA.   1977.   The Yearbook of Agriculture: Gardening for Food and Fun, Part 4.   Home Food Preservation. pp. 295–384.

VAN ARSDEL, W.B., COPELEY, M.J., and MORGAN, A.I.   1973.   Food Dehydration, Vol. 2, Practices and Applications, Chapt. 20. AVI Publ. Co., Westport, Connecticut.

VAS, K.   1977.   Food irradiation.   Technical and legal aspects.   Food Nutr. 3(3), 2–8.

VITA 1970.   Village Technology Handbook.   Volunteers in Technical Assistance.   Mt. Rainier, Maryland.

VON OPPEN, M.   1977.   The sun basket.   Approp. Technol. 4(3), 8–10.

WADSWORTH, J.I., HAYES, R.E., and SPADERO, J.J. 1979. Optimum protein quality food blends. Cer. Foods W. *24*, 274–280, 286.

WALSH, B.H. and BATES, R.P. 1978. Safety of home canning procedures for low-acid foods. J. Food Sci. *43*, 439–443.

WATANABE, K. 1975. An experimental fish drying and smoking plant on Volta Lake, Ghana: Design, construction and economic considerations. Trop. Sci. 17, 75–93.

WEISBERG, S.M. 1973. Exploiting grass-roots food technology in developing countries. Food Technol. *27*(5), 70–72, 80.

WHITAKER, J.R. 1978. Biochemical changes occurring during the fermentation of high protein foods. Food Technol. *32*(5), 175–180.

WORGAN, J.T. 1977. Canning and bottling as methods of food preservation in developing countries. Approp. Technol. *4*(3), 15, 16.

WU, L.C. and BATES, R.P. 1975. Protein-lipid films as meat substitutes. J. Food Sci. *40*, 160–163.

ZAMORA, A. and FIELDS, M.L. 1978. Production of corn and legume malts for use in home fermentation. J. Food Sci. *43*, 205–207, 214.

10

Solar Dehydration

Selçuk I. Güçeri

Introduction
Technical Background
Solar Dehydration Systems
Conclusion
References

INTRODUCTION

Even though solar drying is not a new concept, its large-scale use and intensive research in this field started with the beginning of the energy crunch in the mid-1970s, when the use of renewable energy sources for commercial and residential purposes received considerable attention. Solar energy appears to be a feasible alternative, particularly for low-temperature applications. One such area is dehydration of fruits, grains, and vegetables for preservation and easy transportation.

Solar energy is abundant, but its efficient use with food depends on careful design of the dehydration systems. Analysis and design of solar systems require fundamental knowledge of heat and mass transfer, solar energy, and food dehydration. A selection of books in these areas is given in the references (Özişik 1977; Holman 1981; Duffie and Beckman 1980; Kreith and Kreider 1978; Lunde 1980; Charm 1971; Kirscher 1956). A reader interested in pursuing a vigorous treatment of the subject should consult these and other books and reports.

This chapter is not intended to be a design tool for solar dehydration systems, which vary greatly in size and type of application, but rather to serve as an introduction to basic concepts and to present several examples that are reported to be functional.

TECHNICAL BACKGROUND

Humidity

The rate of dehydration in any drying process is closely related to the moisture content of the air passing over the substance being dried. There are two humidity terms that identify the moisture content: *Specific humidity* "ω" is the ratio of mass of the water vapor in air (m_v) to the mass of dry air (m_a).

$$\omega = m_v/m_a$$

Relative humidity "ϕ," on the other hand, is an identification of how much water vapor air holds, with respect to the maximum amount it can hold if saturated. Relative humidity is numerically expressed as the ratio of the partial pressure of water vapor in air (P_v) to that of the pressure when air is saturated (P_g) at that temperature as given by

$$\phi = P_v/P_g$$

Noting that the amount of water vapor that air can hold increases with increasing temperature, that is, as the partial pressure of water vapor in saturated air increases, it becomes possible to decrease the relative humidity by just increasing the temperature of air; whereas any change in specific humidity must come from an addition or extraction of water vapor to or from the air. The relative humidity is indicative of the drying potential of air and is often the humidity reported in weather information. The specific humidity is used in the thermal analysis of dehydrators. The relations between these two humidities and the air temperature are shown by using psychrometric charts, which are available in many handbooks and textbooks on thermodynamics.

Dehydration

Dehydration of substances is the reduction of their moisture content by evaporation of their water or by mechanical means. Evaporation of water occurs when the partial pressure of water vapor in the air is less than the partial pressure of vapor if the air is saturated, that is, the saturation pressure of water at that temperature. However, in order for liquid water to evaporate, it requires energy that, during the process, is supplied from the surroundings of the dehydrating substance. Per unit mass, the required energy for evaporation of water is known as the *enthalpy of evaporation, h_{fg}* (in kJ/kg). Even though it varies slightly with the temperature, its value can be taken as 2410 kJ/kg for moderate dehydration range. In solar dehydration systems, this energy is mainly supplied from solar energy.

Dehydration of food substances takes place in two distinct regimes. In the first regime, as the water at the surface of the substance evaporates, sufficient quantities can migrate from the internal regions to the surface that dehydration is controlled by the external air and energy flow, that is, by the rate of surface evaporation. This regime is known as the *constant rate period*.

When a certain level of moisture called the critical moisture content is reached, the dehydration rate decreases steadily. This second regime is known as the *falling rate* period. During this period, the rate of dehydration is controlled by the rate of water migration to the surface. The actual mechanism of this migration through the solid substance is a rather complex one; however, it appears that, in most cases for food dehydration, it is the result of diffusion of liquid and/or the vapor in the capillaries of the substance. The different dehydration regimes just mentioned are depicted in Fig. 10.1. More detailed information on this matter is presented by Görling (1958).

In *hygroscopic* materials, part of the water exists in bound moisture form such as water absorbed at solid surfaces, as solutions in cell or fiber walls, or chemically combined with the solid. Therefore, for hygroscopic materials, the falling rate period ends with an equilibrium moisture content rather than zero moisture as in the case of nonhygroscopic materials. Henderson and Perry (1955) suggest the use of the following formula to find the equilibrium moisture content, W_e:

$$1 - P/P_g = \exp[-cT(W_e)^n]$$

where P_g is the partial pressure of water in saturated air at the given

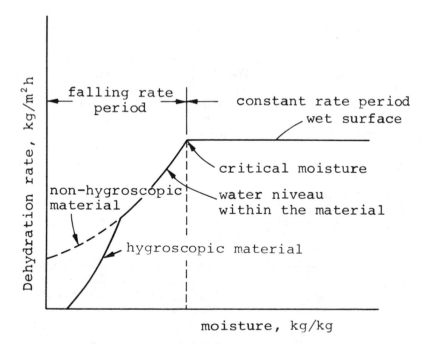

FIG. 10.1   SCHEMATIC ILLUSTRATION OF DEHYDRATION PERIODS.

temperature, c and n are constants for the material being processed. Table 10.1 shows their values for some of the crops.

Some of the food substances are treated prior to dehydration to improve the quality of the product. Also, the maximum dehydration temperature should not exceed a certain allowable value during the process to prevent degradation of the material. One of the damages caused by too high a temperature is known as case hardening, which results from rapid shrinking of the outer cells that prevents the proper flow of the liquid to the surface. Table 10.2 shows the usual pretreatment and maximum allowable temperatures for various food substances.

Radiation and Solar Energy

Any successful application of solar energy requires an understanding of its availability and nature and the fundamental principles governing its transmission. This section intends to give some basic information essential for the general design and performance prediction of solar dehydration systems. Many of the details, which are necessarily omitted, can be found in literature on solar energy (see Duffie and Beckman 1980; Kreidler and Kreith 1977) and heat transfer (see Özişik 1977; Holman 1981).

Objects that are not at *absolute* zero temperature emit energy in the form of radiation as given by

$$q = \sigma \varepsilon T4$$

where T is the temperature measured on the absolute scale, in °K; σ is the Stefan–Boltzmann constant (5.6697×10^{-8} W/m^{2}K^4) and ε is the emissivity, the ratio of the amount of energy emitted from a surface to that of the maximum energy that can be emitted by a surface. Surfaces that emit the maximum energy at a given temperature are called *black bodies* because such objects appear black to the human eye. The emitted radiative energy is not uniformly distributed over all wavelengths but has a distribution that depends mainly on the source temperature; as the source temperature becomes higher, the intensity of the emitted energy increases and shifts to shorter wavelengths. For practical purposes, the sun is assumed to be a perfect emitter at about 5700°K, and most of its energy is carried between the wavelengths 0.3 and 3.0 μm. The visible range of solar radiation is

TABLE 10.1.   VALUES OF c AND n FOR SOME CROPS

Material	c	n
Cotton	4.91×10^{-5}	1.70
Flaxseed	6.89×10^{-5}	2.02
Shelled corn	1.10×10^{-5}	1.90
Sorghum	3.40×10^{-6}	2.31
Soybeans	3.20×10^{-5}	1.52
Wheat	5.59×10^{-7}	3.03

Source: Henderson and Perry (1955).

TABLE 10.2.   PRETREATMENTS·AND MAXIMUM ALLOWABLE TEMPERATURES FOR VARIOUS FOOD SUBSTANCES

Material	Initial moisture (%)	Final moisture (%)	T_{max} (°C)	Pretreatment
Grains:				
paddy, raw	22–24	11	50	—
paddy, parboiled	30–35	13	50	parboiling[1]
maize	35	15	60^2–80	—
wheat	20	16	45	—
millet	21	14	...	—
Vegetables:				
green peas	80	5	65	blanching[3]
cauliflower	80	6	65	slicing
carrots	70	5	75	slicing and blanching
green beans	70	5	75	blanching
onions, garlic	80	4	55	slicing
cabbage	80	4	55	shredding and blanching
sweet potatoes	75	7	75	cubing
potatoes	75	13	...	cubing
leafy vegetables (spinach, cassava leaves, etc.)	80	10	...	—
chilies	...	5	65	—
cassava	62	17	...	cubing
Fruits:				
apples	...	24	70	slicing and sulphuring[4]
apricots, peaches	85	18	65	halving, sulphuring
grapes	80	15–20	70	sulphuring
bananas	...	15	70	longitudinally halving[5]
guavas	...	7	65	halving[5] deseeding
figs	...	24	...	fumigating
Other crops:				
coffee	50–52	11	...	soaking, shelling
cocoa beans	50	7–8	...	fermenting
cotton seed	...	8	...	—
copra	30	5	...	slicing
groundnuts	40	9	...	—

Source: German Appropriate Technology Exchange, 1979.
Legend: . . ., not reported; —, not applicable.
[1]Parboiling: treat with 150% water at 60–70°C for 5–6 hr.
[2]Without germination loss.
[3]Blanching: exposing to steam for 1–5 min. according to size.
[4]Sulfuring: dipping in 1–3% sulphurous acid to prevent discoloration.
[5]Use nonferrous knife for cutting to prevent discoloration.

about 0.4 to 0.7 μm. Objects at the temperatures usually observed in solar dehydration systems emit energy at substantially longer wavelengths. Spectral information is necessary in the design of solar systems because many of the radiative characteristics of the materials depend on the wavelength as well as on the *angle of incidence*, which is the angle between the beam radiation and the local normal to the surface.

In addition to emissivity, three other properties of a surface play an important role in radiative transfer: *absorptivity*, α, is the ratio of the absorbed energy to the total incident radiative energy. A perfect emitter, a black surface, is also a perfect absorber and absorbs all the incident energy regardless of the direction and wavelength distribution of the radiation. *Transmissivity*, τ, is the ratio of transmitted energy to the total radiative energy incident on the surface. Similarly, the *reflectivity*, ρ, is defined as the ratio of the reflected energy to the total incident radiative energy. From the conservation of energy principle, radiative energy reaching a surface is either absorbed, transmitted, or reflected, that is,

$$\alpha + \tau + \rho = 1$$

and consequently, for black surfaces,

$$\alpha_b = 1; \qquad \varepsilon_b = 1; \qquad \tau = 0; \qquad \rho = 0.$$

This characteristic of black body behavior suggests the use of nonreflecting black color for the solar collection elements.

It must be emphasized that this expression is valid for total radiative energy incident on a surface or for the part of it that is contained in a narrow wavelength band or for a portion of it coming from a certain direction. For example, glass has high transmissivity for radiation carried in short wavelengths, where $\lambda < 3.0$ μm (solar radiation), and is essentially opaque for radiation emitted by surfaces at low temperatures and carried over long wavelengths. Solar energy can penetrate into the greenhouses covered with glass, but the radiated energy from the plants and other objects cannot go through the glass in the form of radiation; thus, it acts as a thermic diode for radiative heat exchange. This phenomenon is commonly known as the *greenhouse effect*, as shown in Fig. 10.2. Covering of the solar collector surfaces by glazing materials follows the same reasoning, in addition to preventing convective losses.

Three quantities of solar radiation must be known in order to successfully design and predict the performance of a solar system:

1. Amount of radiation
2. Nature of radiation, i.e., how much of it is *diffuse* and how much of it is *beam* radiation
3. Angle of incidence on a surface of specified orientation as a function of time

The amount of radiation is obtained either from the collected data or from one of the several formulas suggested to predict insolation. If available, the actual data provide the more reliable approach. Radiation data are presented in several forms, possibly hourly, daily or monthly, and yearly average values. When this information is given on a daily basis, prediction of its hourly distribution can be made by using a chart developed by Liu and Jordan (1963).

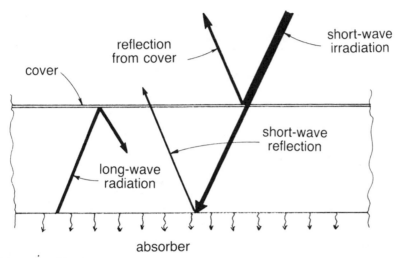

absorber

FIG. 10.2   THE GREENHOUSE EFFECT DUE TO HIGH TRANSMISSIVITY FOR SHORT
WAVELENGTH ENERGY AND LOW TRANSMISSIVITY FOR LONG WAVELENGTH ENERGY
AS EXPERIENCED FOR MANY OF THE COVER MATERIALS. THE MULTIPLE REFLEC-
TIONS ARE NOT SHOWN, FOR CLARITY.

The next important quantity of interest is the amount of diffuse radiation
relative to beam radiation. As the amount of diffuse radiation mainly
depends on the cloudiness and moisture content in the air, it is rather
difficult to predict accurately. A possible approach is to use one of the
empirical expressions available based on the *cloudiness index* and the
clearness factor. These two factors relate the local measured radiation to
that outside the atmosphere at the same latitude. For diffuse radiation, the
radiative properties of surfaces can be approximated by using values for an
incident angle of 60°. From the definition, the amount of diffuse radiation on
a surface does not heavily depend on the orientation of the surface for small
tilt angles. If this angle is large, then ground reflection must be taken into
account as well.

One of the most important quantities related to the performance of a solar
energy system is the angle of incidence for the beam radiation. As pointed
out earlier, the radiative properties of materials strongly depend on the
angle of incidence. Figure 10.3 shows the incidence angle dependence of
transmissivity for various numbers of covers made of glass, with a refrac-
tion index of 1.5. It is clear that, even though there is not too much variation
in the transmissivity characteristics of a cover system for up to 50° of
incidence angle, beyond this value to 90° there is a sharp drop to zero
transmissivity when the beam radiation is parallel to the surface. It is also
clear that the increased number of covers reduces the radiative energy gain
mainly because each cover reflects part of the incident energy. For moderate climates the optimum number of covers is two, and for warm areas one
cover is usually sufficient, but for cold climates triple cover might be

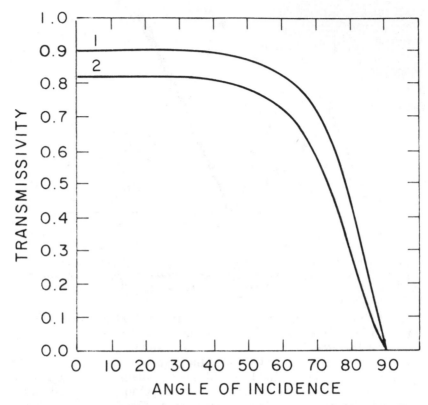

FIG. 10.3   THE TRANSMISSIVITIES OF 1 and 2 GLASS COVER SYSTEMS AS A FUNC-
TION OF ANGLE OF INCIDENCE.

necessary for satisfactory energy collection.

The angle of incidence for solar beam radiation is a function of parameters such as location, time of the day, and time of the year and is given by
Duffie and Beckman (1980) as:

$$\cos \theta = \sin \delta \sin \psi \cos \xi - \sin \delta \cos \psi \sin \beta \cos \gamma$$
$$+ \cos \delta \cos \psi \cos \xi \cos \beta + \cos \delta \sin \psi \sin \xi \cos \gamma$$
$$+ \cos \delta \sin \xi \sin \gamma \sin \beta$$

where ψ is the local latitude, β is the hour angle, and δ is the declination, i.e.,
the angle between the earth's orbital plane and its equatorial plane, that
can be approximated (Cooper 1969) as:

$$\delta = 23.45 \sin[360 (284 + r/365)].$$

with r indicating the day number in a year, January 1 being "1." The hour
angle is positive before noon and negative in the afternoon, being zero at

noon. It is related to the rotational speed of the earth at the rate of 15 deg per hour. γ is the surface azimuth angle and is zero when the surface is oriented toward the south; east is negative and west is positive. Using this expression, a factor R can be established to convert the instantaneous beam insolation data on horizontal surface to that for one tilted toward the south as:

$$\frac{\text{radiation on tilted surface}}{\text{radiation on horizontal surface}} = R$$

$$= \frac{\cos (\psi - \xi) \cos \delta \cos \beta + \sin (\psi - \xi) \sin \delta}{\cos \psi \cos \delta \cos \beta + \sin \psi \sin \delta}$$

For optimum annual energy collection, a surface must be tilted toward the equator at an angle that is about equal to the local latitude. If the energy is needed mostly during summer months, then this angle must be less by an amount up to $10°$; likewise, the tilt angle must be increased for optimum wintertime collection. The effects of the orientation on the annual energy collection are studied by Morse and Czarnecki (1958).

System Performance Simulation

Very often it is desirable to predict the performance of the solar dehydration units. In fact, for large-scale applications, prediction is essential for making investment decisions and design optimization before the system is built. The theoretical simulation of dehydration processes requires the simultaneous solution of two conservation equations, those for conservation of mass and conservation of energy. These equations are coupled through the air moisture content, the dehydration properties of the dehydrating material, and the energy supply.

A performance prediction analysis starts with hourly insolation data at the particular location. Then, depending on the application, a suitable configuration is chosen. According to the orientation and the radiative characteristics of the solar energy collection surfaces, the useful energy available for dehydration is calculated. This energy now becomes an input for the coupled energy and mass conservation equations for the dehydration process, the solution of which gives the desired time-based performance. If the design is not found to be satisfactory, it must be altered and the same calculation pattern followed until satisfactory performance can be predicted. Safety margins must be left because a number of important quantities can only be estimated. A flow diagram showing a possible design sequence is shown in Fig. 10.4.

The conservation of mass equation states that the sum of the dry air and water vapor coming out of a dehydration section is equal to the sum of the

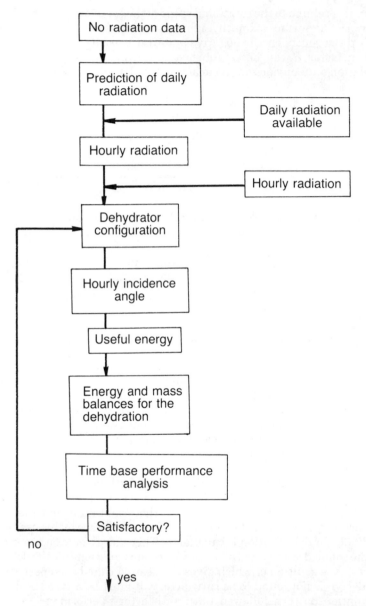

FIG. 10.4   USUAL STEPS IN PREDICTING AND OPTIMIZING THE THERMAL PER-
FORMANCE OF SOLAR DEHYDRATION SYSTEMS.

dry air and water vapor at the inlet plus the amount of water extracted from
the dehydrating substance.

The conservation of the energy principle can be stated as follows:

> Heat consumed to evaporate the water of the dehydrating substance = solar radiation absorbed + net radiative heat exchange with the neighboring substances + net radiative and conductive heat exchange with the surroundings + convective heat transfer between the substance and the air flow

Each of the terms requires detailed analysis to predict accurately the performance of the dehydration system. It should be noted that some of the terms in the expression may be absent or negligible for certain configurations; for example, in a closed chamber dehydration bin, direct solar radiation does not occur. The net energy gain by the dehydrating substance is used to evaporate its water.

If the dehydration is to be performed using air flows in a substantially long channel or tunnel, the complete analysis can be done by dividing the entire dehydration channel (path) into several smaller ones and making the calculations by considering the conservation equations for each section, starting from the first. The inlet conditions for the first section are known. Once the first section is analyzed, then the output conditions for the first section become the inlet conditions for the next one, and so on. This approach may require some iterations for calculating the average values of the properties of air flowing through a section. The outlet conditions from the dehydration bin become the outlet conditions from the last section considered. If the number of sections to be simulated is not very large, an alternate way is to write the conservation equations for each section separately, containing the values related to the neighboring sections, and to solve the resulting set of algebraic equations. A good example of this approach is presented by Selçuk et al. (1974).

SOLAR DEHYDRATION SYSTEMS

Solar energy has been used for drying vegetables, fruits, and grains since antiquity. Several different configurations have evolved through the decades to meet specific demands in dehydration. It is difficult to divide the solar driers and dehydrators into distinct categories, but an attempt will be made to classify them according to their size and way of utilizing solar energy as follows:

Open air, direct radiation driers
Closed chamber, direct radiation dehydrators
Preheated air dehydrators
Industrial-scale crop dehydrators

Open Air, Direct Radiation Driers

Open air, direct radiation driers have probably the longest history among the forms of dehydration. These systems have the advantage of being the least sophisticated, with maximum ease of operation. One area where they are commonly used is in the drying of coffee beans and tobacco. In Colombia, for example, approximately 400,000 tons of coffee beans are dried this way every year. Figure 10.5 shows one such drier, in which the drying trays are fitted with rollers operating on rails so that the trays can conveniently be slid under the protective cover during nights and rainy weather. It is reported that maize and cocoa beans are also dried using these units. The fresh coffee with a moisture content, wet basis, of 50% is loaded on trays, which yields 12.5 kg/m^2 of dry coffee with 11% moisture, wet basis. Table 10.3 shows the results of test runs by Alvero (1975) with different loading densities. This kind of drying is expected to be expensive for large drying loads. One way of simplifying the operation and system complexity is to use cement floors and transparent plastic covers to protect the beans against rain, avoiding the rail mechanism. In such a drier, it becomes necessary to mix the beans occasionally for uniform drying.

Another interesting open air drying setup is one that has been used in Australia to dry grapes since the beginning of this century. This unit consists of racks of steel netting, stretching between wooden posts as shown

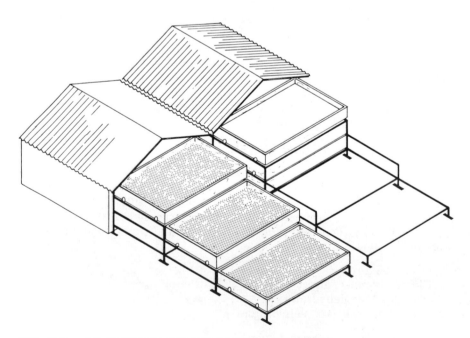

FIG. 10.5   SOLAR DRIER USED FOR COFFEE IN COLOMBIA.

TABLE 10.3. EXPERIMENTS IN DRYING COFFEE

Thickness of coffee beans (mm)	Tray loading kg/m^2 with 11% moisture	Days for drying	Daylight hours (total)	Sunshine hours	Moisture removed (kg/m^2)	Heat required (kwh/m^2)	Total insolation (kwh/m^2)	Efficiency (%)
8.3	3.125	2.78	33.37	16.5	2.90	1.95	14.2	13.73
16.7	6.250	4.07	48.85	25.9	5.60	3.76	20.5	18.41
33.3	12.500	8.45	101.45	39.5	10.85	7.3	36.7	19.87
50.0	18.750	12.11	145.33	53.6	17.05	11.5	50.7	22.56

Source: Alvero (1975).

FIG. 10.6   DRYING OF GRAPES ON RACKS IN AUSTRALIA. COURTESY: J.V. POS-SINGHAM, CSRIO DIVISION OF HORTICULTURAL RESEARCH. 1980.

in Fig. 10.6. The construction and operation of these units are well documented (see Grncarevic and Hawker 1971; CSRIO 1973; Possingham 1975). The complete assembly measures 46–96 m long and has 8–12 horizontal tiers of 5 cm mesh galvanized wire netting. The spacing between the tiers is 18 cm at the top, gradually increasing to 36 cm at the bottom to compensate for the obstruction of the air flow closer to the ground. The intermediate posts are located at 3 m intervals, and heavy end posts support the strong end crosspieces that carry the tiers.

The racks should preferably be aligned in a north–south direction with free space on the sides to provide the necessary air flow. They can operate with or without a roof; if there is one, the roof is oversized and flat to keep rainwater away from the fruit in windy weather. Another function of these covers is to protect the grapes against ultraviolet radiation to yield better quality products for fruits that are sensitive to UV. To further improve this protection, use of hessian side curtains is suggested, with due consideration to avoid mold development.

Following pretreatment, grapes are loaded manually on racks, one bunch thick. Sultanas are generally pretreated by cold-dipping them in a solution of 2.5% food grade potassium carbonate and 1.5–2% of commercial "grape dipping oil," which is a mixture of about 70% of ethyl esters of C_{16} and C_{18} fatty acids with free oleic acid and emulsifiers (Grncarevic and Lewis 1973). This pretreatment reduces the dehydration period from 3–5 weeks long to 8–14 days, with an added advantage of preventing discoloration due to enzymatic darkening. The decrease in dehydration time is believed to be due to the changes in physical and chemical structure of the wax platelets covering the grape surface in such a way as to increase its permeability for water (Chambers and Possingham 1963; Possingham 1972).

Grapes can also be treated after being placed on racks. A multiple-nozzle fork wand is used, as shown in Fig. 10.7, to spray emulsion in such a way as to cover the entire surface of grape berries at the rate of 450 liters per 1000

FIG. 10.7   RACK SPRAYING OF SULTANAS, AN ALTERNATIVE TO BULK DIPPING. COURTESY: J.V. POSSINGHAM, CSRIO DIVISION OF HORTICULTURAL RESEARCH. 1980.

FIG. 10.8   SHAKING DOWN THE DRIED FRUIT. COURTESY: J.V. POSSINGHAM, CSRIO DIVISION OF HORTICULTURAL RESEARCH. 1980.

buckets. When the desired moisture level is achieved, the racks are shaken by a mechanical device mounted on a tractor as shown in Fig. 10.8, and dried grapes fall on to hessian placed underneath. Table 10.4 shows the drying data per 50 m of drying rack for various kinds of grapes.

TABLE 10.4. DRYING DATA FOR CURRANTS AND GRAPES ON RACKS

Types of grapes	Pretreatment	Quantities dried (tons)		Final moisture content, wet basis (%)	Drying time
		Green	Dry		
Currants	None	10	2.5	15.0	2 weeks
Sultanas	Cold dipping[1]	10	2.5	13.5	8–14 days
Walthem Gross, Muscot Gordo, Blanco	Hot dipping[2]	10	2.5	14.0	2 weeks

Source: Possingham 1975.
[1]Cold dip: 10 kilograms (kg) of potassium carbonate in 400 liters of water plus 6 to 8 liters of oil. The oil is a mixture of ethyl ethers of fatty acids and free oleic acids. The solution is used at ambient temperature. The maximum dipping time is 30 min.
[2]Hot dip: a. 1.8 kg of sodium hydroxide per 450 liters of water at 93°C.
          b. 1.4 kg of sodium hydroxide per 450 liters of water at boiling point. The dipping time is 4 sec.

A similar configuration except with vertical trays has been investigated by Roa (1975) for drying of cassava chips. Figure 10.9 shows one of the larger units with vertical wire mesh sidings, supported by angle bars. Cassava chips with an initial moisture of 67%, wet basis, must be dried to 50% moisture in the first day of drying; otherwise, their quality deteriorates rapidly. The cut pieces of cassava $(1-2 \text{ cm} \times 1-5 \text{ cm})$ are first dipped in 50% alcohol solution for 2 min and then placed in trays, with maximum allowable densities depending on the wind velocity and the air relative humidity. The reported advantage is that the vertical driers take about one-half the time required for tray sun drying. It is also suggested that, in the case of air humidity in excess of 75%, supplemental heat should be used.

As mentioned previously, black-painted surfaces absorb most of the radi-

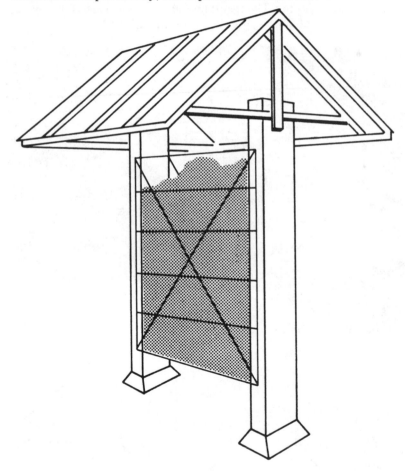

FIG. 10.9   VERTICAL DRYER FOR CASSAVA.

ation incident on them; therefore, it would be logical to paint the trays black when the fruits are to be dried in them. However, a substantial portion of the radiation is still lost because the produce placed on the trays covers most of the available area and the absorptivity of the fruits is far less than that of the black trays. A solution to this problem is suggested by Bolin et al. (1979), as shown in Fig. 10.10. This solar trough dehydrator uses a curved reflective surface under the trays such that solar radiation passing through the opening is reflected back to the bottom of the drying trays, which is made of a black metallic plate to absorb energy and help prevent localized high-temperature spots. With the proper design and orientation, this device can operate as a solar trap for a wide range of incidence angles. The optimum configuration is mentioned to be a half-circle reflecting surface with trays covering half of the opening. The result for dehydrating peaches, in comparison with conventional sun drying, is shown in Fig. 10.11.

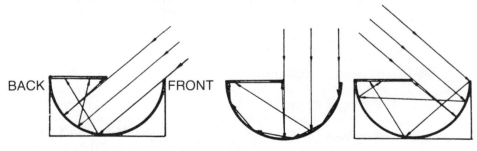

FIG. 10.10   A SOLAR TROUGH DRYER. SOURCE: BOLIN *et al.* (1978).

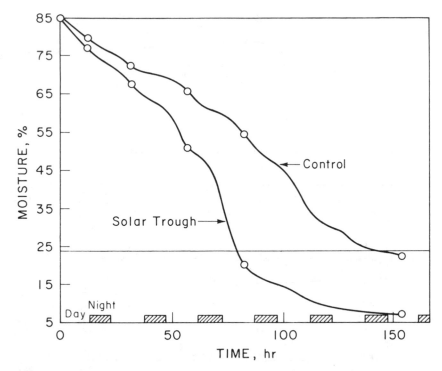

FIG. 10.11   DRYING CURVES FOR PEACHES USING THE SOLAR TROUGH DEHY-
DRATOR AND COMPARISON WITH CONVENTIONAL SUN DRYING. SOURCE: BOLIN
et al. (1978).

Closed Chamber, Direct Radiation Dehydrators

Probably the most important drawback common to the open air driers is
the contamination and infestation of the fruits by insects and airborne dust.
To prevent this, closed-space, direct radiation dehydrators are used in
varying sizes. These dehydrators essentially consist of a transparent cover
system and a tray section that holds the substance to be dehydrated. Inlet
and outlet points must be provided for adequate amounts of air flow. Easy
accessibility to the material being dehydrated for mixing and replacement
is also essential for a successful design. Figure 10.12 depicts one such
device for small-scale food preservation as suggested by Lawand (1966).
This dehydration box has a double-glazed transparent cover and a blacken-
ed interior with insulated sides and bottom. The access doors are located
at the back. Fresh air enters the box through the holes in the base and
leaves through the outlet ports located on the upper sections of the cabinet
by natural convection. The 193 cm × 66 cm experimental unit had 1.1 m^2
drying area. Typical radiation analyses of the performance of the drier for

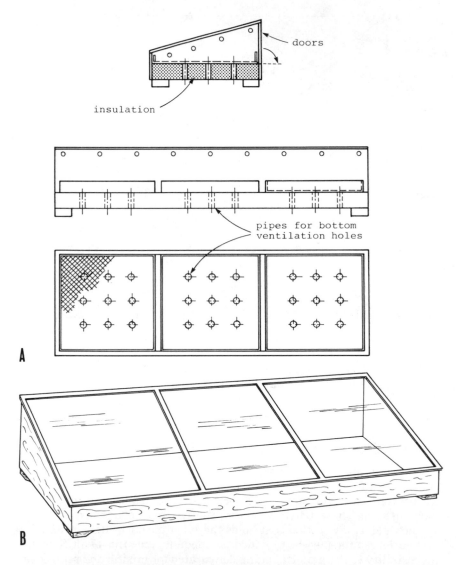

FIG. 10.12   THE SOLAR CABINET DEHYDRATOR. A. SCHEMATICS. B. A VIEW OF THE CABINET. SOURCE: LAWAND (1966).

the Damascus (Syria) area are given in Tables 10.5 and 10.6. Lawand (1966) suggests that the length of the cabinet should be at least three times the width to minimize shading effects, and the tilt angle for the cover must be chosen according to the latitude and with due consideration for the air motion. A watertight cover is necessary to protect the produce against rain, and during operation the temperature must be monitored to avoid

TABLE 10.5.   RADIATION ANALYSIS FOR THE DEYHDRATION CABINET

Hours	Total solar radiation on horizontal, I_H (cal/cm²)	Diffuse solar radiation, I_{DIFF} (cal/cm²)	Direct solar radiation on horizontal I_H-I_{DIFF} (cal/cm²)	Correction factor, R	Total radiation incident on cabinet cover, I_T (kilocals)	Transmittance of direct solar radiation, τ	Energy transmitted through glazings, I_{TR} (kilocalories)
10 a.m. – 11 a.m.	51.5	5.9	45.6	1.31	775	0.795	611
11 a.m. – 12 a.m.	56.2	6.5	49.7	1.33	862	0.805	690
12 a.m. – 1 p.m.	55.5	7.4	48.1	1.33	848	0.805	678
1 p.m. – 2 p.m.	51.1	9.5	41.6	1.31	761	0.795	598
2 p.m. – 3 p.m.	31.7	14.7	17.0	1.35	448	0.755	338

Source: Lawand 1963.

TABLE 10.6.   THERMAL ANALYSIS FOR THE DEHYDRATION CABINET

Solar time (hours)	Average cabinet temperature, T_c (°C)	Ambient air temperature T_a (°C)	Temperature difference $T_c - T_a = \Delta T$ (°C)	Heat Loss from solar panels, Q_{sp} (kilocal/hr)	Heat loss through bottom, Q_b (kilocal/hr)	Heat loss from cover, Q_k (kilocal/hr)	Available heat to dryer, Q_a (kilocal/hr)	Internal effective efficiency, Q_a/I_{TR} (%)	Over-all effective efficiency, Q_a/I_T (%)
10 a.m. – 11 a.m.	73.0	18.6	54.4	38.1	35.2	199.0	338.7	55.3	43.9
11 a.m. – 12 a.m.	84.5	21.6	62.9	44.0	40.5	230.5	375.0	54.3	43.5
12 a.m. – 1 p.m.	89.0	22.8	66.2	46.4	42.6	243.0	346.0	51.0	40.7
1 p.m. – 2 p.m.	85.5	24.2	61.3	42.9	39.5	224.7	290.9	48.8	38.2
2 p.m. – 3 p.m.	66.5	25.2	41.3	28.9	26.6	151.3	122.2	36.1	27.7

Source: Lawand 1963.
Average wind speed during test = 1 meter/second.

TABLE 10.7. PROSPECTIVE OPERATION OF THE DEHYDRATION CABINET

Breakdown of drying time in any season	Days available for drying	Product to be dried	Number of days of each drying cycle	Number of cycles per drying interval	Fresh product charged to dryer per cycle (kg)	Dried product produced per cycle (kg)	Dried Product produced in interval (kg)	Ratio of fresh material to final dried product
April 1–30	30	Parsley herbs or broad beans	1	30	2.4[1]	0.3[1]	9.0	14.0
May 1–June 15	46	Garlic	2	23	2.6	1.2	27.6	3.2
June 16–July 9	24	Apricots	2	12	4.0	0.6	7.2	7.0
July 10–Aug. 5	27	Peaches	3	9	4.5[1]	0.9[1]	8.1	5.3
Aug. 6–31	26	Onions	2	13	3.0	0.6	7.8	8.5
Sept. 1–20	20	Okra	2	10	3.0	0.5	5.0	6.5
Sept. 21–Oct. 22	32	Grapes	4	8	5.7	1.2	9.6	4.8
Totals	205						74.3	

Source: Reported by Lawand (1966) for the vicinity of Damascus, Syrian Arab Republic.
[1] Estimates.

exceeding the maximum allowable temperature for the produce. The dehydration of various substances using this cabinet is shown in Table 10.7.

A similar device with a glass cover has also been suggested by Agrawal and Kapoor (1975). Their drying data are given in Table 10.8 and Figure 10.13. In these and several other types of solar dehydrators the air flow is induced by natural convection; that is, when the air warms up, its density decreases and lighter air moves upward toward the outlet ports, and the fresh and cooler air flows in through the lower inlet ports.

Figure 10.14 shows a larger-scale direct-absorbing chamber type of dehydrator used in Brazil to process cocoa beans. Air flow is by natural convection, entering the unit through the slots on the sides and leaving through the opening at the top. The north–south aligned chamber has a glass cover and two drying platforms with an aisle in between. When necessary, the side entry slots are closed, and air first passes through an auxiliary heating section. It is reported that the midday temperature in the chamber can reach values 20–25°C higher and the minimum relative humidity can be 15–20% lower than the ambient.

To provide higher and more uniform heat and moisture transfer from the produce, crossdraught dehydrators are sometimes used. In this configuration, air flow is through the trays as well as over the surface where the produce is placed. Due to increased obstructions in the air flow path, these dehydrators often require external forcing of air for satisfactory operations. An experimental unit using this principle has been reported by Bailey and Williamson (1975). A schematic of their dehydrator is shown in Fig. 10.15. Air flow is provided by a small fan that draws air from the slots at the bottom edge of the unit.

A larger-scale operation on a similar principle is proposed by Altenkirch (see Atangündüz 1978). Schematics of this crossdraught chamber dehydrator, which is aligned in a north–south direction, are shown in Fig. 10.16. Desiccant materials are placed in trays along the east and west sides of the unit. Before noon, the east side receives solar energy and the west side remains cooler; this temperature difference introduces natural con-

TABLE 10.8. SOLAR DEHYDRATION DATA FOR THE CABINET SUGGESTED BY AGRAWAL AND KAPOOR (1975)

| Material | Quantity Dried (g.) | Pre-treatment | Moisture content | | Maximum Allowable Temp. (°C) | Drying time (hr) |
			Initial (%)	Preferred Final (%)		
Prunes	750	sulfuring	85	15–20	77	18
Peaches	275	none	80	5–6	77	11
Peas	420	blanching	80	5–6	66	5
Cauliflower	200	none	85	5–6	66	2.5

Average temperature attainable inside the cabinet: 75°C.
Average outside temperature: 35°C.

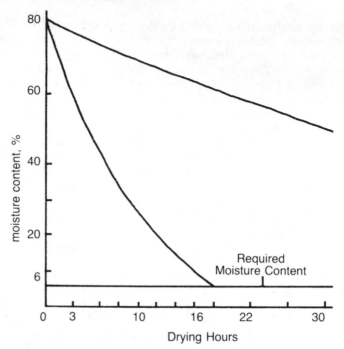

FIG. 10.13 DEHYDRATION DATA FOR PRUNES USING THE SOLAR CABINET DE-
HYDRATOR. SOURCE: AGRAWAL AND KAPOOR (1975).

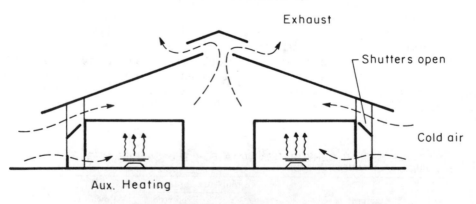

FIG. 10.14 DIAGRAM OF THE GLASS-ROOF DEHYDRATOR WITH TWO PLATFORMS
AND A CENTRAL PASSAGE. SOURCE: GHOSH (1975).

vection from the west side to the east side of the unit. The direction
of the natural convection is reversed in the afternoon. This arrangement
lets the fresh air go through perforated trays containing the desiccant
material before entering the dehydration section, which in turn reduces
the moisture content of the air, decreasing its relative humidity. In the

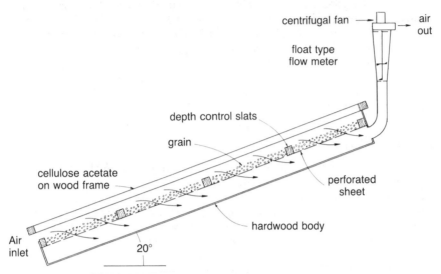

FIG. 10.15   A NATURAL CONVECTION SOLAR DEHYDRATION CABINET USING CROSSDRAUGHT FLOW OF AIR. SOURCE: BAILEY AND WILLIAMSON (1975).

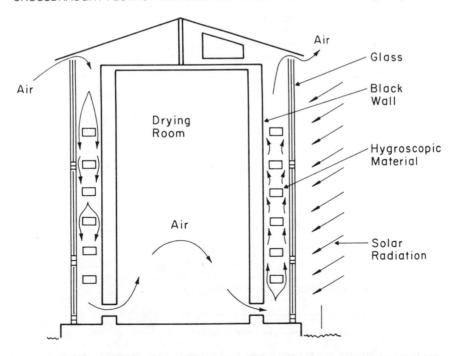

FIG. 10.16   THE ALTENKIRCH SOLAR DEHYDRATION BIN USING DESICCANT MATERIALS. SOURCE: ATAGÜNDÜZ (1978).

meantime, the desiccant material in the outlet path of the air is also subject to solar irradiation; thus, with proper design, solar energy regenerates the desiccant material, making it ready for the reversed flow. With the periodic motion of the sun, the process repeats itself. Experimental results and detailed theoretical analysis have been presented by Atagündüz (1978). One of the advantages of this unit is that the produce is completely protected from direct solar radiation, making it especially suitable for dehydrating ultraviolet-sensitive materials.

Pre-Heated Air Dehydrators

It was pointed out earlier that the main driving force for the dehydration process is the difference in the moisture content of air relative to its saturation state. As the temperature of the air rises, the maximum amount of moisture it can hold also increases; in other words, its relative humidity decreases, thereby increasing the drying potential. Several dehydrators have been reported in which air is first heated by letting it flow through a section that is essentially an air-type solar collector. An example of these preheated air dehydrators is the one investigated and reported with extensive theoretical analysis by Selçuk et al. (1976). Figure 10.17 depicts this crossdraught unit. Air flow is provided by a fan; the air is first heated by being passed through a collector section made of a matrix of steel chips. Auxiliary heaters are used as a back-up energy source.

The results of drying mulberries in this dehydrator are given in Fig. 10.18. Akyurt and Selçuk (1973) reported another similar system supplemented with auxiliary heat for continuous operation. A schematic of this unit is shown in Fig. 10.19. The results of dehydrating green peppers is

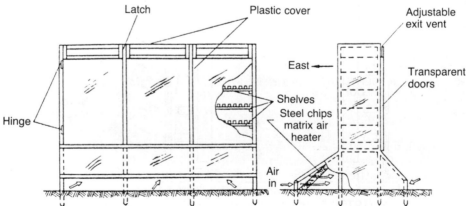

FIG. 10.17   THE MULTIPLE-SHELF SOLAR DEHYDRATOR. SOURCE: SELÇUK et al. (1976).

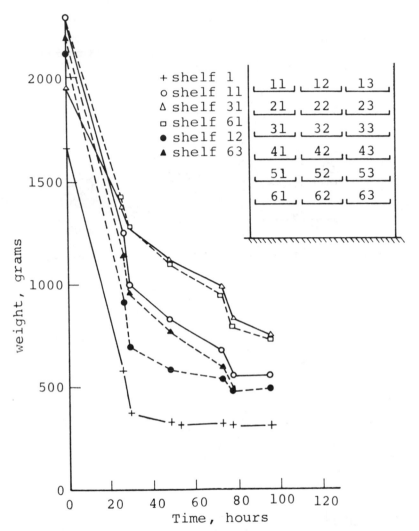

FIG. 10.18   DEHYDRATION OF MULBERRIES IN THE MULTIPLE-SHELF DEHYDRATOR.
SOURCE: SELÇUK (1975).

shown in Fig. 10.20. Another crossdraught, preheated air unit as proposed by Van Dresser (1965) is shown in Fig. 10.21. A wind-powered, rotary-ventilator (attic fan) assisted version of this kind of dehydrator, which helped to increase air flow through the drying section, was investigated by Lawand (1975). A damper can be placed to adjust the air flow, thus regulating the temperature of the dehydrating substance.

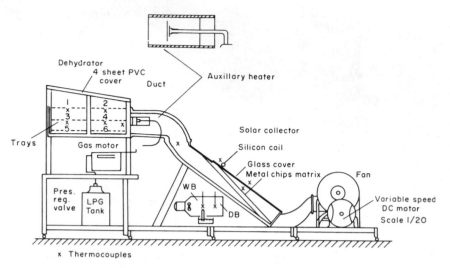

FIG. 10.19 THE SOLAR DEHYDRATOR FITTED WITH AUXILIARY HEATING. SOURCE:
AKYURT AND SELÇUK (1973).

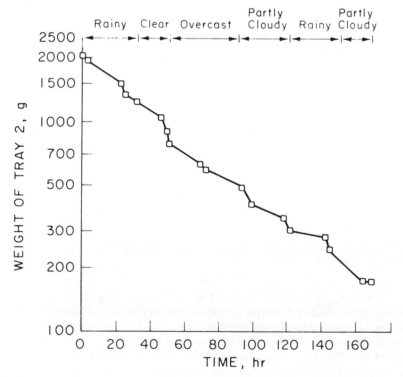

FIG. 10.20 WEIGHT LOSS VS. TIME FOR SLICED GREEN BELL PEPPERS IN THE
SOLAR DEHYDRATOR. SOURCE: AKYURT AND SELÇUK (1973).

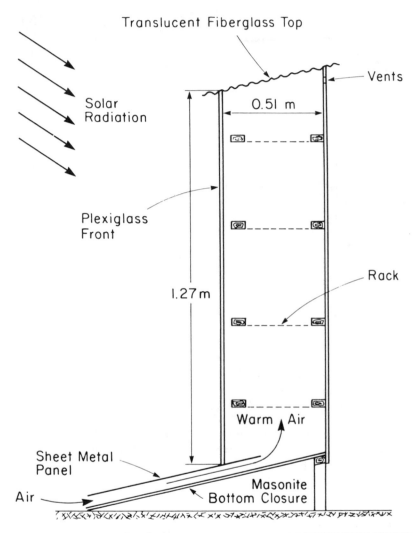

FIG. 10.21   SECTION VIEW OF THE FRUIT AND VEGETABLE DEHYDRATOR. SOURCE: VAN DRESSER (1975).

Larger-scale air preheating is also attractive, especially if the structure of the dehydration bin can be incorporated in the solar energy collection system. Several such units are reported in the literature. Phillips (1965) reported on the operation of a coffee-drying bin, as shown in Fig. 10.22, with reported electricity savings of up to 66% when compared to bins not assisted by the solar energy in the Mayagues (Colombia) area. Air is fed to the system from an opening in the roof of the structure. The flow channel is provided by covering the roof with sheet metal painted black. The tempera-

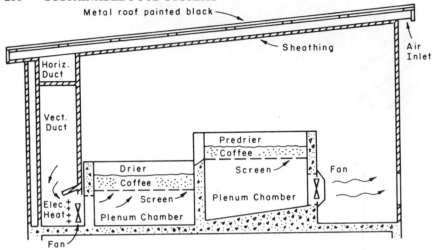

FIG. 10.22   DIAGRAM OF A COFFEE DEHYDRATION BIN USING ITS ROOF AS A SOLAR COLLECTOR. SOURCE: PHILLIPS (1965).

ture increase of air was found to be given by the expression

$$\Delta T(°C) = (0.139)H(1-\exp[-2.46/v])$$

where H is the incident solar energy in W/m^2 and v is the volumetric air flow rate in m^3/min/m^2 collector area.

For an air flow rate of 68 m^3/min, the increase in air temperature exceeds 10°C under favorable conditions. The coffee beans to be dehydrated are placed in two sections. First, the washed beans with 55% moisture (wet basis) are placed in the predrier, where they are skin-dried for 2–3 hours. The final stage of dehydration takes place in the main drier section, where warm air blown through the coffee beans from the bottom to obtain a final moisture of 12% within 24 hours with an air flow rate of 24 m^2/min per square meter of bin area used. The electrical heating elements supplied enough power to maintain the air temperature at around 50°C, which also eliminated the need for frequent stirring. Use of auxiliary power enabled the bin to operate continuously during nights and cloudy days. If a transparent cover is used over the collector area, a temperature increase of 50% more than the uncovered version can be expected. Two other similar operations have been investigated by Peterson (1975) for dehydrating corn. Figure 10.23 shows one of the units with a south-facing roof of 30° slope, located in Sioux Falls, South Dakota (latitude 44°34′N). In this application, the flat-black-painted roof sheeting acted as the collector plate and provided temperature increases of about 5–12°C when covered with a plastic glazing stretched 8 cm above the roof. It is reported that 1 m^2 of collector area is required for 2 m^3 of shelled maize to provide an acceptable rate of dehydra-

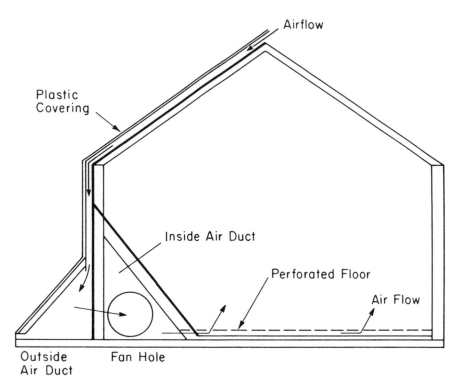

Airflow

Plastic
Covering

Inside Air Duct

Perforated Floor

Air Flow

Outside   Fan Hole
Air Duct

FIG. 10.23.   SOLAR SUPPLEMENTAL HEAT DEHYDRATION BIN. SOURCE: PETER-
SON (1975).

tion with 25% initial moisture. The fan must supply 2 m³/min of air per m³ of
maize. The main feature of the unit is the use of low temperature air flow for
slow dehydration in the fall season. If maize is dehydrated during the
warmer months, it must be done in one week to prevent deterioration,
which would require high air flow rates. In low temperature dehydration,
the important part is to supply sufficient air flow to advance the dehydration front through the grain fast enough to prevent any damage. It has also
been suggested that the fan operate continuously day and night until the
top grain is down to 20% moisture or less so that the top layers are not
spoiled before the lower layers are dried. Figure 10.24 shows another
solar-assisted steel dehydration bin investigated by Peterson (1975). The
diameter of the unit is 5.5 m, and it has a 110 m³ capacity. Air drawn in by a
fan through two channels created by covering two-thirds of the side of the
bin with black-painted aluminum covered with transparent plastic, using
spacers. On both sides of the aluminum absorber plate, the air flow rate is
28.3 m³/min. The warm air thus collected is supplied to the dehydration bin
after passing through an auxiliary heating section operated with electricity
and then blown through the perforated floor and the shelled corn. During

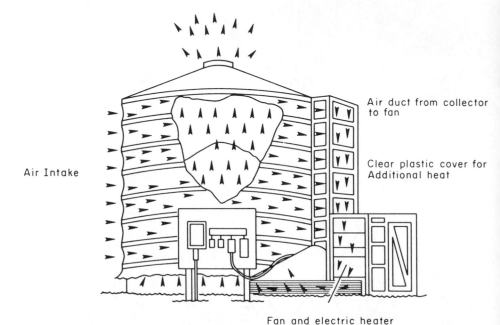

Air duct from collector to fan

Air Intake

Clear plastic cover for Additional heat

Fan and electric heater

FIG. 10.24   A DEHYDRATION BIN USED TO DRY CORN. SOURCE: PETERSON (1975).

the test runs, energy savings of 50% were estimated when the average outdoor temperature was 5°C with 71% relative humidity. A view of the unit is shown in Fig. 10.25.

Air heating for dehydration can also be accomplished by utilizing solar collectors separate from the dehydration bin. Operation on such a system has been investigated by Roa and Macedo (1976) for drying 600 kg of cocoa beans. Their experimental bin is shown in Fig. 10.26; it is 1 m in diameter and has a perforated floor. The fan draws in air through 8 m of collectors and supplies it to the bin at a rate of 7.8 m/min. The design objective was a 15°C average increase in the air temperature. The authors also reported extensive theoretical modeling of the operation, which was compared with the collected data. The results are shown in Fig. 10.27 at various locations in the bin.

A solar fruit dehydrator using an innovative solar collector has been reported by Bolin et al. (1978). The dehydrator used two polyethylene tubes; the 0.9 m diameter, black-painted inner absorbing tube is covered by a 1 m diameter clear tube, providing a 5 cm air gap between them. Air is blown through the inner tube that collected the heat absorbed by the black tube. The 24 m long collector assemblies are made by heat-sealing 4 or 6 ml thick polyethylene sheets. The dehydrator (measuring 0.75 m × 1.5 m × 1.0 m), which contains 12 trays, is attached to the end of the tubing as shown in Fig. 10.28. The maximum temperature increase for air is reported to be 15°C. To

FIG. 10.25 A VIEW OF THE CIRCULAR STEEL DEHYDRATION BIN. COURTESY W.H. PETERSON, UNIVERSITY OF ILLINOIS, URBANA-CHAMPAIGN.

obtain higher temperatures, part of the air is recirculated through the system. The results of an apricot dehydration experiment in Suisun, California, are shown in Fig. 10.29.

Industrial-Scale Crop Dehydration

One of the most challenging applications of solar energy is in industrial scale crop dehydration. Recently there have been several activities in this area. A well-documented (Carnegie *et al.* 1979; Niles *et al.* 1978; Carnegie and Pohl 1979; California Polytechnic State University 1977, 1978; Stine and Carnegie 1979) case is located in Fresno, California, for raisin and prune dehydration. The system is designed by the California Polytechnic State University in cooperation with TRW, Inc., for the Lamanuzzi & Pantaleo, Inc., plant. Figure 10.30 shows the schematic of the solar energy system used to supply about 80% of the heating requirements for one of the dehydration tunnels in one season, from August to January. A unique

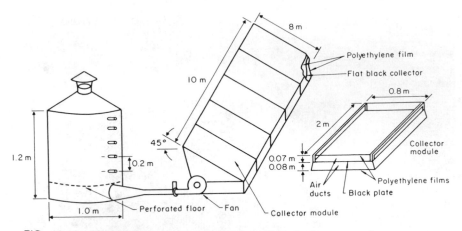

FIG. 10.26 DEHYDRATION OF CARIOCA BEANS IN BINS USING ONLY SOLAR ENERGY, WHICH IS COLLECTED BY COLLECTORS SEPARATE FROM THE BIN. SOURCE: RAO AND MACEDO (1976).

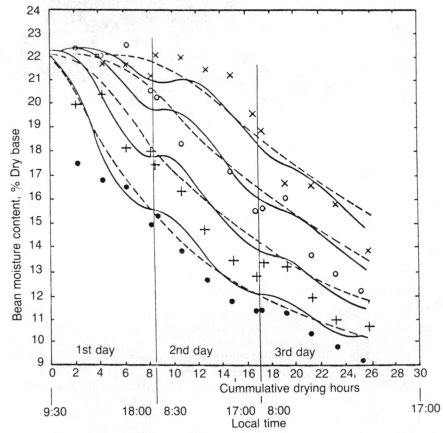

FIG. 10.27 EXPERIMENTAL AND THEORETICAL VALUES OF MOISTURE CONTENT.—— SIMULATION (VARYING CONDITIONS); ---SIMULATION (AVERAGE CONDITIONS); EXPERIMENTAL, 20 CM LEVEL; +, EXPERIMENTAL, 40 CM LEVEL;), EXPERIMENTAL, 60 CM LEVEL; X, EXPERIMENTAL, 80 CM LEVEL. SOURCE: RAO AND MACEDO (1976).

FIG. 10.28 A SOLAR-HEATED DEHYDRATOR CONSTRUCTED OF TWO POLYETHYLENE TUBES. PART OF THE HEATED AIR CAN BE RECIRCULATED TO OBTAIN HIGHER TEMPERATURES. COURTESY: H.R. BOLIN, USDA SCIENCE AND EDUCATION ADMINISTRATION, WESTERN REGIONAL RESEARCH CENTER. 1979.

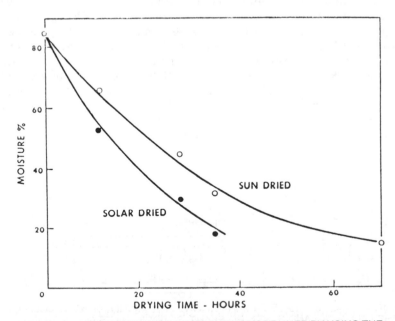

FIG. 10.29 APRICOT DEHYDRATION CURVES OBTAINED BY USING THE POLYETHYLENE TUBES AS SOLAR COLLECTORS. SOURCE: BOLIN *et al*. (1979).

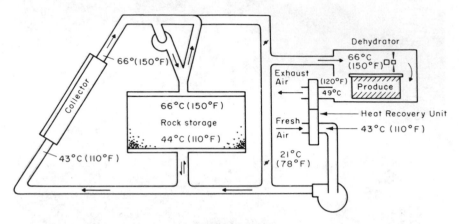

FIG. 10.30   SCHEMATICS OF THE SOLAR DEHYDRATION SYSTEM IN THE LAMANUZZI AND PANTALEO PLANT IN FRESNO. SOURCE: NILES *et al.* (1978).

feature of this design is the use of rock-bed thermal storage for storing the excess solar energy during peak insolation hours. The collectors used single glazing, as shown in Fig. 10.31; a view of the 1951 m^2 collector field is shown in Fig. 10.32. The air flow rate is 566 m^3/min, providing an average dehydration temperature of 62°C. The rock-bed storage unit contained 396 m^3 (699 tons) of 25.4 mm (1 in.) commercial grading riverbed granite pebbles. The total volume of the unit is 657 m^3 and has 8.86 GJ (8.4 × 10^6 BTU) storage capacity for a temperature differential of 16.7°C. The exhaust temperature of air from the dehydrator section is about 48.9°C; therefore, a Corn's Heat Wheel energy recovery unit is installed. The monthly breakdown of the total energy consumption for the operation season of August 1978 to January 1979 is shown in Fig. 10.33. The results of a complete computer simulation of the performance is also reported (Carnegie *et al.* 1979). An energy analysis shows that the energy payback time of this system is 4.8 operating seasons, that is, after this length of time it will become a net energy source and will have paid back the original energy

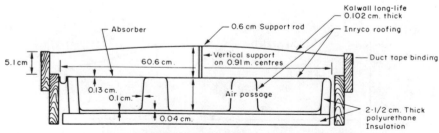

FIG. 10.31   THE CROSS-SECTIONAL VIEW OF THE SINGLE GLAZED COLLECTORS IN THE LAMANUZZI AND PANTALEO PLANT. SOURCE: NILES *et al.* (1978).

FIG. 10.32 A VIEW OF THE COLLECTOR FIELD OF 1951 M² COLLECTION AREA.
COURTESY: E.J. CARNEGIE, CALIFORNIA POLYTECHNIC STATE UNIVERSITY, 1979.

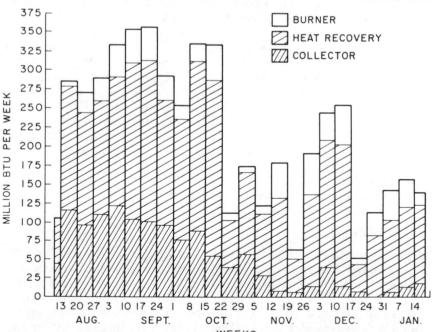

FIG. 10.33 THE WEEKLY DISTRIBUTION OF ENERGY CONSUMPTION FOR THE
LAMANUZZI AND PANTALEO PLANT IN FRESNO, CALIFORNIA. SOURCE: CARNEGIE
et al. (1979).

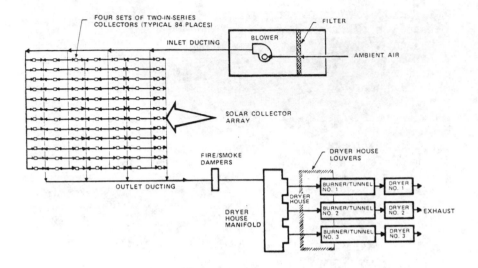

FIG. 10.34   THE SCHEMATICS OF THE SOLAR ENERGY DEHYDRATION SYSTEM OP-
ERATING IN THE GOLD KIST SOYBEAN DEHYDRATION PLANT. SOURCE: GUINN
AND FISHER (1977); FORWALTER (1978).

investment. The economic payback time is estimated as 11 to 17 years,
depending on incentives and economic variables.

Another industrial-scale application of solar energy is in the Gold Kist,
Inc., soybean dehydration plant at Decatur, Alabama, which was originally
designed for fuel oil operation. The system description presented by Guinn
and Fisher (1977) is shown in Fig. 10.34. The 1217 m² collector field is made
of 672 Solaron collectors and has 15° slope. As all the solar energy collecta-
ble is used immediately, thermal storage is not used. The rate of air
flow is 764.4 m³/min. A positive pressure system is used to prevent dust
intrusion and the consequent possibility of having explosive mixtures in
the collectors. Collectors are made with single glazing, which also reduces
the stagnation temperatures about 15°C, increasing safety. The estimated
amount of energy savings for the year 1975–1976 was 6.4% of the energy
requirement of one dehydrator (see also Forwalter 1978).

CONCLUSION

Because of the required advanced technology and system complexity, the
cost of energy obtained from solar radiation increases as the temperature at
which it is to be delivered increases. At the present, processes taking place
at low to medium temperatures can use solar energy effectively and economically. Dehydration of foodstuff thus recommends itself as an area
suitable for solar energy applications. In the preceding sections, an overview of various forms and sizes of solar dehydration systems is presented.

The available configurations vary according to the purpose and local traditions as well as available technology. In many cases, the design and improvement of solar dehydrators depend on trial-and-error methods. There is a definite need for a more systematic approach, perhaps in the form of unified, computerized design codes that would have the flexibility to handle different design goals. These computer-aided design and analysis codes should be user oriented and should be widely available, as are the various codes now publicly available for residential heating and cooling using solar energy (P.L. Versteegen and D. E. Cassel 1979). An added advantage of this approach would be the possibility of design optimization without going through the trial-and-error sequence.

For energy conservation on a large scale, the use of solar energy in industrial dehydration processes remains a challenging field. Further studies and applications in this area can be expected to unveil more economical and efficient systems.

REFERENCES

AGRAWAL, H.C. and KAPOOR, S.G.   1975.   *See* Brace Research Institute.

AKYURT, M. and SELÇUK, M.K.   1973.   A solar dryer supplemented with auxiliary heating system for continuous operation.   Solar Energy *14*.

ALVERO, V.   1975.   *See* Brace Research Institute.

ATAGÜNDÜZ, G.   1978.   Utilization of solar energy for drying agricultural and industrial products.   Proceedings, International Symposium-Workshop on Solar Energy, Cairo, Egypt, June.

BAILEY, P.H. and WILLIAMSON, W.F.   1975.   *See* Brace Research Institute.

BOLIN, H.R., STAFFORD, A.E., and HUXSOLL, C.C.   1978.   Solar heated fruit dehydrator.   Solar Energy *20*, 289–291.

BOLIN, H.R., STAFFORD, A.E., and HUXSOLL, C.C.   1979.   Solar through dryer.   Solar Energy *22*, 455–457.

BRACE RESEARCH INSTITUTE.   1975.   Technical Report T99, McDonald College of McGill University, Quebec, Canada, December.

CALIFORNIA POLYTECHNIC STATE UNIVERSITY.   1977.   Research on the application of solar energy to industrial drying or dehydration processes. Final Phase I Report.   San Luis Obispo, California, March.

CALIFORNIA POLYTECHNIC STATE UNIVERSITY.   1978.   Research on the application of solar energy to industrial drying or dehydration processes. Final Phase II Report.   San Luis Obispo, California, September.

CARNEGIE, E.J. and POHL. J.   1979.   Solar Energy Technology Handbook, Edit. Dickinson/Cheremisinoff, Marcel Dekker, Inc. Pub. Co., New York. Chapters 7–9.

CARNEGIE, E.J., NILES, P.W., and STINE, W.B.   1979.   Operation of an industrial solar drying system.   Proceedings, ISIS Annual Solar Energy Conf., Atlanta, Georgia.

CHAMBERS, T.C. and POSSINGHAM, J.V.   1963.   Studies on the fine structure of the wax layer of Sultana grapes.   Aust. J. Biol. Sci. *16*, 818–825.

CHARM, S.E.   1971.   The Fundamentals of Food Engineering.   AVI Publishing Company, Westport, Connecticut.

COOPER, P.I.   1969.   The absorption of solar radiation in solar stills.   Solar Energy *12*.

CSRIO.   Dried Fruits Processing Committee, 1973.   Grape drying in Australia.   ISBN 0-643-00053-4.   Melbourne, Australia.

DREW, M.S. and SELVAGE, R.B.G.   1979.   Solar heating system performance estimation using sinusoidal inputs.   Solar Energy *23*, 435–442.

DUFFIE, J.A. and BECKMAN, W.A.   1980.   Solar Engineering of Thermal Processes.   John Wiley & Sons, New York.

FORWALTER, J.   1978.   13,174 sq. ft. of solar panels will provide 10,400,000 BTU/day for drying.   Food Processing, June.

GERMAN APPROPRIATE TECHNOLOGY EXCHANGE.   1979.   Devices for drying: state of techology report on intermediate solutions for rural applications.   Report M: 4/1, Munchen, West Germany.

GÖRLING, P.   1958.   Physical phenomena during the drying of foodstuffs.   Macmillan Co., New York.

GRNCAREVIC, M. and HAWKER, J.S.   1971.   Browning of sultana grapes during drying.   J. Sci. Fd. Agric. *22*, 270–272.

GUINN, G.R. and FISHER, P.N.   1977.   Soybean drying using heat from solar energy.   Solar Industrial Process Heat Symposium, University of Maryland, Proceedings, ERDA, September.

HENDERSON, S.M. and PERRY, R.L.   1955.   Agricultural Process Engineering. John Wiley & Sons, New York.

HOLMAN, J.P.   1981.   Heat Transfer.   McGraw-Hill Book Co., New York.

KIRSCHER, O.   1956.   Wissenschaftlichen Grundlagen der Trocknungstechnik.   Springer Verlag.

KREITH, F. and KREIDER, J.F. 1978. Principles of Solar Engineering.   McGraw-Hill Book Co., New York.

LAWAND, T.A.   1966.   A solar cabinet dryer.   Solar Energy *10*, 158–164.

LAWAND, T.A.   1975.   *See* Brace Research Institute.

LIU, B.Y.H. and JORDAN, R.C.   1963.   The long-term average performance of flat-plate solar energy collectors.   Solar Energy *7*.

LUNDE, P.J.   1980.   Solar Thermal Engineering.   John Wiley & Sons, Inc., New York.

MORSE, R.N. and CZARNEKI, J.T.   1958.   Flat plate solar absorbers: the effect on incident radiation of inclination and orientation.   Report E.E.6 of Engineering Section, Commonwealth Scientific and Industrial Research Organization, Melbourne, Australia.

NILES, P.W., CARNEGIE, E.J., POHL, J.G., and CHERNE, J.M.   1978.   Design and performance of an air collector for industrial crop dehydration.   Solar Energy *20*, 19–23.

ÖZIŞIK M.N.   1977.   Basic Heat Transfer.   McGraw-Hill Book Co., New York.

PHILLIPS, A.L.   1965.   Drying coffee with solar heated air.   Solar Energy *9*, 213–216.

PETERSON, W.H.   1975.   *See* Brace Research Institute.

PETERSON, W.H.   1980.   Illinois solar grain drying systems.   Proceedings, Grain Conditioning Conference, University of Illinois, Urbana–Champaign.

POSSINGHAM, J.V.   1975.   *See* Brace Research Institute.

ROA, G.   1975.   *See* Brace Research Institute.

ROA, G. and MACEDO, I.C.   1976.   Grain drying in stationary bins with solar heated air.   Solar Energy *18*.

SELÇUK, M.K.   1975.   *See* Brace Research Institute.

SELÇUK, M.K., ERSAY, O., and AKYURT, M.   1976.   Development, theoretical analysis and performance evaluation of shelf type solar dryers.   Solar Energy *16*, 81–88.

STINE, W.B. and CARNEGIE, E.J.   1979.   Long term performance of a 635 ton pebble bed in continuous operation.   Proceedings, Solar Energy Storage Options Workshop, Trinity University, San Antonio, Texas.

VANDRESSER, P.   1975.   *See* Brace Research Institute.

VERSTEEGEN, P.L. and CASSEL, D.E.   1979.   A survey of existing solar system simulation methods.   Proceedings, Annual Meeting of ISES, Atlanta, Georgia, 1979.

11

Recycling of Nutrients from Food Wastes

Dietrich Knorr

Introduction
Amount and Origin of Food Wastes
Reduction of Food Wastes
Recovery of Nutrients from Food Processing Wastes
Recovery Methods for Specific Nutrients and Sources
Suggestions for Further Research
Conclusions
References

INTRODUCTION

Wastes and by-products[1] leading to environmental disruption originate in collective human activities. Through increasing population, industrialization, and centralization such products are concentrated locally to an extent exceeding nature's capacity to take care of them, and thus they create a pollution problem (Kwon 1974). Many types of wastes result from the production, distribution, preparation, and consumption of food. These wastes also represent a loss of valuable nutrients. If nutrients could be recovered or food wastes could be converted into nutrients for human beings, animals, or plants, total nutrient resources could be vastly increased and at the same time the waste disposal problem could be minimized (Kramer and Kwee 1977).

AMOUNT AND ORIGIN OF FOOD WASTES

Estimates for the percentage of food waste in the United States by weight of various foods in processing, storage, distribution, and consumption during World War II (Table 11.1) were given by Kling (1943), who concludes his study with the following statement:

[1] Once a waste stream achieves some measure of value it is commonly called a by-product (Tannenbaum and Pace 1976).

TABLE 11.1. ESTIMATED PERCENTAGE OF FOOD WASTAGE IN THE UNITED STATES DURING WORLD WAR II

Food	Farm	Transportation	Storage	Processing	Wholesale	Retail	Consumer	Total
				Losses (%)				
Dairy products	17.5[1]	0.3	*	1.0[1]	*	0.25	1.5	20.55
Meat, poultry, and fish	1.5[2]	0.3	0.5	2.5	1.0	1.5	7.0	14.30
Eggs	1.0	1.0	0.5	*	0.25	0.25	1.0	4.00
Potatoes	7.0	1.0	5.0	1.0	1.0	3.0	10.0	28.00
Dry legumes and nuts	9.0	*	5.0	34.0	*	0.25	2.0	50.25
Tomatoes and citrus fruits	7.0	3.0	2.0	5.0	2.0	8.0	6.0	33.00
Leafy, green, and yellow vegetables	12.5	3.0	1.0	5.0	2.0	7.0	12.5	43.00
Other vegetables	8.0	2.0	1.0	5.0	1.0	4.0	8.0	29.00
Deciduous fruits	8.0	3.0	1.0	3.0	1.0	7.0	3.0	26.00
Cereals and flour[3]	13.0	*	4.0	14.0	1.5	1.5	5.0	39.00
Sugars and syrup	1.0	*	*	1.0	*	*	2.0	4.00
Butters and fats	1.0	*	*	0.5	*	*	5.0	6.50
Coffee, tea, chocolate, and spices,	—	*	1.0	1.0	*	*	5.0	7.00
All foods	9.1	0.9	1.5	4.3	0.8	2.4	4.75	23.70

After Kling 1943, Roy 1976.

[1] Quantities of dry skim milk used for feed on farms are included only at the farm level and not at processing.
[2] Including waste on fishing vessels.
[3] Excluding grains used for feed with the exception of wheat.
[4] Weighted by the average per capita consumption of different food groups in the period 1936–1941.
[5] Estimated at 15% of food purchased by the housewife.
* Less than 0.25%.
Note: Where relative wastes occur in the form of feeding edible food to livestock, a net waste was computed by making allowance for the livestock products produced by the feed. Grains fed to livestock, with the exception of wheat, were not considered as being wasted.

more food is wasted than is consumed by our Armed Forces and Lend-Lease Shipments. Waste is much greater than any feasible increase of food production in 1943 or 1944. Every bit of food ordinarily wasted which is conserved is the equivalent of so much production. Although it is true that only a part of the total food waste is recoverable, conservation of only a portion could probably add more to the nation's food supply at the present time than any other program.

Goodman and Pimentel (1979) recently showed that in the United States 18 million metric tons of dry biomass from food processing wastes (pods, hulls, cobs, chaff, and other by-products) are readily available for energy conversion and only an estimated 20–30% of the vegetable plant is utilized directly for human consumption (Kramer and Kwee 1977).

An indication of the annual quantities of wastes from some crop plants is given in Table 11.2.

Post-harvest Losses

A rough estimate of world post-harvest is 20% (Pimentel *et al.* 1975), ranging from 9% in the United States to 40% and 50% in some of the less-developed countries (LDC's) in the tropics (May 1977). Part of these losses is also due to wastage during storage and handling of the products (Tables 11.1, 11.3, and 11.4).

Examples of data on food wastage in the United Kingdom are given in Tables 11.3 and 11.4.

Food Processing Waste

Large amounts of nutrients are accumulated and commonly wasted in many food processes such as fruit and vegetable processing or meat processing (see Tables 11.1, 11.2, and 11.3). It is estimated that approximately 5 million metric tons of tomato cannery wastes accumulate at factory sites in the United States alone. This constitutes a total of almost 100,000 metric tons of protein and 400,000 tons of carbohydrates (Kramer and Kwee 1977). If these wastes were to be utilized completely for human food, they would

TABLE 11.2.   ANNUAL WORLD PRODUCTION OF CARBOHYDRATES IN WASTES FROM CROP PLANTS

	Carbohydrate (10^6 tons)	
	Agricultural waste	Processing waste
Wheat straw	287	—
Wheat bran	—	57.3
Maize stover	120	—
Maize cobs	—	30.1
Sugar cane bagasse	—	83.0
Molasses	—	9.3

After Morgan (1977).

TABLE 11.3.   WASTAGE OF POTATOES AS PERCENTAGE OF WEIGHT OF EDIBLE MATERIAL ENTERING A PARTICULAR STAGE OF THE SUPPLY SYSTEM

Source of wastage	Wastage (%)
Pests and diseases prior to harvesting	17
Harvesting	21 [1]
Storage	10 [2]
Marketing	5
Preparation (peeling: 7–25%)	12
Cooking	2 [3]
Kitchen and plate waste	4
Total wastage:	
cultivation to consumption (including peelings, 6.7%)	53.6
harvesting to consumption (including peelings, 8.5%)	44.1

After Roy (1976).
[1] Includes potatoes left in the ground and potatoes damaged too severely to be marketed.
[2] Includes losses due to rotting and evaporation.
[3] Excluding water loss. Note that deep-fried potatoes lose about 42% of their weight as evaporation (Chappell 1954).

TABLE 11.4.   WASTAGE OF WHITE BREAD AND OF WHEAT PRODUCTS USED IN ITS PREPARATION AS PERCENTAGE OF WEIGHT OF EDIBLE MATERIAL ENTERING A PARTICULAR STAGE OF THE SUPPLY SYSTEM

Source of wastage	Wastage (%)
Wheat:	
Pests, diseases, weeds	16
Harvesting	1
On-farm storage	1.25
Storage and transport	0.4
Flour:	
Milling rejects (to animal feed)	3.2
Milling offals (to animal feed)	24.5
Bread-making	5
Bread:	
Marketing	0.1
Kitchen and plate waste	6.5
Total wastage:	
Cultivation to consumption	47.2
Farm-gate to consumption	35.4
Adjusted wastage (allowing for by-products used as feed):	
Cultivation to consumption	42.8
Farm-gate to consumption	29.9

After Roy (1976).

provide minimal total energy (calorie) requirements for a population of 2.5 million and minimum protein requirements for 5 million people. Strolle (1977) estimated that 2.7 to 3.2 x 10^6 kg starch is discharged annually in U.S. potato-processing waste effluents.

Food waste in fruit and vegetable canning is given as an example for food and nutrient losses during processing of foods in Tables 11.5 and 11.6.

TABLE 11.5.   WASTAGE IN FRUIT AND VEGETABLE CANNING

	Edible material (% purchased wt.)	All material (% purchased wt.)
Apples	12	45
Pears	12	45
Apricots	8	25
Peaches	20	40
Oranges	3	45
Lemons	3	45
Grapefruit	3	58
Green beans	5	12
Butter beans	6	85
Beets	7	35
Sprouts	10	—
Cabbages	5	25
Carrots	18	50
Peas	6	—
Potatoes	5	—
Sweetcorn	20	80
Tomatoes	5	25

Source: USDA 1965.

TABLE 11.6.   NUTRIENT LOSSES IN VEGETABLE CANNING

	Blanching loss		Lost in canning liquor		Total losses	
	Sugars	Protein	Fats	Protein	Energy	Protein
Green beans	22	8	—	15	22	22
Carrots						
whole	12	10	—	16	12	24
sliced	24	31	—	16	24	42
Peas	15	6	5	14		19
Sweetcorn			1.5	8	1.5	8
Dried beans	10	2			10	2

After Ben—Gera and Kramer (1969).

During the 1974–1975 season, 2.1 million metric tons of coffee berries were processed in Central America, resulting in 415,000 metric tons of dried dehulled coffee (Aquirre *et al.* 1977). The whole material produced consisted of 830,000 metric tons of pulp, 415,000 metric tons of mucilage, 70,000 metric tons of hulls, and 1 to 14 million metric tons of process water (containing approximately 0.5–2.0% total solids). Another example is potato starch production in the Netherlands, where 25,000 metric tons protein, 25,000 metric tons minerals, 25,000 metric tons nonprotein nitrogen, and approximately 8,000 metric tons of sugar could be produced from the potato starch mills alone every year (Knorr 1977A).

Wastage in Marketing

Wastage in marketing is low and is estimated to be usually below 1% (Roy 1976). Smaller shops may incur much greater losses than supermarkets. The differences, however, between supermarkets and small shops may be more apparent than real, as small shopkeepers often trim and pack foods themselves whereas supermarkets receive their stocks already cleaned, trimmed, and packeted.

Waste in Consumption

Five to ten % of edible food (measured as calories or weight) is lost or wasted after purchase (Roy 1976). Much of the material discarded in the preparation of food (Table 11.7) is inedible (e.g., bones, peelings, shells) but cannot be considered as absolute waste, as these materials do contain nutrients that could be utilized. Estimates of the amount of kitchen and plate waste vary widely. Harrison *et al.* (1975) indicated that householders discard at least 9−10% of edible food purchased. Over half of this discarded food is "straight waste" (e.g., a whole steak, half a loaf of stale bread, unopened packages of food), the rest being plate scrapings and edible material discarded during preparation.

A pilot study of British civil servants indicated that about 5% of the edible calories purchased were discarded (Anon. 1968). This compares with 7−10% waste of calories from middle-class American households in 1960 (Adelson *et al.* 1963) and 2−3% from British households in the 1930s (Cathcart and Murray 1939).

LeBovit and Boehm (1979) judged that an average of 20% of the calories in food purchased in the United States at retail are discarded. Overconsumption and the fact that some diets are more wasteful than others represent additional types of food waste. The average daily food intake for most developed countries is well above 3000 kcal.[2] For example, nearly twice as much fossil energy is expended for a nonvegetarian diet (with a

TABLE 11.7.   MATERIAL DISCARDED DURING PREPARATION OF FOOD

Food item	Material discarded (% purchased wt.)
Broad beans	75
Plaice	70
Peas	60
Cod	45
Bananas	40
Chicken	30
Herrings	30
Cabbage, cauliflower	30
Beef (stewing)	25
Oranges	25
Sprouts	25
Sweetcorn	22
Apples	20
Pork	15
Potatoes (old)	14
Carrots	14
Eggs	12
Bacon	12
Cheese	5
Potatoes (new)	3

After Roy (1976).

---

[2]For example, the average daily food intake per capita is 3300 kcal in the United States (USDA 1977) and approximately 3050 kcal in the Federal Republic of Germany (Ernährungsbericht 1976).

predomination of animal protein) than for a lacto-ovo diet where eggs, milk, and milk products are the only animal protein eaten (Pimentel and Pimentel 1979).

REDUCTION OF FOOD WASTES

Food wastes may be reduced by prevention of waste and by the utilization of wastes for food, feed, fertilizer, and other products.

Prevention of food wastes may be technical, financial, legislative, organizational, or educational. Considerable knowledge already exists on technical measures for minimizing wastage in production, storage, processing, and distribution, ranging from biological controls for crop pests and diseases to new processing and storage techniques. Less is known about the effectiveness of economic measures designed to discourage the hoarding or dumping of food or educational measures such as publicity to promote less wasteful cooking and eating habits (Roy 1976). Much waste at all stages of the food system occurs simply because disposal is often the cheaper alternative (Burch et al. 1963). Similar major food losses occur because the cost of preventive action (e.g., investing in new storage facilities) is expected to exceed the value of the food saved. Food wastage may also be reduced by increasing the consumption of edible parts of various foods (e.g., organs such as heart, liver, kidney) by humans and/or by switching to a more vegetarian diet. Another possibility for preventing food waste is by changing certain food quality criteria. Perhaps, as Pyke (1975) has argued, the search for uniform, unblemished, and hygienic food in the industrialized countries has gone beyond what is really necessary or even desirable.

As far as waste utilization is concerned, farms, households, eating establishments, and the food industry are the main sources of under-used waste. Farm wastes can be either reused in polycultural (often cyclic) agricultural systems such as eco-farming ("organic" farming) in the form of feed, manure, and compost (Besson and Vogtmann 1978; Merrill 1976; Oelhaf 1978) or they can be converted into protein products such as leaf protein concentrates (LPC), single cell protein (SCP), and fungal protein (Pirie 1971; Tannenbaum 1977; Birch et al. 1976). Roy (1976) stated that active research is under way on the utilization of farm wastes, especially straw and animal manures, and on improved methods of conserving winter feed to reduce the need for imported animal feed. Adoption of these waste-saving measures is likely to encourage a gradual swing away from the specialization of the 1960s back toward a pattern of mixed farming. There are also proposals (Worgan 1976) of leaf protein extraction accompanied by microbiological conversion (Table 11.8) and the Bioplex concept where organic waste is treated by a stream of processes so that the waste from one would become the raw material for another (Forster and Jones 1976). The Bioplex concept could convert refuse, sewage, and farm wastes into various foods and feedstuffs.

Reducing household wastes will require reduction in over-consumption

TABLE 11.8. PROTEIN YIELDS FROM CONVENTIONAL CROPS AND FROM CROP BY-PRODUCTS

Yield of protein (kg/ha)

| | Seed | Leaf protein | Fungal protein from | | | Total |
			leaf juice	leaf fiber	maize cobs	
Maize:						
Conventional crop	352	—	—	—	—	352
Combined with waste recovery	352	300	110	1290	80	2132
Peas:						
Conventional crop	400	—	—	—	—	400
Combined with waste recovery	400	625	125	1366	—	2546

After Worgan (1977).

and consumer education in shopping, preparation, and eating habits of foods. Utilization of household wastes is mainly dependent on efficiently collecting food wastes. This would require either small-scale operations such as feeding household wastes directly to animals (e.g., pigs) or sophisticated food-waste collecting operations. Economic factors are usually the main barrier to food waste reduction. For example, whether a food processor decides to use or to dump his wastes depends on whether the expected cost of installing a new plant for utilization minus the value of the processed waste is less than the cost of disposal (Burch *et al.* 1963). Waste effluents of large food processing plants are the most concentrated form of readily available food wastes, which also cause large waste disposal problems. Because of the importance of food processing wastes they will be discussed in more detail. Any policy for tackling food wastage would require a combination of prevention and utilization measures because, although losses can be reduced to a minimum, the complete elimination of waste in any process is not possible. Ideally, wastage of those parts of agricultural products and foods directly edible by people would be minimized by preventive measures and the inedible parts used for animal feed or other purposes (Roy 1976).

RECOVERY OF NUTRIENTS FROM FOOD PROCESSING WASTES

It has already been stated earlier that large amounts of nutrients, especially proteins and carbohydrates, accumulate in food processing wastes and that these can be the source of major food losses, particularly from large food processing plants. Also these wastes can be a severe pollution problem.

Several workers have reported on the recovery of nutrients from various food process wastes. Protein, carbohydrate, fats, organic acid, amino acid, inorganic salts, flavor, and pigment recovery have been noted by Altschul (1976), Friedman (1975), Pirie (1971), Birch *et al.* (1976), Kramer and Kwee (1977), Lotrakul (1978), and Anon. (1979). Protein concentrates[3] were the products most commonly derived from food processing plant effluents (Birch *et al.* 1976). Several methods have been used and developed to produce food proteins from food processing wastes. Some established and some potential sources for food protein concentrates are listed in Table 11.9.

RECOVERY METHODS FOR SPECIFIC NUTRIENTS AND SOURCES

Potato Processing Waste: A Case Study

Composition.   The main nutrients in potato processing waste effluents are carbohydrates, proteins, amino acids, minerals, and organic acids. The

---

[3]Protein products with 65–90% (d.m.) crude protein are usually called protein concentrates; protein products with a crude protein concentration above 90% are referred to as protein isolates.

TABLE 11.9.   ESTABLISHED AND POTENTIAL SOURCES FOR FOOD PROTEIN
CONCENTRATES AND ISOLATES FROM FOOD PROCESSING WASTES

Protein source	Reference
Fruit and vegetable processing waste	Righelato *et al.* (1976)
	Tannenbaum (1977)
Tomato processing waste	Kramer and Kwee (1977)
Potato processing waste	Meuser and Smolnik (1979)
	Knorr (1977 A)
Rice bran	Saunders and Kohler (1975)
Wheat gluten processing waste	Finley (1977)
Corn gluten processing waste	Phillips and Sternberg (1979)
Grape seeds	Fantozzi and Betschart (1979)
Sesame seeds	Johnson *et al.* (1979)
Rapeseeds	Ohlson and Anjou (1979)
Soybeans	Circle and Smith (1975)
Sunflower	Sosulski (1979)
Safflower	Betschart (1979)
Coconut	Hagenmaier (1979)
Groundnut	Oke *et al.* (1975)
Dairy waste	Coton (1976)
Fish processing waste	Pigott (1976); Pariser *et al.* (1978)

composition of a typical potato starch processing waste is shown in Table 11.10. About 35 to 60% of the crude protein is heat coagulable (Oosten 1976) and about one-third of the dry solids are amino acids, amides, and peptides (DeNoord 1976). The main minerals are potassium and phosphorus, usually in the form of K_2HPO_4 (Peters 1972). Typical volumes and biochemical oxygen demand of potato processing waste effluents are given in Table 11.11, along with an indication of the large differences in the wastes of plants processing different potato products.

Economics of Nutrient Recovery.   Meister and Thompson (1976) reported that a process for the recovery of protein from waste effluent of potato chip processing should be economical if combined with starch recovery. Heisler *et al.* (1959) reported two benefits resulting from the recovery of useful nitrogenous compounds from potato starch factory waste water. First, the pollution effect of the waste effluent (usually called "protein water" or fruit water) would be reduced. Second, the economics of potato starch processing would be improved through the creation of marketable by-products. Stabile *et al.* (1971) presented an economic analysis of the alternative methods for processing potato starch effluents (Table 11.12) based on a starch plant effluent of 2% solids. At the time of the study only concentration of effluents by evaporation appeared economically feasible. Meanwhile, with the introduction of new starch manufacturing processes (Verberne 1977), protein recovery from potato starch factory effluents apparently is economically feasible (Strolle 1980).

Converting starches from potato processing wastes into single-cell protein was indicated (Anon. 1976) as a promising new source of profit because the wastes could yield product worth over 50 cents/kg at a 50% conversion rate.

Recycling of Nutrients.   Carbohydrates have been successfully converted

TABLE 11.10.   COMPOSITION OF POTATO STARCH PROCESSING WASTE

Waste Contents	Percentage found in waste			
	(1)[1]	(2)	(3)	(4)
Solids	0.7	5	5	2–5
	(% dry solids)	(%)	(%)	(% dry solids)
Carbohydrate	80	—	0.8	35
Crude protein	8	2–3	2.7	35
Minerals	—		0.6	20
Organic acids	—		—	4

[1]Literature source: 1. Righelato *et al.* (1975). 2. Oosten (1976). 3. DeNoord (1976). 4. Knorr (1977 A).

TABLE 11.11.   VOLUME AND BIOCHEMICAL OXYGEN DEMAND (BOD) OF POTATO PROCESSING WASTE EFFLUENTS

	Potato starch processing[1]	French fries and granules processing[2]	
Waste water capacity (m³/hour)	80	20	
Waste water dry matter content (%)	0.7	2	3
Waste water BOD (mg/liter)	400	10,000	20,000

[1] From Righelato *et al.* (1976).
[2] From Skogman (1976).

into *Candida* or *Torula* yeast by the symbiotic growth of *Endomycopsis fibuliger* and *Candida utilis. Endomycopsis fibuliger* produces the amylase necessary to hydrolize the starch into glucose, which is then metabolized by the *Candida* yeast. By this symbiotic action most of the carbohydrates in the starchy waste streams are utilized in one step, avoiding a costly prestep of hydrolysis by either acid or enzyme (Skogman 1976). This so-called Symba Process reduces organic matter in the starch-carrying stream by well over 90% and the inorganic salts containing nitrogen and phosphorus by over 50%. Residence time in the fermenter is approximately 10 hr and BOD reduction is about 90%. Yield of single-cell protein based on dried solids is 55% of the starch present (Anon. 1976). The recovery of proteins from potato processing wastes using protein coagulation (precipitation), separation (dewatering), and drying will be discussed in more detail. A combination of protein recovery by heat coagulation and an ion exchange and recovery process for various potato processing waste components (Fig. 11.1) has been investigated by Stabile *et al.* (1971). Ascorbic acid, amino acids, and amides have been recovered by ion exchange (Jackson 1962; Xander and Hoover 1959); Schwartz *et al.* (1972) studied the recovery of organic acids and phosphate from waste effluents of potato processing plants.

Recovery of Potato Proteins

A process to recover proteins from potato processing water includes three main steps: (1) protein coagulation (precipitation); (2) separation (dewatering); and (3) drying (Fig. 11.2).

TABLE 11.12.   COMPARISON OF SOME ALTERNATIVE METHODS FOR PROCESSING POTATO STARCH EFFLUENTS

Alternative method	Resulting product	Use	Fixed capital cost (US$)	Total operating cost (US$/year)	Sales (US$/year)
Concentration by evaporation	Concentrate with protein	feed	514,000	148,500	186,700
Protein recovery and biological treatment	Protein	feed/food	807,000	198,100	44,000
Protein recovery and concentration by evaporation	A. Protein B. Concentrate without protein	feed/food feed	881,000	281,500	165,000
Protein recovery and ion exchange and biological treatment	A. Protein B. Amino acid mixture C. Organic acid mixture D. K_2SO_4 and $(NH_4)_2SO_4$ E. $(NH_4)_2SO_4$	feed feed/food beverages fertilizer fertilizer	2,550,000	755,750	444,000

After Stabile *et al.* (1971).

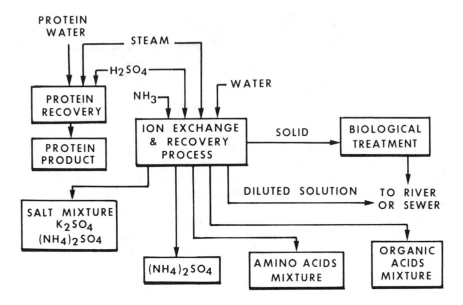

FIG. 11.1.   COMBINATION OF NUTRIENT RECOVERY AND BIOLOGICAL WASTE
TREATMENT FROM POTATO STARCH PLANT EFFLUENTS. AFTER STABILE *et al.* 1971.

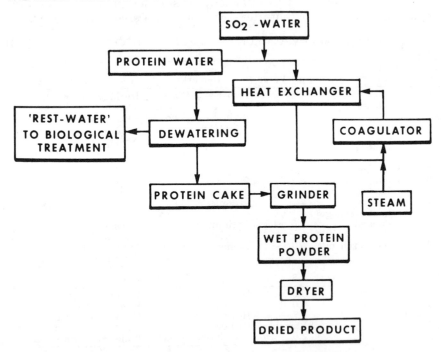

FIG. 11.2.   SCHEME OF POTATO PROTEIN PLANT. AFTER PETERS 1972.

Protein Coagulation. The most common way to coagulate proteins is by heat. As shown in Table 11.13 steam injection is normally used to heat the protein water. The temperatures applied range from 75° to 120°C but most processes use 95° to 100°C. More recently several workers (Meister and Thompson 1976; Knorr 1977A; Finley and Hautala 1976; Knorr 1979) suggested protein coagulation at ambient temperatures.

A simplified flow diagram based on pilot plant experiments (Knorr et al. 1977) for the recovery of potato protein concentrates at room temperature is shown in Fig. 11.3.

The influence of pH (1 to 7) and heat (23°–98°C) on protein precipitation from waste effluents of potato chip processing has been documented by Meister and Thompson (1976). The highest temperature was most effective in recovering protein at all but the low pH values. In these experiments an optimal pH range of 3.5 to 4.5 was indicated. At lower pH values, room temperature (23°C) gave better recoveries than the heat treatments. Heating to 80°C or acidification to pH 3.0 or slightly below did not give optimal results; rather, heat (80°–90°C) at pH values of 4.0 to 4.5 was most effective for protein recovery.

Heat coagulation has been proposed by several other authors (Vlasblom and Peters 1958; Borud 1971; Strolle et al. 1973). In some cases a combination of heat and pressure treatments have been applied (Landwirtschaftliche Kartoffelverwertungs-AG 1957).

Potato proteins can be precipitated by physicochemical procedures. Precipitation of protein concentrates from potato processing waste water by

TABLE 11.13.   PROTEIN COAGULATION FROM POTATO PROCESSING PLANT WASTE EFFLUENTS

Temperature (°C)		pH Value	Remarks	References
95–105	(steam)	4.8–5.0	Presence of SO_2	Huchette and Fleche (1975)
95	(steam)	—	—	Vlasblom and Peters (1958)
90–100		—	Adding H_2SO_4 or Ca $(OH)_2$	Alton and Tobias (1976)
75–95		—	—	Xander and Hoover (1959)
80–90	(waterbath)	4.0–4.5	Laboratory scale	Meister and Thompson (1976)
100	(steam)	3.5	Sulfuric acid added	Stabile et al. (1971)
80	(steam and heat exchange)	4.5	Presence of SO_2	Peters (1972)
121	(steam and heat exchange)	—	Presence of SO_2	Rosenau et al. (1978)
99	(steam)	5.5 or less	Optimum conditions found	Anon. (1968); Masters (1972)
120	(heat exchange)	5.0	Preheating 40–50°C	Landwirtschaftliche Kartoffelverwertungs-AG (1957)
98	(steam)	4.8	HCl, presence of SO_2	Knorr et al. 1977
20–22		3.0	HCl or $FeCl_3$	Knorr et al. (1977)
20–22		4.0	Citric acid	Knorr (1979)
Ambient		4.7	HCl and chlorine	Grunewald (1954)
23°C		Variable	HCl or $FeCl_3$	Meister and Thompson (1976)
4°C		2.0	Polyphosphoric acid	Finley and Hautala (1978)

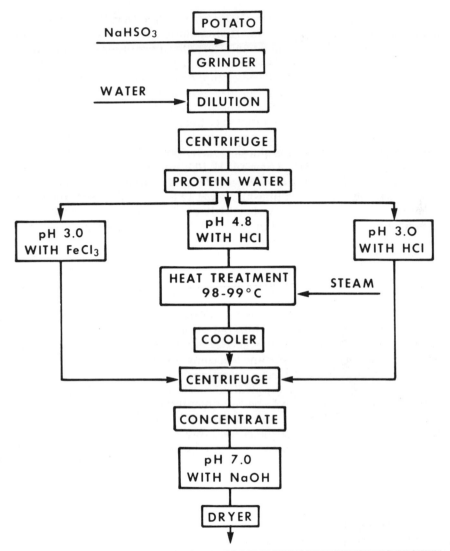

FIG. 11.3.   SIMPLIFIED FLOW DIAGRAM FOR THE RECOVERY OF POTATO PROTEIN
CONCENTRATES WITH DIFFERENT COAGULATION PROCEDURES. AFTER KNORR *et
al.* 1977.

polyphosphoric acid has been described by Finley and Hautala (1976).
Meister and Thompson (1976) compared $FeCl_3$ with HCl, and HCl with
H_3PO_4 as coagulants. The same workers attempted to raise the pH with
lime solution $Ca(OH)_2$ followed by lowering the pH value with either
H_3PO_4 or $FeCl_3$ for recovery of proteins from waste effluents of potato
chip processing. When HCl was substituted for H_3PO_4, results were almost

identical. Meister and Thompson (1976) also showed that $FeCl_3$ compared favorably with hydrochloric acid. Hydrochloric acid would be preferred from a cost point of view and as an alternate to adding H_3PO_4 to public water. Ferric chloride is one of the principal coagulants in sewage work; it is relatively inexpensive and has acidic properties, and the trivalent iron ion is a good nucleating site for large floc formation. Another advantage of ferric chloride is that no additional energy for heating is required. Protein recovery was satisfactory when lime treatment was followed by H_3PO_4 or $FeCl_3$ treatment. However, because of the high amount of calcium in the precipitated material, the usefulness of such a protein product is questionable. A serious disadvantage of lime and H_3PO_4 treatment is that water must be neutralized before being discharged. Moreover, although phosphate can be readily precipitated with lime above pH 11.8, its solubility is increased below pH 9 (Meister and Thompson 1976). Finley and Hautala (1976) used calcium chloride and removed the precipitated calcium phosphate by centrifugation. Potato protein from starch manufacture wastes was prepared by Alton and Tobias (1976) by adding H_2SO_4 or $Ca(OH)_2$. Jackson (1962) stated that acid precipitation was preferable to heat precipitation because it preserved the ascorbic acid, gave a more desirable product on drying, and inhibited foaming.

Significantly higher vitamin C values (Table 11.14) were found in potato protein concentrates (PPC) precipitated at ambient temperature than in HCl/heat precipitated samples (Knorr et al. 1977). However, certain sensory quality criteria (e.g., taste) and ash content were not fully satisfactory, especially when using $FeCl_3$ as a coagulant. Increased protein solubility indicates that the protein concentrates were less denatured during processing and are more likely to be functionally active in food systems in which protein solubility is a prerequisite. Table 11.15 shows that all the coagulable protein (36.6% of the crude protein in the protein water) was recovered by HCl/heat treatment as well as by ferric chloride and citric acid at room temperature. Protein yield with HCl and $Al_2(SO_4)_3$ as coagulants was lower.

Concentration and Protein Separation (Dewatering).   Meister and Thompson (1976) studied the effect of concentration and heat treatment on settling of potato protein precipitates. In an experiment where residual crude protein was measured over a time span of 80 min, sedimentation was faster in heat-treated samples than in samples treated at room temperature, but differences beyond 60 min were not significant. The initial sedimentation in low protein concentrates was faster, but the percentage of protein settled during the entire period was lower. The importance of temperature in the evaporation step was recently shown by Strolle et al. (1980); and Della Monica et al. 1975 showed that the concentrates are unstable and a drying step is required. Strolle et al. (1973) also investigated the influence of pH and concentration. Oosten (1976) described coagulation of the protein in the ultrafiltration concentrate by mixing the concentrate with steam. Schmidt

TABLE 11.14.   RECOVERY OF PROTEINS WITH DIFFERENT PRECIPITATION METHODS, APPROXIMATE ANALYSES, AND PROTEIN SOLUBILITY OF POTATO PROTEIN CONCENTRATES

	Composition of protein concentrates (% dry matter)		
	Hydrochloric acid at 20−22°C (pH 3.0)	Ferric chloride at 20−22°C (pH 3.0)	Hydrochloric acid at 98−99°c (pH 4.8)
Total solids (%)	93.7	94.7	95.4
Nitrogen	10.5	9.2	12.5
Crude fat	2.3	1.3	2.4
Ash	24.5	25.1	7.2
Total sugars	3.6	2.6	1.3
Total carbohydrates	7.2	7.1	7.1
Total vitamin C (mg/100g)	18.1	14.9	0.01
Iron	0.10	4.32	0.12
Calcium	0.14	0.04	0.14
Magnesium	0.20	0.11	0.10
Sodium	4.25	3.85	1.53
Protein solubility (pH 7)	56.0	87.5	11.5

After Knorr et al. (1977).

et al. (1976) reported spray drying of the ultrafiltration concentrate as well as acid precipitation of the protein followed by diluting and spray drying of the precipitate. Results of experiments in treating potato peeling water by hyperfiltration and ultrafiltration were presented by Minturn (1975).

The precipitated proteins can be separated by using a continuous rotary filter (Strolle et al. 1973; Stabile et al. 1971), plate and frame type filter press (Strolle et al. 1973), by gravity settling (Meister and Thompson 1976; Peters 1972), or by centrifugation using continuous conveyor-discharge centrifuges (Meister and Thompson 1976; Huchette and Fleche 1975; Peters 1972). Strolle et al. (1973) have compared filtration and centrifugation methods (plate frame filter press, continuous rotary filter, and a bench-type air-driven "Sharples" super centrifuge) and recommended the use of the plate frame filter press. After dewatering by filteration, they further recommended drum drying or freeze drying; and after (solid bowl) centrifugation, air drying, freeze drying, or the use of a drying system for heavy paste dispersions as described by Baran (1964). The filter cake can be disintegrated and dried in a pneumatic dryer, and liquid concentration from a separator can be worked up in a spray dryer (Peters 1972).

Air drying studies (Stroller et al. 1973) with wastes from potato starch manufacturing in a conventional tray drier gave a dried product that was black, hard, hornlike, and very difficult to grind; double drum drying gave a fairly soft, grayish product. Freeze drying gave a white soft product; however, this method is undoubtedly uneconomical (Strolle et al. 1973). Spray drying was reported by Anon. (1968), Masters (1972), Huchette and Fleche (1975), and Schmidt et al. (1976) to yield soft, yellowish products (Giokas 1976) with superior water solubility to equivalent drum dried products (Schmidt et al. 1976). The crude protein content of the dried product ranged from about 70 to 80% (N x 6.25) (Huchette and Fleche 1975; Finley and Hautala 1976).

TABLE 11.15. PERCENTAGE YIELD OF POTATO PROTEIN FOR VARIOUS TREATMENTS AS A FUNCTION OF pH

Treatment	pH 2	pH 3	pH 4	pH 5	pH 6
			Yield (%)		
HCl/heat (98°C)	82	96	99	96	98
Citric acid (20−22°C)	86	104	63	10	0
Al$_2$ (SO$_4$)$_3$ (20−22°C)	—	76	76	38	—
HCl (20−22°C)	16	16	7	0	0
FeCl$_3$ (20−22°C)	98	104	10	0	—

After Knorr (1979).
Note: All data obtained starting with a 1.1% solution of crude protein. 100% yield means all trichloracetic acid heat-coagulable protein (36.6% of the crude protein) precipitated. — indicates treatment not done.

The influence of different drying techniques (freeze drying, spray drying and drum drying) on the functionality of potato protein concentrates was studied by Knorr and Betschart (1982). Heat coagulation (HCl/heat treatment) was used for protein precipitation and processing of potato protein concentrates as outlined in Fig. 11.3.

Freeze drying was conducted in a modified Stokes vacuum oven. Spray drying was carried out using a Bowen laboratory model conical type dryer with inlet and outlet temperatures of 210° to 220°C and 105° to 110°C respectively. A steam heated (125°C) Buflovak double drum drier with stainless steel drums of 30 cm diameter by 45.5 cm length was used for drum drying. All protein concentrates were ground in a hammermill to pass through a 0.28 mm sieve.

Results of analyses and data of functional properties of potato concentrates dried by three different procedures are shown in Table 11.16. No significant differences were found in the composition of the protein concentrates, but differences were significant for some of the functional properties, especially for water absorption capacity, fat absorption capacity, farinograph absorption, specific loaf volume, and crumb texture. Water absorption capacity as well as farinograph absorption decreased and loaf volume and crumb texture increased in the direction freeze → spray → drum dried samples. Water absorption capacity was also influenced by various pH levels of concentrates (Fig. 11.4). The effect of drying on protein solubility of different protein coagulates at various pH levels is shown in Fig. 11.5. Drying had no effect on the protein solubility of heat coagulated protein concentrates (potato protein concentrates, rice bran protein concentrates) but markedly affected soy protein concentrates that had received minimum treatment during processing. These data indicate that additional heat treatment during different drying processes does not further affect the degree of protein denaturation that occurs during heat coagulation. It is interesting to note that the effect of drum drying on protein solubility was comparable to the effect of heat coagulation, while spray drying and freeze

TABLE 11.16.   RESULTS OF PROXIMATE ANALYSES OF FUNCTIONAL
PROPERTIES OF HEAT COAGULATED POTATO PROTEIN CONCENTRATES DRIED
BY DIFFERENT METHODS[1]

	Potato protein concentrates (pH 7.0)		
	Freeze dried	Spray dried	Drum dried
Total solids (%)	96.6	95.4	93.6
Total nitrogen [3]	12.5	12.5	12.5
Ash [3]	7.11	7.16	7.26
Carbohydrates [3]	6.90	6.99	7.41
Crude fat (acid hydrolysis) [3]	5.62	5.46	6.10
Protein solubility [3]	11.5±1	10.5±1	11.0±1
Water absorption capacity (% increase in weight)	365±8	273±6	247±5
Fat absorption capacity (% d.m.)	158±9	110±10	135±16
Specific loaf volume[2] (ml/100g)	147±21	193±5	261±17
Farinograph absorption[2] (%)	70.6	69.6	63.4
Crumb deformation[2] (%)	13±1	14±2	28±1

[1] From 2 to 5 replications.
[2] 10% replacement level of wheat flour.
[3] % dry matter.

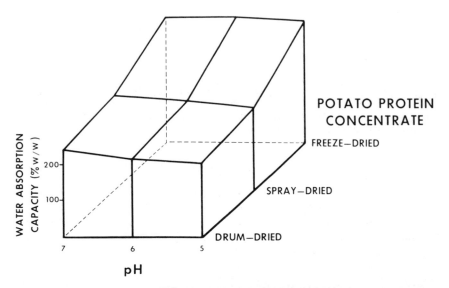

FIG. 11.4.   WATER ABSORPTION CAPACITY OF FREEZE, SPRAY, AND DRUM DRIED
POTATO PROTEIN CONCENTRATES AT DIFFERENT pH LEVELS.

drying resulted in highly soluble products. The higher drying temperature
(125°C) and the long drying time (approximately 30 sec) during drum
drying are the most likely explanations for the occurring protein denaturation, and low drying temperature and extremely short drying time are the

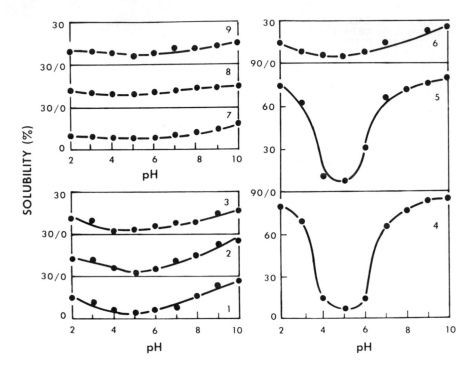

FIG. 11.5.   RELATIONSHIP BETWEEN PROTEIN SOLUBILITY AND pH OF VARIOUS PROTEIN CONCENTRATES DRIED BY DIFFERENT METHODS: 1–3, RICE BRAN PROTEIN CONCENTRATE; 4–6, SOY PROTEIN CONCENTRATE; 7–9, POTATO PROTEIN CONCENTRATE. FREEZE-DRIED SAMPLES: 1, 4, 7; SPRAY-DRIED SAMPLES: 2, 5, 8; DRUM-DRIED SAMPLES: 3, 6, 9.

main reasons for high solubility of protein concentrates dehydrated by freeze and spray drying respectively.

In summary, the protein recovery process has an essential influence on the composition and functionality of potato protein concentrates. The effects of coagulation and drying on nitrogen solubility, water absorption capacity, and baking properties are most important for the application of potato protein concentrates in food systems.

Utilization of Potato Protein Concentrates

Potato protein concentrates are recovered commercially from European potato starch processing plants. A typical composition of such (heat coagulated) products is given in Table 11.17.

The protein quality of potato protein concentrates is, in general, at least comparable to that of casein. Protein Efficiency Ratio (PER) values up to 2.63 (casein = 2.50) and "Biological Values" between 67 and 73 have been

TABLE 11.17.   TYPICAL COMPOSITION OF A COM-
MERCIAL POTATO PROTEIN PRODUCT

	Concentration (% w / w)
Moisture	9.2
Crude protein (N × 6.25)	81.5
Pure protein	79.7
Digestible protein	56.6
Ash	3.58
Fat	0.96
Sugar	0.28

After Knorr et al. (1976).

reported. The results of PER studies with two commercially processed heat coagulated potato protein concentrates are given in Table 11.18. Product A was spray-dried, and Product B was hot-air dried. The means of the PER for both products were higher than the casein value, although the differences were not significant. This protein quality and the high lysine content of potato protein concentrates (Knorr 1978) would make them a very valuable protein source, especially as a supplement for cereal proteins, which are low in lysine. Unfortunately, the potato protein concentrates usually have a pronounced taste and flavor, which is described as a raw and earthy potato flavor or as smell of cooked potatoes (Knorr et al. 1976; Meuser and Smolnik 1979). Furthermore, horny protein particles formed during commercial protein precipitation are responsible for an impression of "sandiness" during consumption (Meuser and Smolnik 1979). Huchette and Fleche (1975) also found dried potato protein products with a sulphur dioxide[4] content of 500 ppm and a solanin content of 1000 to 1500 ppm.

Because of these deficiencies, potato protein concentrate is currently used as animal feed, mainly as chicken and pig feed and as a milk powder replacement in cattle feeding.

Major applications of high quality potato protein products could include the following (Fig. 11.6):

a. use in human food as a major ingredient or supplement;
b. application to enhance product nutritive value, product functionality and acceptability;
c. use in animal feeds as a substitute for other proteins;
d. use in industrial applications such as adhesives, coatings in paper processing, etc.

In Europe and in the United States several studies are under way to examine the potential use of potato protein concentrates for human consumption. The three main areas investigated are (1) improvement of functional properties, (2) purification of protein concentrates, and (3) use of potato protein concentrates as a food supplement.

---

[4]SO_2 is commonly used to inhibit darkening reactions during potato protein processing.

TABLE 11.18. PROTEIN EFFICIENCY RATIO (PER) AND DIGESTIBILITY OF POTATO PROTEIN CONCENTRATES (PPC) [1]

Dietary source of protein [2]	Final body weight [3] (g)	Total feed consumption (g)	Per Actual	Per Adjusted
Casein (ANRC protein)	203±8	436±17	3.38±0.08	2.50
PPC Sample A	188±10	388±32	3.43±0.13	2.54
PCC Sample B	217±5	452±8	3.56±0.05	2.63

After Knorr (1978).
[1] PER assay 28 days; digestibility data from 6th through 13th days of test.
[2] All diets calculated to contain 10% protein.
[3] Five male weanling rats per test groups, 10 per control group, Sprague–Dawley strain; initial age = 21 days, initial weight = 56 grams.

Note: PPC source: Österreichische Agrar-Industrie GmbH., Vienna, Austria.

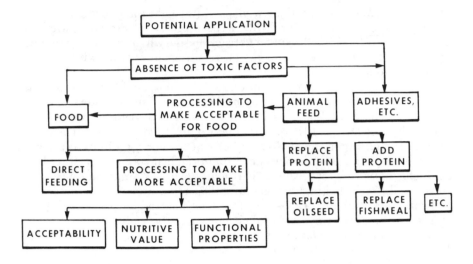

FIG. 11.6.   POTENTIAL APPLICATION FOR POTATO PROTEIN PRODUCTS.

The earthy, raw potato flavor of commercial potato proteins was significantly reduced by using a method that combined extraction with diethylether: ethanol: water, and steam treatment, or an extraction with hydrochloric acid and diethylether: ethanol: water (Knorr et al. 1976). The
aroma of the resulting spray dried potato protein products was not influenced by drying conditions such as inlet/outlet temperature or pH value
of the coagulates (Giokas 1976).

The color of potato protein is influenced by the use of SO_2 or H_2SO_3 added
to the potatoes or to the protein water (Huchette and Fleche 1975). Antioxi-
dants such as butylhydroxytoluene, ascorbic acid, and a-tocopherol are also
claimed to influence the color of the recovered protein (Huchette and Fleche
1975). The influence of different drying methods on product color was
described by Strolle et al. (1973) and was mentioned before. The effect of pH
(4, 6, and 8) during drying on the color of a spray dried product was studied
by Giokas (1976), who found that the lightest-colored product was obtained
at the lowest pH value. The use of citric acid as protein coagulant resulted
also in light colored, fluffy products (Knorr 1979). Protein solubility of a
protein concentrate recovered from potato cut water by using polyphosphoric acid was 98.2% (Finley and Hautala 1976), whereas Giokas (1976)
found that protein solubility of a product derived from potato starch effluents was significantly influenced by the drying temperature and pH value
during spray drying. The positive effect of protein coagulation at ambient
temperature has been shown earlier in this paper (see Table 11.14).

Meuser and Smolnik (1979) recommend the following two-step purification procedure to prepare "pure potato protein, neutral in taste and smell."
In the first step the heat precipitated coagulate is suspended in warm water

in order to remove most of the low molecular weight components responsible for flavor and taste. This will increase the crude protein content to approximately 90%. A subsequent extraction step with ethanol will remove the rest of the undesired components, resulting in product with a crude protein content of 93–95%.

As a food supplement potato protein could find possible use in protein enrichment of bread, snacks, crisp bread, cookies, and crackers. Experiments describing protein enrichment of bread with potato protein have been published (Knorr 1977B, 1978; Meuser and Smolnik 1979). The influence of partial replacement (5–20%) of wheat flour by a protein product recovered from potato starch waste effluents on loaf volume, moisture loss, and deformation of bread was studied during 96 hr of storage time on breads baked at different baking temperatures. The results showed a strong relationship between moisture loss and storage time, and low relationships in the cases of storage time versus deformation and specific loaf volume.

Depression of loaf volume is commonly reported in protein enriched breads. This has been observed in various degrees with many plant protein sources. The decrease of specific loaf volume when potato protein/concentrates were added (especially above a replacement level of 10%) was reported earlier (Knorr 1977A). There are several possible explanations for the depression in loaf volume brought about by the protein concentrates. One generally used explanation for these effects is the "dilution" of the wheat flour with protein. This theory suggests that protein supplements dilute the gluten, with a resultant loss in strength of the gluten structure. A study by Knorr and Betschart (1978) examined the role of an inert substance upon loaf volume of breads enriched with potato protein/concentrates, soy protein concentrates, and rice bran protein concentrates. The loaf volume depression (between 0 and 40% replacement level) for the protein concentrates was greater than the depression with an inert substance (sand). One possible explanation for the greater depression in loaf volume brought about by the protein concentrates when compared with sand at similar concentrations is that the dilution effect may be functioning in combination with one or more additional factors.

The same authors also investigated the influence of levels of water added on loaf volume of protein fortified breads. Additional water (0–16%) was added (flour basis) to the amount of water usually added to reach 500 farinograph units. Up to 8–12% water addition increased the loaf volumes, whereas at levels greater than 12% the dough became too sticky and difficult to handle. The specific loaf volume at the 12% level increased up to 34% when compared to the specific loaf volume of the standard breads (volume of the bread made with the dough that had 500 B.U.). The influence of potato protein fortification of wheat flour breads on their baking quality can be roughly summarized as follows: The various coagulants used for the protein precipitation apparently do not affect loaf volume, but the loaf volume is affected by heat treatment during and after coagulation. Heat treatment involved during drying also increased the loaf volume in the direction freeze dried → spray dried → drum dried PPC (see Table 11.16),

thus the differences in loaf volume are presumably related to protein denaturation. Loaf volume decreases with increasing replacement levels of
wheat flour (0–40% potato protein concentrates). The loaf volume depression for the potato protein containing breads was greater than the depression with an inert substance (sand). The dilution of the gluten of wheat flour
is one generally used explanation for the loaf volume depression. This may
be functioning in combination with one or more additional factors. The loaf
volume of potato protein enriched bread increased when levels of water
were added to the dough at levels higher than the amount commonly used
(to reach 500 B.U.) were added. The results indicate that up to an approximately 10% replacement level, it is possible to produce PPC enriched breads
with little change in bread quality.

SUGGESTIONS FOR FURTHER RESEARCH

In agreement with Krochta *et al.* (1975) and with Milner *et al.* (1977), it is
highly recommended that the reclaiming of organic wastes of all kinds for
food and feed use be a major effort in food and agriculture related research.
Major reasons for the reclamation of wastes include:

1. The increasing cost of agricultural and industrial food production
2. The worldwide need for high quality protein
3. The need for reduction of pollution from food wastes
4. The decreasing supply of high quality drinking water and
5. The increasing concern about wastage of energy

This leads to an urgent need for using our (sometimes already limited)
food sources (including water) more carefully and more efficiently. Specific
research is needed to:

1. examine the exact amount of food wastes at different stages of the
   food chain
2. study and develop methods to collect and/or concentrate food that
   would otherwise be wasted
3. develop appropriate/intermediate food processing technologies for
   intermediate and small-scale waste recycling or recovery operations.
4. study and develop energy- and cost-effective food waste and water
   recycling processes (e.g., heat coagulation versus protein coagulation at ambient temperatures)
5. investigate toxic and risk factors (e.g., environmental pollutants)
   and nutrient quality of the recycled products for human and/or
   animal consumption
6. develop methods to reduce or eliminate risk and toxic factors to
   increase or preserve nutrient quality during the nutrient recovery
   process
7. examine and improve functional properties in order to use the recycled products as highly functional food or food ingredients

8. investigate and apply innovative food processing techniques for the utilization of recycled nutrients
9. study consumer acceptance of newly developed food products containing recycled nutrients
10. develop definitions and regulatory standards and procedures for these products

CONCLUSIONS

The concept of recycling nutrients and producing food from waste is attractive and could create many innovative approaches in food science and technology. The existing data indicate that such products will find a place in food and feed markets of the future. There is a demand for new and additional food sources and for higher efficiency during the production, processing, distribution, and consumption of food. The recycling of nutrients from food wastes also plays an important role in new concepts of food production, which include ecological approaches in agricultural production, environmentally sound technologies during food processing, and the reduction of pollution associated with food wastes. One way to reduce food wastes is by recycling and making them (again) useful for human and animal consumption. However, this concept should be understood as only a short-term solution and should, in the long run, be directed only toward areas in the food chain where wastes are inevitable. The main goal of our efforts to increase the quality and the amount of the food supply has to be aimed toward the avoidance of food wastes from production to consumption rather than the recovery of often carelessly wasted food or food components.

REFERENCES

ADELSON, S.F., DELANEY, I., MILLER, C., and NOBLE, I.T. 1963. Discard of edible food in households. J. Home Economics 55(8), 633−638.

ALTON, L.V. and TOBIAS, V. 1976. Thermal and chemical precipitation of protein from potato juice. Chem. Abstr. 85, 92421.

ALTSCHUL, A.M. 1976. New Protein Foods. Vol. 2, Part B. Academic Press, New York.

ANON. 1968. Protein recovery from potato starch. Process Biochemistry, 3(5)51.

ANON. 1976. Fermentation pays off in transforming waste to protein. Food Engineering 48(11) 66−67.

ANON. 1979. Proceedings—World Conference on Vegetable Proteins. J. Am. Oil Chem. Soc. 56(3) 99−484.

AQUIRRE, F., MALDONADO, O., ROLZ, C., MENCHU, J.F., ESPINOSA, R., and DE CABRERA, S. 1977. Protein from waste. Chemtech 7, 636−642.

BEN-GERA, I. and KRAMER, A. 1969. Utilization of food industries waste. Advances in Food Research 17, 77−152.

BESSON, J.M. and VOGTMANN, H.   1978.   Towards a Sustainable Agriculture.   Verlag Wirz, Aarau.

BETSCHART, A.A.   1979.   Development of safflower protein.   J. Am. Oil Chem. Soc. *56*, 454–457.

BIRCH, G.G., PARKER, K.J., and WORGAN, J.T. (Editors).   1976.   Food from Waste.   Applied Science Publishers Ltd., London.

BORUD, O.J.   1971.   Verwertung von Abfällen der kartoffelverarbeitenden Industrie. Die Stärke. *23*, 172–176.

BURCH, J.E., LIPINSKI, E.S., and LITCHFIELD, J.H.   1963.   Technical and economic factors in the utilization of waste products.   Food Technol. *54* (10) 54–60.

CATHCART, E.P. and MURRAY, A.M.T.   1939.   A note on the percentage loss of calories as waste in ordinary mixed diets.   J. Hygiene *39*, 45–50.

CIRCLE, S.J. and SMITH, A.K.   1975.   Soybeans: Processing and products. *In* Food Protein Sources.   N.W. Pirie, (Editor).   Cambridge University Press, Cambridge and New York.

COTON, S.G.   1976.   Recovery of dairy waste.   *In* Food From Waste.   G.G. Birch, K.J. Parker, and J.T. Worgan, (Editors).   Applied Science Publishers, Ltd., London.

DE NOORD, K.G.   1976.   Recovery of protein in potato starch manufacture. *In* Chemical Engineering in a Changing World.   Koetsier, W.T. (Editor). Elsevier Sci. Publ. Co., Amsterdam.

ERNÄHRUNGBERICHT.   1976.   Deutsche Gesellschaft für Ernährung. E.V., Frankfurt/Main.

FANTOZZI, P. and BETSCHART, A.A.   1979.   Development of grapeseed protein.   J. Am. Oil Chem. Soc. *56*, 457–459.

FINLEY, J.W.   1977.   Protein removal from gluten-starch wash water.   Cereal Chem. *54*, 131–138.

FINLEY, J.W. and HAUTALA, E.   1976.   Recovery of soluble proteins from waste streams.   Food Product Development *10*(3) 92–93.

FORSTER, C.F. and JONES, J.C.   1976.   The bioplex concept.   *In* Food From Waste.   G.G. Birch, K.J. Parker, and J.T. Worgan, (Editors).   Applied Science Publishers Ltd. London.

FRIEDMAN, M. (Editor) 1975.   Protein Nutritional Quality of Foods and Feeds. Part 2.   Marcel Dekker, Inc., New York.

GIOKAS, S.   1976.   Zerstäubungstrocknung eines aus Kartoffelfruchtwasser gewonnenen Proteinproduktes.   University of Agriculture, Thesis, Vienna, Austria.

GOODMAN, N. and PIMENTEL, D.   1979.   Biomass energy conversion as an alternative energy source.   Compost Science/Land Utilization *20*, 28–31.

GRUNEWALD, A.   1954.   Die Behandlung des Kartoffelfruchtwasses und die industrielle Gewinnung der Albumine.   Stärke *6*, 182–186.

HAGENMAIER, R.   1979.   Experimental coconut protein products.   J. Am. Oil Chem. Soc. *56*, 448–449.

HARRISON, G.G., RATHJE, W.L., and HUGHES, W.W.   1975.   Food waste behavior in an urban population.   J. Nutr. Education. 7(1) 13–16.

HEISLER, E.G., SICILLIANO, J., TREADWAY, R.H., and WOODWARD, C.F. 1959. Recovery of free amino compounds from potato starch processing water by use of ion exchange. Am. Potato J. *36*, 1–11.

HUCHETTE, M. and FLECHE, E.G. 1975. Verfahren zur Gewinnung von Kartoffelproteinen, die dabei erhaltenen Produkte und deren Verwendung. BRD Offenlegungsschrift 25 00 2000.

JACKSON, M.L. 1962. Research ideas and cost estimates for utilizing the potato industrially. Ind. Eng. Chem. *54*(2) 50–56.

JOHNSON, L.A., SULEIMANN, T.M., and LUSAS, E.W. 1979. Sesame Protein: A review and prospectus. J. Am. Oil Chem. Soc. *56*, 463–468.

KLING, W. 1943. Food waste in distribution and use. J. Farm Economics, pp. 848–859.

KNORR, D. 1977A. Protein recovery from waste effluents of potato processing plants. J. Food Technol. *12*, 563–580.

KNORR, D. 1977B. Potato protein as partial replacement of wheat flour in bread. J. Food Science *42*(6) 1425–1427.

KNORR, D. 1978. Protein quality of the potato and potato protein concentrates. Food Sci. and Technol. *11*, 109–115.

KNORR, D. 1980. Protein recovery from food wastes: The influence of various methods of protein coagulation upon yield, quality and properties of potato protein concentrates. J. Food Sci. *45*, 1183–1186.

KNORR, D. and BETSCHART, A.A. 1982. The relative effect of an inert substance and protein concentrates upon loaf volume of breads. Food Sci. and Technol. *11*, 198–201.

KNORR, D. and BETSCHART, A.A. 1980. Effect of dehydration methods on the functionality of plant protein concentrates. Stärke (in press).

KNORR, D., HOESS, W., and KLAUSHOFER, H. 1976. Ergebnisse von Untersuchungen zur Verminderung von Geruch und Geschmack bei handelsüblichem durch Hitzekoagulation aus Kartoffelfruchtwasser gewonnenen Protein Trockenprodukt. Confructa *21*, 166–180.

KNORR, D., KOHLER, G.O., and BETSCHART, A.A. 1977. Potato protein concentrates: The influence of various methods of recovery upon yield, compositional and functional characteristics. J. Food Processing and Preservation *1*, 235–247.

KRAMER, A. and KWEE, W.H. 1977. Utilization of tomato processing wastes. J. Food Science *42*, 212–215.

KROCHTA, J.M., RUMSEY, T.R., and FARKAS, D.F. 1975. Defining food R and D needs as a guide for the future. Food Technol. *29*(10), 74–84.

KWON, T.W. 1974. By-product recovery as a resource. *In* Environmental Quality and Food Supply. P.L. White, and D. Robins, (Editors). Futura Publishing Co., Mount Kisco, New York.

LANDWIRTSCHAFTLICHE KARTOFFELVERWERTUNGS-AG. 1957. Verfahren zur Gewinnung von Kartoffeleiweiss. Austrian Patent Nr. 193704.

LeBOVIT, C. and BOEHM, W.T. 1979. Changes to meet the dietary goals. National Food Review, NFR-8, 24–26.

MASTERS, K. 1972. Spray Drying. CRC Press, London.

MAY, R.M. 1977. Food lost to pests. Nature 267, 669–670.

MEISTER, E. and THOMPSON, N.R. 1976. Physical-chemical methods for the recovery of protein from waste effluents of potato chip processing. J. Agric. Food Chem. 24, 919–923.

MERRILL, R. (Editor). 1976. Radical Agriculture. Harper and Row, New York.

MEUSER, F. and SMOLNIK, H.D. 1979. Potato protein for human food use. J. Am. Oil Chem. Soc. 56, 449–450.

MINTURN, R. 1975. Advanced techniques for aqueous processing and pollution abatement. Oak Ridge Natl. Lab. (U.S.) ORNL-NSF-EP 1975.

OELHAF, R.C. 1978. Organic Agriculture. Halsted Press, New York.

OHLSON, R. and ANJOU, K. 1979. Rapeseed protein products. J. Am. Oil Chem. Soc. 56, 431–437.

OKE, O.L., R.H. SMITH, and A.A. WOODHAM. 1975. Groundnut Food Protein Sources. Cambridge University Press, Cambridge.

OOSTEN, B.J. 1976. Protein from potato starch mill effluent. In Food From Waste. G.G. Birch, K.J. Parker, and J.T. Worgan. Applied Science Publishers Ltd., London.

PARISER, E.R., WALLERSTEIN, M.D., CORKERY, C.J., and BROWN, N. 1978. Fish Protein Concentrates: Panecea for Protein Malnutrition. The MIT Press, Cambridge, Massachusetts, and London.

PETERS, H. 1972. Measures taken against water pollution in starch and potato processing industries. Pure and Applied Chemistry 29(1–3) 129–141.

PHILLIPS, R.D. and STERNBERG, M. 1979. Corn protein concentrate: Functional and nutritional properties. J. Food Sci. 44, 1152–1161.

PIGOTT, G.M. 1976. New approaches to marketing fish. In New Protein Foods. A.A. Altschul, (Editor). Vol. 2, Part B. Academic Press, Inc., New York.

PIMENTEL, D., DRITSCHILO, W., KRUMMEL, J., and KUTZMANN, J. 1975. Energy and land constraints in food protein production. Science 190, 754–761.

PIMENTEL, D. and PIMENTEL, M. 1979. Food Energy and Society. Edward Arnold, Ltd., London.

PIRIE, N.W. 1971. Leaf Protein: Its Agronomy, Preparation, Quality and Use. Blackwell Scientific Publications, Oxford and Edinburgh.

PYKE, M. 1975. Fit to eat. BBC Radio 3, 11. November (after Roy, M. 1976).

RIGHELATO, R.C., IMRIE, F.K.E., and ULITOS, A.J. 1976. Production of single cell protein from agricultural and food processing wastes. Resource Recovery Conservation. 1, 257–269.

ROSENAU, J.R., WHITNEY, L.F., and HAIGHT, J.R. 1978. Upgrading potato starch manufacturing wastes. Food Tech. 32, 37–39.

ROY, R. 1976. Wastage in the UK food system. Earth Resources Research Ltd., London.

SAUNDERS, R.M. and KOHLER, G.O. 1975. Concentrates by wet and dry processing of cereals. *In* Food Protein Sources. N.W. Pirie, (Editor). Cambridge University Press, Cambridge, England.

SCHMIDT, P., GIESEMANN, H., and SNIJDER, H.H.   1976.   Verfahren zur Gewinnung von wasserlöslich em Eiweiss aus Kartoffelfruchtwasser.   BRD Offenlegungsschrift 25 42 155.

SCHWARTZ, J.H., KRULICK, S., and PORTER, W.L.   1972.   Potato starch factory waste effluents III.   Recovery of organic acids and phosphate. J. Sci. Food Agric. *23*, 977–985.

SKOGMAN, H.   1976.   Production of symba-yeast from potato wastes.   *In* Food From Waste.   G.G. Birch, K.J. Parker, and J.T. Worgan, (Editors). Applied Science Publishers, Ltd., London.

SOSULSKI, F.   1979.   Food uses of sunflower proteins.   J. Am. Oil Chem. Soc. *56*, 438–442.

STABILE, R.L., TURKOT, V.A., and ACETO, N.C.   1971.   Economic analysis of alternative methods for processing potato starch plant effluents.   Second National Symposium of Food Processing Wastes.   March 23–26, Denver, Colorado.

STROLLE, E.O.   1977.   Precipitating carbohydrate from potato processing. Paper presented at 61st Annual Meeting of the Potato Association of America, Fredericton, New Brunswick, Canada.

STROLLE, E.O.   1980.   Personal Communication.   February 26, 1980.

STROLLE, E.O. CORDING, J., and ACETO, N.C.   1973.   Recovering potato proteins coagulated by steam injection heating.   J. Agric. Food Chem. *21*, 974–977.

TANNENBAUM, S.R.   1977.   Single-cell protein.   *In* Food Proteins.   J.R. Whitaker, and S.R. Tannenbaum; (Editors).   AVI Publishing Company, Inc. Westport, Connecticut.

USDA.   1977.   National Food Situation.   U.S. Department of Agriculture. Econ. Research Service, NFS-158.

VERBERNE, P.   1977.   A new hydrocyclone process for the production of potato starch with lowest fresh water production.   Starch *29*:303–306.

VLASBLOM, M. and PETERS, H.   1958.   Recovery of proteins from potato wash water.   Dutch Patent No. 87, 150.

WORGAN, J.T.   1976.   Wastes from crop plants as raw material for conversion by fungi to food or livestock feed.   *In* Food from Waste. G.G. Birch, K.J. Parker, and Worgan, J.T. (Editors).   Applied Science Publishers, Ltd., London.

WORGAN, J.T.   1977.   Protein production by micro-organism.   *In* Plant Proteins. G. Norton (Editor).   Butterworths, London.

XANDER, P.A. and HOOVER, E.F.   1959.   Methods of producing protein and protein hydrolyzate from potatoes and potato waste.   U.S. Patent 2, 879, 264.

12

Challenging the Modern U.S. Food System: Notes from the Grassroots

Michael Schaaf

INTRODUCTION

The structure of the food production, processing, and marketing industries has changed radically since World War II. Farms are fewer, larger, and highly specialized and mechanized. Food processing and distribution has become a sophisticated industry that generates thousands of new products annually. Ownership of these sectors has become more concentrated, too.

The "Mom and Pop" stores that once serviced most American consumers are being rapidly replaced by streamlined, vertically integrated superettes. Supermarket fresh tomatoes—greener and firmer than yesteryear's—are shielded from human grasp by ever-present packaging. Family farms have been consolidated into megafarms whose banks, suppliers, and markets are no longer local.

A new pattern of ownership and control of food production and marketing has emerged. The corner stores, farm fresh foods, and the local farmer are all being pushed aside by thoroughly integrated, richly capitalized, nationally focused, and highly technologized alternatives. The changes wrought by this industrialized structure—built on motives that often have little to do with food—have altered the very fabric of rural society and the premises by which food is grown and distributed.

Modern alternatives may not offer the public anything better. For example, "convenience" stores have rapidly replaced the Mom and Pops, yet their appeal, according to the U.S. Department of Agriculture, "is based on convenience of location, quick service, and long hours"—though they have higher prices, less brand selection, and higher profit margins (USDA 1972). What they have described is the old Mom and Pop store, only Mom and Pop are now workers rather than owners.

Contradictions of this sort have infected those of us who eat the food as well as those of us who grow it. Consumers have been subjected to unprecedented food price inflation simultaneously with a growing body of changes in food quality. Meanwhile, they are faced with a sophisticated food marketing industry that relentlessly offers a bevy of new products. Producers have watched their numbers dwindle radically while those who remain are compelled to accommodate the modern agricultural trends of specialization, bigness, and mechanization. As they have evolved into cogs of the vast food production machine, farmers have been surrounded, on one hand, by the interests of farm input suppliers and, on the other hand, by food processors and marketers.

These social and economic changes in all links in the food chain have created a crisis—a "Food Crisis."

Many consumers and producers have responded by attempting to shape the food system to their own terms. New food distribution systems, family food production, and ecological production techniques are common targets of citizen action. Because the tentacles of government now reach deep into the workings of the economy, food activists have also entered legislative halls in an effort to enhance their efforts.

In contrast to the industrial economy of food, food organizing has sought to create more local food links. Organizations have been established that often service both producers' and consumers' needs through relying on popular resources and direction. But the food producing and distribution system is not so simply organized. The challenge that food crisis organizing faces can be fully appreciated only in the setting of the economic structure and trends of the overall food industry.

Contrary to the popularizing thrust of food projects, the food industry, like finance and manufacturing, is becoming increasingly concentrated in large corporate hands. The question is, "What is the potential of food organizing to substantively affect the food system structure?" This chapter examines the nature of the food crisis and popular responses and analyzes the character of this organizing.

A CLOSER LOOK AT THE FOOD CRISIS

All facets of the food system—how and by whom food is produced, processed, and marketed—have been revolutionized over the past few decades.

Food Production

In 1945, there were 5.9 million farms and a farm labor force of nearly 11 million; today, there are 2.7 million farms and about 4 million workers (Congressional Budget Office 1978).

Through "economic cannibalism from within agriculture" (Congressional Budget Office 1978), small farms are being replaced by much larger farms using modern machines and production practices. From 1950 to the present, average farm acreage and total assets increased by almost 100% and 150%, respectively. Meanwhile, farms of $100,000 sales volumes have increased their share of farm receipts from 17% in 1960 to 52% in 1977 (Belden *et al.* 1979).

The underlying dynamic can best be described as industrialization. World War II labor scarcity helped initiate a wave of farm mechanization that radically increased productivity. The economies of the new machines required farm expansion: purchasing or leasing a neighboring farmer's land was a favorite option. Farmers and farm workers were displaced and farm size grew, capitalized by an ever-enlarging farm debt. This, in addition to spiralling land prices and rising production costs, often means that the initial investment for land and operating costs can be close to $400,000, an entry cost prohibitive for new farmers. Meanwhile, the exit of farm families results in the decline of farm-related services and industries and their once stable rural communities.

Industrial production practices have also affected the farm resource base. Loss of topsoil due to erosion proceeds at a Dust Bowl pace: eight times its replacement rate (Belden *et al.* 1979). The remaining soil is so drained that more synthetic fertilizer is required to produce the same yield. The volume of irrigation water has increased over 150% since 1940 (Belden *et al.* 1979). Other artificial inputs, such as pesticides and herbicides, have also increased in volume dramatically. Growing dependence on all these fossil-fuel-based inputs has resulted in higher energy inputs per unit of output and continuing energy-sensitive production costs.

Along with the growth in artificial inputs, nonfarm interests are increasingly penetrating the farm sector. In 1970, only 17% of the food supply was produced under corporate contract; the American Agricultural Marketing Association estimates that this will triple by 1980 (Belden *et al.* 1979). On-farm production of inputs has been replaced by purchased inputs, which now account for 70% of the total farm input package, as compared to 44% in 1950. Significantly, only 15 companies account for 60% of all farm input revenues.

These pervasive changes in the structure of agriculture have not been merely a result of impersonal economic forces. The policies of the U.S. Department of Agriculture, as well as other public agencies, have played a critical role in fostering these trends. Secretary of Agriculture Bob Bergland agreed, "tax laws, credit programs, government regulations, farm marketing arrangements, yes, even agricultural research, are skewed to favor the big farm over the small and medium sized farm" (Bergland 1979A).

This "bigger is better" philosophy has had the approval, if not the active support, of big business leaders. In 1962, the Committee on Economic Development, an association of 200 prominent businessmen and educators whose purpose is to "guide business and public policy," issued "An Adaptive Program for Agriculture" (Committee on Economic Development 1962). The report advocated decreasing farm numbers and increasing capital investment. Members of CED's Subcommittee on Agriculture subsequently held high-level positions such as Secretary of the Treasury and membership on the Council of Economic Advisors. A later CED report describing the results of earlier policy recommendations concluded, "In general, policies of this nature have been pursued by the U.S. government" (Ritchie 1979), in a partnership of government and big business.

Food Processing

Industrialization and concentration has also proceeded in the food processing and distribution sectors. The existence of 30,000 food processing firms implies healthy competition, but the 50 largest food concerns controlled 64% of manufacturers' assets in 1978, up from 42% in 1963. These firms also corner 90% of the manufacturers' profits. Control of the market for a multitude of common grocery items is frequently shared by just three brand names.

The efficiency criterion that has rationalized the growth of food marketing giants is contradicted by the impact on the consumer. Recent research by Federal Trade Commission economist Russell Parker concludes that lack of competition in the food marketing industries adds $15 billion to annual consumer food expenditures, 7% of the national food budget (Consumers Opposed to Inflation in the Necessities 1979). Parker and a USDA economist, John Conner, further estimate that 20% of these overcharges end up in the profit margins of the food giants (Hightower and DeMarco 1978).

The big-business journal *Fortune* reports that the giant food processors "must respond to the consumer—by generating new products, abandoning old ones, whatever—in such a way as to continue growing despite the maturity of the overall industry" (Kiechall 1978). Roughly 500 new items are introduced every month, of which about 500 survive annually (U.S. Department of Energy 1978). Each new product offers a processing nuance that, not coincidentally, increases the value-added and profit margins while decreasing dependence on agricultural commodities. Basic food products are low-profit, slow-growth items that hold no fascination for the money machines dominating the industry.

Critics Hightower and DeMarco summarize (Hightower and DeMarco 1978),

[Our] food is becoming little more than a low quality medium to which food manufacturers add coloring and flavoring to give the stuff minimal consumer appeal, a dozen or so basic vitamins to give it "nutrition," several chemicals to hold it together, preservatives to give it shelf-life probably greater than your own allotted years, sugar to cover up any mistakes and a package to make it "convenient."

Food Retailing

When the food finally arrives at the supermarket, the consumer still does not fare well. A few supermarket chains maintain control of retailing in such major cities as Denver, Washington, D.C., and Milwaukee. The result is familiar; a 1977 Congressional Joint Economic Committee study of food retailers concluded that "in many markets, consumers are paying large dollar overcharges due to their market power." This estimate of national monopoly overcharges ranged to $622 million in 1974 (Consumers Opposed to Inflation in the Necessities 1979).

A consumer coalition, Consumers Opposed to Inflation in the Necessities, estimates that aggregating the total cost of concentration of food manufacturing and retailing industries reveals that an average American family of four is overcharged at least $313 annually (Consumers Opposed to Inflation in the Necessities 1979).

FARMERS AND CONSUMERS RESPOND

Except for the corporate giants that produce, process, or distribute food, no one has been spared the burdens of the Food Crisis. Reduced to dependent cogs in the food system, farmers who have not been forced out of business are pressed by financial and ecological burdens. Consumers are pawns for industry marketing maneuvers that often provide less than nutritious food at inflated prices.

Motivated by a need to relieve these conditions, food producers and eaters have been stirred to action. People who have never grown food before have launched latter-day Victory Gardens. Farmers who have relied on traditional outlets have developed alternatives. No systematic survey of motivations is available, but the available evidence sheds some light.

Stretching the Food Budget

Consumers are concerned about the prices and availability of foodstuffs. According to the Consumer Price Index, food prices rose 111% from 1967 to 1979. This inflation is particularly burdensome for low- and moderate-income people whose consumption patterns give little flexibility to "buy down" as prices soar. In 1972–1973 the 10% of American families with the lowest incomes spent 35% of their incomes on food, compared to 10% of income expended by the top 10% group. (National Advisory Council on

Economic Opportunity 1979) Moreover, evidence suggests that the foods that moderate-income people tend to purchase rose in price faster than "luxury" food (Manchester and Brown 1977). The price of artichokes rose more slowly than the price of french fries, and the cost of beefsteak more slowly than the cost of hot dogs.

The route for escaping this food-price spiral is not altogether apparent to people reared with the belief that the existing U.S. food system is the best in the world. One strategy has been to grow some of your own food. The Gallup Poll reports that in 1978, 41% of all households had gardens, which produced a Gross Home Garden Product of $11 billion, or $330 net per garden (Gardens for All 1979A.)

However, gardening requires resources, in particular land, which are not available to many urban dwellers. Gardens for All, a national gardening association, estimates that two million people have implemented a community solution to this obstacle by gardening on about one million community gardening plots in 1978 (Gardens for All 1978). Furthermore, a survey of community garden coordinators revealed that 31% of participating gardeners were involved primarily because of the money saved.

Community gardens are sponsored by community organizations, local governments, and private employers. The Staley Gardens are community gardens sponsored by Staley Manufacturing Company of Decatur, Illinois. In 1979, the Gardens consisted of 135 plots, 25 ft by 75 ft each, covering a total of 5.5 acres. The company is very supportive of the gardens, providing soil tests and enrichments, information, and basic cultivation. The 110 participating gardeners consist of employees, families, and retirees. A garden committee of three retirees and three employees assigns plots yearly; participants are responsible for plots from sowing to cleanup. Gardeners participate for many reasons: A secretary asserts, "I garden because I like to feed my family fresh produce." Another participant reports that she can feed a family of three on her harvest. She gardens to save money, and her home yard is too small. An employee speaks for just about everyone, "Part of the fun of gardening is neighboring" (Gardens for All 1979B).

Another strategy for saving money is to organize systems to buy direct from farmers. There are apparently benefits to consumers and producers alike through minimizing marketing costs and some market functions by relating directly. These functions, spanning all food processing and distribution activities, have gobbled up 72% of the 1970 to 1978 food inflation.

Declining farm profit margins and expanding middleman shares have inspired vegetable and fruit farmers to retaliate by establishing farm stands on the urban fringe through which farm products can be sold directly to the public. As direct access to urban customers became necessary, farmers have collaborated with consumers in organizing farmers markets.

As farmers principally offer locally produced foods, there is considerable variation in prices across the nation, reflecting local production conditions. Nonetheless, smart consumers have consistently been rewarded with savings through farmers market shopping: in Hartford, Ct., prices average 24%

lower than supermarket prices (Taylor 1979); in the California farmers markets, the supermarket price averaged over all items was 71% higher. Up the coast in Seattle, the average price for produce items at the Pike Place Market was 19% lower than the supermarket price (Sommer 1979).

Improving the Family Diet

Participants in the community gardens or farmers markets are not singular in their motivation. Pecuniary concerns such as those just discussed are frequently melded with food quality or personal satisfactions.

Over the past several years criticism has been mounting regarding the quality of the American diet. The term "junk food" has become associated with old favorites: hot dogs, candy, white bread. Discussions about banning of Red Dye Number 2, sodium nitrate, and saccharine have stirred concern about the rest of the 3900 additives that are part of our diet. Then, too, critics point out that six out of the top ten causes of cancer are diet related (Jones 1978).

Dietary criticisms, once considered fringe issues by the nutrition establishment, advanced in respectability with the publication of "Dietary Goals for the United States" by the Senate Select Committee on Nutrition and Human Needs (1977). The American diet was criticized for insufficient fiber and excessive fats, calories, cholesterol, salt, and sugar. In short, Americans, according to the committee, have been eating too many highly processed foods.

Although the relationship between food characteristics and health is subtle, a vocal group of concerned nutritionists has elevated the issue to a new level of public and governmental awareness. The findings of the Center for Science in the Public Interest (CSPI), a national public interest group, preceded the "official" criticisms by several years. In the mid-1970s, CSPI launched annual "Food Day," which provided an occasion for local action and education about a whole range of food issues, including the effects of diet on health. Patterned after Earth Day, which dramatically enhanced popular recognition of the environmental crisis, Food Day was opportunity for a variety of local food projects, whether ongoing or ad hoc, to act in concert.

Alarmed consumers have been compelled to seek alternatives to the supermarket whose shelves are stocked with giant food processors' products. In addition to their monetary benefits, home-based food production and farmer-to-consumer marketing can be a means to improve food quality. Gardens for All (1979A) reported that community garden coordinators estimate that 14% of their participants garden primarily in order to produce better food. Recent studies in Illinois, Alabama, Colorado, Arizona, Ohio, and Florida consistently report that customers like to buy directly from farmers in such outlets as farmers markets because of some combination of freshness and quality (Watkins 1979).

One of the more popular alternative food distribution mechanisms is consumer food cooperatives. These are local businesses that buy food whole-sale and resell it at less than retail price by minimizing distribution costs and amenities. The organizations are controlled by their members, often utilize volunteer labor, and provide supportive services.

The history of the food cooperative movement can be conceptually divided into three eras: (1) the Depression era co-ops, which are few in number but in some areas are a significant economic force; (2) the New Wave co-ops that emerged during the early 1970s and tend to feature smaller units emphasiz-ing the social/political aspects of cooperation, such as strong member partic-ipation, member education, and anticorporate politics; and (3) the Third Wave, which are New Wave co-ops that have attempted to meld the two previous eras by building more viable business units yet preserve the actualization of important social/political motives.

The New Wave co-ops are presently the elite of the movement. Typically, they are small buying club units of perhaps 15 to 100 families that collec-tively purchase food on a periodic basis and distribute it from donated space such as a church basement. Although food co-op spokespeople articulate several goals for the movement, the food quality objective may be para-mount, considering the food commonly sold. Natural foods, which are less processed than their mainstream counterparts and have limited appeal to most Americans, are a vital component of the movement. The buying clubs do save members dollars. In Chicago, the Self-Help Action Center, which has assisted over 300 co-ops to get started, estimates that co-opers save 30% in the winter and 50% in the summer. The Center's 35 constituent co-ops are comprised of almost 8000 household members.

Buying clubs, which experienced a spurt of growth during the period of rapid food price rises in 1973–1974, have occasionally spawned small storefronts. However, this growth has apparently stabilized or declined in many areas. It has been difficult for the largely volunteer organizations to establish a stable base of membership and organization from which to build. The Third Wave co-ops have attempted to respond to these business short-comings.

Arcata Cooperative is an example of a young storefront food co-op strug-gling to harmonize cooperative business and social objectives. Located in Arcata, a rural town in northern California, the Co-op, which has a membership of 3600 drawn from a cross-section of the community, "was established to meet our community's need for wholesome, nutritious food at fair prices" (Arcata Cooperative, Inc., undated). The average inventory of $125,000 turned over $4.6 million of products in 1979 by emphasizing natural foods; it also includes produce, dairy items, groceries, alcoholic beverages, and meat.

Membership in the Co-op is defined by purchase of one share of $10 stock, which entitles the member to elect the governing Board of Directors and receive a proportion of the surplus (profit) money remaining at year's end. Management of the enterprise is innovatively designed to maximize demo-cratic control and the accountability of workers and members alike. The

Co-op pursues social objectives through consumer information services, a newsletter, food workshops, lobbying, and aid to emerging co-ops. The member-controlled organization keeps its food dollars in the community by buying 50% of its produce from neighboring farmers.

The Arcata Cooperative is part of a much larger, diverse, national food co-op movement featuring both sophisticated co-op food markets that transact over $70 million in sales annually and pre-pay buying clubs that transact as little as $7000 worth of business annually. A network of warehouses vertically integrates the retail operations. Although limited national data are available, food co-ops surely comprise the bulk of the 1.2 million members of consumer goods co-ops in 1977 (Schaaf 1977).

Saving the Family Farm

In addition to food price and quality motives, concern about the plight of farmers, particularly smaller and family producers, has provoked citizen action. Only 2.2 million farms feed 210 million people and produce exports. Farmers are resisting further reductions in their numbers and their growing dependence on nonfarm sectors that often have little sensitivity to a farmer's needs.

In that the government is heavily involved in supporting and regulating food production, an important dimension of farmer response has been political. The American Agriculture Movement (AAM), composed principally of Midwestern family farmers, dramatically protested their income squeeze by blockading Washington during the summer of 1979. The guaranteeing of production costs, "parity," through federal price supports was the basic issue.

Smaller producers, who enjoy neither the staying power nor the political appeal of the larger family firms, must seek remedies that are usually less illustrious than those of the AAM. They have occasionally entered the political fray, but they tend to be issue oriented. National Land for People, for instance, is an organization of small farmers and sympathizers seeking reinterpretation of California water irrigation rights, which have been manipulated to favor corporate rather than small farmers, contrary to the original legislation. Other regional as well as national small-farm advocacy groups have also emerged.

Apparently, small and family farm political action has made some impact. Their issues have been projected to national prominence. A multitude of federal and state legislation has been proposed and enacted in order to reverse these trends (Belden et al. 1979). Farm taxation, financing, ownership, and marketing have been frequent legislative issues. Religious groups (United Presbyterian Church 1979) and public interest organizations such as Rural America and the National Rural Center have highlighted the issues and proposed remedies. Recognizing that federal agricultural policy is responsible for much of the current situation, Secretary of Agriculture Bergland scheduled a "full-scale national dialogue on the future of

American Agriculture." He has questioned whether the Department's policies have contributed to "an unending trend toward larger and larger and fewer and fewer farms that will increasingly dominate and control production" (Bergland, 1979B).

Yet action projects are frequently the root of the political efforts. Historically, farmers have organized various kinds of cooperatives to improve their economic strength. Consistent with agricultural trends toward bigness, these farmer cooperatives have decreased in number and increased in size. Many have grown extremely large, with several (such as Agway), among the *Fortune* 500. The business arena of most cooperatives is national. While there are notable exceptions, such as localized cooperatives in the Southeast, the predominant regional or national focus often separates these organizations from the immediate needs of farmers. At least one large farm organization, the National Farmers Organization, is engaged in developing farmers' market power through cooperative action.

The more marginal producers, who do not usually produce for export, large processors, or transnational distribution systems, have frequently turned to local solutions. Recognizing that the modern marketplace was bypassing their capabilities and advantages, farmers have turned to direct farmer-to-consumer marketing outlets.

In Philadelphia, farmers or "Tailgate" markets have grown rapidly. In 1978, markets were launched in three locations through the sponsorship of Nutritional Development Services, an agency of the Archdiocese of Philadelphia. The first day at one of the markets, 1000 people quickly purchased the truckloads of the surprised farmers who sold milk, eggs, produce, baked goods, honey, and assorted other items. The farmers markets now total four, all strategically located on church parking lots.

A full-time coordinator helps organize the markets, oversees management, and assists in promotions. The farmers are responsible for a $47 annual fee in addition to pricing their goods and maintaining their stalls.

Farmers estimate that their profit from market sales ranged from 33 to 45% higher than what they would have gained from the farm wholesale price (Hanssens 1979). Of course, their marketing costs are higher, too.

Another attraction is the mere ability to sell. The Philadelphia Daily News explains (Diehl 1978):

The tailgate solution arises from the problem that small farmers have had lately getting their produce sold. It seems that most big East Coast supermarkets would rather buy from big West Coast growers who can ship great quantities of fruits and vegetables year-round. The little farmer—and Pennsylvania has more family farmers than any other state—gets left out in the cold, with few outlets for his more seasonally and spacially limited crops.

As they are a means to bring farmers and consumers in direct contact, the Tailgate markets provide an opportunity for producers to educate their customers about farm problems and needs.

Limited evidence verifies farmers' monetary benefits from farmers markets. In Colorado, farmers received 44% higher gross returns selling through the farmers market than if they had sold through wholesale channels (USDA 1979).

The farmers market and direct marketing phenomenon is nationwide. A survey conducted by the American Vegetable Grower in 1978 revealed that there were 782 farmers markets in the 36 states that responded. Figures on gross volume are not available, but the 60% of American households that transacted with direct market outlets in 1977 undoubtedly purchased a good deal of food. In some states such as New Jersey, where over 64% of the farmers sell direct, farmer retailing is an important option for many farms. Yet Whedon Barton, Director of the Office of Energy, USDA, estimates that direct marketing, because of convenience limitation and narrow product lines, can perhaps market 2% of all foodstuffs (Department of Energy 1978). Within the context of current consumption habits and constraints, this is perhaps correct. However, sophisticated direct marketing areas such as Pennsylvania and California have demonstrated that there is much room for expansion.

The plight of the small farmers is a special target of concern. Local and regional development groups are active in small farm development. Community development corporations, such as Central Coast Counties in Santa Cruz, California, work directly with minority farmers to launch their individual and collective enterprises. In the South, the Southern Cooperative Development Fund provides attractively packaged capital in addition to technical assistance to area farmers and cooperatives. In some cases, small farmer institutions, such as the practical education facility the Graham Center, have been established.

Grower groups have taken action also. In Vermont and New Hampshire, the Natural Organic Farmers Association (NOFA) has organized cooperative orders of nonchemical soil amendments, helped establish direct and cooperative marketing, and provided educational services.

Next door to NOFA, in Maine, a practical focus is married to a political one. The Maine Consortium for Food Self-Reliance is an alliance of five rural organizations composed of farmers and consumers alike. The organization seeks to diversify and expand food production in a state that imports 85% of its food and has experienced drastic agricultural decline. Not only are food prices 11% higher in Maine than the national average, but per capita income is desperately low. The objective is to provide jobs and income from producing food while minimizing food prices through bypassing the transnational, inflation-prone marketing system that feeds the state.

The Consortium has conducted some background research that defines the needs for new policy directions to combat projected continuing decline. At the same time, innovative legislation requiring state institutions to buy local foods was successfully shepherded through the legislature. An additional project linked producers with food co-ops.

Democratizing the Food System

A fourth motivating force in food organizing is concern about the structure of the food production and distribution industries. These issues are the heart of the food crisis, but corporate boardrooms appear far removed from the daily struggles of the farmer or the squeezed budget of the consumer. Democratizing the food system involves redistributing concentrated power.

There are only two roads to the center of power: either an authority as powerful as corporate food producers and marketers legally intercedes on the growers' and eaters' behalf, or the latter parties address the issues where they unfold, in the local community. In the case of the powerful authority alternative, neither the federal nor state governments have yet taken decisive action. The U.S. Attorney General, for instance, has not moved on charges of anticompetitive behavior within the food marketing industry. Official responses range from palliatives to sincere but fragmented attempts to address far-reaching problems, undoubtedly largely because very powerful interests are not relinquishing their privileged status without a fight. The tremendous defensive political response of large landowners to the agitation of the National Land for People for irrigation rights illustrates this.

National groups such as Rural America as well as the alliance of unions and consumer and environmental groups that have formed COIN (Consumers Opposed to Inflation in the Necessities) have shown leadership in tackling these broad issues.

A more popular angle for dealing with the issue of the structure of the food industry has been involvement in community projects. In a small way, participating in a food co-op or selling at a farmers market helps. As one Hartford Farmers Market shopper asserts, "I come here to buy because I want to support the idea of a farmers market here. My husband and I are interested in food issues. We have our own community garden, and we eat a lot of fruits and vegetables" (Giuca 1979). New Wave food co-ops in particular are havens for these broad, more political concerns.

However, political objectives motivate only part of the movement. Leaders, who inherently must transcend narrow interests, are often more interested than the general membership in larger political/economic issues. Participants are drawn to projects for concrete purposes or issues; leaders, on the other hand, tend to address the relationship of issues to one another and operate from a more comprehensive critique. Leader-oriented action manuals connect the immediate task to larger issues. For example, the Boston Urban Gardeners manual does not just address food production in the city. "For what city people cannot produce themselves, our local farmers could be our best allies for obtaining fresher and more reasonably priced foods. We all benefit from strengthening our farm economy and saving more of our state (and regional) farmland" (Boston Urban Gardeners 1978).

An organization involved in assisting in the establishment of farmers markets in the South, the Agricultural Marketing Project, uses more potent rhetoric (Agricultural Marketing Project 1977):

Rural development has become a primary goal for both public and private institutions in the past several years. . . . If development means exploitation of labor, an end to small farm operators, and resource spoilage without an equitable return to the communities, then rural development will be an empty promise. . . . AMP is empowering the poor and powerless by building viable economic alternatives and constructing lasting socio-political coalitions. The key to building such alternatives is working with community leadership, whether it consists of small farmers or urban consumers, to assist them in obtaining the skills they need to deal with the governing political and economic structures.

How sympathetic community gardeners are to the plight of Massachusetts farmers or farmers marketers to the politics of rural development represent the continuing tension between the more practical and ideological aspects of the movement.

SOME CHARACTERISTICS OF FOOD PROJECTS

Born of imposing conditions in the food production, processing, and marketing industries, farmer and consumer organizing has struggled to build institutions independent of the dominant food economy. This community empowerment has utilized a unique blend of assets. Before analyzing this strategy, several caveats must be appreciated.

The character of local organizing is elusive. Much local food organizing concentrates on the action agenda to the exclusion of self-analysis of performance. Pausing for an analytical snapshot seems like a luxury.

Local organizing also tends to be both transient and fragmented, a reaction to a particular issue in a particular setting. Although all community gardens have common elements, differences in climate, topography, political environment, ethnic participation, and resources may dictate widely varying organizing strategies. It is difficult to compare projects that are disparate in so many important aspects.

A result of all these factors is a lack of reliable data. Few rigorous studies of project motivation, organization, operation, benefits, shortcomings, and accomplishments have been conducted. Perhaps most important, a communicable sense of what these projects are and what can be done to facilitate them is often lacking. Given all these obstacles to a thorough assessment, the following examination of characteristics must be considered a tentative analysis.

A Strategy for Independence

The strategy for attacking the food crisis has several outstanding dimension. First, much of the organizing joins consumer and producer issues instead of treating them in isolation. Consumer food projects often acknowledge the plight of producers and sometimes translate rhetoric into action. Several New England food co-ops, for instance, give preference to local producers who face marketing difficulties. Farmers, on the other hand, promote direct farmer-to-consumer marketing with consumers' benefits in mind. This recognition of complementary interests, though still very limited in scope, portends the breaking down of the traditional hostility between producer and consumer camps.

An underlying theme of this entente is the essential harmony of consumer and farmer interests. The fact is that middlemen functions consume 60% of the food dollar, a margin that, in recent years, has consistently eaten up food price rises. This serves neither farmers nor consumers who are having their "buttons pushed" by giant middlemen. Moreover, farmer-oriented policies, which slow the trend toward reducing farm numbers and sustaining rural livelihood, entail negligible food price impacts. In the words of the Congressional Budget Office, "The highly publicized conflict between farmers and consumers—higher commodity prices versus lower retail food prices—may not be a primary consideration in decisions concerning the future structure of agriculture" (Congressional Budget Office 1978).

A second thrust is diversity of the projects and broad popular involvement. Prior to the 1960s and 1970s activism that mobilized all sectors of society, attempts to remedy food problems tended to focus either on food for the needy in urban areas or on farmer organizing in rural areas. Revealing the concerns of a broad spectrum of socioeconomic classes, this new generation of organizing has attacked food problems from numerous perspectives: a slowing of concentration of production in few farms, alternative food distribution networks such as food co-ops, and "natural foods." Of course, the stated purposes of the various projects are not necessarily consistent with one another—a co-op's "cheap food" policy apparently contradicts an income-maximizing opportunity of a farmers market. The objectives of participants are perhaps even more diverse. Yet this multifaceted concern could be the grounds for some political consensus about a reorientation of the food system toward basic food grower and food eater needs, rather than big business priorities.

Another distinctive strategic characteristic is the strong local focus of the efforts. Although the impacts and sources of the "food crisis" can be defined in far-reaching terms, the response has frequently been local. This may be attributed to the immediate impact of changes in the way food is produced and distributed. A housewife does not have to be fully aware of the monopolistic character of the food industry to seek relief from soaring food prices. Many Americans also appear to feel that there is little they can do to remedy the fundamental causes of inflation and other society-wide problems. Better to take care of the symptoms close to home. This more skeptical belief is complemented by the growing possibility of effective local action around concrete issues: the politics of everyday life.

The local focus is not necessarily parochial, precluding the participation of outside organizations. A common strategy for launching local projects is through multi-community or statewide organizations that can provide technical assistance and funding, share experiences, and help work out the philosophical underpinnings. Food co-op federations, for example, help launch or strengthen projects of member co-ops.

As described earlier, not all recent food activities have taken the local approach. Many statewide, regional, and national organizations have emerged that do not have strong local ties and are essentially concerned with the same kinds of issues as the local efforts. These tend to be more politically oriented groups that attack problems through legislation, advocacy, and public education.

The strategic objectives of recent food organizing are also distinctive. In the past, food relief was provided through church or local government welfare channels. The more recent approach emphasizes self-help. It seeks to build organizations that can provide better services in a self-reliant manner, without continual subsidization. People grow their own food instead of relying on charity. Participants are the policymakers of these self-help efforts, rather than conduits for implementing priorities identified from above.

Self-help is motivated by a twofold distrust, first, of the commitment of responsible organizations to perform the needed tasks and, second, of the ability of the profit-driven food system to meet people's needs. Thus, food crisis organizing is change-oriented. It seeks to establish alternative institutions and approaches to problems. Political offspring of action projects often deal with adverse interests head on.

A frequent shortcoming of the self-help strategy is the capability of those most in need, low-income families, to use it. The building of durable organizations requires a longer-term perspective that those concerned about the source of the next meal do not have the privilege to enjoy. Then, too, agencies charged with low-income assistance are compelled by political pressure to provide short-term support that often does not allow these social groups to arise in concerted challenge to their oppressive conditions.

These strategic thrusts—producer-consumer linkages, diverse approaches, local orientation, and self-help—represent an attempt to attack the food system at a vulnerable juncture—the loss of community autonomy and accountability in food production and distribution. By seeking to build durable, multipurpose local institutions that respond to both farmers and consumer interests, the strategy builds power, the ability to influence basic relationships.

The Means to Build Power

Power is a function of resources and the ability to influence the use of them. Food crisis organizing has tended to utilize power as a means to establish independent institutions. Unique approaches to generating resources and establishing control have unfolded. Given the vulnerability and weakness of these emerging bases of power, outside assistance has been required.

The use of internally generated resources has been emphasized. Financial, technical, and human resources are the basic fuel of organizing. Who provides resources is critical to project participation and effectiveness. Healthy projects tend to have freedom to pursue their own objectives, but limited availability and external control of resources can compromise or even undermine this autonomy.

For example, financial institutions have historically not looked favorably on food cooperatives. Cooperative business tends to be perceived as too much of an aberration for the more conservative lending institutions. When co-ops do manage to secure capital from a conventional bank, they often find that enterprise decision-making is partly relinquished to the noncooperatively oriented banks. For instance, banks do not appreciate co-op education, such as Arcata's program, as a marketing tool (Committee on Banking, Currency and Housing 1976). It is frowned upon as a business expense. This kind of problem has been one factor leading to the recent federal government creation of the National Consumer Cooperative Bank (Committee on Banking, Currency and Housing, 1976).

Most food projects rely heavily on the resources of participants. Food co-ops typically require members to work, and farmers market growers put up funds to promote the market. Certainly, sizeable ventures cannot be expected to generate all their own capital or labor. But experience has shown that a healthy portion of members' equity capital—money that members loan to the business as a condition of membership—can secure greater freedom to allow the venture to pursue its own course. Swedish consumer cooperatives, which stress the accumulation of equity capital, have effectively challenged concentrated private economic power by building competing enterprises (Schaaf 1977). Farmer cooperatives, some of which are prominent firms nationally, also have recognized the importance of equity investments in storage, processing, and transport equipment.

Utilizing internally generated resources has allowed food projects to give participants a role. To feel a part of a project, individuals need to feel they are contributing something of value. This does not have to be capital as in the Swedish case; it may be a share of routine work or a role in decision-making and administration.

An opportunity to contribute has not usually meant a flood of resources. Local food projects chronically suffer from insufficient resources; soil is thin in community gardens; food banks find their shelves depleted long before new stocks arrive. In many cases they operate outside the mainstream and have far-reaching dreams. Dependency on largess is the only way to survive. Survivors of the "grants economy" report that this is a precarious, draining way to exist and certainly not a strategy for building durable institutions. The plight of projects bucking the present economic order demonstrates that they can never expect to have enough.

Though insufficient resources often mean that important tasks are left undone, they also may mean that meager resources are effectively utilized. When you have little, you make sure that it goes as far as possible. But too much too soon does not work either. Food projects can "finally receive funding" and then slip into sated passivity or bewilderment: budget discipline is relaxed, volunteers' contributions contract, or hired management innocently usurps members' decision-making.

The importance of internally generated resources for community food ventures does not automatically relegate food projects that are more richly endowed or receive outside resources to an inferior status. Where there is need, an abundance of resources can be effectively utilized without jeopardizing participation or effectiveness. Boston Urban Gardeners, one of the more sophisticated and successful urban gardening development groups in the country, was launched with a huge infusion of outside resources (Boston Urban Gardeners 1978):

One of the first activities of this group was "Earthmoving Week" in May of 1977, when 500 cubic yards of topsoil, donated by the Metropolitan District Commission (MDC), were delivered to gardens. . . . BUG members managed to involve the U.S. Army, the National Guard, the MDC, the Turnpike Authority, the Department of Public Works, Massport, and several outlying towns and private contractors to donate trucks, labor and time to transport topsoil and compost. The deliveries of soil have been estimated to total over $25,000 worth of contributions.

In the nation's poorer communities, outside resources are essential for any projects. What is important is whether these resources complement or smother a project's resources and undermine local capacity. Outside resources can only extend, rather than replace, participant resources.

Food crisis organizing often relies on local initiative to establish a foundation of resources and commitment. The inspiration for food organizing tends to be more a function of community than of state or federal initiative. Without town, neighborhood, city, or area initiative and the resources that come with it, projects are launched without community acceptance. Although a community can grow to accept a project that is adapted to its needs and practices, local initiative has proven to be more durable.

Experiences in cooperative development demonstrate the pitfalls of neglecting this lesson. For example, in early 1900s the Right Relationship League, a quasipolitical organization centered in the northern Midwest, attempted to establish a cooperative network by travelling from community to community to buy out stores and hire management. However, cooperative business is more than dollars and sense; local commitment was never secured through education and organization. The movement failed (Schaaf 1977).

The "community" that initiates activity differs from one local food project to another. Boston Urban Gardeners is a citywide organization that has inspired and assists local projects. Sometimes a local government has played an initiatory role. Occasionally, state or national organizations or government have successfully started local projects if local initiative has been catalyzed and other factors such as local resources have been integrated in a productive fashion. The California Department of Food and Agriculture, for instance, has fostered rapid expansion of farmers markets in a state whose agriculture is dominated by export commodities.

Outside agencies can stimulate community food projects by communicating experiences in other localities and by providing organizational assistance and seed money.

Though critical to amassing power, internally generated resources and local initiative are catalyzed by participant control of the project. Whether it is a food project or other community effort, people do not feel comfortable committing their money, time, or energy unless they expect an opportunity to influence how those inputs will be utilized.

Consider the case of an old farmers market. For decades it was controlled and administered by the city government. Fees were collected but not used to benefit either the sellers or buyers at the market. The market was shifted to a different location every few years to accommodate priority concerns of the city, usually developers' interests. Farmer participation suffered and the once sought-after stall became a pork barrel for city fathers. The ailing venture lost all hope of revival with the failure of a petition urging the city to enforce a long-neglected ordinance that would allow only locally grown produce at the market. The farmers left the market to the hucksters when this last-ditch effort to prevent unfair competition was frustrated. No participant could rationalize further selling below cost.

The distinction between influence and control is important. Control implies dominance whereas influence implies a sharing of control with some outside party. In order for community ownership to emerge, it does not appear necessary for total control of the project to exist, particularly in the case of government-supported programs. The principal function of such programs is to provide funding and, to a lesser extent, professional resources. As previously mentioned, poorer communities can seldom develop projects without such infusion of resources. The "strings" attached to government programs are often a subject of complaint, but, if subject to negotiation or accepted before a project is initiated, these constraints have not uniformly undermined a healthy measure of community control. For instance, an urban garden must typically rely on the local government to supply the land, and strings are usually attached. Restrictions regarding who may garden there or how long the lot is available are sometimes imposed.

The Community Food and Nutrition Program of the Community Services Administration (CSA) was a large funder of local food projects, providing $22 million in 1978. Funds were provided for a variety of projects, accompanied by CSA administrative and program guidelines. Regardless of these constraints, the funds were, in many instances, used to complement local resources to launch successfully food co-ops, community gardens, small farmers' projects, and a myriad of other variations. Sometimes funding conditions impose discipline on projects, which contributes to success.

But government programs do not necessarily act to build local capacity. Consider food stamps, for example. Eligible families are given a subsidy of coupons usable as money in purchasing food at certified food outlets. Decisions about income guidelines, allotment levels, and so on are made nationally. Apart from outreach services, the only local responsibility is to administer the distribution of the coupons, with guidelines that can seriously affect the amount of coupons distributed. This program requires little local initiative or internally generated resources. It is not subject to community control, beyond manipulation of eligibility regulations. It is not a food project that embodies new attitudes or relationships in the food system. This does not mean, however, that it does not serve real needs, but only that it is not an indicator or tool of change.

In the end, the balance between influence and control cannot be rigidly defined. It is a dialectic in which the influence that one community needs to experience ownership may be different from another community's or even different from its own at another point in time. But without that sense of ownership, lackluster and dependent efforts appear to result.

The notions of local initiative, internal resources, and participant control are organically interwoven. Initiative begets resources that, in turn, beget member control, which is necessary for further initiative. Together, these strategy elements compose a base of power beholden to no one but participants. Their interrelationships are delicate, but outside intervention is possible if the objective of empowerment is mindfully addressed.

DIRECTIONS FOR RESEARCH AND DEVELOPMENT

The scope of farmer and consumer food projects is undeniably modest relative to the volume of foodstuffs moved through conventional channels. Research and development must focus the unique qualities of the movement while advancing it as a means of handling food. The questions of how we can help people help themselves, what are viable models, and how opportunities can be created and attacked need to be taken up by researchers.

The fundamental challenge is recognizing the nature of the task. Ignoring contrary evidence, apologists for the dominant food industry explain that this structure is necessary to achieve efficiency and prosperity. But data do not make policy; people do. If food project participants desire to broaden the impacts of their efforts, a recognition of who has power and how it can be combatted is absolutely essential. This recognition is political. Vested big business interests will continue to steer the food system along their path unless confronted.

Two kinds of actions are needed. First, the institutions already in place—the food co-ops, the farmers markets, the community gardens, and so on—need to be advanced to new levels of service. For example, farmers markets must graduate to producer wholesaling cooperatives capable of handling more food. At the same time, the pool of resources must be expanded. Food co-ops, producer co-ops, and even advocacy groups must gather equity that can be used to launch other projects.

Public resources can complement local resources, if sensitively applied. The government sponsorship of the farmer-owned Production Credit Association, which historically has provided sorely needed credit and services, is an example of such creative programming. Another critical capital institution, the National Consumer Cooperative Bank, is in place. Cooperators must be vigilant in guiding its performance.

Practical acknowledgment of the nature of the task is required. Development schemes must be carefully planned. Businesses must be sound, yet the qualities that distinguish food projects must be maximized. Collaboration between projects, such as growers and food co-ops, must be pursued. Member self-interest must be built upon as a source of verve and direction.

Research can be supportive of building alternative organizations. Manuals tell how to organize various food projects but do not specify the "secrets of success" in concrete terms. For instance, what is the optimum arrangement for integrating member labor in a storefront co-op that relies primarily on hired employees? How can community garden production be maximized? There are untold other questions.

Background research for planning is critical. The basis for clearheaded strategizing is often absent. It is not altogether clear what growth direction an energetic food co-op might pursue, for instance. What are the weak points in the food distribution system that co-ops can most readily penetrate? The appearance of natural foods on supermarket shelves augurs the coming of sophisticated competition for that market niche. Another area for practical research involves the diversification of local agriculture.

The second kind of action is overtly political. While organization-building is fundamental, it alone does not adequately speak to the challenge facing food crisis organizing. It is imperative that participants realize the larger purpose of their efforts. A farmers market is not just a quaint shopping place, nor is a community garden merely a lovely way to enjoy a Saturday afternoon.

Local projects need to recognize the mutual goals shared by other sectors of the movement. A common motivational thread knits many food projects together. Farmers who cannot see the way to collaborating with consumers against middlemen who dominate the food economy display a myopic vision that will ultimately do little to lift them out of their marginal status. The allies are too few and the adversary too strong to alienate them glibly. The stage has been set for coalescing urban–rural linkages and building regional food systems through more self-reliance.

As more and more people seek such remedies, conventional systems will be increasingly called into question. Those who presently control the food production and distribution systems will not idly watch their dominant position eroded. A graphic example is the struggle that the Senate Select Committee on Nutrition and Human Needs faced when they made preliminary announcement of their investigation results: Americans should eat less meat. The livestock industries made sure that this recommendation, despite its scientific validity, never achieved official status.

Strength will undoubtedly be required to withstand big business challenges and to leverage needed support. The vulnerability for cooptation is great when resources are scarce and the broader picture is murky. Already a consortium of major corporations is rapidly entering into the small farm development theater by selling helpful services. Hard questions regarding benefit distribution, control, and obviating public services need to be asked.

Perhaps the greatest political challenge will be leveraging the government whose resources are essential for building and protecting viable alternative organizations. A reallocation of services would help in addition to new initiatives. The federal Farmer-to-Consumer Direct Marketing Act was one step in the right direction. Other public assistance is long overdue: an antimonopoly legal attack on food processors and retailers, for example. The sophisticated research capabilities of the land grant system and the USDA must be mobilized.

The target of these political efforts is not necessarily national. Some federal action cannot be dispensed with, but state and local jurisdictions are an expanding opportunity for obtaining resources and favorable legislation.

While the challenge is formidable, some cornerstones have been laid: concrete projects, committed participants, a growing assortment of supportive organizations, and some illustrious political gains. There is still more to tap. America's spirit of cooperation and self-help lies largely undisturbed. The roots descend to the founding era of the nation, when these attitudes were necessary for survival. This spirit needs to be synthesized into a new vision as growing concentration in the economy challenges our democratic traditions.

The impact of food projects is unquestionably small. But their unique strategy, abetted by a political vision and benevolent public policy, can shape the direction of the food system. Much work needs to be done.

REFERENCES

AGRICULTURAL MARKETING PROJECT.   1977.   Statement of Purpose. Nashville, Tennessee.

ARCATA COOPERATIVE INC.   Undated.   Arcata's Community Store.   Arcata Cooperative, Inc., Arcata, California.

BELDEN, J., EDWARDS, G., GUYER, C., and WEB, L.   1979.   New Directions in Farm, Land and Food Policies: Conference on Alternative State and Local Policies.   Washington, D.C.

BERGLAND, B.   1979A.   It's Time to Rethink Our Farm Policy.   Blair and Ketchum's Country Journal 6,(11).   Brattleboro, Vermont.

BERGLAND, B.   1979B.   The Structure of American Agriculture.   Issue Briefing Paper No. 16.   U.S. Department of Agriculture, Washington, D.C.

BOSTON URBAN GARDENERS.   1978.   A City Gardeners Guide.   Boston, Massachusetts.

COMMITTEE ON BANKING, CURRENCY AND HOUSING, 1976. U.S. House of Representatives, Hearings before the Subcommittee on Financial Institutions Supervision, Regulation and Insurance, Ninety-Fourth Congress, Second Session, H.R. 14512. U.S. Government Printing Office, Washington, D.C.

COMMITTEE ON ECONOMIC DEVELOPMENT. 1962. An Adoptive Program for Agriculture. New York.

CONGRESSIONAL BUDGET OFFICE. 1978. Public Policy and the Changing Structure of American Agriculture. Government Printing Office. Washington, D.C.

CONSUMERS OPPOSED TO INFLATION IN THE NECESSITIES (COIN). 1979. There are Alternatives: A Program for Controlling Inflation in the Necessities of Life. COIN, Washington, D.C.

DIEHL, A. 1978. Tailgate markets take a front seat. Philadelphia Daily News. July 26. Philadelphia, Pennsylvania.

GARDENS FOR ALL. 1978. Community Gardens—1978. Gardens for All News 1(3). Burlington, Vermont.

GARDENS FOR ALL. 1979A. Community Gardening—1978: Complete Results of the Gardens for All Survey of Community Garden Coordinators. Burlington, Vermont.

GARDENS FOR ALL. 1979B. The Statley Gardens. Gardens for All News. 2(3). Burlington, Vermont.

GIUCA, L. 1979. Farmers Bring Native Produce to City Market. Hartford Courant. August 1. Hartford, Connecticut.

HANSSENS, C. 1979. Direct Marketing in Philadelphia: The Tailgate Market Project. Nutritional Development Services, Archdiocese of Philadelphia. Philadelphia, Pennsylvania.

HIGHTOWER, J. and DeMARCO, S. 1978. Corporate Chefs Cook Consumer's Goose. National Catholic Reporter. November. Kansas City, Missouri.

JONES. 1978. Conference on Nutrition and the American Food System. National Food Review. NFR-4, U.S. Department of Agriculture, Washington, D.C.

KIECHALL, W. 1978. The food giants struggle to stay in step with consumers. Fortune Magazine. September. New York.

MANCHESTER, A. and BROWN, L. 1977. Do the Poor Pay More? National Food Situation. NFR-1, U.S. Department of Agriculture. Washington, D.C.

NATIONAL ADVISORY COUNCIL ON ECONOMIC OPPORTUNITY. 1979. 11th Annual Report: Inflation and the Poor. Washington, D.C.

RITCHIE, M. 1979. The Loss of Our Family Farms. San Francisco, California.

SCHAAF, M. 1977. Cooperatives at the Crossroads. Exploratory Project for Economic Alternatives. Washington, D.C.

SENATE SELECT COMMITTEE ON NUTRITION AND HUMAN NEEDS. 1977. Dietary Goals for the United States. Government Printing Office, Washington, D.C.

SOMMER, R.   1979.   Farmers' Markets—Myths and Realities.   California Agriculture.   February.   Sacramento, California.

TAYLOR, S.   1979.   Direct Marketing in Hartford.   Connecticut Public Interest Research Group.   Hartford, Connecticut.

UNITED PRESBYTERIAN CHURCH IN THE U.S.A.   1978.   Who Will Farm? Church and Society Program.   United Presbyterian Church.   New York.

USDA.   1972.   Market Structure of the Food Business.   Marketing Research Report No. 971, Economic Research Service.   United States Department of Agriculture.   Washington, D.C.

USDA.   1979.   Annual Report: Farmer-to-Consumer Direct Marketing Program.   Agricultural Marketing Service.   United States Department of Agriculture.   Washington, D.C.

U.S. DEPARTMENT OF ENERGY.   1978.   Energy and Food.   Office of Consumer Affairs.   Department of Energy.   Washington, D.C.

WATKINS, E.   1979.   Why Direct Marketing?   American Vegetable Grower 27(6).   Willoughby, Ohio.

Part IV

Quality and Quality Control

13

Organically Grown Foods

Joseph A. Maga

INTRODUCTION

In any society there are groups of people who, for various reasons, consume diets thought by most to be irrational or strange; usually these individuals are termed food faddists. The United States has had its share of such personalities. It is interesting how these groups are treated by the majority. For example, few would condemn a Jewish family for not eating pork products because that is part of their religious belief but, on the other hand, most meat-eaters think that a family that practices vegetarianism has lost its ability to reason.

Interestingly, the number of people who have been attempting new dietary patterns has been growing, a good indication that they are either dissatisfied with or concerned over their present food consumption patterns. One possible reason for change is that Americans represent an affluent society and can afford to experiment with their eating habits. Perhaps they are overwhelmed by the vast number of food items available to them and find a simpler diet based around a home-prepared-foods psychology much more satisfying. Presently, approximately 7800 different food items are available, with 3000–4000 new, modified, or improved items introduced each year (von Elbe 1972).

Another potential reason for the "revolt" of the American consumer over traditionally processed foods may be the frustration associated with the numerous ways of marketing the quality of foods. A prime example of this concept was cited by von Elbe (1972), whereby Grade A for milk refers only

305

to sanitary quality whereas Grade A for vegetables implies quality attributes such as texture, color, flavor, size uniformity, and absence of defects. In yet other foods, the top grade is called prime, fancy, or even Grade AA. Labeling requirements also present confusion to the consumer: some products covered by standards of identity are not required to have ingredients listed, although some processors list these ingredients anyway.

The progress made in the science of nutrition has also made the public more aware of food nutrients. Unfortunately, this awareness usually occurs through the mass media, which may overemphasize minor conclusions to a point that many people feel guilty about their diet. There is no question that the general dietary pattern in the United States should be modified, in view of the obvious evidence of obesity within the population. Some people are suddenly and dramatically changing their dietary habits to improve the status of their health. One such group is the "organic food consumer," who in 1972 was estimated to number seven million people (von Elbe 1972). Certainly some people have been consuming "organically grown foods" for years, probably because they were in a position to grow or obtain such products at reasonable prices.

The promotion of organically grown foods in the United States is believed to have been started by Jerome I. Rodale, a native of New York City, who was owner of Rodale Press (Jukes 1977). He believed that organic gardening, which emphasizes the use of animal and vegetable waste as fertilizer, produced crops that were superior to conventionally grown foods. Rodale is credited with introducing the term "organically processed food," which eventually became shortened to organic food. Through his popular publications, the organic movement and terminology were routinely accepted by the general public. In addition, terms such as natural foods and health foods also appeared.

Today organic food consumers are calling for agricultural producers to revert to organic methods and for food processors to abstain from adding chemicals to our food supply, because they feel that these chemicals are polluting the environment and/or are a threat to our health. They firmly believe that organically grown food tastes better, is better nutritionally, and is safer to their health than conventionally grown, processed, and marketed foods. Because of these claims, they are willing to pay a premium for such foods. There are no legal definitions pertaining to these products, except for health conditions associated with the marketing of such items that are common to all foods. A believer in organic foods may not be completely assured that he is indeed purchasing organically grown food.

In light of the practical and emotional confusion that exists relative to the claims and counterclaims associated with organically grown food, this chapter shall attempt to review pertinent scientific literature to guide the reader in making a rational decision as to both the overall and the individual merits of such claims.

DEFINITIONS

One topic that should be resolved is to define, from both a scientist's and a layman's standpoint, a number of terms that have been used interchangeably by many people. This should serve both to verify that the author and reader are writing and reading of the same things and to point out some of the potential legal problems if such terminology ever becomes part of the law.

A scientist would normally define the word organic as applying to the chemistry of substances that contain carbon in their structure or to compounds that can be synthesized by living things, namely plants and animals. Since we normally consume plants and animals as a food source, we can state that all food is organic. However, because of the popularization of the term organic food, some people now define organic as "food that is grown without pesticides; grown without artificial fertilizers; grown in soil whose mineral content is increased with applications of natural mineral fertilizers; has not been treated with preservatives, hormones, antibiotics, etc." The definition was supplied by R. Rodale, son of J.I. Rodale, during public hearings in New York City on organic foods. It has also appeared in print (Anon. 1972). Since all food is organic, whether grown by conventional or by organic farming techniques, it is technically more correct to say "organically grown foods" when referring to foods produced by organic farming methods.

"Natural foods" is another interesting term. By the simplest definition, health foods are made by nature. In practice, a natural food is defined as food made exclusively from ingredients that are readily recognized as foods.

Interestingly, the terms organic food and natural food should not be used interchangeably. A prime example is the case of a major conventional food processor who has marketed a natural cereal (made from ingredients that can be identified as food) yet in its package advertising claimed that it is not organic (the natural ingredients were not organically grown). One would think that this marketing approach borders on deception, unless one reads the fine print. This approach opens the door for a whole series of pseudo-natural foods, which eventually may be disowned by both proponents and opponents of organically grown food. Some traditional food processors do not feel that they can market organically grown foods under their own label, for fear of admitting that the claims made by opponents of conventional foods are true. Yet recently, numerous traditional food processors have introduced natural and/or organic lines to complement and to compete with their traditional lines.

Still another category is "health foods," which can be defined as foods that suggest both physiologic and psychologic health. However, since all edible foods can be instrumental to health when properly used in a balanced diet, whether grown by conventional or by organic methods, it has been proposed that one cannot legally define a health food (Stare *et al.* 1972). From a practical standpoint, health foods usually connote diet supplements such as wheat germ lecithin, low-salt and low-sugar foods, yeast, alfalfa, rice, bran, and yogurt. A major claim made for health foods is that they can maximize one's resistance to stress, infection, and disease, which from a controlled scientific standpoint would be extremely difficult to prove. From a marketing standpoint it should be noted that health foods are natural, but not necessarily organic.

These definitions, for the most part, appear to be logical and straightforward. However, they become almost useless when considered from a legal standpoint. In any event, attempts have been made to pass legislation defining the terminology.

Because California is the leader in both the production and the consumption of organically grown foods, it is logical that attempts were first made there in 1972 to have such items defined by law.

A proposal to define terms for labeling was introduced and assigned to the California Assembly, as Bill Number 450. It had an impressive list of supporters, including the State of California Department of Consumer Affairs, the California State Department of Agriculture, and the Food and Drug Bureau of the Department of Public Health of California, as well as a major producer of organic rice. Undoubtedly, organic producers and marketers would have had much to gain if such a bill were passed because, if their products were officially recognized by law, it would add merit to claims that their products were better and safer than traditionally grown products. However, the bill was dropped even before being voted upon.

At the same time, a bill introduced into the California Senate also attempted to define terms and to establish the legal groundwork for organic farming and marketing. The bill would have required the Secretary of Agriculture to inspect each organic farm no fewer than two times a year, for each crop grown that year, and to measure the minimal humus and mineral content of the soil where the crops were grown. If the bill had passed, a major workload of the State Department of Agriculture would have been to collect data from organic farms.

In 1973 the Oregon Department of Agriculture issued a proposed Standard of Identity and Requirement for Organic Foods.

The burden of proof rested with both the producer and the marketer of organically grown foods if their claims were challenged. Undoubtedly, the extra paperwork and laboratory analyses required if such system were engaged would add significantly to the cost of such items. Any potential legal claims, especially in the area of pesticide residue, would be virtually impossible to resolve unless in a case of obvious fraud because of the widespread appearance of pesticides in the general environment. The practical problems with enacting any such proposed legislation can perhaps best be appreciated by the fact that to date no legal definitions exist.

THE PROBABILITY OF ORGANICALLY GROWN FOOD

As many opponents of organically grown food can be accused of opposing something that they do not understand, an attempt will be made in this section to explain in both a practical and a theoretical way what organic farming entails. Where appropriate, the methodology will be compared with conventional methods and the advantages and disadvantages of each discussed. At this point, it would also perhaps be useful to restate the general philosophy of organic farming, which has usually been taken to mean the production and marketing of food crops without the use of manufactured chemicals, either as plant nutrients or as pesticides. Insect pests are usually controlled by biological or physical means. If pesticides are employed, they are usually organic compounds produced by living organisms. With organic farming, it is assumed that mineralization of decaying organic matter and the resulting solvent effect on naturally occurring soil minerals are the only sources of mineral salts or ions that plants can absorb from the soil in the building of organic plant substances. If soils are deficient in certain minerals needed for plant growth, these can be supplied from various natural sources, which include ground limestone, oyster shells, raw phosphate rock, or wood ashes. The keys to successful organic farming have been reported to be animal manures, composts, and crop rotation. A summary of the theoretical advantages and disadvantages of such a system (Schoonover 1972) is shown here:

Advantages:

- The fertilizers used are relatively safe from the standpoint that the potential for burning plants with strong chemical fertilizers usually does not occur with organic fertilizers.
- No concern is shown for residual pesticides due to inaccurate chemical measurement and/or distribution.
- Organic fertilizers help to improve soil structure.
- It makes use of wastes and residues.
  Disadvantages:
- Continuous long-term production of food crops, except for perhaps legumes, cannot be maintained by recycling only the organic residues produced on the same plot.
- Organic fertilizers, to be completely effective, have to be fully worked into the soil.
- Decay of organic matter is gradual; thus, nutrients can be released at times or at rates not optimum for plant growth.
- More attention and labor, and thus cost, are required of the organic method as compared to the conventional method.
- Certain manures and composts may not be good sources of micronutrients.
- Manure can pollute ground water.

• Organic farming is not as efficient as conventional farming, especially on marginal soils.

Native soils throughout the world can be classified into thousands of different kinds from a scientific viewpoint. They can differ from each other in such attributes as color, depth, particle size, mineral composition, and level of organic matter. Thus, no one fertilizer, whether organic or inorganic, can be optimum for all soils. An important consideration is the organic matter, or humus, which usually arises from the decomposition of vegetable and animal matter. It has been clearly demonstrated that organic fertilizers can improve the physical condition of soil, permeability of water, and aeration, thus allowing an increased oxygen supply to the roots as well as increasing the organic matter of soil and improving the ion exchange capacity (Peavy and Greig 1972). In addition, organic matter is very important to soil microorganisms because it makes water, energy, and other essential nutrients available to their population.

A total of 16 chemical elements are believed essential for plant growth (Utzinger et al. 1970). These are carbon, hydrogen, oxygen, nitrogen, phosphorus, potassium, sulfur, calcium, magnesium, iron, zinc, boron, molybdenum, manganese, copper, and chlorine. Aside from proper manipulation of drainage, irrigation, and modification of the physical condition of the soil, man can do little to influence the levels of three of the nutrients, namely, carbon, hydrogen, and oxygen, to plants since these are primarily derived from air and water. Carbon, hydrogen, and oxygen are also the most abundant elements in plants, usually consisting of 94–99.5% of the total plant weight, with the other elements listed comprising, as a group, from 0.5 to 6% of the plant.

Plant nutrients can also be divided as being primary, secondary, and micronutrients. The primary nutrients consist of nitrogen, phosphorus, and potassium, which are required by plants in relatively large amounts and thus usually have to be continuously supplied to the highly cultivated plant in the form of fertilizer, as most soils do not normally contain sufficient amounts of these nutrients to sustain continual cultivation. The secondary nutrients are calcium, magnesium, and sulfur and are usually required at approximately the same level as phosphorus. However, in soils with optimum acidity for plant growth, these secondary nutrients seldom limit plant growth. The remaining required elements are called micronutrients because they are usually required by most plants in only small amounts.

Soil pH has a significant influence on the availability of these nutrients to the plant. Most plants grow best in soils with a pH range of 6.0–6.8. However, in more acidic soils, nitrogen, phosphorus, potassium, sulfur, calcium, magnesium, and molybdenum are made less available to the plant, whereas if the soil pH is above 7.0, the elements iron, manganese, boron, copper, and zinc are less available. In general, soils are acidic; therefore, the process of liming, the addition of calcium or magnesium carbonate, is practiced. Liming also supplies calcium and/or magnesium, as well as reducing the levels of aluminum, manganese, and iron, which are usually associated with acidic soils. In addition, liming tends to favor microbial activity, which is essential to the breakdown of organic matter, and to accelerate the release of nutrients from organic matter, as well as to improve soil structure.

Interestingly, oxygen is the only element that can be used directly by plants, with all other elements having to be converted to ionic form before they are absorbed and metabolized by plants. Thus, it does not matter if these ions originated from the decomposition of organic fertilizers or from the dissolving of inorganic fertilizers.

Because organic matter has to be broken down before its nutrients are released, organic fertilizers work more slowly than inorganic ones. Their use requires coordination so that the proper amounts of nutrients are readily available to the plant when required. Also, application of compost that is not properly decomposed can result in additional essential nutrients being tied up and thus not made available to the plant. Another potential problem with the breakdown of organic fertilizers is the fact that their rate of decomposition is governed by soil temperature. In the spring, when soil temperatures are normally cool, few nutrients may be released, thereby potentially resulting in stunted plant growth. In contrast, inorganic fertilizers make their nutrients available as soon as they are applied, as the soil usually contains sufficient moisture to dissolve them.

On a per unit weight of nutrient, inorganic fertilizers are less expensive than organic fertilizers. It must be remembered that even though some organic fertilizer materials can be obtained for little or no actual cost, there are indirect cost factors, such as transportation, time, and labor. Because of their usual low nutrient content per unit weight, a larger amount of organic fertilizer material is usually required as compared to the equivalent amount of nutrients derived from inorganic fertilizer sources. It has also been argued that inorganic fertilizers can increase soil organic matter more effectively than organic fertilizers because they generally increase plant growth more than organic fertilizers. From an efficiency standpoint, the use of inorganic and organic fertilizers in combination has been shown to be more effective than either method used individually.

Man, in his imaginative way, has thought to utilize various materials as sources of organic fertilizers; however, some have found little practical application because they may be naturally limiting in certain nutrients. Probably the most effective organic fertilizer is crops themselves, or their residue. There are several broad categories of these types of organic fertilizers. One is usually called green manure, which represents crops that are directly plowed back into the soil in their entirety. They have the merits of applying organic matter, improving soil conditions, and providing nutrients for succeeding crops. However, their major disadvantage is the fact that the soil in which they are grown cannot be used to produce marketable crops while the green manure is being grown; thus, continuous production of food usually cannot be achieved using this technique. A compromise is to turn nonmarketable crop residues directly into the soil. However, if this is practiced, additional organic fertilizer will have to be applied, as most of the nutrients were removed in the marketable portion of the crop. This step is usually accomplished by composting, which will be discussed in detail later.

Another major source of organic fertilizer is various animal manures; they can vary in composition as can be seen in Table 13.1. Their primary advantage is the fact that, in the fresh state, their high moisture content and microflora encourage further biological degradation, making their nutrients readily available. However, application of fresh, raw manure to crops near harvest can result in fecal bacteria contamination of the crop, which is, according to general food laws, a health violation. Fresh manures can also significantly contaminate surface water sources. The alternative of dry manure can also present problems, as many nutrients may have already

TABLE 13.1.   PRIMARY NUTRIENT COMPOSITION OF VARIOUS ORGANIC FERTILIZERS

	Primary nutrient		
	Nitrogen (%)	Phosphorus (%)	Potassium (%)
Bulky organic materials:			
Alfalfa hay	2.50	0.50	2.10
Peat and muck	2.30	0.40	0.75
Peanut hulls	1.50	0.12	0.78
Alfalfa straw	1.50	0.30	1.50
Winery pomaces	1.50	1.50	0.80
Bean straw	1.20	0.25	1.25
Olive pomaces	1.20	0.80	0.50
Sheep manure (fresh)	1.05	0.40	1.00
Timothy hay	1.02	0.20	1.50
Poultry hay (fresh)	1.00	0.85	0.45
Cotton bolls	1.00	0.15	4.00
Horse manure (fresh)	0.65	0.25	0.50
Seaweed (kelp)	0.60	0.09	1.30
Grain straw	0.60	0.20	1.10
Cattle manure (fresh)	0.55	0.15	0.45
Hog manure (fresh)	0.50	0.35	0.45
Sawdust and wood shavings	0.20	0.10	0.20
Organic concentrates:			
Dried blood	13.0	1.5	0.8
Hoof and horn meal	12.0	2.0	0.0
Fish meal	10.0	6.0	0.0
Bat guano	10.0	4.5	2.0
Animal tankage	9.0	10.0	1.5
Wool wastes	7.5	0.0	0.0
Soybean meal	7.0	1.2	1.5
Caster pomace	6.0	1.9	0.5
Cottonseed meal	6.0	2.5	1.5
Fish scrap	5.0	3.0	0.0
Bone meal	4.0	23.0	0.0
Sewage sludge	3.0	2.5	0.4
Cocoa shell meal	2.5	1.5	2.5
Garbage tankage	2.5	1.5	1.5
Bone charcoal	1.5	32.0	0.0
Tobacco dust and stems	1.5	0.5	5.0
Steamed bone meal	0.8	30.0	0.0
Wood ashes	0.0	2.0	6.0

From Utzinger *et al.* (1970).

leached during drying. Another interesting point to be made from Table 13.1 is the fact that the nutrient levels of most organic fertilizers are not high. Large amounts may need to be applied if the crops to be grown are to achieve maximum yield. The only exception to this last statement is the growth of legume crops such as beans, peas, and soybeans, as these crops are capable of obtaining a major portion of their nitrogen requirement from the atmosphere in conjunction with certain soil bacteria by a process called fixation. Two organic fertilizers listed in Table 13.1, bone charcoal and wood ashes, are primarily inorganic because they are burned before use, but they are derived from organic sources.

In contrast to organic fertilizers, most common inorganic fertilizers, as seen in Table 13.2, can give good nutrient yields, especially if used in combinations. It is also interesting to note that some of the inorganic fertilizers listed in Table 13.2, like rock phosphate, green sand, and basic slag, even though truly inorganic, are commonly used by organic farmers. On the other hand, urea, a natural organic compound, is commonly produced from inorganic chemicals.

Another technique commonly used by organic farmers is the application of mulch. Mulching is considered to be an effective way of conserving soil moisture and prevent weed growth. Common organic mulches used include straw, hay, leaves, grass clippings, and sawdust. However, some types of sawdust, cedar, may be toxic to certain plants, while others, alder, can encourage rot on woody plants. Sawdust is also generally slow to break down and may require the application of additional nitrogen, which is used as an energy source for soil microorganisms. If this is not done, the microorganisms will utilize nitrogen that should be used for plant growth, resulting in stunted and yellowed plant growth.

TABLE 13.2. PRIMARY NUTRIENT COMPOSITION OF VARIOUS INORGANIC FERTILIZERS

Fertilizer	Primary nutrient		
	Nitrogen (%)	Phosphorus (%)	Potassium (%)
Ammonium nitrate	33.5	0	0
Ammonium sulfate	21	0	0
Calcium nitrate	16	0	0
Sodium nitrate	16	0	0
Urea	45	0	0
Ammonium phosphate	11	48	0
Diammonium phosphate	18	46	0
Basic slag	0	8	0
Rock phosphate	0	5	0
20% superphosphate	0	20	0
Concentrated superphosphate	0	45	0
Superphosphoric acid	0	76	0
Green sand (Glauconite)	0	1	6
Muriate of potash	0	0	60
Potassium sulfate	0	0	50
Potassium nitrate	13	0	44

From Utzinger et al. (1970).

Plastic film has also been utilized as an effective mulching agent. Aside from controlling weeds and conserving soil moisture, it also increases soil temperature, making breakdown of organic matter more rapid, and results in cleaner products with fewer rot problems. However, its major disadvantages are initial cost and the fact that it has to be removed at the end of the growing season and cannot be recycled in an organic fashion.

The organic farming advocate has cited numerous reasons that mulching is superior to the use of chemical herbicides in the control of weeds. For example, because no one herbicide is effective for every weed in every crop, an extensive inventory of such compounds is required. In addition, herbicides must be applied at the proper time and in the proper amount. If not enough is applied, weed control is not effective, and thus, money and material have been wasted. However, if too much is applied, severe crop damage may result with residues in the soil, possibly causing damage to different crops planted on the same plot at subsequent plantings. In addition, overuse is wasteful and expensive. Lastly, some weeds can only effectively be controlled using herbicide rates that may also damage plants. The users of herbicides counter the above claims by stating that, to minimize misuse of herbicides, only experienced applicators should use them.

Composting

As mentioned earlier, the concept of composting is quite important to the organic farming techniques (Poincelot 1975). At this point, some of the history, biochemistry, and methodology associated with this process will be discussed. Composting has been described as nature's way to soil improvement and is thus of special significance to the organic farmer.

Composting is nothing new, as reference to its use was made in biblical times, but it currently represents an area of active research. In theory it presents a method of giving economic value to various types of waste products that up to now were considered worthless and were actually causing environmental and expense problems associated with their conventional disposal.

Major scientific improvements in the process were reported (Howard 1935) in the mid-1930s, which resulted in the Indore process. This event is thought to have started J.J. Rodale, the father of organic farming in America, on his lifelong pursuit in the area. Since then, the technique has been modified and expanded and is currently being used in the disposal of refuse at various locations (Spitzel 1967).

In its simplest form, composting consists of mixing carbonaceous wastes, such as leaves, hay, straw, sawdust, paper, or cornstalks with nitrogenous wastes, such as grass clippings, vegetable wastes, garbage, manure, or soil, and permitting microbiological breakdown of the organic matter.

As might be expected, numerous factors can have a significant influence on the time required and the resulting compost quality. One of the byproducts of composting is heat generation, and the temperature in turn is controlled by the size of the mass being reacted, as well as its composition. Temperature will also control rate of decomposition. Optimum decomposition temperatures during composting can range from 48 to 70°C (Jeris and Regen 1973). If the temperature exceeds 70°C, there is a good possibility of killing the active microorganisms.

The moisture content of the fermenting mass is also quite important, and for most composting products should be maintained at 50–60%. If lower than 40%, decomposition will be slow; and if higher than 60%, anaerobic decay will begin, resulting in offensive odors (Wiley 1957). Rate of decomposition can also be hastened by grinding the materials, which in effect increases reactive surface area. Aerobic fermentation is encouraged by frequent turning of the compost pile. Major by-products of the process are carbon dioxide and water, thus resulting in volume loss as high as two-thirds of the original materials.

Probably the most important factor governing the overall reaction is the ratio of carbon to nitrogen, as the microorganisms involved require carbon for growth and nitrogen for protein synthesis. A ratio of 30 parts carbon to 1 part nitrogen has been reported as optimum (UCB 1953). However, ratios between 26 and 35 have been reported to be acceptable (Cornfield 1958). If the ratio is much below 26, nitrogen is lost in the form of objectionable-smelling ammonia gas; if higher than 35, a long composting time is required. Typical carbon to nitrogen ratios, along with the nitrogen content of various materials used in composting are shown in Table 13.3. Thus, it can be seen that for optimum composting, the C/N ratios for quite a few waste products require adjustment. It is also interesting to note that refuse and garbage from individual cities also differ significantly in C/N ratios.

As would be expected, numerous chemical changes occur during composting. All or most sugars, starches, and water-soluble materials are utilized by the microorganisms. Lipids undergo major changes, while cellulose and hemicellulose change to a lesser degree. Lignin is fairly resistant to chemical change, but pH also changes dramatically. At the beginning, pH is usually near 6, slightly acidic, but during decomposition the formation of acids reduces it further to 4.5–5.0. However, as these acids are further broken down, the pH increases, with the final pH of the compost being on the alkaline side at pH 7.5–8.5 (Kochtitsky et al. 1969). As mentioned earlier, most plants prefer an acidic situation. However, continuous usage of compost may gradually increase soil pH.

Another factor that changes during composting is the microbiological population, with regard to both type and number (Chang and Hudson 1967). During the early mesophilic stages of composting, many acid-producing bacteria and fungi appear. However, as temperature increases, thermophilic bacteria, actenomycetes, and thermophilic fungi take over. As the internal temperature reaches 70°C, spore-forming bacteria become active. Then, as temperature begins to fall, mesophilic bacteria and fungi again appear. In addition, protozoa, nematodes, ants, springtails, millipedes, and worms appear during the last mesophilic stage. Typical mesophilic and

TABLE 13.3.   PERCENTAGE NITROGEN AND CARBON/NITROGEN RATIOS OF VARIOUS WASTE MATERIALS

	Nitrogen (% dry wt.)	C/N ratio
Total residential refuse including garbage:		
Berkeley, CA	1.07	33.8
Savannah, GA	1.30	38.5
Raleigh, NC	—	51.5
Chandler, AZ	0.57	65.8
Johnson City, TN	0.60	80.0
Garbage only:		
Louisville, KY	2.90	14.9
Raleigh, NC	1.92	15.4
Garbage/paper (fresh wt. ratio)		
5/1	1.13	40.2
9/1	1.25	34.6
Sewage sludge (moisture free)		
Activated	5.60	6.3
Digested	1.88	15.7
Fruit wastes	1.52	34.8
Wood (pine)	0.07	723
Paper	0.25	173
Grass clippings	2.15	20.1
Leaves	0.5–1.0	40–80
Sawdust	0.11	511
Lumber mill wastes	0.31	170
Pharmaceutical wastes	2.55	19

From Poincelot (1975).

thermophilic bacteria, fungi, and actenomycetes that are active during composting are summarized in Table 13.4. Interestingly, up to 25% of the final weight of compost is made up of dead and living microorganisms (Satria 1974; Poincelot and Day 1973).

Health Concerns

A health concern long associated with compost, especially when sewage sludge or manure is added, is the presence of animal and human pathogens (microorganisms that can cause disease). The destruction of these organisms is dependent on both time and temperature (Wiley 1962). For example, one day at 65°C was found to be required to destroy *Salmonella* species (Knoll 1961). However, for other pathogenic organisms, more severe time/temperature relationships are required. For example, destruction of *Bacillus anthracis* takes 3 weeks at 55°C and at least 40% moisture. However, some pathogenic fungi can even survive these conditions (Golueke and McGauhey 1970). The key factor in this area is a minimum temperature for a minimum time period. If either or both are not met, there exists the possibility of contaminating food crops, especially those normally consumed raw, with pathogenic organisms. Others (Knoll 1961) have reported that elevated temperature is not the only means of insuring pathogen destruc-

TABLE 13.4. MICROOGANISMS ISOLATED FROM COMPOST

Mesophilic Bacteria:	Mesophilic Fungi: *Cont.*
Cellumonas folia	*Aspergillus niger*
Chondrococcus exiguus	*Aspergillus terreus*
Myxococcus virescens	*Geotrichum candidum*
Myxococcus fluvus	*Rhizopus nigricans*
Thiobacillus thiooxidans	*Trichoderma viride*
Thiobacillus Denitrificans	*Trichoderma harzianum*
Aerobacter species	*Oospora variabilis*
Proteus species	*Mucor spinescens*
Pseudomonas species	*Mucor abundans*
Thermophilic bacteria	*Mucor variens*
Bacillus stearothermophilis	*Cephalosporium acremonium*
Thermophilic Acinomycetes:	*Chaetomium globosum*
Micromonospora vulgaris	Glomerularia *species*
Nocardia brasiliensis	*Pullularia*
Pseudonogardia thermophila	*Fusidium* species
Streptomyces rectus	*Actinomucor corymbosus*
Streptomyces thermofuscus	*Mucro jansseni*
Streptomyces thermophilus	*Talaromyces variable*
Strepyomyces thermoviolaceus	*Helminthosporium satirum*
Streptomyces thermovulgaris	Thermophilic Fungi:
Streotomyces violaceoruber	*Aspergillus fumigatus*
Thermoactinomyces vulgaris	*Humicola insolens*
Thermomonospora curvata	*Humicola griseus* var. *thermoideus*
Thermomonospora fusca	*Humicola lanuginosa*
Thermomonospora glaucus	*Mucor pusillus*
Thermopolyspora polyspora	*Chaetomium thermophile*
Mesophilic Fungi:	*Absidia ramosa*
Fusarium culmorum	*Talaromyces duponti*
Fusarium roseum	*Talaromyces emersonii*
Stysanus stemonitis	*Talaromyces thermophilus*
Corpinus cinereus	*Sporotrichum thermophile*
Coprinus megacephalus	*Sporotrichum calorinum*
Coprinus lagopus	*Mycelia sterilia*
Clitopilus pinsitus	*Stilbella thermophila*
Coprinus labopus	*Malbranchea pulchella* var. *sulfurea*
Clitopilus pinsitus	*Dactylomyces crustaceous*
	Byssochlamys species
	Torula thermophila

From Poincelot (1975).

tion. Some are just killed out by competition from other more prevalent microorganisms. It is also suggested that compost be permitted to "rest" or "ripen" after fermentation. This can take from 2 to 7 weeks (Gerretsen *et al.* 1956). If not, compost that is applied not fully decomposed will require soil nitrogen to complete the process, thus robbing it from plants.

Thus, it can be appreciated from the brief discussion on composting that much science is involved if it is to be done properly. Because of the time, up to 6 months for certain materials, and attention required, compost cannot be considered an inexpensive source of organic fertilizer. Some suggest that one should just let nature take its course in manufacturing compost, but this can take over 2 years.

In the area of solid waste disposal, cellulose, in the form of paper products, can represent approximately half of typical municipal refuse. As shown in Table 13.3, cellulose requires a reduction in its C/N ratio before it can effectively be composted. However, even under ideal conditions, 40% of the cellulose associated with municipal compost was found to be resistant to microbial attack after 8 weeks (Stutzenberger *et al.* 1970). The search for microorganisms that have higher cellulolytic activity is quite an important research area (Chang 1967; Fergus 1964; Stutzenberger 1971).

The use of various forms of sewage sludge has been practiced for centuries as a form of organic fertilizer. Recently, with growing concern over various forms of environmental pollution, many municipalities have sought other methods to dispose of their sewage. One such logical use was the recycling of these products onto and into the soil.

Various types of sewage sludge are available from most municipal sewage treatment plants. One type is raw sewage, which because of its potential for containing pathogenic organisms and its offensive odor, is not normally recycled. Two other basic forms are also available, namely, digested sludge, which is essentially raw sewage that is anaerobically decomposted, and activated sludge, which has undergone aerobic decomposition. Ideally most treatment plants attempt to produce activated sludge, as its odor is less offensive than that of digested sludge.

However, the exclusive use of sewage sludge can result in the accumulation of certain metals in food crops. The Woburn Market-Garden experiment was started in 1942 to demonstrate the feasibility of applying various organic fertilizer sources in the growing of food crops (LeRiche 1968). Sewage sludge that had come from mainly a residential area had been used. The use of sewage sludge was abandoned in 1961, and crops grown in 1967 still displayed high levels of certain potentially toxic metals. Thus, as observed in England, the use of sewage can be shown to be quite effective. However, with time, the buildup of certain metals may make the technique of little value and actually quite harmful to human health.

Other studies (Braids *et al.* 1970; King *et al.* 1974) have also demonstrated that levels of metals potentially toxic both to the growth of certain plants and to humans ingesting these plants or their produce, increase with the application of sewage sludge. This has occurred even though it was believed that most heavy metals associated with raw sewage are precipitated during secondary sewage treatment (Baier and Fryer 1973). However, some heavy metals can combine with organics in raw sewage and, as such, are not effectively precipitated. Another important fact is that certain industries can at times discharge high levels of certain metals into sewage systems (Hvisingh 1974), thus adding to the problem. The dietary consumption of certain metals, such as cadmium, mercury, and lead, are currently close to suggested maximum intake values (FAO-WHO 1972), which means that any system that tends to increase these levels may result in significant health problems.

Plant Diseases

Disease control can present certain problems to the organic farmer. It is granted that the most effective way of controlling most plant diseases is through the use of selective fungicides. As these are not utilized by the organic farmer, he has to search out other methods to effectively control diseases or face serious economic losses. One approach, which is also used in conventional farming, is to choose plant varieties that have the genetic capability to resist certain troublesome diseases. These are continually being developed by the plant breeder. However, a plant's resistance to certain diseases can be dramatically altered by mutation of plant pathogens, and thus a plant variety that has demonstrated resistance for years may suddenly be attacked by a modified disease.

Rotation of crops has also been used as a technique to control certain plant diseases. However, from a practical standpoint, there are only so many food crops that an organic farmer can economically grow during certain seasons of the year. To stay in yearly production, he may find himself planting similar crops year after year, thus increasing the potential for certain diseases. In addition, certain families of food items, such as tomato, potato, pepper, and eggplant, are prone to the same diseases, which can also result in economic disaster.

General field sanitation is an important aspect to consider in controlling certain plant diseases, as some pathogens can survive from season to season in plant refuse. This also presents a potential problem if diseased plants are used in composting and if the composting conditions obtained are not sufficient to destroy the pathogenic organism. Weeds in crop rows or along a field's border can also act as hosts to certain virus and wilt-promoting organisms.

Insect control can also present major problems. It is usually accepted that a certain amount of a crop grown under organic conditions will be subject to insect damage, thus reducing yield (Taber *et al.* 1976). However, certain nonsynthetic insecticides are available to the organic farmer. For example, pyrethrins, which are derived from the dried flowers of certain chrysanthemum species, have been available for quite some time. Problems with their use include that they only kill insects by contact, have a very short residual effect and thus must be used often, will not control mites, and are especially harmful to fish. Rotenone is another naturally derived insecticide from the root of the Derris plant, which is native to tropical Africa and South America. It is considered to be the best general-purpose nonsynthetic insecticide available. However, it is not effective against spider mites and soil insects and is highly toxic to most cold-blooded animals.

Nicotine, which is derived from the tobacco plant, has also been used by the organic farmer. However, it is not effective against most chewing insects or when applied in cool weather, and it has only short residual effects. It will control aphids, soft-bodied sucking insects, thrips, and some types of caterpillars.

The application of various petroleum oils to control certain insects has been practiced since the eighteenth century; however, their use is limited to woody plants such as fruit trees and some berry varieties. They are effective against aphids and mites. Soapsuds also have been used to control aphids.

Many organic farmers believe that various biological controls are an alternative to the use of synthetic pesticides. These controls can be a disease organism, a predacious or parasitic insect, predacious spiders and mites, insect-feeding birds, rodents, toads, and other vertebrates. Some of these usually occur naturally, but certain farmers have attempted to increase their numbers by introducing additional members in food crops during various phases of their growth cycle. However, most of these attempts have met with only limited success, as the presence of these biological agents cannot be easily contained to one specific area; if the supply of their food, insects, is limited, they will "seek greener pastures." They are usually most effective in heavily infected crops, which if infected near harvest, will certainly limit their economic value.

It is hoped that from this brief discussion on the techniques associated with organic farming, the reader can appreciate that to be effective and be able to compete with conventional methods, a great deal of science and time can be involved to just obtain a product for market. Also, as with most enterprises, the larger it becomes, the more complicated it becomes. Thus, if organic farming were going to be the method of choice, its techniques are going to have to be expanded and improved upon quite dramatically if the system is going to supply adequately our current food needs.

THE ORGANIC FOOD CONSUMER

Perhaps at this point a few words should be said as to why the organic food movement appears to be expanding. Fox (1970) believes that advertising has been the key because, of all industries, the food industry is by far the largest and even minor changes in dietary patterns can involve millions of dollars. Others (NDC 1973) feel that as the science of nutrition is not very old, its scientific data are vulnerable to distortion and misinterpretation. Thus, it becomes quite difficult for the layman to sort through theories as well as basic nutrition data just collected and to separate fact from fiction.

As pointed out by Sipple and King (1954), misinformation can be corrected only through effective and accurate nutritional education. However, the major problem in this area is the fact that numerous people claim to know something about or even be experts in nutrition and are more than willing to donate their time in spreading the word. In addition, several health food manufacturers have prepared literature that tells what is wrong with your current conventional diet with assurances that their diet plan will change your life.

Several large surveys (FDA 1972; National Analysis Inc. 1972) have clearly demonstrated that the American public is generally not aware of sound nutritional facts. The latter study had a section dealing specifically with topics that are primary claims used by the organic food movement against conventional foods. The specific statements, which were to be answered true or false, are shown in Table 13.5; the distribution of responses, relative to educational level and dietary habits, are summarized in Table

TABLE 13.5.   NUTRITION AND HEALTH FOOD QUESTIONS USED ON SURVEY

1. The chemicals added to our manufactured food take away much of its value for health.
2. Man-made vitamins are just as good as natural vitamins.
3. Much of our food has been so processed and refined that it has lost its value for health.
4. Chemical sprays that farmers use make our food a danger to health, even if they are used carefully.
5. There is no difference in food value between food grown in poor, worn-out soil and food grown in rich soil.
6. Many foods lose a lot of their value for health because they are shipped so far and stored so long.
7. Food grown with chemical fertilizers is just as healthful as food grown with nautral fertilizers.

From National Analysis, Inc. (1972).

13.6. As can be seen, the health food group averaged 86% wrong answers for the seven questions. Interestingly, the general public answered the same questions improperly approximately 60% of the time. Also, general educational level did not have any dramatic influence in the manner in which the statements were judged. Thus it can be concluded that the general public, and especially organic food users, need an intensive nutritional education program.

SENSORY CONSIDERATIONS

The sensory properties of conventional and organically grown foods have often been claimed to be different. Organically grown foods are said to be more flavorful and to taste fresher. Numerous factors should be considered before arriving at an overall decision in this important area. One can argue that the sensory properties of a food (appearance, aroma, flavor, and texture) comprise a primary factor in governing food acceptability. One could further reason that this in turn can significantly influence food intake, which in turn can be correlated with nutritional status. It can be seen that such a claim can have far-reaching implications.

Perhaps the most difficult parameter to measure is the psychological factor. For example, if one has a strong persuasion for or against organically grown foods and one is told that he is consuming a conventional product, his decision as to its sensory acceptance may not be completely subjective and rational.

Another important factor to consider is maturity or ripeness at time of harvest relative to time of purchase and/or consumption. It is a well-accepted fact that most conventionally grown perishable foods are harvested prior to peak maturity or ripeness in order that the food can withstand further handling and marketing. Thus, when comparing the sensory properties of, say, conventionally grown peaches from California to organically grown peaches harvested and marketed at peak ripeness from an operation in New York undoubtedly the New York product would taste and probably look better. However, when perishable organically grown foods are marketed away from their traditional roadside stand situation, they

TABLE 13.6. RESPONSES (%WRONG) TO STATEMENTS FROM TABLE 13.5 AS INFLUENCED BY EDUCATION LEVEL AND DIETARY HABIT.

Statement[1]	Total public	College graduates	Less than high school	Health food users
1. Additives (F)	48	37	52	86
2. Synthetic Vitamins (T)	65	53	74	85
3. Refining (F)	60	56	65	89
4. Pesticides (F)	57	52	63	88
5. Worn-Out Soil (T)	85	88	83	93
6. Storage (F)	73	68	77	86
7. Chemical Fertilizers (T)	56	44	66	77
AVERAGE	57	57	69	86

From National Analysis, Inc. (1972).
[1] Statement was true (T) or false (F).

face similar problems relative to sensory acceptability as the conventionally grown food items.

Varietal differences can also play an important role in the sensory properties of food items. For example, during Prohibition it was quickly learned
that certain California thin-skinned grape varieties that produced some
exceptionally fine wines could not be shipped great distances because of
resultant bruising. Therefore, thicker-skinned varieties, that some felt
produced wines of only average quality, were utilized for shipping.

The same claim has been made of certain tomato varieties. Individuals
claim that the flavor has been bred out of commercial tomato varieties. In
most instances, the tomato varieties in question were not originally developed to be utilized as fresh sliced tomatoes but rather in processed tomato
products.

It has been clearly demonstrated that the levels of various flavor compounds vary with tomato variety (Nelson and Hoff 1969). Data of these type
are summarized in Table 13.7. In addition, to complicate matters, it has also
been demonstrated that harvest date can also significantly influence the
levels of volatiles, or flavor compounds, found in tomatoes so that the
discriminating connoisseur of tomatoes may be able to detect differences in
tomato flavor throughout the harvest season even if these tomatoes are
grown in his own back yard. Also, factors that humans have little control
over, such as temperature and amount of sunshine, can also significantly
influence the sensory properties of foods.

Also, to be economically feasible, varietal factors such as disease resistance, ease of harvest, and, most importantly, yield have to be considered.
Using the tomato as an example, perhaps the breeder has not placed major
emphasis on certain sensory properties; however, the economic incentive to
date has not been great enough to merit this attention. Currently, few will
dispute the claim that a ripe tomato harvested from your own garden,
whether grown by conventional or organic means, tastes better than a
slightly pink tomato purchased at a supermarket chain, regardless of variety. This has been scientifically demonstrated by Bisogni et al. (1976) and is
summarized in Table 13.8.

The sensory properties of foods are usually highly subjective among a
population, yet there is no question that something harvested at its peak or
freshly processed will be judged better than products that have not under-

TABLE 13.7. INFLUENCE OF TOMATO VARIETY ON THE LEVELS
(PPM) OF SELECTED VOLATILES

Compound	Variety		
	Roma	Rutgers	H 1350
Acetaldehyde	0.21	0.48	0.92
Acetone	0.64	1.03	0.76
Methanol	125	177	229
Ethanol	14	56	62
Isopentanal	0.44	0.87	0.42
Hexanal	2.82	1.32	3.44

From Nelson and Hoff (1969).

TABLE 13.8.   EFFECT OF RIPENING AND HARVEST DATE ON THE FLAVOR AND OVERALL QUALITY OF TOMATOES

Harvest date	Flavor		Overall quality	
	Ripened in:		Ripened in:	
	Room[1]	Field[2]	Room[1]	Field[2]
June 25	3.2[3]	2.4[3]	3.7[3]	2.5[3]
July 7	3.4	2.1	3.9	2.1
July 15	4.0	2.3	4.1	2.1

From Bisogni et al. (1976).
[1] Harvested at mature green stage and ripened in humidified air at 20°C until firm red stage.
[2] Harvested from field at firm red stage.
[3] 5-point acceptability scale with 1 being excellent and 5 very poor.

gone optimum conditions. However, not everyone can have a garden or harvest fresh produce throughout the year, and certain sensory sacrifices are to be expected.

Again, using tomatoes as an example, numerous volatile or aroma components have been identified. In fact, today the number is in excess of 150 such compounds. Shah et al. (1969) have proposed that the typical aroma of field-ripened tomatoes is composed of 32% carbonyls, 10% short-chain alcohols, and 58% hydrocarbons. They have reported on the volatile composition of field-ripened, artificially ripened, and overripened tomatoes and observed differences in the amounts of certain volatiles that contribute to tomato flavor. For example, artificially ripened tomatoes had higher levels of butanol, 3-pentanol, 2-methyl-3-hexanol, isopentanal, 2,3-butanedione, propylacetate, and isopentyl butyrate than field-ripened tomatoes. In contrast, levels of nonanal, decanal, dodecanal, neral, benzaldehyde, citronellyl propionate, citronellyl butyrate, geranyl acetate, and geranyl butyrate were higher in field-ripened tomatoes as compared to artificially ripened tomatoes. When field-ripened and overripened tomatoes were compared, it was found that isopentyl butyrate, cironellyl butyrate, and geranyl butyrate increased with overripening. Shah et al. (1969) concluded that short-chain compounds were formed to their maximum concentration during the early stage of maturation and that artificial ripening could mean that long-chain flavor compounds would not be synthesized at appreciable levels.

Artificially ripened tomatoes have also been shown to be higher in acid content and lower in sugar than field-ripened ones (Boe et al. 1968), which would certainly also influence flavor. In addition, Dalal et al. (1967), through the use of gas chromatography, concluded that artificially ripened tomatoes had less volatile compounds than corresponding field-ripened tomatoes.

It might be of interest to the reader to see where tomato flavor is derived. From Figure 13.1, it can be seen that the mechanism is very complex. In addition, the amounts of end-products (flavor compounds) can be significantly influenced by factors such as sunlight, nutrient availability, and enzymatic activity.

In the future, the food scientist will probably find a way to protect or

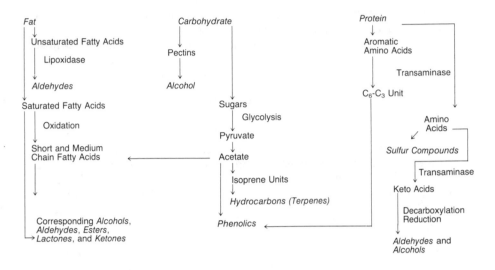

FIG. 13.1. PATHWAYS FOR THE FORMATION OF TOMATO VOLATILES.
FROM SALUNKHE *et al.* 1974.

preserve the fine flavor of fully ripe tomatoes on their way to market, which will probably involve the use of chemicals, which in turn will add fuel to the belief that already too many chemicals are added to our food supply.

The discussion has centered primarily around highly perishable foods. However, if processed foods such as flour and canned goods are considered, one must assume that, independent of method of production, they were harvested at their peak. Thus, any obvious sensory differences in the processed product could be attributed to the basic differences in concept of production (conventional versus organically grown).

In searching the literature for actual data comparing the sensory properties of conventional and organically grown foods, one finds that some of the potential problems described, such as varietal differences and degree of maturity and ripeness, are inherent because in most such studies the products evaluated were obtained at the retail level and thus product history was not completely available. On the other hand, one could argue that this is the manner by which most consumers obtain these products and that these data are thus quite valid. From a purely scientific point of view, though, it is suggested that this question can only be resolved beyond any question of doubt by growing numerous products at various locations around the world side by side, using conventional and organically grown techniques during a long-term period (10 years) and subjecting the products to both subjective and objective sensory evaluation. Some will argue that this has been already done, which can be countered by the fact that the studies were rather informally done without adequate collection and evaluation of all data. Undoubtedly, such a study would involve a great deal of time and effort, both of which are not fully justified relative to other more pressing food-related problems facing our society.

At this point, data reported in the literature relative to specific sensory comparisons on conventionally and organically grown foods will be presented and discussed. Perhaps the most frequently quoted data in this area were reported by Appledorf *et al.* (1974), who compared preferences for color, odor, flavor, texture, and overall acceptability of 25 food items purchased in a health food store with those for comparable items purchased in a traditional food store. It should be noted that from the standpoint of a well-designed experiment, several areas can be criticized. For example, they utilized a 20-member panel and acknowledged that an unspecified number of these had previously consumed health foods. From this statement, one cannot assume that an equal number of the panel currently consumed either organically grown food or conventionally grown food and in turn conclude that the panel was biased. In addition, one would have difficulty in attempting to duplicate this study because experimental detail relative to the manner and amount of food items served are not reported. Further confusion can result from the lack of complete descriptions relative to certain food items. The panel was reported to have met 3–4 times a week for 3 months, but it is not clear from the data presented how many times each product was evaluated. In any event, a large number of data were generated and statistically evaluated. These are summarized in Table 13.9. From these data, the authors concluded that none of the foods purchased from health food stores were judged to be statistically superior ($p < .05$) in overall acceptability to their conventional counterparts. In contrast, 13 of the conventional foods were judged to be significantly superior in overall acceptability to the corresponding health food store items.

When other specific sensory attributes were evaluated, it was found that, in general, conventional foods scored higher than organically grown foods. Thus, if one overlooks some of the potential problems in experimental design and reporting apparent in this study, one can conclude that in general, the sensory properties of the food items purchased in health food stores, which would imply that they were organically grown, were not found to be statistically superior to those of conventionally grown foods.

A later study of much better design was reported by Schutz and Lorenz (1976). They evaluated overall sensory preferences for raw lettuce and carrots and cooked green beans and broccoli of known varieties that had been grown at the same site under depleted, organically fertilized, and inorganically fertilized conditions. Their panel consisted of 25 female and 25 male California college-age students. Although it was not reported, one would expect to have a number of individuals who consume organically grown foods in this group. Another variable investigated was the effect of mislabeling products. In this latter portion, they found that labeling vegetables as being organically grown caused a statistically significant increase in product ratings. Thus, a psychological factor of expecting a certain product, in this case organically grown produce, to be a better product

TABLE 13.9.   COMPARISON OF THE SENSORY PROPERTIES OF HEALTH AND CONVENTIONAL FOODS

Class/food		Overall acceptance	Color	Aroma	Flavor	Texture
Fruit Products:						
Apple Butter	(T)	6.1a	6.6a	6.8a	6.1a	5.7a
	(H)	6.2a	6.7a	7.1a	6.4a	6.2a
	(T)	4.8a	6.2a	5.4b	4.9a	6.0a
Dried apples	(T)	6.8a	6.4a	6.1a	6.6a	6.2a
	(H)	5.0b	4.4b	4.8b	5.6a	4.4b
Apple juice	(T)	7.4a	7.0a	7.2a	7.2a	7.4a
	(H)	4.2c	3.8c	6.0b	4.6c	4.3c
	(H)	5.6b	5.1b	6.6ab	6.0b	5.9b
Apple sauce	(H)	4.6a	5.8b	6.8a	4.4b	5.7b
	(T)	8.0b	7.6a	6.6a	7.9a	7.3a
Dates	(T)	6.7a	6.6a	6.3a	6.8a	6.5a
	(H)	7.1a	6.4a	6.0a	7.1a	6.8a
Milk products:						
Cheddar cheese	(H)	6.7a	5.1b	6.5a	6.8a	6.5a
	(T)	6.8a	7.5a	6.2a	6.5a	6.7a
	(T)	6.6a	7.1a	5.8a	6.4a	7.0a
Swiss cheese	(T)	6.8a	7.1a	7.1a	6.6a	6.7a
	(T)	6.4a	7.2a	6.6a	6.6a	6.4a
	(H)	5.2b	6.7a	6.7a	5.2b	5.6a
Ice cream	(H)	6.7b	6.6b	6.2b	6.7b	7.5b
	(T)	8.4a	7.9a	7.6a	8.3a	8.2a
Powdered milk	(H)	5.7a	6.8a	5.7a	5.8a	6.6a
	(T)	5.9a	6.6a	5.9a	5.8a	6.8a
Cheese pizza	(T)	6.5a	7.4a	6.4b	6.4a	6.3a
	(H)	6.7a	5.8b	7.4a	6.6a	6.4a
Cereal products:						
Bread	(T)	6.9a	6.9a	7.2a	6.9a	6.8a
	(H)	7.1a	7.4a	6.9a	6.9a	6.8ab
	(T)	7.2a	7.4a	7.0a	7.0a	7.5a
Cereal	(T)	7.1a	6.8a	7.0a	7.1a	5.6a
	(H)	5.9b	6.2a	5.3b	5.5b	5.4a
Corn chips	(H)	5.2b	5.3b	4.8b	5.0b	5.6b
	(T)	7.7a	7.4a	7.0a	7.4a	7.3a
	(T)	7.0a	7.1a	6.0a	7.0a	6.9a
Fig bars	(H)	7.0a	6.5a	7.0a	7.0a	7.0a
	(T)	7.4a	7.4a	7.8a	7.2a	7.0a
	(T)	6.6a	7.0a	6.2b	6.7a	6.2a
Rice	(H)	5.9a	5.4b	6.8a	5.9a	5.5b
	(T)	6.2a	7.0a	7.1a	6.0a	7.0a
Sesame chips	(H)	6.2b	6.8a	5.7a	6.1b	6.0b
	(T)	7.0a	7.0a	6.8a	7.2a	7.4a
Miscellaneous:						
Beans/tomato sauce	(T)	7.2a	7.4a	7.0a	7.2a	7.3a
	(H)	6.8a	7.3a	7.2a	6.7a	7.4a
Cashews	(H)	6.1b	5.2b	5.5b	6.0b	6.4a
	(T)	7.8a	6.8a	6.6a	7.8a	7.3a
Coconut	(H)	4.9b	7.8a	6.7a	4.6b	5.2b
	(T)	8.1a	8.0a	7.8a	8.1a	8.1a
Dates	(T)	6.7a	6.6a	6.3a	6.8a	6.5a
	(H)	7.1a	6.4a	6.0a	7.1a	6.8a
Honey	(T)	7.0a	8.4a	6.2a	6.8a	7.4a
	(H)	6.8a	7.0a	6.3a	6.2a	7.2a
	(T)	7.4a	7.2a	6.8a	7.2a	7.5a
Ketchup	(H)	7.6a	7.9a	7.0a	7.7a	7.6a
	(T)	7.2a	7.0b	7.2a	7.4a	7.0a
Mayonnaise/potatoes	(H)	6.8a	6.8a	6.8a	6.6a	7.0a
	(T)	6.5a	6.8a	6.8a	6.4a	6.6a

(continued)

TABLE 13.9.   *(Cont.)*

Class/food		Overall acceptance	Color	Aroma	Flavor	Texture
Mayonnaise/tomato	(H)	5.8b	7.6a	7.0a	6.0b	7.4a
	(T)	7.4a	7.6a	7.2a	7.6a	7.0a
Peanut butter	(H)	4.8b	6.1b	6.6a	5.3b	4.2b
	(T)	7.2a	7.3a	7.7a	7.3a	7.4a
	(H)	4.0b	5.8b	6.4a	3.9c	4.5b
	(T)	6.4a	7.7a	6.9a	6.3b	7.6a
Tomato juice	(T)	7.2a	7.4a	7.4a	7.1a	6.9a
	(H)	3.0b	5.8b	5.4a	2.8b	5.8b

From Appledorf et al. (1974).
Symbols: 9-point hedonic scale with 1 = dislike extremely to 9 = like extremely. T = traditional; H = health.
Values for each food product attribute which are followed by the same letter are not different at $p < 0.05$.

resulted in significant results. Thus it was demonstrated that the mind is more influential than the mouth!

Schutz and Lorenz also reported that statistical evaluation of the preference data for properly labeled produce demonstrated that no significant difference was observed for lettuce and green beans as influenced by type of fertilizer applied. In the case of carrots, product grown with no added fertilizer and with inorganic fertilizer was preferred to that grown with organically applied fertilizer. However, organically grown broccoli was preferred to broccoli grown under depleted fertilizer conditions as well as inorganic fertilizer. Thus, it is apparent from this study that for certain products, organically grown can be demonstrated to be statistically superior in overall sensory acceptability to conventional products. However, it should be emphasized that this appears to be the exception rather than the rule, at least based on the results of the study.

This latter piece of evidence can serve to add fuel to the claim that inorganically grown vegetables taste better; but before the claim can be declared a fact, many more studies on different food items as well as different processed forms, such as canned and frozen, are required before a clearcut decision can be made.

A study by Maga *et al.* (1976) investigated the influence of fertilizer types and amounts, as well as processing, on the sensory properties of spinach, using both subjective and objective techniques. Spinach was grown using no nitrogen application, mineral-based fertilizer (ammonium sulfate) at two levels, and two corresponding levels of organic fertilizer (dried bloodmeal), along with a late application of mineral fertilizer. The resulting spinach was harvested and each fertilizer treatment evaluated against the other using raw, freshly cooked, and freshly cooked/frozen samples. A 25-member college-age panel employing a sensory triangle test procedure, whereby three samples are served to each panel member with two of the samples being identical and the other being different, was used. The number of correct judgments in choosing the different sample can then be used to determine if the samples are statistically different.

As can be seen in Table 13.10, processing in general did not statistically alter the sensory properties of the products independent of fertilizer treatments. It can also be seen that at the same fertilizer application level, no significant sensory differences resulted between organic and mineral fertilizers. However, in most cases, lack of fertilizer, as compared to the other fertilization treatments, did result in significantly different sensory properties independent of processing.

The authors also performed, using raw spinach, a preliminary analysis of the headspace volatiles associated with each fertilizer treatment. It can be argued that headspace volatiles are not necessarily correlated with overall aroma and/or flavor intensity, as the odor thresholds (minimum concentration of a compound required for it to be identified by smelling) are not the same for all volatiles. It can also be pointed out that all volatiles do not significantly contribute to the sensory properties of a specific food. Since the authors did not report on the identification of the specific peaks separated by gas chromatography, nor were the data evaluated statistically, the data can be argued to be of limited value. As seen in Table 13.11, fertilizer type and amount did dramatically alter total peak area. The authors did state that no qualitative chromatographic differences were apparent among treatments. In any event, the authors did present chemical evidence for the amount of volatiles produced by the various fertilizer treatments investigated.

This author is not aware of any published work identifying the specific compounds responsible for spinach flavor. Also, the volatiles associated with heated spinach were not compared in the preceding study and thus should serve as the focal point for an interesting study. It should be noted that the study just described dealt only with spinach and thus the conclusions reached should not and cannot be applied to all vegetables.

It is also interesting to note that from a research standpoint, spinach is an

TABLE 13.10.   TRIANGLE TEST SENSORY DIFFERENCES OF SPINACH AS INFLUENCED BY TYPE AND AMOUNT OF FERTILIZER APPLICATION AND METHOD OF PROCESSING

Fertilizer type/amount	No. correct responses out of 25		
	Raw	Cooked	Frozen
No nitrogen vs. normal level of mineral	12	11	12
No nitrogen vs. high level of mineral	18[1]	22[1]	19[1]
No nitrogen vs. normal level of organic	9	11	8
No nitrogen vs. high level or organic	15[1]	19[1]	17[1]
No nitrogen vs. late mineral	14[1]	14[1]	13[1]
Normal mineral vs. high mineral	8	10	10
Normal mineral vs. normal organic	11	11	12
Normal mineral vs. high organic	10	8	11
Normal mineral vs. late mineral	9	9	9
High mineral vs. normal organic	6	8	8
High mineral vs. high organic	12	12	11
High mineral vs. late mineral	4	5	7
Normal organic vs. high organic	7	5	6
Normal organic vs. late mineral	8	10	10
High organic vs. late mineral	6	8	5

From Maga et al. (1976).
[1] Significantly different at $p < 0.05$.

TABLE 13.11.   INFLUENCE OF FERTILIZER TYPE AND AMOUNT ON RAW SPINACH HEADSPACE PEAK AREAS

Fertilizer type-amount	Peak area (cm^2)
No fertilization	426
Normal level of mineral-based	514
High level of mineral-based	981
Normal level of organic-based	503
High level of organic-based	986
Late application of normal level of mineral-based	962

From Maga *et al.* (1976).

easy model to work with, as it has a relatively short maturation time as compared to other vegetables. However, organic fertilizer sources have a problem in that they have to be chemically broken down before they are available to plants. This process occurs much more rapidly with inorganic fertilizers and thus comparisons of inorganic versus organic fertilizers when applied to quickly maturing crops may have an inherent bias against the organic fertilizer. Obviously, this potential problem can be minimized by growing several harvests of the crop in question.

One of the major objectives of American agriculture has been to increase product yield, and the primary manner in which this has been accomplished for most crops has been through the increased use of fertilization. However, as will be discussed in detail, the use of high nitrogen levels with some food crops can result in adverse sensory properties. Thus, a situation may exist whereby these crops are compared to organically grown products that, because of the fertilizer source, which is usually lower in nitrogen, appear to be significantly different in sensory attributes.

The use of excessive levels of nitrogen in the production of potatoes has been reported to adversely affect their sensory properties both directly and indirectly. Indirect results of high nitrogen levels (in excess of 200 lb of nitrogen per acre) include less resistance against mechanical damage at harvest and during transport of potatoes as well as a decline in the keeping quality during storage and an increase in enzymatic graying of pre-peeled potatoes and consequent discoloration after cooking. Direct effects include loss of typical potato flavor and loss of texture after cooking (Schuphan 1972; Enge and Baerug 1971; Baerug 1971).

Similar results have been reported for canned tomato juice. A seven-member flavor evaluation panel ranked juice made from tomatoes receiving no or low levels of ammonia nitrogen as better than tomatoes receiving a high level of 120 pounds of nitrogen per acre (Saravacos *et al.* 1959).

Nitrogen level in the form of liquid ammonium nitrate has been shown to influence the general appearance of cantaloupes (Pew and Gardner 1972). Their data are summarized in Table 13.12. It was concluded that up to 100 lb of nitrogen per acre could result in a significant improvement in overall cantaloupe appearance. Thus, for some products high nitrogen levels appear to exert a positive influence on sensory properties, whereas with other products the opposite is true.

TABLE 13.12.   EFFECT OF NITROGEN APPLICATION LEVELS ON THE
APPEARANCE OF CANTALOUPE

Pounds nitrogen applied/acre	Cantaloupe general appearance
0	5.8[1]
50	6.6
100	7.4
150	7.8

From Pew and Gardner (1972).
[1] Ranked from 1 to 9 with 9 being most desirable.

Using peanuts as a model, Pattee and Singleton (1972) have demonstrated that the level of certain volatile compounds can vary dramatically
as influenced by geographic location of growth. Their data for the compound
methanol are summarized in Table 13.13. It is interesting to note that most
of the foreign varieties were low in methanol as compared to the American
ones. Thus, their data indicate that location of growth, as well as variety,
can significantly influence the volatiles associated with a food, which in
turn would make even a scientific study designed specifically to evaluate
the effect of fertilizer type (inorganic versus organic) difficult to evaluate
even if the plots used were side by side.

Relative to sensory differences, at this point in time, it would be safe to
say that no significant differences are apparent when the potential of other
variables that may influence sensory properties are considered.

NUTRITIONAL CONSIDERATIONS

The claim that organically grown foods are more nutritious than conventionally grown foods is frequently heard. Usually upon further debate it

TABLE 13.13.   EFFECT OF PEANUT VARIETY AND LOCATION
OF GROWTH ON PERCENTAGE METHANOL COMPOSITION

Variety	Location	Methanol (%)
Colorado–Manfredi	Argentina	8.7
Natal Common	South Africa	18.7
Red Spanish	Australia	7.6
Virginia Bunch	Australia	9.8
Shulamith	Israel	6.8
Tainan No. 9	Taiwan	26.6
	United States:	
Argentine	Virginia	36.8
Argentine	Georgia	29.1
Argentine	Oklahoma	32.8
NC-2	Virginia	30.3
NC-2	Georgia	14.5
Early Runner	Virginia	36.2
Early Runner	Georgia	15.7
56R	Virginia	37.8
56R	Georgia	20.2
Florispah	Virginia	34.3
Pearl	Virginia	53.2
61R	Georgia	19.8

From Pattee and Singleton (1972).

is resolved that perhaps certain people are confusing nutrition with food safety, as the presence of intentional food additives in most cases has nothing to do with the nutritional value of the resulting food.

Another logical explanation for this claim is that in some situations organically grown foods may be more nutritious because they are commonly sold at roadside stands and probably are fresher and thus have lost fewer nutrients than a product that has been transported to market over 3,000 miles. However, this unique situation cannot be translated to mean that all organically grown foods are better nutritionally than all conventionally grown counterparts.

Certain branches of the government have as part of their assigned tasks the nutritional well-being of the general public and thus constantly hear the concerns of the people. It is interesting to note that Leverton (1973) in her function as USDA science advisor filed the following statement at an Open Hearing on Organic Food held by the Attorney General for the State of New York on December 1, 1972:

There is no proved, substantiated basis for claiming that plants grown with only organic fertilizer have a greater nutrient content than those grown by conventional methods. The type of fertilizer used—whether organic or inorganic—is not a determining factor in the nutritive value of the plant.

The nutrient content of a plant is based on its genetic nature. The genes in a carrot cause it to develop a relatively large amount of vitamin A-value, just as the genes in an orange are responsible for its high ascorbic acid content. Climate (including the amount of light), together with the kind and amount of nutrient material available to the plant for growth, and the stage of maturity at harvest are the other chief factors involved.

Nutrient material must be in the inorganic form to be absorbed by the plant. This means that organic fertilizer must be broken down into its inorganic components before the elements are absorbed. Also, most of the nutrients present, except for the mineral elements, are synthesized in the plant rather than being absorbed from the soil in the performed state.

Maintaining or preserving the nutritive value of fresh vegetables and fruits from the time they are harvested until they are marketed and then until they are consumed requires great care. Maintaining "freshness" is the key to maintaining nutritive value. But maintaining freshness, including the desirable flavor which it connotes, has nothing to do with the manner in which the vegetables or fruits are fertilized and grown. Freshness depends on the manner and the time of harvesting, control of such factors as temperature and humidity, packaging, speed of transportation, and thereafter the handling at the wholesale and retail levels and in the home.

The nutritive superiority of most whole grains over their more refined counterparts, i.e., whole wheat flour vs. white flour, is well recognized. This superiority, however, is in no way related to the type of fertilizer used or the use of pesticides or additives. The process of refining removes some of the nutrients in varying degrees, especially the B vitamins, iron, and trace minerals. Often products are "enriched" by adding certain purified B vitamins and iron. This is not done, however, for the trace minerals and vitamin E lost in refining.

Increased use of cereals in the whole grain form is commendable. It can be promoted on the basis of increased nutritive value but not as related to fertilizer and processing methods.

Several important domestic groups, representing various phases of the food industry, have also felt it necessary to issue position papers. One such group is the Institute of Food Technologists (IFT) in their report (IFT 1974), prepared as "A scientific status summary of the IFT expert panel and CPI" (Committee on Public Information). They conclude that fertilizer type does not influence the fat, carbohydrate, protein, or vitamin content of plants. However, they do grant that fertilizer type can influence the mineral composition of plants. Thus, it can be argued that certain nutritional differences can occur between organically grown and conventionally grown foods, depending primarily on geographical location.

The National Dairy Council (NDC 1973) has also published a review/ position paper on the nutritional aspects of organically grown food that agrees with the preceding work (White 1972; Jukes 1971). Several other reports have appeared that state essentially the same theme—that it is believed that no difference in nutritional attributes exist and that even if any did, they would be minor (Utzinger *et al.* 1970; von Elbe 1972). However, people who strictly follow a new diet program, whether it consists of organically grown foods or not, usually physically and/or psychologically experience an improvement in health. In most cases, the new diet is usually more balanced and at a lower total caloric intake than their former diet, thus resulting in detectable improvements.

Undoubtedly the most emphatic was a statement prepared by Stare *et al.* (1972). They point to specific studies of fertilizers.

One can cite many studies, some very large, cooperative studies carried out by many investigators in different parts of our country. The results uniformly show that while fertilization is most important for crop yields, it has only a minor effect, if any, on nutritive quality and that there is no difference between chemical and organic fertilizers which supply the same amounts of available inorganic nitrates, phosphates, and potassium compounds.

We might refer to only two such studies:

1. What is usually referred to as the Southern Cooperative Group carried out a coordinated research effort for a 10-year period between 1943 and 1953. It involved Agricultural Experiment Stations in Arkansas, Georgia, Louisiana, Mississippi, North Carolina, Oklahoma, Puerto Rico, Texas, and the U.S. Plant, Soil, and Nutrition Laboratory at Cornell. Several vegetables were involved in these studies using different types of storage and cooking procedures. It was found that fertilizer effects on the vitamin content of vegetable matter represent at most only a small part of the total environmental effect on the plant.

The vegetables studied in this large cooperative project included sweet potatoes, cowpeas, lima beans, and turnip greens—these because they make a major contribution to the vitamin and mineral content of diets in the South.

2. Another major 10-year study was carried out at Michigan State University. The results were summarized in a publication in 1955 from Michigan State University entitled *Nutrition of Plants, Animals, and Man.* This study was designed to determine whether soil fertility influences the nutritional quality of crops and, in turn, whether such effects can be measured in terms of the nutrition of the animal (dairy cows) and the nutritional value of the milk produced.

The results of the experiment lend confidence to the observation that, regardless of the quality of the feed furnished the cow, if sufficient feed is available to support lactation, the milk produced will be high in nutritive value. The study again emphatically points to the value of a fertile soil in increasing agricultural productivity but not to influencing the nutritive quality of the foods.

The relatively recent report by Appledorf *et al.* (1973) has been used extensively as evidence to demonstrate that organically grown foods are not nutritionally superior to conventionally grown foods. The authors concluded, based on the data shown in Table 13.14, that only minor differences were detected in approximate composition. The authors made note of the fact that, in some instances, the similarity in chemical composition was quite marked, especially when both samples came from the same processor, as was the case for honey. Other noted differences in composition were attributed to formulation and processing rather than to inherent differences between samples. However, as alluded previously, studies of this type do not really answer the question beyond a shadow of a doubt, as a complete analytical nutritional analysis was not performed. Vitamin and essential trace mineral analyses would have added greatly to the overall validity, value, and conclusions reached in the above study.

Data have appeared in the literature for some food items indicating that certain nutritional changes can be observed as influenced by both fertilizer types and amounts. However, the problem comes in defining nutrition—is it the complete nutritional value of all nutrients potentially available in a product, or is it one or two specific nutrients? Overall it can be argued that normally one product is not consumed alone, except in some nonrecommended diets, so that a certain nutritional inadequacy specific to that product probably will not have a pronounced nutritional impact on one's life.

Data shown in Table 13.15 demonstrate that the type and amount of inorganic fertilizer applied to tomato plants can influence the level of ascorbic acid, or vitamin C, and certain nutritionally important minerals in tomato juice. As can be seen, ascorbic acid levels were lower in the fertilized plants as compared to a nonfertilized control and especially lower in the cases where anhydrous ammonia (NH_3) was used. In the case of minerals, no

TABLE 13.14. APPROXIMATE COMPOSITION (%) OF VARIOUS HEALTH (H) AND TRADITIONAL (T) FOODS

Food	Moisture		Protein		Fat		Ash		Carbohydrate	
	H	T	H	T	H	T	H	T	H	T
Almonds	4.1	3.6	26.0	25.5	46.3	47.3	3.0	3.0	20.7	20.6
Apple butter	50.9	53.2	0.5	0.4	0.0	0.0	1.7	0.3	46.9	46.1
Apples, dried	13.8	16.6	1.0	0.8	0.2	0.2	1.5	2.7	83.5	79.7
Apple juice	88.6	87.5	0.4	0.1	0.3	0.1	0.2	0.2	10.5	12.1
Brazil nuts	2.4	2.2	18.7	19.1	60.8	24.8	3.5	3.4	14.6	50.5
Bread, whole wheat	36.8	35.4	11.9	12.2	1.9	2.2	2.6	2.2	46.9	48.0
Cashews	3.8	2.5	20.1	18.7	45.2	47.7	2.2	6.1	28.8	25.1
Cereal, whole wheat	11.9	9.2	11.8	12.6	0.6	0.7	2.3	1.5	73.4	75.9
Cheese, cheddar	38.2	37.7	22.6	24.0	30.0	29.9	3.3	3.4	5.9	5.0
Coconut	2.6	16.1	8.6	4.8	63.0	21.7	1.8	0.9	24.0	56.5
Corn snacks	6.7	2.0	9.4	5.5	28.2	28.8	4.6	2.7	51.1	61.0
Dates	20.8	20.5	2.0	1.4	0.1	0.1	1.4	1.6	75.7	76.4
Fig bars	16.6	14.3	5.4	5.7	4.3	5.9	5.4	1.6	68.3	72.5
Honey, tupelo	15.1	15.1	0.3	0.3	0.2	0.2	0.1	0.1	84.4	84.4
Ice cream, peach	56.3	53.4	4.2	4.4	7.4	14.7	0.7	0.7	31.4	26.9
Mayonnaise	8.7	9.4	2.5	2.4	80.9	79.8	1.3	1.2	6.6	7.2
Milk, dry	4.3	5.3	34.3	34.1	0.1	0.1	7.9	7.6	53.3	52.9
Pancake mix	8.4	8.0	14.7	10.9	2.9	9.3	4.6	4.3	69.5	67.5
Peanut butter	0.2	0.5	28.9	28.9	47.7	48.4	2.7	3.4	20.6	18.8
Pecans	3.3	3.1	13.2	12.0	67.1	68.9	1.8	1.6	14.6	14.5
Preserves, blackberry	32.9	26.9	0.9	0.8	0.1	3.4	0.2	0.2	65.9	68.7
Rice	10.8	11.8	8.1	8.4	0.6	0.5	1.4	0.5	79.0	78.8
Rice cereal	16.9	9.1	5.8	5.8	0.7	0.5	0.8	0.3	75.8	84.2
Tomato juice	95.6	91.0	0.8	0.9	0.0	2.3	0.7	1.0	2.9	4.8

From Appledorf et al. (1973).

TABLE 13.15.   INFLUENCE OF FERTILIZER APPLICATION ON RESULTING TOMATO
JUICE ASCORBIC ACID AND MINERAL COMPOSITION (mg/100 ml)

Fertilizer	Nutrients added			Juice composition			
	N	P_2O_5	K_2O	Ascorbic Acid	K	Ca	P
None	0	0	0	18.0	215	4.9	9.9
NH_4NO_3	120	0	0	16.8	213	5.8	12.7
NH_4NO_3 + $CaHPO_4$	120	120	0	16.5	225	6.0	13.4
NH_4NO_3 + $CaHPO_4$ + K_2SO_4	120	120	120	17.2	221	6.6	12.9
NH_3	60	0	0	14.5	228	4.7	14.3
NH_3	120	0	0	15.3	231	5.3	13.0
NH_3 + $CaHPO_4$	120	120	0	15.2	237	5.6	12.2
NH_3 + $CaHPO_4$	60	60	0	14.3	217	5.9	11.1

From Saravacos et al. (1959).

trend was noted for potassium. However, fertilization resulted in increased
levels of calcium and phosphorus noted in tomato juice derived from fertilized tomatoes as compared to nonfertilized tomatoes.

The mineral content of tomatoes has been reported to increase with
growth and maturation (Salunkhe et al. 1974) because of increased cell
organization and permeability, increased acid-base balance, an the activa-
tion of enzyme systems. Although minerals represent a small fraction of the
tomato, they play an important role relative to the nutritional composition
of the tomato.

It has been demonstrated that the protein content of tomatoes is influenced by both maturity and the level of nitrogen available to the plant (Aziz
1968) as well as the amount of enzymatic activity. Protein content was
found to increase with increasing nitrogen level and to also increase with
maturity. However, protein level can be shown to decrease in overripe
tomatoes because of protein degradation, which can serve as a precursor for
flavor compounds (Salunkhe et al. 1974).

The type of fertilizer administered to tomato plants has been shown to
influence the free amino acid composition of tomatoes (Hoff et al. 1974). Free
amino acid composition of a food is important not only from a nutritional
standpoint but also because free amino acids can enter into chemical reactions during processing. However, from the data presented in Table 13.16, it
is interesting to note that the free amino acid composition did not significantly change during ripening, within fertilizer treatment. In contrast to
this study, Davies (1966) observed that both glutamic and aspartic acids
increased by factors of 10 and 2, respectively, as tomatoes passed from the
mature green to red stage of ripeness. An earlier study by Davies (1964)
indicated that glutamic, aspartic, and pyrrolidone-carboxylic acids were all
increased in tomatoes by the application of increasing levels of nitrogen but
were decreased by increasing applications of phosphate.

Corn is probably the crop that has been shown to be most dependent upon
nitrogen application as a means of improving yield. However, as shown in
Table 13.17, nitrogen rate can also influence the level of several macro and
micro minerals associated with corn.

Walker and Hymowitz (1972) have attempted to correlate the organic and

TABLE 13.16.   EFFECT OF FERTILIZER TYPE ON THE FREE AMINO ACID COMPOSITION IN RIPENING TOMATOES

Amino acid	NO$_3$		NH$_4$	
	Green	Ripe	Green	Ripe
Aspartic	0.32	0.45	0.32	0.60
Glutamic	0.70	0.80	1.76	1.76
Pyrrolidone-5-Carboxylic	0.17	0.20	0.72	0.73
Alanine	0.06	0.07	0.17	0.07
Arginine	0.00	0.04	0.08	0.04
γ-Aminobutyric	2.75	2.83	2.76	2.30
Serine	0.09	0.16	0.29	0.15
β-Alanine	0.01	0.02	0.03	0.03
Glycine	0.02	0.03	0.04	0.02
Isoleucine	0.04	0.05	0.27	0.12
Leucine	0.14	0.15	0.23	0.17
Lysine	0.04	0.04	0.20	0.13
Methionine	0.02	0.03	0.07	0.05
Phenylalanine	0.09	0.15	0.47	0.33
Proline	0.01	0.01	0.06	0.02
Tryptophan	0.00	0.00	0.01	0.00
Tyrosine	0.06	0.10	0.17	0.14
Valine	0.08	0.09	0.37	0.19
TOTAL	4.66	5.25	8.37	6.96

From Hoff et al. (1974).

TABLE 13.17.   EFFECT OF NITROGEN RATE ON THE MINERAL COMPOSITION AND YIELD OF CORN

	Mineral composition of corn (lb/20,000 plants)				
	0 lb N/acre	80 lb N/acre	160 lb N/acre	240 lb N/acre	320 lb N/acre
Nitrogen	55.00	91.00	94.00	96.00	109.00
Phosphorus	5.40	8.90	8.30	9.10	13.80
Potassium	95.00	103.00	117.00	141.00	154.00
Calcium	20.00	23.00	27.00	23.00	24.00
Magnesium	11.00	15.00	17.00	14.00	15.00
Manganese	0.17	0.20	0.23	0.18	0.35
Iron	0.50	0.56	0.58	0.60	0.57
Zinc	0.08	0.13	0.16	0.12	0.22
Boron	0.05	0.06	0.08	0.06	0.08
Copper	0.03	0.03	0.04	0.04	0.06
Yield (bu/acre)	118	146	139	153	156

From Walker and Peck (1972).

mineral components of beans, peanuts, and cowpeas in an attempt to uncover any possible linear relationship that could be useful to the plant breeder in improving the overall nutritional quality of these crops. They found that most correlations among oil, total sugar, sucrose, raffinose, and stachyose with 10 different minerals were negative. The only relationship that exhibited a positive correlation was between stachyose, a sugar that is believed to be partly responsible for the flatulence associated with most legumes, and the nitrogen content of beans.

Nitrogen source has also been shown to significantly influence the composition of cultivated mushrooms. Substitution of ammonium nitrogen in the form of ammonium sulfate with urea resulted in mushrooms that contained higher levels of ash, potassium, urea, aspartic acid, manine, valine, and sulfur-free amino acids and a decrease in the free and protein amino acid levels of proline and arginine. As seen in Table 13.18, the nitrogen source also influenced the fatty acid composition of the resulting mushrooms.

As seen in Tables 13.19 and 13.20, the incorporation of small amounts of sulfur into the soil where soybeans are grown can result in a statistically significant increase in the level of protein as well as an increase in the levels of sulfate-containing amino acids such as lysine and methione that have an important nutritional role. It can also be seen from Table 13.20 that the levels of certain nonessential amino acids dropped with sulfur addition. The role of sulfur in plant nutrition and composition has been thoroughly reviewed by Beaton (1966). It is interesting to note that most inorganic fertilizers have sulfur added because of its overall importance; sulfur deficiencies can become a real problem if organic farming is followed exclusively.

Peavy and Greig (1972) conducted an interesting study with spinach in which both mineral and organic fertilizers were applied and the levels of certain nutrients compared over three harvests that lasted over 2 years. Thus, the organic fertilizer (feedlot manure) had a chance to be broken down and made available to the plant. They found that the mineral fertilizer,

TABLE 13.18.   INFLUENCE OF NITROGEN SOURCE ON FATTY ACID COMPOSITION (%) OF CULTIVATED MUSHROOMS

	Fatty Acid in Mushrooms (%)	
Fatty acid	Urea	Ammonium sulfate
Capric	Trace	Trace
Lauric	Trace	Trace
Myristic	0.71	0.40
Pentadecanoic	0.79	0.60
Palmitic	15.79	13.24
Palmitoleic	0.28	0.07
Eptadecanoic	0.89	0.82
Stearic	3.30	2.94
Oleic	2.31	1.38
Linoleic	71.03	78.32
Linolenic	0.50	0.50

From Maggioni et al. (1968).

TABLE 13.19.   INFLUENCE OF SULFUR ADDITION ON THE YIELD AND PROTEIN CONTENT OF SOYBEANS

	Sulfur added			
	0 ppm	10 ppm	20 ppm	40 ppm
Yield (g/plant)	2.4	3.3	3.2	3.0
Protein	33.4	35.8	38.4	33.8

From Sharma and Braford (1973).

TABLE 13.20.   EFFECT OF SULFUR ADDITION ON THE AMINO ACID COMPOSITION OF SOYBEANS

Amino acid	Added sulfur			
	0	10	20	40
Aspartic	6.94	6.19	5.14	4.95
Threonine	3.05	3.27	2.89	2.66
Serine	3.28	2.66	2.59	3.07
Glutamic	7.30	6.14	6.00	7.31
Glycine	2.87	2.07	1.77	1.54
Alanine	3.52	2.92	2.54	2.40
Valine	3.49	3.25	3.43	2.06
Cystine	0.30	0.34	0.38	0.30
Methionine	0.25	0.49	0.48	0.27
Isoleucine	2.58	2.93	2.38	2.08
Leucine	4.08	3.04	2.91	3.37
Tyrosine	0.35	0.15	0.35	0.48
Phenylalanine	0.94	1.06	0.94	1.01
Lysine	3.14	3.30	2.74	4.52
Histidine	4.05	2.47	1.89	2.11
Arginine	4.01	4.03	4.05	4.36

From Sharma and Bradford (1973).
Notes: Indigenous level of sulfur was 6 ppm. Composition expressed as % protein.

when applied at the same nutrient rate as the organic fertilizer, resulted in a greater yield and higher concentration of nitrogen than the organic fertilizer. The organic fertilizer significantly increased phosphorus concentration as compared to the mineral fertilizer for all three crops. Mineral fertilizer was found to increase calcium uptake the first and third crops only as compared to the organic fertilizer. On the other hand, the organic fertilizer significantly increased iron uptake over the mineral fertilizer for the second and third crops as well as significantly increasing sodium levels for all crops. Thus, this study clearly demonstrates the type of problem one can have in arriving at a definite conclusion relative to the nutritional superiority of organic versus mineral fertilizer. Depending on which side you want to defend, data are presented that can be used by both sides. Therefore, this author finds it personally difficult to arrive at a clearcut statement concerning the nutritional claims that have been voiced by both proponents and opponents of organically grown foods.

Another study (Salomon 1972) has appeared showing that in the case of green snap beans, the vitamin C content decreases during their second harvest when mineral fertilizer is used as compared to an actual increase in vitamin C content at the second harvest when compost is used as the fertilizer source (Table 13.21). In the case of carrots, no significant differ-

TABLE 13.21.   EFFECT OF HARVESTING TIMES AND FERTILIZER SOURCE ON THE VITAMIN C CONTENT OF GREEN SNAP BEANS

Fertilizer	Vitamin C content (mg/100 g)	
	First harvest	Second harvest
Compost	26.1	28.6
Matching mineral level	28.7	24.5

From Salomon (1972).

ences in the levels of vitamin C and carotene, which is a precursor for vitamin B_1, were noted when compost and mineral fertilizers were compared.

Several earlier reports (Scheunert *et al.* 1934; Scheunert 1935) have appeared where rats were used to compare the nutritional adequacy of foods raised either organically or conventionally. The authors concluded or observed that the rats (over 1000) on the inorganic fertilized foods lived longer, were more fertile, and showed greater resistance to infectious diseases as compared to the organically grown food group. However, as pointed out by Schuphan (1972), information relative to varieties, location of growth, and statistical significance were not reported, making the apparently extensive study of limited value.

Later studies (Dost and Schuphan 1944; Wendt 1938) involved the use of humans; however, Schuphan (1972) has also criticized these studies because they were of short duration. They compared the use of barnyard manure as a fertilizer source to barnyard manure fortified with inorganic fertilizer. Analysis of the products revealed that the fortified fertilizer source resulted in higher crude protein, carotene, and minerals but lower sugar and vitamin B levels than products raised on barnyard manure alone. The two classes of products were concluded to have no significant influence on the nutritional status and health of adults. However, in the case of infants, the fortified fertilizer was superior to the barnyard fertilizer alone with respect to average daily weight gain, vitamin C, and carotene levels in the blood, teething, red blood count, and serum iron.

Thus, it would appear that these early studies, although not perhaps the best of the experimental design, should have served as some sort of evidence that potential differences, as influenced solely by fertilizer type, could exist. With today's sophisticated scientific technology, it seems somewhat foolish to have the two basic groups making claims and counterclaims about the nutritional quality of their respective products and not yet have a clear scientific understanding as to what the argument is about. Perhaps the current status of the situation has been best summarized by Salomon (1972) who said "I really don't question their equality but rather I am skeptical about their superiority."

As defined earlier, "health foods" are believed to be good sources of to-date unidentified nutritional factors that may be lacking or deficient in certain of our conventionally processed foods. (Engel and Copeland 1952; Ershoff *et al.* 1969) However, to date, definite experiments to substantiate completely these observations have not been reported. Areas like this present additional problems to both sides, because of free and interchangeable use of terms such as health foods, natural, and organic.

ECONOMIC CONSIDERATIONS

It is assumed that the sensory and nutritional qualities of conventional and organically grown foods are essentially the same; one would assume that their cost should be approximately the same. However, the few surveys that have been published clearly point out that the prices of organically grown foods tend to be higher than those of conventionally grown foods, although some exceptions can be found. Thus, it should be noted that no extensive national survey covering at least one year's food prices has been made available to the general public, although several single-city surveys have been published. Also, it should be noted that these surveys are now at least 5 years old and considering how much food prices have changed during this time period, they may not be completely valid today.

One such study was conducted in the Gainesville, Florida, area in 1973 (Appledorf *et al.* 1973). As seen in Table 13.22, eight of the 24 items purchased in traditional stores were more expensive than the same items purchased in health food stores. However, even more interesting is the fact that, as a 24-item group, the items purchased in a health food store cost 70% more than if purchased in a conventional supermarket with some of the same items costing as much as 4.5 times more. Based on the similarity of the proximate composition of these items, which was also part of this study, the authors seriously questioned whether the extra cost of food items purchased in health food stores was justified.

In a later study, (Appledorf *et al.* 1974) the same group again compared the prices paid for certain health store purchased versus comparable supermarket purchased foods. As seen in Table 13.23, 23 of the 25 traditional

TABLE 13.22.   COST COMPARISONS OF VARIOUS FOODS PURCHASED AT HEALTH FOOD AND TRADITIONAL STORES

	Cents/oz.	
Food item	Health food store	Traditional store
Almonds	10.4	10.9
Apple butter	5.9	1.3
Apples, dried	8.4	5.6
Apple juice	2.9	0.9
Brazil nuts	7.6	13.0
Bread, whole wheat	3.4	2.1
Cashews	10.6	10.7
Cereal, whole wheat	4.4	3.0
Cheese, cheddar	11.6	6.6
Coconut	3.0	4.9
Corn snacks	14.0	7.5
Dates	3.3	4.1
Fig bars	4.2	3.0
Honey, tupelo	8.1	3.6
Ice cream, peach	4.3	0.9
Mayonnaise	4.7	4.0
Milk, dry	4.3	5.1
Pancake mix	3.7	1.9
Peanut butter	5.6	4.2
Pecans	15.3	16.5
Preserves, blackberry	6.8	3.7
Rice	1.8	1.2
Rice cereal	6.5	7.0
Tomato juice	2.9	1.0

From Appledorf *et al.* (1973).

foods were equal to or significantly less in cost than the same foods purchased in a health food store. This study also evaluated the sensory properties of these foods, and the authors concluded that the higher price paid for health food store food products could not be justified by the overall general sensory preference of these foods over traditional ones.

The USDA also has published information on the cost of organically grown foods (Office of Consumer Affairs 1972). They reported that a market basket of 29 standard food items purchased in a supermarket cost $11.00, whereas the same food items marketed as being organically grown cost $20.30 in the organic section of a supermarket, $21.90 in a health food store, and $17.80 in a natural food store. A natural food store was defined as a low-profit cooperative type of store where many items were purchased in bulk and repackaged at the store in smaller containers or in containers provided by the consumer. In addition, they published the prices paid for each of 38 items in the four types of stores, which Jukes (1977) nicely converted into percentages based upon the traditional food item price. These data are shown in Table 13.24. Of the 114 potential organically grown food item purchases, only 11 cost less than the corresponding traditionally grown food, with 10 of these items being fresh fruits and vegetables. When the three types of outlets that sold organically grown foods are compared, the organic section in a traditional supermarket only had two lower-priced organic items, the health food store three, and the natural food store six.

TABLE 13.23.   PRICES CHARGED FOR VARIOUS FOODS PURCHASED IN HEALTH FOOD STORES AS COMPARED TO TRADITIONAL STORES

Food item	Cents/oz.	
	Health food store	Traditional store
Apple butter	9.7	1.4
Apples, dried	10.8	8.2
Apple juice	3.3	1.2
Apple sauce	5.0	2.4
Beans/tomato sauce	2.3	1.5
Bread, whole wheat	3.1	2.4
Cashews	9.7	9.7
Cereal	4.9	4.1
Cheese, cheddar	12.0	7.6
Cheese pizza	125.0	111.0
Cheese, swiss	13.4	9.1
Coconut	3.4	7.0
Corn chips	12.2	4.5
Dates	6.1	4.9
Fig bars	4.4	2.2
Honey, orange blossom	5.6	4.2
Ice cream	3.5	1.5
Ketchup	4.6	2.4
Mayonnaise/potatoes	7.4	3.4
Mayonnaise/tomato	7.4	3.4
Milk, powdered	5.6	6.0
Peanut butter	9.5	4.0
Rice	2.6	2.6
Sesame chips	9.8	7.8
Tomato juice	22.5	9.3

From Appledorf *et al.* (1974).

TABLE 13.24. PERCENTAGE FOOD COST COMPARISONS OF ORGANIC FOODS AS INFLUENCED BY STORE OF PURCHASE

Food item	Cost of organic food as percentage of regular food bought in		
	Supermarket	Health food store	Natural food store
Apple juice	224	259	172
Grape juice	198	175	213
Prune juice	236	164	231
Apple sauce	212	236	228
Apple butter	550	600	544
Peach preserves	248	198	220
Plum preserves	212	174	—
Peaches, dried, pitted	181	229	212
Prunes, with pits	162	144	145
Raisins	222	—	175
Pinto beans	295	595	195
Cornmeal	214	314	150
Rice, cream of	134	227	148
Rice, brown, long-grain	188	180	140
Macaroni	316	—	276
Spaghetti	344	—	360
Whole wheat bread	148	148	—
Honey	144	191	91
Peanut butter	165	194	157
Peanut oil	196	227	156
Vinegar, cider	300	239	339
Chicken, fryer, whole	179	227	—
Chicken, fryer, cut-up	167	203	—
Eggs	189	—	189
Fresh fruits and vegetables			
Apples, Rome	150	—	100
Grapefruit	171	218	147
Lemons	83	88	59
Oranges	161	206	111
Asparagus	141	167	129
Carrots	100	116	116
Celery	177	94	94
Cucumber	416	363	300
Lettuce, iceberg	288	188	206
Lettuce, Romaine	140	74	100
Onions	125	150	181
Potatoes	160	230	200
Spinach	131	175	49
Yams	125	150	125

From Jukes (1977).

Another survey (Porter 1975) was conducted in the New York area at approximately the same time. Although not so extensive, it included several vitamin preparations as well as food items. From Table 13.25, it is again apparent that foods and items marked organically grown or processed are in the vast majority of cases significantly more expensive than their traditionally marketed counterparts.

One final cost comparison study (N.Y. State Public Hearing 1972) between organic and regular food will be presented. The cost data (Table 13.26) display the same trend as reported before but have been included to show some of the labeling information presented to consumers of organically grown foods. Some of the verbal descriptions can only attest to the fact

TABLE 13.25.   PRICE COMPARISONS BETWEEN REGULAR AND ORGANICALLY PRODUCED FOODS AND VITAMINS

Item/unit	Regular	Organically produced
Apple juice, qt	$0.37	$0.80
Grape juice, qt	0.37	0.80
Peanut butter, lb	0.99	2.05
Honey, lb	0.53	0.90
Eggs, doz	0.53	1.15
Dried prunes, lb	0.49	1.00
Cider vinegar, qt	0.33	1.00
Wheat bread, lb. loaf	0.43	0.95
C 500 mg, 100 tablets	1.98	3.50
B Complex, 100 tablets	1.79	2.60
E 100 I.U., 100 tablets	2.55	3.30
Multivitamins, 100 tablets	3.45	9.95

From Porter (1975).

that imaginative advertising personnel work for organically grown food companies as well as traditional food concerns.

From the presentation of the cost comparison data, a rational person introduced to this subject for the first time would conclude that the market for organically grown foods must be quite small. However, according to various educated predictions, this is not the case. Wolnak (1977) supplied data indicating that the American public spent between $250 and 300 million on such foods in 1971, $500 million in 1972, and a prediction of $1 billion in 1975, going to $3 billion in 1980. Compared to an expense of $100 billion for conventional foods, the figures seem small, but, as can be noted, their value is growing at a rapid rate.

A primary reason that such sales are growing rapidly is the fact that the number of stores and outlets selling these items is also growing at a fast rate. In the United States the number of such stores has grown from approximately 500 in 1965 to over 3,000 in 1972, with the latter figure not including the number of traditional supermarkets and department stores who have started merchandising these items (Marshall 1974). It has been noted that a similar expansion is apparent in certain European countries, especially the United Kingdom, and to some extent in France and Germany. Some experts (Spaeth 1974) believe that the health food market today is at the same stage as the frozen food industry was 20 years ago and that its further expansion is only a question of time.

Most such outlets in the United States are located on the West Coast, and in California in particular. Two states, namely, California and New York, have 30% of the outlets, while nine states (California, New York, Pennsylvania, Texas, Ohio, Florida, Illinois, Michigan, and New Jersey) have approximately 65% of the national outlets (Spaeth 1974).

The economic importance of the total market for health foods and organically grown foods may be underestimated, as a major portion of the business is conducted by relatively small, independently owned and operated companies, thus making data collection somewhat difficult. The belief that these types of food items do not represent only a passing fad can be sup-

TABLE 13.26. LABELING AND COST COMPARISONS OF ORGANIC AND REGULAR FOODS

Food item	Organic label	Organic food cost		Regular food cost	
Beets	Organic beets	$0.75	10 oz	$0.39	10 oz
Carrots	Grown without chemical artificial fertilizers, fungicides, fumigants or herbs	0.45	1 lb	0.25	1 lb
Cashew nuts	Natural organic, full of nutrition, extra large, superior quality, fresh, shelled, wholesome, flavorful, carefully selected, protein-rich	1.10	8 oz	0.59	6 oz
Relish	Organic chow	0.75	15.5 oz	0.29	22 oz
Dried apricots	No fumigants, no pesticides	1.24	10 oz	0.59	8 oz
Dried prunes	Organic foods	0.35	8 oz	0.49	1 lb
Pickled beets	No tumeric, alum, benzoate of soda, or acids	0.85	15 oz	0.29	16 oz
Raisins	Organic raisins	1.15	16 oz	0.49	15 oz
Sesame candy	An organic chew	0.41	3 oz	0.93	13 oz
Spinach	Unsprayed, organically grown, no chemical residue	0.75	10 oz	0.39	10 oz
Tea	100% natural organic imported orange flower tea	1.49	Box of 40	0.67	Box of 48

From New York State Public Hearing on the Matter of Organic Foods (1972).

ported by the fact that numerous major traditional food processors have also begun to produce and market such food items to compliment their current food lines.

The entire "movement" is even more fascinating if one stops to realize that organically grown foods are not something new. In fact, in light of the history of man, what this author has been calling conventionally grown foods are relatively new, while organically grown foods have been with us since humans started to consume food.

The commercialization of the domestic health food market is also not new. It was started in 1877 by the eminent physician and surgeon, Dr. John Harvey Kellogg, who began feeding baked grain mixtures to patients at his sanitarium in Battle Creek, Michigan. This was the basis for an early prototype of corn flakes, which probably few people today consider to be a health food. One of Dr. Kellogg's patients was named Mr. Post; upon his release, he marketed a cereal-based drink called Postum and a nutlike cereal called Grape Nuts. Some people may be surprised to learn that the granddaddies of the health food movement in the United States were Kellogg and Post. It is also interesting to note that their promotion of what most people considered to be health foods at the time came about because their religious beliefs as Seventh-day Adventists dictated that they be vegetarians. Cereal products were a logical choice to them.

As pointed out by White (1972), health food stores in the past primarily catered to supplying food supplements to older people or providing dietary foods to individuals who experienced food allergies, for example. However, today the organic food movement has been found to be especially popular with younger people, many of whom are antiestablishment and will go to great lengths to avoid purchasing food marketed by the major food companies.

One group (IFT 1974) claims that one reason the cost of organically grown food is more than that of conventionally grown food is the fact that the fertilizer costs are significantly different. From data that is not explained or referenced, they report that nitrogen from garbage compost costs $12 per pound, while nitrogen in dry cow manure costs $5 per pound. In comparison, nitrogen, at the time the article was written, from commercial chemical fertilizer was costing 7.5 to 15 cents per pound.

Others believe that these foods cost more because the demand for them exceeds their supply. In 1972, only 200 farms in the United States were certified organic. Another list published at approximately the same time (Allen 1971) listed 38 certified organic farms that had a combined total of only 1642 acres under cultivation, with 27 of these 38 farms consisting of fewer than 50 acres. Some people have expressed concern about whether all the food that is marketed as organically grown is truly organically grown. Another potential concern is the fact that, as some of these farms are so small, there is a strong possibility of environmental contamination from neighboring farms that are growing crops using conventional methods. Certification that a farm is truly organic involves questionnaires to growers on methods of farming, checking soil samples for residues, and personal visits (Goldstein 1971). Presently, inspection and certification of organically grown foods has been voluntary. However, at least one state has expressed support to effectively control the marketing procedures and certification program for organically grown foods. It has been proposed that organic farmers register with the state each year, be inspected at least twice a year, and pay an inspection fee (Goldstein 1972). If such a proposal became law, it is argued, a large number of inspectors would be required and the expense would either become a taxpayer expense or be passed on to the consumer of organically grown foods. Other factors believed involved in higher prices include the concept that most organic farms are small and require more manual labor. In addition, yields may not be as high, crop losses are greater, and shipping costs tend to be higher because these smaller organizations cannot effectively compete with the established supermarket chains.

One scientist (Howard 1973) has perhaps best summarized the primary reason that people apparently are willing to spend more for organically grown foods than conventional foods. He stated that "knowledge of the emotional value of food is much older than the nutritional value of food; hence, many people will pay the increased price because food has an emotional rather than intellectual value."

REFERENCES

ALLEN, F. 1971. Looking for organic America. Org. Gardening Farming *18*, 75–83.

AMERICAN CHEMICAL SOCIETY. 1969. Cleaning Our Environment, the Chemical Basis for Action. Washington, D.C.

ANONYMOUS. 1972. Organic farmers seal—certifying program launched nationwide. Org. Food Mark. *2*, 2–5.

APPLEDORF, H., PENNINGTON, J., WHEELER, W.B., and KOBURGER, J.A.. 1974. Sensory evaluation of health foods—a comparison with traditional foods. J. Milk Food Technol. *37*, 392–394.

APPLEDORF, H., WHEELER, W.B., and KOBURGER, J.A. 1973. Health foods versus traditional foods: a comparison. J. Milk Food Technol. *36*, 242–244.

AZIZ, A.B.A. 1968. Seasonal changes in the physical and chemical composition of tomato fruits as affected by nitrogen levels. Meded. Landbouwhogeschool Wageningen *68*, 1–14.

BAIER, D.C. and FRYER, W.B. 1973. Undesirable plant responses with sewage irrigation. J. Irrigation Drainage Division, ASAE *99*, 133–137.

BEATON, J.D. 1966. Sulfur requirements of cereals, tree fruits, vegetables and other crops. Soil Sci. *101*, 267–282.

BISOGNI, C.A., ARMBRUSTER, G., and BRECHT, P.E. 1976. Quality comparisons of room ripened and field ripened tomato fruits. J. Food Sci. *41*, 333–338.

BOE, A.A., DO, J.Y., and SALUNKHE, D.K. 1968. Tomato ripening: effects of light frequency, magnetic field and chemical treatments. Econ. Botany 22, 124–134.

BRAIDS, O.C., SOBHAN-ARDAKANI, M., and MOLINA, J.A.E. 1970. Liquid digested sewage sludge gives field crops necessary nutrients. Illinois Res. 12, 6–7.

CHANG, Y. 1967. The fungi of wheat straw compost. II. Biochemical and physiological studies. Trans. Br. Mycol. Soc. 50, 667–677.

CHANG, Y. and HUDSON, H.J. 1967. The fungi of wheat straw compost. I. Ecological studies. Trans. Br. Mycol. Soc. 50, 649–66.

CORNFIELD, A.H. 1958. Composting of straw in small units. Plant and Soil 10, 183–193.

DALAL, K.B., OLSON, L.W., YU, M.H., and SALUNKHE, D.K. 1967. Gas chromatography of field, glass-greenhouse-grown, and artificially ripened tomatoes. Phytochem. 6, 155–157.

DAVIES, J.N. 1965. Effect of nitrogen, phosphorus and potassium fertilizers on the non-volatile organic acids of tomato fruit. J. Sci. Food Agric. 15, 665–673.

DAVIES, J.N. 1966. Changes in the non-volatile organic acids of tomato fruit during ripening. J. Sci. Food Agric. 17, 396–400.

DOST, F.H. and SCHUPHAN, W. 1944. Über Ernährungsversuche mit verschieden gedüngten Gemüsen. Die Ernährung 9, 1–7.

ENGE, R. and BAERUG, R. 1971. Effect of heavy nitrogen fertilizer dressings and crop rotation on yield and quality properties of table potatoes. Joint Report of Farm Crops Inst. (No. 182) and Inst. Fertilization and Soil Management (No. 69) of Norway, page 1.

ENGEL, R.W. and COPELAND, D.H. 1952. Protective action of stock diets against the cancer inducing action of 2-acetylaminofluorene in rats. Cancer Res. 12, 211–215.

ERICKSON, B. 1972. California Home Economics Legislative News Suppl., Oct. 24.

ERSHOFF, B.H., BAJBUA, G.S., FIELD, J.B., and BAVETTA, L.A. 1969. Comparative effects of purified diets and a natural food stock ration on the tumor incidence of mice exposed to multiple sublethal doses of total body X-irradiation. Cancer Res. 29, 780–784.

FAO–WHO Joint Expert Committee on Food Additives. 1972. Sixteenth report, WHO Tech. Rept. Ser. No. 505, Geneva.

FERGUS, C.L. 1964. Thermophilic and thermotolerant molds and actinomyces of mushroom compost during peak heating. Mycologia 56, 267–284.

FOOD AND DRUG ADMINISTRATION. 1972. A study of health practices and opinions, final report. Department of Health, Education and Welfare, contract No. FDA 66–193, Washington, D.C.

FOX, F.W. 1970. Facts, fads and fallacies about food. South African Med. J. 44, 736–737.

GERRETSEN, F.C., KOLENBRANDER, G.J., and MELMAN, T.P. 1956. Composting time in relation to nitrogen activity of ground town refuse compost. Verslagen Van Landbouwkundige Onderzoekingen No. 62.6, pp. 1–24.

GOLDSTEIN, J. 1971. National farmers organization to market organic crops. Org. Gardening Farming *18*, 79–83.

GOLDSTEIN, J. 1972. Pennsylvania seeks ways to aid organic family farmer. Org. Gardening Farming *19*, 75–77.

GOLUEKE, C.G. and McGAUHEY, P.H. 1970. Comprehensive studies of solid waste management. First and Second Annual Reports. Public Health Service Pub. No. 2039, U.S. Bureau of Solid Waste Management, Washington, D.C.

HOFF, J.E., WILCOX, G.E., and JONES, C.M. 1974. The effect of nitrate and ammonium in nitrogen on the free amino acid composition of tomato plants and tomato fruit. J. Amer. Soc. Hort. Sci. *99*, 27–30.

HOWARD, A. 1935. The manufacture of humus by the Indore process, J. Roy. Soc. Arts *84*, 25–33.

HOWARD, H.W. 1973. Why chemicals in food? Food Prod. Dev. 7, 6–8.

HUISINGH, D. 1974. Heavy metals: Implications for agriculture. Ann. Rev. Phytopath. *12*, 375–388.

INSTITUTE OF FOOD TECHNOLOGISTS' EXPERT PANEL ON FOOD SAFETY AND NUTRITION. 1974. Organic foods. Food Technol. *28*, 71–74.

JERIS, J.S. and REGAN, R.W. 1973. Controlling environmental parameters for optimal composting. Compost Sci. *14*, 10–15.

JUKES, T.H. 1971. Fact and fancy in nutrition and food sciences. J. Amer. Dietet. Assoc. *59*, 203–211.

JUKES, T.H. 1977. Organic food. CRC Crit. Rev. Food Sci. Nutr. *9*, 395–418.

KING, L.D., RUDGERS, L.A., and WEBBER, L.R. 1974. Application of municipal refuse and liquid sewage sludge to agricultural land. J. Environ. Quality *3*, 361–366.

KNOLL, K.H. 1961. Public health and refuse disposal. Compost Sci. *2*, 35–40.

KOCHTITZKY, O.W., SEAMAN, W.K., and WILEY, J.S. 1969. Municipal composting research at Johnson City, Tennessee. Compost. Sci. *9*, 5–16.

LEVERTON, R.M. 1973. Nutritive value of "organically grown" foods. J. Amer. Diet Assoc. *62*, 501.

LeRICHE, H.H. 1968. Metal contamination of soil in the Woburn market-garden experiment resulting from the application of sewage sludge. J. Agric. Sci. *71*, 205–207.

MAGA, J.A., MOORE, F.D., and OSHIMA, N. 1976. Yield, nitrate levels and sensory properties of spinach as influenced by organic and mineral nitrogen fertilizer levels. J. Sci. Food Agric. *27*, 109–114.

MAGGIONI, A., PASSERA, C., RENOSTO, F., and BENETTI, E. 1968. Composition of cultivated mushrooms during the growing cycle as affected by the nitrogen source introduced in composting. J. Agric. Food Chem. *16*, 517–519.

MARSHALL, W.E. 1974. Health foods, organic foods, natural foods. Food Technol. *28*, 50–51, 56.

NATIONAL ANALYSIS, INC. 1972. A Study of Health Practices and Opinions, Report No. PB 210978. Philadelphia.

NATIONAL DAIRY COUNCIL. 1973. Food Faddism. Dairy Council Digest *44*(1), 1–6.

NELSON, P.E. and HOFF, J.E. 1969. Tomato volatiles: Effect of variety, processing and storage time. J. Food Sci. *34*, 53–57.

NEW YORK STATE PUBLIC HEARING ON THE MATTER OF ORGANIC FOODS. 1972. Before Attorney General Louis J. Lefkowitz, New York, December 1.

OFFICE OF CONSUMER AFFAIRS. 1972. Consumer News, No. 13, 1–4.

PATTEE, H.E. and SINGLETON, J.A. 1972. Comparison of geographical and varietal effect on the peanut volatile profile by peak-ratio analysis. J. Agric. Food Chem. *20*, 1119–1124.

PEAVY, W.S. and GREIG, J.K. 1972. Organic and mineral fertilizers compared by yield, quality and composition of spinach. J. Amer. Soc. Hort. Sci. *97*, 718–723.

PEW, W.D. and GARDNER, B.R. 1972. Nitrogen effects on cantaloupes, 1972. Comm. Soil Sci. Plant Analy. *3*, 467–476.

POINCELOT, R.P. 1975. The biochemistry and methodology of composting. Conn. Agric. Exp. Sta., New Haven, Bull. 754, 1–18.

POINCELOT, R.P. and DAY, P.R. 1973. Rates of cullulose decomposition during the composting of leaves combined with several municipal and industrial wastes and other additives. Compost Sci. *14*, 23–25.

PORTER, S. 1975. Sylvia Porter's Money Book. Doubleday, Garden City, New York.

SALOMON, R. 1972. Natural foods—myth or magic. Assoc. Food Drug Officials 36, 131–136.

SALUNKHE, D.K., JADHAV, S.J., and YU, M.H. 1974. Quality and nutritional composition of tomato fruit as influenced by certain biochemical and physiological changes. Qual. Plant. Pl. Fds. Hum. Nutr.. *24*, 85–93.

SARAVACOS, G., LUH, B.S., and LEONARD, S.J. 1959. Effect of fertilizers on quality and composition of tomato juice. J. Food Sci. *24*, 648–655.

SATRIANA, M.J. 1974. Large scale composting. Pollution Tech. Rev. No. 12, Noyes Data Corp., Park Ridge, New Jersey.

SCHEUNERT, A. 1935. Vergleichende Unters. Der Physiologischen Wirkungen Fortgesetzten Genusses von Nahrungsmittelin, die mit und ohne Handelsdunger gezogen sind. Angew. Chem. *48*, 42–45.

SCHEUNERT, A., SACHSE, T., and SPECHT, A. 1934. Über die Wirkung fortgesetzter Verfütterung von Nahrungsmitteln die mit und ohne kunstliche Düngung gezogen sind. Biochem. Z. *274*, 372–377.

SCHOONOVER, W.R. 1972. Your Garden: Should it be Organic? Leaflet, Agricultural Extension, Univ. California. Davis, California.

SCHUPHAN, W. 1972. Effects of the application of inorganic and organic manures on the market quality and on the biological value of agricultural products. Qual. Plant Mater. Veg. *21*, 381–398.

SCHUTZ, H.G. and LORENZ, O.A. 1976. Consumer preferences for vegetables grown under "commercial" and "organic" conditions. J. Food Sci. *41*, 70–73.

SHAH, B.M., SALUNKHE, D.K., and OLSON, L.E. 1969. Effects of the ripening processes on the chemistry of tomato volatiles. J. Amer. Soc. Hort. Sci. *94*, 171–176.

SHARMA, G.C. and BRADFORD, R.R. 1973. Effect of sulfur on yield and amino acids of soybean. Comm. Soil Sci. Plant Analy. *4*, 77–82.

SIPPLE, H.L. and KING, C.G. 1954. Food fads and fallacies. J. Agric. Food Chem. *2*, 352–354.

SPAETH, R.S. 1974. Growth of health food sales in the supermarket. Food Prod. Devel. *7*, 28–30.

SPITZER, E.F. 1967. Composting works in Houston. Amer. City *82*, 97–104.

STARE, F.J., HEGSTED, D.M., MAYER, J., GEYER, R.P., GERSHOFF, S.N., HERRERA, M.G., McGANDY, R.B., KERR, G.R., and ANTONIADES, H.N. 1972. "Health" foods: Definition and nutrient values. J. Nutr. Ed. *4*, 94–97.

STUTZENBERGER, F.J. 1971. Cellulase production by Thermomonopora curata isolated from municipal solid waste compost. Appl. Microbiol. *22*, 147–152.

STUTZENBERGER, F.J., KAUFMAN, A.J., and LOSSIN, R.D. 1970. Cellulolytic activity in municipal solid waste composting. Can. J. Microbiol. *16*, 553–560.

TABER, H.G., DAVISON, A.D., and TELFORD, H.S. 1976. Organic gardening. Wash. State Univ. Coop. Ext. Service, Bull. EB 648, pp. 1–16.

UNIVERSITY OF CALIFORNIA AT BERKELEY. 1953. Reclamation of municipal refuse by composting. Sanitary Engineering Research Project, Tech. Bull. No. 9.

UTZINGER, J.D., TRIERWEILER, J., JANSON, B., MILLER, R.L., SADDAM, A., and CREAN, D.E. 1970. Organic gardening. Coop. Ext. Service, Purdue Univ., Bull. HO-70, pp. 1–19.

VON ELBE, J.H. 1972. Organic foods—Another consumer hoax? J. Milk Food Technol. *35*, 669–671.

WALKER, W.M. and HYMOWITZ, T. 1972. Simple correlations between certain mineral and organic components of common beans, peanuts and cowpeas. Comm. Soil Sci. Plant Analy. *3*, 505–511.

WALKER, W.M. and PECK, T.R. 1972. How nitrogen rates affect nutrient content of corn plants as measured in two ways. Illinois Res. *14*, 16–19.

WENDT, H. 1938. Über Ernährungsversuche mit verschieden gedüngten Gemüsen. Die Ernährung *3*, 53–57.

WHITE, H.S. 1972. The organic foods movement. Food Technol. *26*, 29–33.

WILEY, J.S. 1957. High rate composting. Amer. Soc. Civil Engr. Trans. Abst. 2895.

WILEY, J.S. 1962. Pathogen survival in composting municipal wastes. J. Water Pollution Control Federation *34*, 80–90.

WOLNAK, B. 1972. Food industry and FDA face fad food threat. Food Product Devel. *6*, 28–30.

14

Quality and Quality Determination of Ecologically Grown Foods

Dietrich Knorr and Hartmut Vogtmann

Food Production and Food Consciousness
Eco-Foods and Eco-Farming
Quality of Conventionally Grown Foods versus Eco-Foods
Food Quality Criteria
Detection of Eco-Foods
Conclusions
References

FOOD PRODUCTION AND FOOD CONSCIOUSNESS

There are two counteractive trends in current agricultural food production. The first of them is the tendency to a more centralized, mechanized, and capital-intensive agricultural production. Recent developments of the conventional U.S. agricultural system are an example of this development (Anon. 1978). This trend can also be underlined by the following statement (U.S. General Accounting Office 1978):

The agriculture sector is heading toward fewer but larger farms which are capturing a larger portion of total farm sales. Today's farmer is moving away from the self-sufficient, independent, land-owning model of yesteryear into a commercial entrepreneur, specializing in single crops. He is enmeshed in the trends of national and international economics, relying increasingly upon a variety of other specialists to provide capital, new technology, supplies, land, petroleum products, and marketing assistance. Land no longer is the farmer's primary production input as productivity of the land now depends upon the skill and knowledge with which capital is applied.

The second trend is geared towards more ecologically oriented agriculture, where food production is regarded as a cyclic system in which soil, animals, and plants are linked and in which natural regulatory principles play an active part (Merrill 1976). This development is worldwide (Besson and Vogtmann 1978; NGO-Report 1979) and is discussed at various levels (Youngberg 1978; Peters 1979; Oelhaf 1978).

The Federal Republic of Germany, for example, published on the occasion of the 1979 United Nations Conference on Science and Technology for Development (Science and Technology 1979) the following statement:

Population growth and the much needed increased investments mean, for many countries, that continuously higher outputs must be demanded from limited farming land. Mechanization and large inputs of mineral fertilizers seem to be the most suitable instruments—until nature steps in and replies with decreased yields. We have to realise that, in agriculture in particular, interferences with natural processes must be oriented towards ecological necessities and cannot be subject to economic pressures.

Other arguments are frequently used to favor more ecological approaches in food production. First, the consequences of excessive use of chemicals in agricultural production and their application during industrial food processing on the environment as well as on human and animal health is mentioned (Schönbäck 1980; Hall 1974), and second the reported higher nutritional quality of ecologically grown food (Gottschewski 1975).

Some of the currently used food quality criteria such as yield or weight on a fresh weight basis, size and uniformity, appearance and resistance to handling have been reported to be more adapted to the technological needs of an industrial type of agricultural system specializing in single crops in which the soil is regarded as an inert support medium (Matile 1971; Ulbricht 1975) than to nutritional considerations. They may also have been promoted by food processors because they are easily recognized by the consumer ("external" food quality criteria).

The introduction of hard-skinned tomatoes (Hightower 1972) in California in order to resist the physical stress during mechanical harvesting has been given as an example of how efforts to maximize productivity (here yield on a fresh weight basis) and efforts to give higher priority to technological needs than to nutritional ones can be counterproductive to food production as a whole. These tomatoes resulted in higher yields but also increased in water content (Perelman 1976), which had to be added by irrigation. This "productivity improvement" is actually added to the cost of drying out the tomatoes for ketchup, tomato sauce, and other processed tomato products (Knorr 1979A) because 86% of the tomatoes harvested are processed, the first step of which is water removal (Pimentel et al. 1977).

Most of the existing concern about food quality (Merrill 1976; Hall 1974; Verrett and Carper 1974) is directed toward the use of various additives and supplements during agricultural production and during food processing. There is also concern about the foods derived from highly refined ingredients and the effects of such foods on human health and performance. Consequently, the steadily growing interest in natural foods, health foods, and "organic" food increased rapidly during the last few years. Retail sales for such foods in the United States were projected to rise from $500 million in 1972 to $3 billion by 1980 (Anon. 1974).

There are indications that an increasing number of people are becoming more and more concerned about the quality of their food supply (Leinen 1978) and are willing to pay more for higher food quality (Scheer and Krammer 1979; Vogtmann 1979). More than 70% of the Austrian population, for example, stated that they would be willing to pay up to 10% higher price for ecologically (organically) grown products (Scheer and Krammer 1979), which they assumed to be of higher nutritional quality.

In 1978, 61% of the U.S. public said that natural foods are better than other foods (Leinen 1978). That professional journals are now dealing with these products (e.g., Anon. 1974; White 1972; Packard 1978; Knorr 1979B), that various institutions distribute releases on the subject (e.g., IFT 1979; Stephenson 1978), and that health foods and organic foods are now topics in food science textbooks (e.g., Labuza 1977; Peckham and Freeland—Graves 1979), all indicate the increasing interest in the area of natural foods, health foods, and organic foods.

There is also increasing interest among food processors within the scientific and professional community and governmental agencies (Anon. 1974; Stephenson 1978) for natural and organic foods. Despite this interest few facts exist on the quality of conventionally versus ecologically grown foods. This leads to confusion and controversy among consumers, producers, government regulators, and researchers.

ECO-FOODS AND ECO-FARMING

The terms natural foods and health foods are perceived in no official legal definition and are often used interchangeably (Stephenson 1978). It is commonly understood that these foods are minimally processed or have not been processed at all (Knorr 1979A). Organic foods (organically grown foods, or better, biologically or ecologically grown foods) will be referred to as eco-foods in this chapter. Eco-foods are defined as those foods which result from environmentally sound resource efficient and sustainable (over the long term) agricultural systems. This very broad definition includes "organic"foods but separates them from natural foods and from health foods and separates them from foods that have been ecologically grown but have been processed conventionally. These products result from"organic farming" (sometimes also called cyclic farming, biological farming, eco-farming, ecological farming) in its most general sense (Lockeretz and Wernik 1979).

Although practitioners of these systems sometimes distinguish between these terms, there are no clearly agreed-upon definitions. In Europe there have been several attempts to define the terms and to regulate the methods for the production of eco-foods (Vogtmann 1979; Aubert 1979). Eco-foods are probably less undefined than health and natural foods and should be strictly separated from them. There are no legal definitions of these terms. *Health foods* are commonly understood as special foods with implied unique health claims. Health food is also used as a general term that seems to encompass natural and organic foods. *Natural foods* are commonly understood as products that are minimally processed and that contain no artificial or synthetic ingredients.

Advocates of organic farming or farming "without inorganic fertilizers"[1] or synthetic pesticides claim, largely on the basis of anecdotal reports, that organic farming is safer and more environmentally sound, uses less fossil fuel, and has lower production costs (Youngberg 1978; Lockeretz and Wernik 1979). Opponents on the other hand, have cautioned that nonchemical farming is neither profitable nor productive enough to meet our food needs. For example, White–Stevens (1977) wrote:

To deny American farmers the use of artificial fertilizers . . . would require the removal of 100 million Americans . . . it would also become necessary to open up some 250 million acres of new land, pressing wildlife into further extinction, return some 20 million non-rural people back to the toil of the soil and stop labor, to reduce the present standard of living by at least 50% and to retreat to the way of life of a century ago.

The controversy over the value of organic farming has been prolonged by the virtual lack of recent research on the topic. The first effort in the United States to study commercial-scale farming (Klepper *et al.* 1977; Lockeretz *et al.* 1975, 1978) examined field crop production on Corn Belt organic farms. The study also examined the production methods, cost, and energy requirements of organic farming as well as social characteristics of organic farmers (see Chapter 4). One of the most important findings of this study was that crop production was comparably profitable on organic and conventional farms. More recent studies (Bernardi 1978; Krate 1979) reached roughly comparable conclusions. The results of these studies, while far too incomplete to provide sufficient information about the consequences of large-scale conversion to organic methods, provide no support for White–Stevens' (1977) prediction.

Youngberg (1978) indicated that the future of ecological agriculture may depend more upon the future costs of chemically based, energy-intensive agricultural production than it does upon the political effort of the alternative agricultural movement. Rising energy prices and uncertainties associated with conventional agriculture have forced many farmers to reexamine some of the older methods of soil husbandry and some newer methods of composting, integrated pest control, mixed cropping systems, renewable energy resources, and the reintegration of livestock with agronomy (Merrill 1976; Youngberg 1978). According to Youngberg (1978), promoters and

---

[1]The term organic fertilizer commonly includes urea, an organic compound, but not rock phosphate or other inorganic minerals, which are generally regarded as acceptable by organic farmers. There is no contradiction in this, as the word organic has several meanings besides its specifically chemical one (Lockeretz and Wernik 1979).

practitioners of ecological farming firmly believe that ecological agriculture is destined to play an increasingly important role in the future of agriculture, and most alternative agriculturists seem genuinely convinced that time and circumstances are on their side. As also reported by Youngberg (1978) and by Besson and Vogtmann (1978), their efforts have already begun to bear fruit and they definitely intend to "keep fighting the battle" (Youngberg 1978), possibly even with governmental support (Staff Report 1978). The 1974 U.S. Department of Agriculture Yearbook of Agriculture formally acknowledged the existence of "organic" farming (Leverton 1974), and in 1977 the Secretary of Agriculture suggested that alternatives to the heavy use of pesticides and other petroleum-based agricultural inputs must be found (Youngberg 1978). The 1978 Senate staff report prepared for hearings on USDA agricultural research priorities stated:

The Department of Agriculture's research program has provided enormous benefits to the country and to farmers, but its stress on one mode of production—the large-scale, energy, capital, chemical intensive farm—has come at a considerable cost. Alternative models, including small family farms and organic and similar farming techniques, offer great potential in areas such as the preservation of rural society, the protection of the environment, human health, the maintenance of an independent, alternative life style for farm families, and the conservation of the soil and other natural resources. The dismissal of these alternatives by the research establishment is contrary to the evidence presented on their behalf, and, we believe, to good public policy (Staff Report 1978).

QUALITY OF CONVENTIONALLY GROWN FOODS VERSUS ECO-FOODS

One of the most controversial areas of organic farming is the question of whether eco-foods are of a quality superior to that of conventionally grown food. On the one hand, there are several claims by producers and consumers and researchers of organic products that they are superior in nutritive value and sensory quality, but on the other hand there are statements by members of the scientific and professional community that no nutrient differences exist between conventionally grown foods and eco-foods. A Scientific Status Summary by the Institute of Food Technologists (Anon. 1974) states, for example; "Organically grown foods are identical in nutrition to those grown by conventional methods using inorganic chemicals. There is no scientific evidence that can demonstrate any difference."

Packard (1978) writes, referring to organic and conventional farming, "No nutrient differences exist in food crops grown under the two different methods—none. Those who suggest otherwise are clearly and grossly in error, whether purposely so or out of innocent ignorance."

However, Schuphan (1972) cautioned, "Detrimental consequences in quality (obviously in market quality and not visible in intrinsic value) may occur by the use of exclusively mineral fertilizers in excess, e.g., of nitrogen in cultivating vegetables: Decreases in taste, flavor, in keeping during storage, in resistance against diseases and pests as well as lowering of the biological value of products.

Comparative Studies

A number of comparative studies have been carried out to examine the influence of "organic" and mineral fertilization and the influence of "organic" and conventional farming on crop yield and food quality (McCarrison 1926; Abele 1973; Wistinghausen 1973; Schuphan 1974; Lockeretz et al. 1975; Svec et al. 1976; Pettersson 1978; Samaras 1977; Aehnelt and Hahn 1973).

Many of these studies lack an adequate design for sufficient comparisons. A common problem is the insufficient duration of the studies. Most of them were of one or two years duration. It usually takes three to five years until the environment is satisfactorily adjusted to the new farming conditions (Preuschen et al. 1977). Examples of long-term experiments are the food composition and yield studies by Schuphan (1974) during 12 years and the 5 year nutritional quality studies by Gottschewski (1975).

Some of the frequently cited studies were also misinterpreted (Anon. 1974; Packard 1978; Stephenson 1978). The Michigan study (Dexter 1955) compared crops from depleted and mineral-fertilized soil and not organic and mineral fertilizer application, and the twenty-five year program of the U.S. Plant Soil and Nutrition Laboratory (Brandt and Beeson 1951) compared the results of two harvests.

Feeding Studies

McCarrison (1926) investigated the effect of fertilizing conditions on the nutritive values of millet and wheat on weight maintenance of pigeons and growth of rats. The treatment of the soil with (1) no manure, (2) complete chemical manure, and (3) organic (cattle) manure resulted in higher nutritive values for the products grown on soil treated with organic manure.

The differences in growth of the animals used, a reflection of the nutritive value of the grains, ranged between 10 and 17%. These differences were suggested to be due, in considerable part, to differences in vitamin A content in wheat and vitamin B content in millet. (Note that the study was performed in 1926 when knowledge of B vitamins was in its infancy.) Figure 14.1 shows the percentage loss of weight in groups of pigeons, of the same initial aggregate weight, when fed on a basal diet. The basal diet of rice, assumed to be "insufficient in vitamins, suitable proteins and inorganic salts," was fed to adult pigeons with addition of small amounts of millet grown under the three different conditions. The least weight loss was the criterion for optimal nutrition. The addition of the "no manure" millet increased the rate at which body weight was lost and hastened the time of death as compared with the controls that received no millet. "Organic

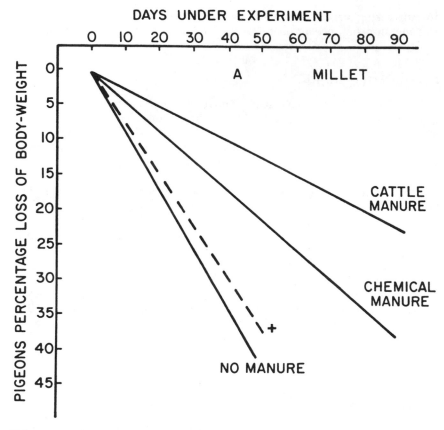

FIG. 14.1.   WEIGHT LOSS OF PIGEONS FED A BASAL RICE DIET SUPPLEMENTED
WITH MILLET GROWN ON SOILS FERTILIZED BY THREE DIFFERENT TECHNIQUES.
*CONTROLS. AFTER McCARRISON 1926.

manure" millet was markedly superior to either of the other millets in
preventing the loss of weight caused by a diet of rice. Comparisons of growth
of young rats receiving 1 g of "organic manure wheat" daily with that of
others receiving 1 g of "chemical manure" wheat daily in addition to commercial basal diet are demonstrated in Fig. 14.2.

Miller and Dema (1958), feeding successive generations of rats on a
supplemented ($CaCO_3$, NaCl, Vitamin A) wholemeal wheat flour diet failed
to detect a difference in the reproductive performance of these animals
using wheat grown with no manurial treatment, artificial fertilizers, or
farmyard manure. Scott et al. (1960) found evidence suggesting a difference
in the growth rate and reproductive performance of mice receiving supplemental whole wheat that had been produced by organic and chemical
methods of farming. The litter size at birth, the weaning ability of the

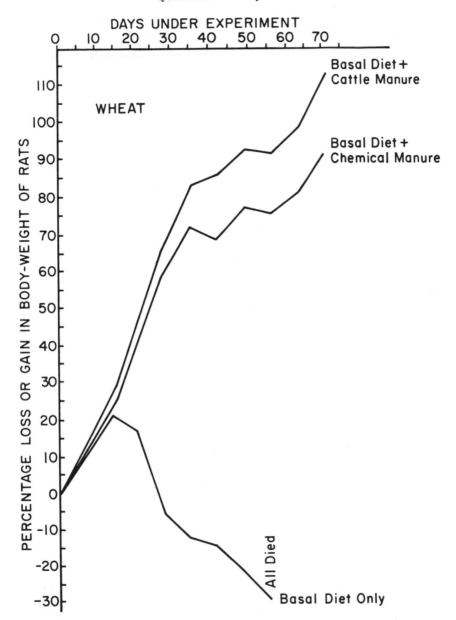

FIG. 14.2.   GROWTH OF RATS FED A BASAL DIET (MEAT RESIDUES, PURIFIED STARCH, OLIVE OIL, SALT MIXTURE) SUPPLEMENTED BY WHEAT GROWN ON DIFFERENTLY FERTILIZED SOILS AND A NONSUPPLEMENTED DIET. AFTER McCARRISON 1926.

mother, and the time interval between successive litters of mice receiving wheat flour, grown on "organic" or stockless (chemical) treated soil, were compared by McSheehy (1977). Analyses of the results failed to detect a difference on these parameters resulting from diets containing wheat grown under different conditions. However, the weaning weights of the offspring of the animals receiving these various diets were significantly different.

Gottschewski (1975) compared a common diet, which was a commercial preparation, with one of similar components that were organically grown. The findings after three years showed a significantly higher number of rabbits born alive and the highest number of rabbits born alive to mothers on the organic diet. The percentage of stillborn animals was highest in the common diet group (Table 14.1). Schiller (1971) studied the relationship between intensive application of mineral fertilizers on pastures and the fertility of cows. He found significant differences in the compositions of plants grown on pastures treated with different concentrations of mineral fertilizers and supposed that increasing mineral fertilization was the reason for higher sterility rates found in cows. Aehnelt and Hahn (1973) found similar results when studying bulls; here the intensive mineral fertilization of the pastures resulted in decrease of the quality of the bull sperm.

Food Composition

Increasing amounts of mineral fertilizer application usually results in an increase of the crude protein content (total N × factor) of the products (Schuphan 1976; Pomeranz et al. 1977; Macleod 1965; Rending and Mickelsen 1976). It was found that nonprotein-nitrogen concentration and the concentration of nonessential amino acids increased with increasing mineral nitrogen application while the concentration of some essential amino acids decreased (MacLeod 1965; Schuphan 1976). Pettersson (1978) showed

TABLE 14.1.   COMPARISON OF OFFSPRING OF RABBITS FED A STANDARD PELLET DIET, A DIET OF CONVENTIONALLY GROWN INGREDIENTS, AND A DIET OF ORGANICALLY GROWN INGREDIENTS.

	Diets		
	Pellet standard N = 40	Conventional N = 32	Organic N = 31
Rabbits born:	264	167	150
alive (no.)	170	99	119
(%)	64	59	79
dead (no.)	94	68	31
(%)	36	41	21
Rabbits alive at			
90 days postpartum:	132	80	110
as % of total			
live births	78	81	92
as % of total			
births	50	48	73

After Gottschewski 1975.

lower crude protein content, but higher true protein content and higher Essential Amino Acid Index (EAA index) for organically grown potatoes compared with conventionally grown ones.

A decrease of protein quality (EAA index) with increasing mineral nitrogen application, resulting in increasing crude protein content and decreasing dry matter content (Fig. 14.3), was found in spinach and lettuce (Schuphan 1976).

McCarrison (1926) as well as Pettersson (1978) showed that true protein content was lower after nitrogen, phosphorous, potassium fertilizer (NPK) application when compared to organic fertilizer application. Svec *et al.*

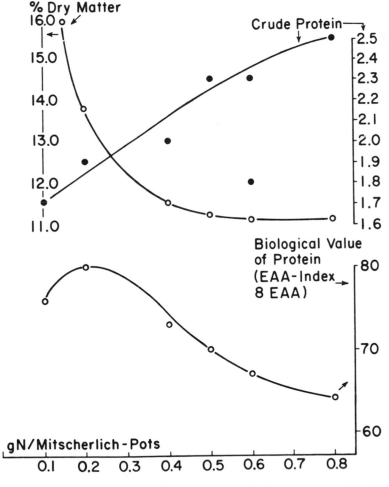

FIG. 14.3.   CHANGES OF CRUDE PROTEIN CONTENT (N × 6.25), DRY MATTER CONTENT, AND BIOLOGICAL VALUE OF PROTEIN OF LETTUCE WITH INCREASING LEVELS OF MINERAL NITROGEN APPLICATION. AFTER SCHUPHAN 1976.

(1976) found no differences in the ascorbic acid concentration of some raw and home-processed vegetables grown under organic and conventional conditions, and no significant differences due to treatment were detected for ascorbic acid and carotene content of seedling rye (Brandt and Beeson 1951). Higher vitamin C concentration for eco-foods were reported as a result of long-term experiments by Schuphan (1976), and about 3.6 times more vitamin C and 2.3 times more βcarotene were found in ecologically grown leek and carrots respectively (IFOAM 1977). Additional data on the composition of ecologically and conventionally grown food are given in Table 14.2.

Wilberg (1972) found slightly higher nitrate concentrations in ecologically grown spinach when compared with conventionally grown. According to Schuphan's (1974) 12-year experiments, nitrate-nitrogen of vegetables from "ecologically" treated soil was 16 times less than that of conventionally grown products. More recent Swiss studies (Schudel *et al.* 1979; Schmid *et al.* 1979) also showed that different plant varieties can respond differently to mineral fertilizer or to compost treatment resulting in higher nitrate content when NPK fertilizer is used (Table 14.3). It should be noted that too high amounts of organic as well as too high amounts of mineral fertilizers generally deteriorate plant quality. Peavy and Greig (1972) reported an increase in iron uptake and decrease of nitrate-nitrogen of organically grown spinach when compared with mineral fertilizer application.

Yield

Yields resulting from comparative studies were either higher than, equal to, or lower than those for the eco-foods when compared to conventionally

TABLE 14.2.   RESULTS OF ANALYSES OF ECOLOGICALLY AND CONVENTIONALLY GROWN FOOD.

	Farming system	
	organic	conventional
Crude protein (% dry matter)	7.7[2]	10.4[2]
True protein (% of crude protein)	65.8[2]	61.0[2]
	59[1]	53[1]
EAA Index	62.8[2]	58.9[2]
Methionine (% of crude protein)	2.2[1]	1.8[1]
	2.6[1]	1.8[1]
Ascorbic acid (mg/100 g[4])	32[1]	23[1]
	18.1[2]	15.5[2]
Vitamin A (I.U./100 g[4])	1660[3]	1230[3]
	645[3]	425[3]
Total sugar (% dry matter)	4.9[1]	4.8[1]
	2.0[1]	1.4[1]
Nitrate-nitrogen (%)	1.8[1]	28.9[1]

[1] After Schuphan (1976).
[2] After Pettersson (1978).
[3] After IFOAM (1977).
[4] Fresh weight.

TABLE 14.3.   RESULTS OF FIELD EXPERIMENTS WITH SPINACH GROWN ON CHEMICAL FERTILIZED OR COMPOST TREATED SOIL.

Variable	Vitamin C content (mg/100 g dry matter)		Nitrate content (mg/100 g dry matter)	
	cv Nores	cv Nobel Original	cv Nores	cv Nobel Original
Compost from cattle manure:				
100 kg N/ha	685	769	1247	590
300 kg N/ha	728	800	929	541
Compost from plant wastes:				
100 kg N/ha	—	769	—	413
300 kg N/ha	—	805	—	629
NPK:				
100 kg N/ha	680	771	2672	1900
300 kg N/ha	691	693	3968	3580

After Schudel 1979.

grown foods (Schuphan 1974; Pettersson 1978; Abele 1973; Ronnenberg 1973; Lockeretz et al. 1975; Rothamsted Report 1978; Wistinghausen 1973; Maga et al. 1976).

Probably the most extensive comparative study was done with wheat and began in 1843 (Rothamsted Report 1968). Some of the data of this still ongoing experiment on wheat and straw are given in Table 14.4. The data from 1852 to 1967 show that yield of wheat and straw was generally superior to NPK and the control when farmyard manure was applied.

Yield, however, is influenced by many factors, and caution is needed to discuss the data (Schuphan 1976). Schudel et al. 1979) showed, for example, that the variety of spinach has a dominant influence on its yield (Table 14.5).

Most of the results dealing with comparison of yield were reported on a fresh weight basis, which can be an unreliable criteria for comparisons because the water content is variable (Schuphan 1974; Knorr 1978) and might be lower in eco-foods (Schuphan 1974, 1976; Schudel et al. 1979).

Storage Stability

Wistinghausen (1973) as well as Pettersson 1978) compared the yield of ecologically grown potatoes with the yield of conventionally grown ones (NPK fertilizer application) after harvest and after winter storage. As indicated in Table 14.6, the yields immediately after harvesting were higher for the conventionally grown potatoes but the storage losses were higher than for those grown ecologically. Thus, final yields of the ecologically grown potatoes were superior to the traditionally grown ones. Furthermore, the starch content of the eco-food was higher and consequently also the starch yield after storage was higher (22%). Samaras (1977), who compared storage losses for various organically and conventionally grown

TABLE 14.4. RESULTS OF GRAIN AND STRAW YIELD FROM THE BROAD BALK EXPERIMENT 1852–1967

Broadbalk, wheat: grain yields, 10-year means, 1852–1967 Total grain, (cwt/acre)

Treatment	1852–1861	1862–1871	1872–1881	1882–1891	1892–1901	1902–1911	1912–1921	1922–1925	1926–1934	1934–1944	1945–1954	1955–1964	1965–1967
FYM[1]	19.2	21.3	16.3	21.2	22.7	20.9	16.7	13.1	16.4	20.8	23.6	23.7	27.0
CONTROL[2]	8.9	8.2	5.7	6.9	7.1	6.4	5.3	3.1	8.1	10.4	10.8	12.6	13.0
NPK	18.6	20.0	15.1	18.3	16.8	18.9	13.5	10.5	15.9	18.5	18.8	18.9	20.6

Broadbalk wheat: straw yields, 10-year means, 1852–1967 Total straw (cwt/acre)

Treatment	1852–	1862–	1872–	1882–	1892–	1902–	1912–	1922–	1926–	1934–	1945–	1955–	1965–
FYM[1]	33.9	34.0	28.0	34.8	38.7	40.9	31.7	28.4	47.0	49.0	49.7	36.9	40.2
CONTROL[2]	15.2	11.5	8.5	8.5	9.1	9.6	7.3	5.2	14.0	17.6	18.6	15.0	15.1
NPK	34.3	33.3	27.6	31.9	28.5	35.9	26.2	23.1	40.0	39.2	37.2	29.6	30.8

After Rothamsted Report 1968.
[1] Farmyard manure
[2] No fertilizer applied

TABLE 14.5.   INFLUENCE OF VARIETY AND FERTILIZATION IN THE YIELD OF SPINACH

Fertilizer	Yield (metric tons dry matter per ha)	
	cv. Nores	cv. Nobel Original
Compost from cattle manure:		
100 kg N/ha	1.12	1.82
300 kg N/ha	1.25	1.95
Compost from plant wastes:		
100 kg N/ha	—	1.44
300 kg N/ha	—	1.80
NPK:		
100 kg N/ha	1.72	1.84
300 kg N/ha	2.05	1.87

After Schudel *et al.* (1979).

TABLE 14.6.   YIELD AND STORAGE LOSSES OF POTATOES GROWN UNDER VARIOUS CONDITIONS

	Fertilizer treatment	
	organic	NPK
Initial yield (metric tons/ha)	35.2	35.6
Losses during winter (%)	15.9	26.1
Final yield after storage (metric tons/ha)	29.6	26.3
Final starch content (%)	13.3	12.1
Final starch yield (metric tons/ha)	3.9	3.2

After Wistinghausen (1973).

TABLE 14.7.   STORAGE LOSSES OF VARIOUS VEGETABLES GROWN UNDER ECOLOGICAL AND CONVENTIONAL CONDITIONS[1]

Product	Storage losses (%)		Reference
	Conventional	Ecological	
Potatoes	24.5	16.3	Åberg 1976
Potatoes	30.2	12.5	Pettersson 1978
Potatoes	26.1	15.9	Wistinghausen 1973
Carrots	45.5	34.5	Samaras 1977
Turnips	50.5	34.8	Samaras 1977
Beets	59.8	30.4	Samaras 1977

[1] Partly only comparisons of different manuring.

vegetables, found an average of 54% higher storage losses resulting from decay and shrinkage and 10.5% higher weight losses for products from mineral fertilized soil (Table 14.7).

Pesticide Residues

Currently, approximately 3 kg of pesticides/capita/year are used in the United States (Pimentel *et al.* 1977).

Pesticide residues were also found in eco-foods (Stephenson 1978). This is not surprising, as Pimentel and Goodman (1974), for example, reported that often less than half of the pesticide applied reaches the intended target area and less than 1% hits the target pest when applied by airplane. About two-thirds of the pesticides applied in the United States in 1973 was applied by airplane (Pimentel and Goodman 1974).

It is interesting to note that a study by Aubert (1975) in which the concentration of chlorinated hydrocarbons was examined in milk from mothers who consumed in part or in total eco-foods showed that the concentration of chlorinated hydrocarbons decreased with increasing concentration of eco-foods in the mother's diet (Fig. 14.4). Unfortunately, limited information was provided about the experimental design of this study.

Sensory Quality

Very little and apparently no sufficiently objective information exists in the area of sensory evaluation of eco-foods versus conventionally grown foods.

Schutz and Lorenz (1976), who studied mainly fresh vegetables, detected no differences in sensory quality due to growing conditions for lettuce. There was a significant preference for the commercial samples over the organic carrots in one of the studies but not in the other one. Organic broccoli was preferred over mineral-fertilized samples. No significant sensory differences resulted between spinach grown on organic and on mineral-fertilized soil (Maga et al. 1976).

Schuphan (1976) stated that eco-foods are of higher sensory quality than conventionally grown ones. Pettersson (1978) reported that organically grown potatoes got higher ranking for taste (especially after storage), when compared with conventionally grown ones.

One of the main problems concerning sensory quality data (Svec et al. 1976; Von Elbe 1972; Schutz and Lorenz 1976) is the lack of comparative studies including a taste panel adapted to ecologically grown foods that might have introduced a consistent bias. This would be less likely if half the judges would have a personal familiarity with conventionally grown food and half be familiar with eco-foods.

In summary, the results of studies on the quality of eco-foods presented indicate possible differences in the nutritive value, the sensory quality, the storage stability, and the degree of pesticide contamination between eco-foods and conventional foods. The magnitude of the confusion and the high level of consumer interest in organic foods make a strong case of the need of well-designed research studies. Their results could help to stop the arguments about the quality of eco-foods on the basis of assumptions and anecdotal reports.

FOOD QUALITY CRITERIA

There is the problem of discovering more about the chemical composition of both processed and unprocessed foods. Surprisingly little is known about this. For

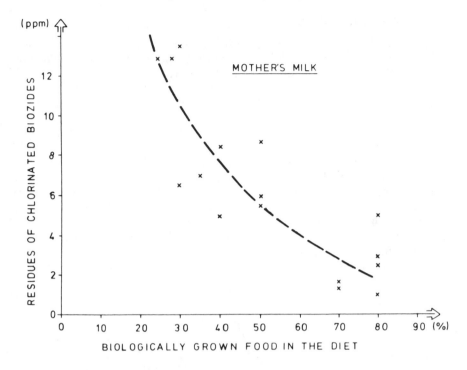

FIG. 14.4.   RELATIONSHIP BETWEEN THE PERCENTAGE OF BIOLOGICALLY GROWN FOOD IN MOTHER'S DIET AND CONCENTRATION OF CHLORINATED HYDROCARBONS IN MOTHER'S MILK. AFTER AUBERT 1975.

example, it is extremely difficult to obtain information on nutrients such as zinc, folic acid and trace elements; data for other food constituents such as dietary fiber or sugar are lacking for almost all foods. (Nutrition Research Alternative 1978)

This result of an analysis of nutrition research alternatives by the Office of Technology Assessment, Congress of the United States, indicates the lack of knowledge about the composition and nutritive value of most foods. Because of this lack of knowledge, one has also to ask about the nutritional relevance of currently used food quality criteria.

The quality criteria advertised most are, besides basic legal and sanitary requirements, "external" quality criteria that can be easily measured and can be easily detected by the consumer. Examples for these "external" food quality criteria are yield or weight on fresh weight basis, size, appearance, and color.

Examples from two areas may illustrate the complex situation.

Yield, Weight, and Size

Yield or weight on a fresh weight basis is influenced by many factors (Schuphan 1976). Knorr (1976), for example, showed that lower yields for ecologically grown food found by Schuphan (1974) became almost equal to that of conventionally grown products when calculated on a dry weight basis, because the dry matter content of the ecologically grown products was higher. The decrease of dry weight of wheat with increasing mineral nitrogen was shown recently by Pearman *et al.* (1978) and confirmed Schuphan's (1976) findings with lettuce (see Fig. 14.3).

The increase in yield on a fresh weight basis with increasing application of mineral fertilizers has been partly related to an increase of water content of the products (Vogtmann 1979), which was also related to the decrease of the vitamin C (Figure 14.5) concentration in plants (Schudel *et al.* 1979).

Because the water content of plants can vary, depending on the agricultural production system used, the yield or weight on fresh weight basis is not an appropriate criterion for the comparison of productivity of conventional versus ecological farming nor for the nutrient content of the resulting

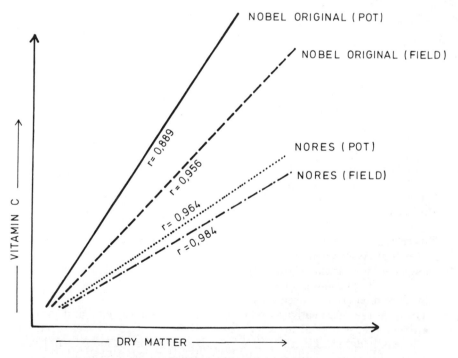

FIG. 14.5.   RELATIONSHIP BETWEEN VITAMIN C CONTENT AND DRY MATTER IN SPINACH. AFTER SCHUDEL *et al.* 1979.

products. These comparisons should be evaluated on yield or weight on dry matter basis. It seems necessary to consider nutrient density or concentration of essential nutrients on a dry weight basis and to replace grading on a fresh weight basis as food quality criteria. Schuphan (1976) reported, for example, a 96% decrease of the vitamin C content from the lightest (smallest) towards the heaviest (biggest) samples of red cabbage collected at the same field unit (Fig. 14.6). As certain food processing industries already use starch content or sugar content as the basis for their payment, this principle could be expanded to other products and could also be made available to the consumer.

Appearance

Most of the fruits and vegetables in the supermarkets today have little or no insect damage on their surfaces. Since 1945, greater emphasis has been given to the cosmetic appearance of fruits and vegetables, partly because of the increased availability of insecticides.

Processors will not allow more than 1% fruit worm damage, and some processors accept only perfect fruit (Van den Bosch et al. 1975). Yet 90% of the processed tomatoes are used for paste, sauce, ketchup, juice, and puree—products in which the consumer could not possibly detect any insect damage (Pimentel et al. 1977).

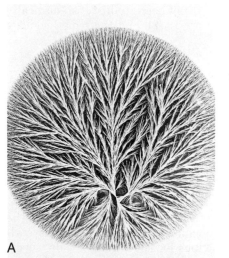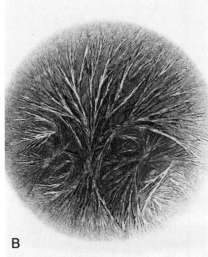

FIG. 14.6.   DETECTION OF CONVENTIONALLY AND ECOLOGICALLY GROWN SPINACH (POT EXPERIMENTS) WITH THE CUPRIC-CHLORIDE CRYSTALLIZATION METHOD. A= COMPOST (100 kg N/ha); B= NPK FERTILIZER (100 kg N/ha). AFTER SCHUDEL 1979.

An estimated 10 to 20% additional insecticide is used on fruits and vegetables overall to reduce the incidence of insects on foods and/or to meet the required cosmetic appearance standard. Pimentel *et al.* (1977) reported that the intensified insecticide use reduced insect tolerances for this cosmetic appearance standard and for other insect control purposes has resulted in:

A greater proportion of food contaminated with insecticide residues than in the past
A larger number of human pesticide poisonings annually (14,000 in the United States)
Continued environmental pollution problems from insecticides
Increased use of energy in pesticide production and pest control
Increased food costs for the consumer

DETECTION OF ECO-FOODS

Methods commonly used in food quality control have also been applied to determine the functional properties, chemical composition, and nutritive (biological) value of eco-foods (Schutz and Lorenz 1976; Von Elbe 1972; Schuphan 1976; Aehnelt and Hahn 1973; Schudel *et al.* 1979; Scott *et al.* 1960; McSheehy 1977; Gottschewski 1975). We will discuss only those methods used specifically for the determination of eco-foods or applied to compare conventionally grown foods with eco-foods. Some of these methods have been used since the beginning of eco-farming (Kolisko and Kolisko 1939; Selawry and Selawry 1957) but have not been studied systematically until recently (Schudel et al. 1979; Knorr 1982), and their methodology is still in its infancy.

Cupric-Chloride Cystallization

The patterns in which salts crystallize from solutions have been shown to be influenced by the presence of impurities (Morris and Morris 1939). Several authors have studied the process that takes place in the formation of specific dendritic configurations of hydrated cupric chloride ($CuCl_2 \cdot 2H_2O$) during the slow evaporation of its aqueous solutions containing additives of biological origin (Beckmann 1959; Selawry and Selawry 1957; Engquist 1970; Leray 1968). Morris and Morris (1941) as well as Beckmann (1959) showed the specific influence of amino acids and proteins on the crystallization pattern of cupric chloride, and Pettersson (1967, 1968) studied the influence of various concentrations of aqueous plant extracts on the crystallization pattern of cupric chloride. Various foods such as cereals, seeds, potatoes, peas, and milk prepared in various ways were tested with the cupric-chloride crystallization method sometimes called the diagnostic crystallization method (Friess 1944; Merten et al. 1959; Pettersson 1970; Selawry and Koepf 1964; Schmidt 1969; Koepf and Selawry 1963A, 1963B). The influence of products resulting from different farming methods on the crystallization patterns has been examined by Pettersson (1970) and by Koepf and Selawry (1963B). Pettersson believes, on the basis of his studies, that both protein concentration and protein composition have a significant influence on the crystallization pattern of cupric chloride. Cupric-chloride crystallization experiments of conventionally and ecologically grown spinach were carried out by Schudel (1979) (Fig. 14.6). However, the evaluation of crystallization patterns and the detection of food quality based on such morphological comparisons is difficult to evaluate. The fundamentals of this method are not yet fully explored and need further research. The high sensitivity of the method and the resulting variability might be limiting factors for an appreciation of the cupric chloride crystallization method in routine analyses (Knorr 1982).

Paper Chromatographic Methods

Two paper chromatic methods have been used to determine the quality of eco-foods in a more holistic way than by estimating isolated food compounds (Kolisko and Kolisko 1939). One method, commonly called *capillary dynamolysis,* or capillary-dynamic technique, or "Steigbild," is an ascending paper chromatographic method. The other method, the so-called *circular chromatographic* method, or just the *chromatographic* method, is a radial paper chromatographic method (Kolisko and Kolisko 1939; Pfeiffer 1960).

Capillary dynamolysis has been mainly applied to plants and soil samples and has been used on human animal feces for diagnostic purposes (Kolisko and Kolisko 1939; Hauschka 1967). The circular chromatographic method has been used for the evaluation of soil and plant samples (Pfeiffer 1960; Pettersson and Wistinghausen 1977) and as an assay for the analysis of vitamins (Smith 1972). A detailed description of the application of the circular chromatographic method for the determination of soil quality is given in this book by W.F. Brinton.

These methods are two-step procedures using a plant extract obtained by extracting plant particles with an aqueous solution of sodium hydroxide and aqueous solutions of salt such as gold chloride, silver nitrate, mercury chloride, ferrous sulfate, cupric sulphate, and stannic chloride. Silver nitrate is the most commonly used one. The plant extract follows either the treatment of the paper with one of the previously mentioned salt solutions, or the paper is "sensitized" with the salt solution after treatment with the plant extract (Kolisko and Kolisko 1939; Pfeiffer 1960). The color and the pattern (form) that usually develop within several hours after drying of the paper are used to interpret the resulting chromatograms.

It has been reported by Pfeiffer (1960) that "the spokes protruding from the outer ring area toward the center [see Fig. 14.7] are caused by proteins and indicate quantity as well as quality of protein." Systematic experiments on the comparison of conventionally and organically grown plants as well as on the fundamentals of the circular chromatographic method have been initiated recently (Knorr 1982). Preliminary results of still ongoing studies with collard plants indicated differences in the patterns of chromatograms obtained from conventionally and ecologically grown plants (Fig. 14.7). The evaluation of these chromatograms is also based on subjective morphological comparison, and so far no quantitative results can be obtained with this method.

 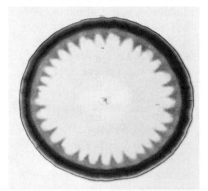

FIG. 14.7.   DETECTION OF CONVENTIONALLY AND ECOLOGICALLY GROWN COLLARD PLANTS (FIELD EXPERIMENTS) WITH THE CIRCULAR CHROMATOGRAPHIC METHOD. A= ECOLOGICALLY GROWN; B= CONVENTIONALLY GROWN. AFTER KNORR 1982.

The results of recent studies (Knorr 1981) indicate that this method can be used for the quantitative determination of proteins in plant material. Linear and highly significant correlations ($r = 0.936$ to 0.954) were found between the area of lowest optical density of the chromatograms and protein concentration of model systems (albumin, casein, and hemin solutions). The addition of nitrates, which are commonly found in plant material (up to 10 mg of $NaNO_3$/mg protein), did not interfere with the results.

According to Brinton (see Chapter 15), the main reaction pathway of this method involves the formation of silver hydroxide and almost immediately silver oxide, the oxide form being insoluble and causing a yellow precipitate. The weakly soluble silver hydroxide causes a partial blocking of the chromatographic paper's pores, resulting in a streaking effect that is enhanced by the presence of larger organic molecules (e.g., proteins). Furthermore, the reaction of silver nitrate with certain amino acids and the formation of a silver–ammonia complex has been reported by Blundell and Jenkins (1977).

Drop Picture Method

The drop picture method, which can be applied as an indicator for water quality, is based on the formation of an unstable ring-vortex flow on the surface and within the layer of a viscous liquid caused by a drop fluid (e.g., drinking water) falling into the liquid layer (Smith 1975).

Bioassays

Bioassays have been carried out by Aehnelt and Hahn (1973), Gott-schewski (1975), Samaras (1977), and Schiller (1971).

Gottschewski (1975) stated that the difficulty in testing food and soil additives results mainly from the "multitude of additives in its synergism and additiveness and from the adaptation (regeneration and resistance capacity) of the organism in question." Consequently the influence of soil and food additives was investigated as a whole, and market food was compared with food from"organic" farms. It was found that the sensitivity of embryonic life is higher than in fetal and adult systems and that there are also remarkable similarities between the development of different mammalian species. One disadvantage of Gottschewski's (1975) experimental design is the fact that foods from different locations (and maybe even different varieties) have been used for comparisons. However, the use of embryonic systems might be developed into a helpful tool to study the nutritional quality of ecologically grown foods.

CONCLUSION

If one assumes (1) that fossil fuels are exhaustible, (2) that an important role of agriculture is to sustain farmlands with ecologically wise methods, and (3) that the single strategy of farm chemicals and mechanized cultivation is open to discussion and alternatives, then, according to Merrill (1976), one is led into new areas of agricultural research. One alternative and its effects on food quality has been discussed in this paper.

The data presented in this chapter indicate differences in composition, nutritive value, functional properties, and storage stability of conventionally and ecologically grown foods as well as between products of soils treated with mineral or organic fertilizer. Many problems are involved in the interpretation and use of these results because of the lack of sufficient data comparing the two agricultural systems (conventional and ecological farming). Examples of the limitations of most studies presented are: (1) the too short duration of the experiments (usually only one to two years), which does not provide enough time for sufficient environmental changes; (2) pot and/or plot experiments instead of comparisons of complete agricultural systems; and (3) use of a variable basis (fresh weight) for comparisons of yield and food quality instead of comparisons on a basis of dry matter or essential nutrients.

Another limitation in comparisons of data for the quality of products resulting from conventional or ecological farming systems is the potential bias of variety of plant. Plant varieties selected for optimal growth in one agricultural system may show different responses in another. This might also influence plant quality factors. Growth rates of plants may also differ under different farming conditions, and the equal growth periods usually provided in comparative studies may lead to plants differing in maturity, which affects plant quality. In addition, quality of conventionally and eco- logically grown plants may be affected by different photoexposure due to different foliage coverage, which in turn may be influenced by fertilizer treatment or farming system.

There is increasing interest in "natural" products and an increasing demand for them (Leinen 1978). It also seems inevitable that the recent trend of consumerism will continue (Sloan 1980).

Furthermore, in European countries and in less developed countries (LDCs), government agencies and individuals tend to increase their self- sufficiency for food supplies, which leads toward a more manifold agricul- tural production than the present one (Knorr 1978; NGO Report 1979; Science and Technology 1979). In addition there is also a worldwide in- creasing need for food production processing, as well as for equipment that is small in scale, labor intensive, capital sparing, and simple to operate (Bourne 1978; Appropriate Technology 1979). See also Chapter 9, Appro- priate Food Technology, by R.P. Bates.

There is a gap between interest and demand for eco-foods and/or knowl- edge about them. Well-designed long-term comparisons of organic farming and conventional farming methods are needed to evaluate the nutritional quality of these products grown or raised under these conditions. In addi- tion, methods are needed to differentiate between conventional and organ- ically grown foods (eco-foods) in order to define and regulate eco-foods and, most importantly, to provide protection of the consumer.

REFERENCES

ABELE, U. 1973. Vergleichende Untersuchungen zum konventionellen und biologisch-dynamischen Landbau unter besonderer Berücksichtigung von Saatzeit und Entitäten. Ph. D. thesis. Justus-Liebig Universität, Giessen.

AEHNELT, E. and HAHN, J. 1973. Fruchtbarkeit der Tiere—eine Möglich- keit zur biologischen Qualitätsprüfung von Futter- und Nahrungsmitteln? Tierärztl. Umschau 4, 1–16.

ANON. 1974. Organic Foods. Food Technol. 23, 71–74.

ANON. 1978. The new American farmer. New York Times Magazine 12(19), 92–102.

APPROPRIATE TECHNOLOGY. 1979. A program plan of the National Sci- ence Foundation. Prepared for the United States House of Representatives. National Science Foundation, Washington, D.C.

AUBERT, C. 1975. Die Muttermilch, ein erschreckender Stand der Toxi- zität. Leb. Erde 1(7), 8–13.

AUBERT, C. 1979. Personal communication.

ÅBERG, E. 1976. Alternativa växtodlingsformer, Skogs-o., Lautbr.-akad. Tidskr. *115*, 315–331.

BECKMANN, H. 1959. Über Keimbildung, Einkristallwachstum und Auffächerungswachstum von Cu Cl₂·2H₂O in rein wässrigen und eiweisshaltigen Lösungen. Ph.D. thesis. Friedrich Wilhelm Universität, Bonn.

BERNARDI, G.M. 1978. Organic and conventional wheat production: examination of energy and economics. Agro-Ecosystems *4*, 367–376.

BESSON, J.M. and VOGTMANN, H. 1978. Towards a sustainable agriculture. Verlag Wirz, A.G. Aarau.

BLUNDELL, T.L. and JENKINS, J.A. 1977. The binding of heavy metals to proteins. Chem. Society Reviews *6*, 139–171.

BOURNE, MC. 1978. What is appropriate/intermediate food technology? Food Technol. *41*(4), 77–80.

BRANDT, C.S. and BEESON, K.C. 1951. Influence of organic fertilization on certain nutritive constituents of crops. Soil Science *71*, 449–454.

DEXTER, S.T. 1955. Nutritive values of crops and cow milk as affected by soil fertility. *In* Nutrition of plants, animals and man. Michigan State University Centennial Symposium, 1855–1955. East Lansing.

ENGQUIST, M. 1970. Gestaltungskräfte des Lebendigen. V. Klostermann Verlag, Frankfurt.

FRIESS, H. 1944. Über eine neue krystallographische Methode zun Nachweis von Veränderungen in konservierten pflanzlichen Lebensmitteln. Z. Lebensmitteluntersuch. u. Forsch. *87*, 19–26.

GOTTSCHEWSKI, G.H.M. 1975. Neue Möglichkeiten zur größeren Effizienz der toxikologischen Prüfung von Pestiziden, Rückstanden und Herbiziden. Qual. Plant. *25*, 21–42.

HALL, R.H. 1974. Food for nought: the decline in nutrition. Random House, Inc., New York.

HAUSCKA, R. 1967. Nutrition. Stuart R. Watkins, Ltd., London.

HIGHTOWER, J. 1972. Hard tomatoes, hard times. The failure of the Land Grant College complex. Agribusiness Accountable Project, Washington, D.C.

IFOAM. 1977. Analyse organisch und konventionell gezüchteter Nahrungsmittel. IFOAM-Bulletin, No. 23.

IFT. 1979. Advertising guidelines for dealing with technical issues regarding food safety and nutrition. Institute of Food Technologists, Chicago.

KLEPPER, R., LOCKERETZ, W., COMMONER, B., GERTLER, M., FAST, S., O'LEARY, D. and BLOBAUM, R. 1977. Economic performance and energy intensiveness on organic and conventional farms in the corn belt: a preliminary comparison. Am. J. Agric. Econ. *59*, 1–12.

KNORR, D. 1976. Konsum and Umwelt-Zustandsanalyse am Beispiel Labensmittel. *In* Umwelt und Gesellschaft. Institut f. Wissenschaft und Kunst, Vienna.

KNORR, D. 1978. Landwirtschaftliche Produktion und Lebensmittel qualitaet. Report prepared for the Ministry of Agriculture and Forestry. Institute Advanced Studies, Vienna.

KNORR, D. 1979A. Ecologically grown food: towards the development of more appropriate quality criteria. (Unpublished manuscript).

KNORR, D. 1979B. Quality of ecologically grown food. Food Sci. and Technol. *12*, 350–356.

KNORR, D. 1981. Feasibility of a circular paper chromatographic method for protein determination. Nutrition & Health *1*, 14–19.

KNORR, D. 1982. Use of a circular chromatographic method for the distinction of collard plants grown under different fertilizing conditions. Biological Agriculture and Horticulture (in press).

KOEPF, H. and SELAWRY, A. 1963A. Application of the diagnostic crystallization method for the investigation of quality of food and fodder. II. Biodynamics, No. 65, 1–12.

KOEPF, H. and SELAWRY, A. 1963B. Application of the diagnostic crystallization method for the investigation of quality of food and fodder. III. Biodynamics, No. 67, 1–12.

KOLISKO, E. and KOLISKO, L. 1939. Agriculture of tomorrow. Kolisko Archieve, Stroud.

KRATE, S.L. 1979. A preliminary examination of the economic performance and energy intensiveness of organic and conventional small grain farms in the Northwest. M.A. thesis, Washington State University, St. Louis.

LABUZA, T.P. 1977. Food and your well being. West Publishing Co., St. Paul.

LEINEN, N.J. 1978. Survey reports significant jump in "natural is better" consumer attitude. Food Process. *39*(3), 28–29.

LERAY, J.L. 1968. Growth kinetics of hydrated cupric chloride. J. Crystall. Growth. *3/4*, 344–349.

LEVERTON, R.M. 1974. Organic, inorganic: what they mean; shoppers guide. 1974 Yearbook of Agriculture, USDA, Washington, D.C.

LOCKERETZ, W., KLEPPER, R., COMMONER, B., GERTLER, M., FAST, S., O'LEARY, D. and BLOBAUM, R.A. 1975. A comparison of the production, economic returns, and energy intensiveness of Corn Belt farms that do and do not use inorganic fertilizers and pesticides. Center for the Biology of Natural Systems, Washington University, St. Louis.

LOCKERETZ, W., SHEARER, G., KLEPPER, R. and SWEENEY, S. 1978. Field crop production on organic farms in the Midwest. J. Soil and Water Conservation *33*, 130–134.

LOCKERETZ, W. and WERNIK, S. 1979. Commercial-scale organic farming in the corn belt in relation to conventional practices and alternative agricultural systems. Unpublished. Northeast Solar Energy Center, Cambridge, Mass.

MacLEOD, L.B. 1965. Effects of nitrogen and potassium on the yield and chemical composition of alfalfa, bromegrass, orchard grass, and timothy grown as pure species. Agron. J. *57*, 261–266.

MAGA, J.A., MOORE. F.D. and OSHIMA, N. 1976. Yield, nitrate level and sensory properties of spinach as influenced by organic and mineral nitrogen fertilizer levels. J. Sci. Food Agric. *27*, 109–114.

QUANTITY AND QUALITY DETERMINATION   377

MARINE, G. and VAN ALLEN, J.   1973.   Food pollution.   The violation of our inner ecology.   Holt, Rinehart and Winston, New York, Chicago, San Francisco.

MATILE, P.   1971.   Wege der Biologie.   Symp. Umweltprobleme und Landwirtschaft, Berne.

McCARRISON, R.   1926.   The effect of manurial conditions on the nutritive values of millet and wheat.   Indian J. Med. Res. *14*, 351–378.

McSHEEHY, T.W.   1977.   Nutritive value of wheat grown under organic and chemical systems of farming.   Qual. Plant. *27*, 113–123.

MEILI, E.   1979.   Was denken konventionelle Bauern zum biologischen Landbau.   Institut f. Geschichte und Soziologie d. Land-u. Forstwirtschaft, Swiss Federal Technical University, Zürich.

MERRILL, R. (Editor).   1976.   Radical agriculture.   Harper and Row, Publishers, New York.

MERTEN, D., LAGNOI, H. and PETERS, K.H.   1959.   Über den Einfluss von Milch und Milchbestandteilen sowie Milchprodukten auf das Kupferchlorid—Kristallisationsbild.   Kieler Milchwirt. Forsch. *11*, 69–79.

MILLER, D.S. and DEMA, I.S.   1958.   Nutritive value of wheat from the Rothamsted Broadbalk field.   Proc. Nutr. Soc. *17*, xciv.

MORRIS, D.L. and MORRIS, C.T.   1939.   Glycogen in the seed of Zea Mays (variety Golden Bantam).   Am. J. Biol. Chem. *130*, 535–544.

MORRIS, D.L. and MORRIS, C.T.   1941.   The modification of cupric chloride crystallization patterns by traces of proteins.   Am. J. Biol. Chem. *132*, 515–521.

NGO-REPORT.   1979.   Final NGO-report on the United Nations Conference on Science and Technology for Development.   Prepared by a study group of the NGO-Committee on Science and Technology for Development.   NGO-Forum.   New York.

NUTRITION RESEARCH ALTERNATIVES.   1978.   Office of Technology Assessment.   Congress of the United States.   Washington, D.C.

OELHAF, R.C.   1978.   Organic agriculture economic and ecological comparisons with conventional methods.   Allanheid, Osmun & Co., Montclair, New Jersey.

PACKARD, V.S.   1978.   Natural?   Organic?   What do they really mean?   Professional Nutritionist *10*(3) 1–3.

PEARMAN, I., THOMAS, S.M. and THORNE, G.N.   1978.   Effect of nitrogen fertilizer on growth and yield of semidwarf and tall varieties of winter wheat.   J. Agric. Sci. (Cambridge) *91*, 31–45.

PEAVY, W.S. and GREIG, J.K.   1972.   Organic and mineral fertilizers compared by yield, quality and composition of spinach.   J. Am. Soc. Hort. Sci *96*, 718–723.

PECKHAM, C. and FREELAND–GRAVES, J.H.   1979.   Foundations of Food Preparation.   Macmillan Publishing Co., Inc. New York.

PERELMAN, M.   1976.   Efficiency in agriculture.   The economics of energy.   *In* Radical Agriculture. R. Merrill, (Editor).   Harper and Row, Publishers, New York.

PETERS, S.   1979.   Organic farmers celebrate organic research: a sociology of popular science.   *In* Counter-movements in tghe sciences.   H. Nowotny and R. Hilry. (Editors).   Sociology of the Sciences.   Vol. III.   D. Reidel Publishing Co.

PETTERSSON, B.D.   1967.   Beiträge zur Entwicklung der Kristallisationsmethode mit Kupfer-chloride nach Pfeiffer.   II.   Lebendige Erde No. 1, 3–18.

PETTERSSON, B.D.   1968.   Beiträge zur Entwicklung der Kristallisationsmethode mit Kupfer-chlorid nach Pfeiffer.   IV.   Lebendige Erde, No. 6, 2–16.

PETTERSSON, B.D.   1970.   Die Einwirkung von Standort, Düngung und wachstumsbeeinflussenden Stoffen auf die Qualitätseigenschaften von Speisekartoffeln.   Leb. Erde 3/4.

PETTERSSON, B.D.   1978.   A comparison between conventional and biodynamic farming systems as indicated by yields and quality.   Proc. Internat. Res. Conf. IFOAM.   Wirz Verlag, Aarau.

PETTERSSON, B.D. and WISTINGHAUSEN, E.   1977.   Bodenuntersuchungen von einem langjährigen Feldversuch in Jarna, Schweden.   Forschungsring. f. biol.-dyn. Wirschaftsweise, Darmstadt.

PFEIFFER, E.E.   1960.   Chromatograms of grain and flour.   Bio-dynamics, No. 54, 2–35.

PIMENTEL, D., DRITSCHILO, W., KRUMMEL, J. and KUTZMANN, J.   1975.   Energy and land constraints in food protein production.   Science *190*, 754–761.

PIMENTEL, D. and GOODMAN, N.   1974.   Environmental impact of pesticides.   *In* Survival in toxic environments.   M.A.Q. Khan and J.P. Bederka. (Editors).   Academic Press, New York.

PIMENTEL, D., TERHUNE, C., DRITSCHILO, W., GALLAHAN, D., KINNER, N., NAFUS, D., PETERSON, R., ZAREH, N., MISITI, J. and HABERSCHAIM, O.   1977.   Pesticides, insects in foods and cosmetic standards.   Bio-Science *27*, 178–185.

POMERANZ, Y., ROBBINS, G.S., GILBERTSON, J.T. and BOOTH, G.D.   1977.   Effects of nitrogen fertilization on lysine, threonine, and methionine of hulled and hull-less barley cultivars.   Cereal Chem. *54*, 1034–1042.

PREUSCHEN, G., BRAUNER, H., STORNAS, R. AND WILLI, J.   1977.   Gesunder Boden = leistungsstarker Betrieb.   Leopold Stocker Verlag, Graz and Stuttgart.

RENDING, V.V. and MICKELSEN, D.S.   1976.   Plant protein composition as influenced by environment and culture practices.   University of California at Davis, Special Publications No. 3058, Davis, California.

RONNENBERG, A.   1973.   Ökonomische Aspekte der biologischen Wirtschaftsweise—Konsequenzen für den Einzelbetrieb und für den Produktmarkt.   Thesis.   Universität Göttingen.

ROTHAMSTED EXPERIMENTAL STATION REPORT.   1968.   Part 2.   Lawes Agricultural Trust, Harpenden.

SAMARAS, I.   1977.   Nachernteverhalten unterschiedlich gedüngter Gemüsearten mit besonderer Berücksichtigung physiologishcer und mikrobiologishcher Parameter. Ph.D. thesis. Justus-Liebig Universität Giessen.

SCHEER, G. and KRAMMER, J. 1979. Der biolgische Landbau—eine wirtschaftliche Chance. Ergebnisse einer Marktuntersuchung. IFOAM-Bulletin 29, 12–13.

SCHILLER, H. 1971. Grüdlanddüngung und unspezifische Rindersterilität. Oberösterreich. und Landw.-Chem. Bundesversuchsanstalt, Linz.

SCHMID, O. et al. 1979. Erhebungen über Nährstoffangebot im Boden und Inhaltsstoffe von Gemüsen. Enquete auf 10 biologischen Betrieben. Zwischenbericht über drei Erhebungsjahre. Forschungsinstitut für biol. Landbau, Oberwil.

SCHMIDT, G. 1969. Qualitätsuntersuchungen an Getreide und Getreideprodukten mittels der Kristallisations methode mit $CuCl_2$. Vitalstoffe. No. 3, 7–16.

SCHÖNBÄCK, W. (Editor). 1979. Gesundheit im gesellschaftlichen Konflikt. Urban and Schwarzenberg, Vienna and Munich.

SCHUDEL, P. 1979. Qualitätsvergleich an Spinat aus Düngungsversuchen (Kompost-und NPK-Düngung) mit Hilfe der Methode der "Empfindlichen Kristallisation." Schlußbericht an das Eidg. Volkswirtschaftsdepartement, Abt. Landwirtschaft, Bern.

SCHUDEL, P. et al. 1979. Über den Einfluß von Kompost- und NPK-Düngung auf Ertrag, Vitamin-C- und Nitratgehalt von Spinat und Schnittmangold. Schweiz. Landw. Forschung 4, 337–349.

SCHUPBACH, M. 1979. Umweltschutz, Landwirtschaft, Gesundheit. Paper presented at a meeting of the Schweizer Gesellschaft f. Umweltschutz. Zürich, 6 April.

SCHUPHAN, W. 1972. Effects of the application of inorganic and organic manures on the market quality and on the biological value of agricultural products. Qual. Plant. 21, 381–398.

SCHUPHAN, W. 1974. Nutritional value of crops as influenced by organic and inorganic fertilizer treatments—results of 12 years' experiments with vegetables. Qual. Plant. 23, 333–358.

SCHUPHAN, W. 1976. Mensch und Nahrungspflanze. Der biologische Wert der Nahrungspflanze in Abhängigkeit von Pestizideinsatz, Bodenqualität und Düngung. Dr. W. Junk B.V. Verlag, Den Haag.

SCHUTZ, H.G. and LORENZ, O.A. 1976. Consumer preference for vegetables grown under "commercial" and "organic" conditions. J. Food Science 41, 70–73.

SCIENCE AND TECHNOLOGY FOR DEVELOPMENT. 1979. Contributions by the Federal Republic of Germany, published on the occasion of the United Nations Conference on Science and Technology for Development in Vienna. German Agency for Technical Cooperation, Eschborn.

SCOTT, P.P., GRAVES, J.P. and SCOTT, M.G. 1960. Reproduction in laboratory animal as a measure of the value of some natural and processed foods. J. Reprod. Fertil. 1, 130–138.

SELAWRY, A. and KOEPF, H. 1964. Zur kristallmorphologischen Eiweisstestung von Samen. Experientia 20, 54–56.

SELAWRY, A. and SELAWRY, O. 1957. Kupferchlorid-Kristallisation in Naturwissenschaft und Medizin. Gustav-Fischer-Verlag, Stuttgart.

SLOAN, E. 1980. Joining the health care team. Cereal foods world 25, 681.

SMITH, H.J. 1975. The hydrodynamic and physico-chemical basis of the drop picture method. Bericht 8/75. Max Planck Institut für Strömungsforschung. Göttingen.

SMITH, M.J. 1972. Further research into a chromatographic technique for vitamin analysis. Human Dimensions 2(1) 2–7.

STAFF REPORT. 1978. Priorities in agricultural research of the U.S. Department of Agriculture: A summary report of the hearings before the subcommittee on Administrative Practices and Procedures of the Judiciary Committee. United States Senate. U.S. Government Printing Office, Washington, D.C.

STEPHENSON, M. 1978. The confusing world of health foods. HEW Publication No. (FDA) 79-2108.

SVEC, L.V., THOROUGHGOOD, C.A. and HYO CHUNG S. MOK. 1976. Chemical evaluation of vegetables grown with conventional or organic soil amendments. Commun. Soil Science and Plant Analysis 7, 213–228

ULBRICHT, T.L.V. 1975. Systems of agricultural production. 8th Int. TNO conference, "Effects on industry of trends in food production and consumption," Rotterdam.

UN-UNIVERSITY. 1979. An issue paper contributed by the food study group of the goals, processes and indicators of development project. Joint workshop on goals, processes and indicators for food and nutrition policy and planning. Massachusetts Institute of Technology, Cambridge, Mass.

U.S. GENERAL ACCOUNTING OFFICE. 1978. Changing character and structure of American agriculture: an overview. CED-78-178. General Accounting Office, Washington, D.C.

VAN DEN BOSCH, R.M., BROWN, M., McGOWAN, C., MILLER, A., MORAN, M., PELZER, D. and SWARTZ, J. 1975. Investigation of the effects of food standards on pesticide use. Draft report, Environmental Protection Agency, Washington, D.C.

VERRETT, J. and CARPER, J. 1974. Eating may be hazardous to your health. Simon and Schuster, New York.

VOGTMANN, H. 1979. Zum Beitrag: Konventioneller und alternativer Landban—Vergleichende Untersuchungen über die Qualität der Ernteprodukte. In Der ökologische Landbau: eine Realität. Stiftung ökologischer Landbau (ed.), Verlag, C.F. Müller, Karlsruhe.

VON ELBE, J.H. 1972. Organic foods—another consumer hoax? J. Milk and Food Technol. 35, 669–671.

WHITE, H.S. 1972. The organic food movement. Food Technol. 26, 29–33.

WHITE–STEVENS, R. 1977. Perspectives on fertilizer use, residue utilization and food production. In Fertilizer and agricultural residues. R.C. Loehr, (Editor). Ann Arbor Science, Ann Arbor, Michigan.

WILBERG, E.   1972.   Uber die Qualität von Spinat aus "Biologischem An-bau."   Landw. Forschung. *25*, 167–169.

WISTINGHAUSEN, E.   1973.   Vergleichende Ertrags-und Qualitätsunter-suchungen.   Lebendige Erde, No. 1, 3–11.

YOUNGBERG, G.   1978.   Alternative agriculturists: ideology, politics, and prospects.   *In* The new politics of foods.   D.F. Hadwiger and W.P. Browne. Lexington Books, Lexington.

15

A Qualitative Method For Assessing Humus Condition

William F. Brinton, Jr.

Introduction
The Circular Chromatographic Method
Interpretation of chromatograms
Conclusions
References

INTRODUCTION

Concern for the propriety of carbon cycling in the food chain is currently promoting a rapid increase of interest in the practical significance of organic matter cycling in soils (Lunin 1977; Flaig *et al.* 1977). Additionally, the primary role that organic matter and humus play in maintenance of soil productivity and the losses attendant upon their removal are becoming widely recognized (Eckholm 1976; Aina 1979).

Concomitant with this renewed interest in the fate of organic materials is the need for laboratory techniques that enable rapid evaluation of the condition and quality of humifying organic matter, particularly in view of composting and soil recycling. A wide array of existent methods for evaluating organic matter and humus include carbon:nitrogen and photometric analysis as well as more sophisticated techniques such as infrared spectrometry and pyrolysis–gas chromatography (Schnitzer and Khan 1972). Despite their usefulness and adaptability, many modern methods are expensive and time consuming, require a fairly high level of technical sophistication, and may give results that are difficult to translate into practice. It may also be apparent that strictly analyzing organic content *per se*, as commonly practiced with soils, will not provide information regarding its condition or quality, information that may be indispensable to interpreting the fate of added organic material (Brinton 1979). For example, amending an acid, podzol soil with organic matter may involve entirely different

382

pathways of decomposition and fixation—implicating soil structure and productivity—than may be the case in a soil of calcareous or alkaline nature (Martin *et al.* 1979; Pauli 1967; Khantulev *et al.* 1968).

THE CIRCULAR CHROMATOGRAPHIC METHOD

The objective of this paper is to report on the technique and use of a circular chromatographic method, which is a simple and fairly rapid qualitative tool for evaluating food material, compost, and soil humus, developed by Pfeiffer (1959). Though the method has been applied to qualitative analysis of plant material and food products (Pfeiffer 1960; Sabarth 1962; Smith 1973), our discussion will be confined to its use in investigating humification in composts and soils as reported by Pfeiffer and others (Koepf 1964; Smith 1973; Stickelberger 1975; Hertelendy 1973).

To date, efforts in evaluating the chromatograms have largely revolved around drawing inferences based upon knowledge of other features of the material being examined. For example, Pfeiffer (1959) and Sabarth (1962) observed that chromatograms performed on organic material during a composting process would change in accordance with the characteristic breakdown and subsequent stabilization of the organic material. This suggested that the chromatograms could be applied as a complement to analytical data to give a characteristic pictorial representation of the degree of ripening of the humifying material. Similar relationships were drawn with soils, particularly by comparing acid soils with near-neutral soils of varying organic content (Koepf 1964). These efforts led to establishing various chromatogram patterns as typical of a certain type of *humus condition*, such as "acid, carbonaceous," "stable, matured," and "poor, mineralized" (Pfeiffer 1959; Koepf 1964). Notwithstanding this work, there is an evident paucity of information proving a link between the appearance of the chromatograms and the humus condition—the latter not having been strictly defined—nor is there information that relates to the nature of the chemical reactions that occur at the time of chromatographing.

Our laboratory has made use of this particular chromatographic method for a number of years, chiefly in conjunction with soil and compost testing. As an additional basis for this paper we draw on preliminary results from a research project undertaken more recently in which we explored more closely some of the problematic areas related to methodology and interpretation. Using 20 randomly selected soils primarily from the northeastern United States and Canada, we have attempted to draw correlations between the appearance of the chromatograms of these soils and some of their chemical and biological features. In particular, we looked at such aspects as mineral content, pH, mobility of humus, and the humic–fulvic acid ratio of the humus. Humus mobility, defined as the solubility of soil organic matter, is highly indicative of past soil-forming processes that may or may not lead to the complexation of newly formed humus molecules with inorganic soil constituents (Springer 1949; Kononova 1966). The humic:fulvic acid ratio of humus is similarly characteristic of soil type and is indicative of a soil's tendency to retain organic matter in a more mobile, less decomposed state (fulvic acid type) or to humify it further to a darker and more stable form (humic acid type) (Kononova 1966; Schnitzer and Kahn 1972; Freytag 1962). Our results, though preliminary, do give positive indications that the appearance of the chromatograms relates to these important soil features; and we use these findings to underscore our recommendations for the method.

Experimental Data

As originally proposed by Pfeiffer (1959), the method utilizes circular (15 cm diameter) Whatman #1 chromatographic paper or, alternatively, square 15×15 cm sheets. Paper wicks, rolled from 20×20 mm squares of the same grade of paper, are pushed through a small punctured hole in the center of the disks. Prior to this step, pencil dots indicating radial distances of 35 mm and 50 mm have been placed on the sheets, as shown in Fig. 15.1, and serve to gauge when to stop the moving liquid front. The liquid is eluted into the paper via the wick from a watch glass placed inside a 100 mm petri dish on which the paper sheet rests.

Reagents used include 0.25 N sodium hydroxide for extracting organic matter and 0.5% silver nitrate for sensitizing the filter paper prior to eluting the humic extract. The main reaction pathway involves the formation of silver hydroxide and almost immediately silver oxide, the oxide form being insoluble and causing a yellow-brown precipitate to form. The weakly soluble silver hydroxide causes a partial blocking of the paper's capillary pores, resulting in a streaking effect that is enhanced by the presence of larger organic molecules in the extracts; consequently, a fairly dramatic ray-like appearance is produced. This effect does not occur when extracting solutions lacking hydroxides are used.

Deposition of Reagent and Humic Extract.   The two-step procedure involves (1) prior sensitization and preconditioning of the paper with the silver nitrate solution and (2) elution of the humic extract with the sodium hydroxide solution. Sensitization is accomplished by wicking approximately 1 ml of the silver nitrate solution into the paper to the nearer radius of 35 mm, at which point the paper is removed, the wick taken out and discarded, and the paper allowed to dry for $2-4$ hours in subdued light at a temperature not exceeding 29°C. The nature of the drying period is very important in influencing the final chromatograph. This effect is due in part to the fact that partial reduction of the silver occurs at this time, possibly causing a swifter and more complete reaction in response to eluting the humic extracts later on. We standardize this "preconditioning" phase by allowing the partial silver reduction to reach the point where the first faint signs of yellow silver oxide appear, at which point the humic extract, prepared in advance, is promptly chromatographed. This is accomplished

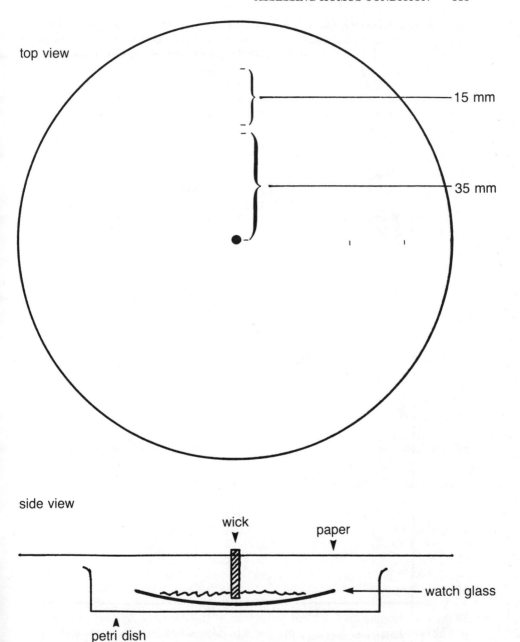

top view

15 mm

35 mm

side view

wick

paper

watch glass

petri dish

FIG. 15.1.   SCHEMATIC VIEW OF THE BASIC ARRANGEMENTS FOR THE CIRCULAR
CHROMATOGRAPHIC METHOD.

by placing a fresh wick into the disk and eluting the humic extract. This part of the procedure should be carried out at approximately 21°C and at a relative humidity of not less than 70%, preferably done inside a temperature- and humidity-controlled chamber. The necessity of high and constant humidity during this period cannot be underestimated. At completion, the paper is removed and hung to dry at room temperature and diffused daylight. After two or more days of further reduction of incompletely reacted silver (including free silver ions and silver hydroxide formed by reaction with the extracting reagent) the chromatogram has stabilized and may be used for interpretation.

Humus Extraction. The mobility and extractability of organic matter with NaOH is a feature sharply dependent on the pH of the sample (Kononova 1966). The relationship we have observed between pH and extractability of organic matter (using an 8 hr extraction period) is shown in Fig. 15.2. The generally low recovery of soil organic matter is partly ex-

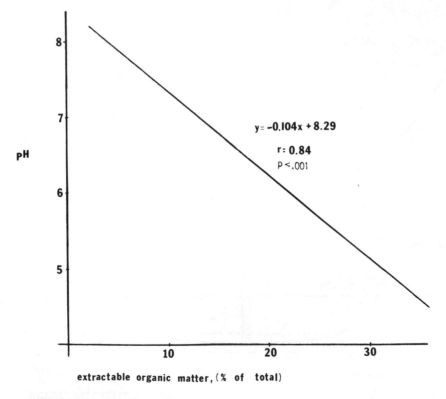

FIG. 15.2. RELATIONSHIP BETWEEN pH AND EXTRACTABILITY OF ORGANIC MATTER OF HUMUS.

plained by the fact that a relatively large percentage of the humus may be present as alkali-insoluble mineral-bound *humins* (Kononova 1966; Najmr 1962; Ricardo 1967). Additionally, under near-neutral conditions a portion may be bound by prominent cations (e.g., calcium) as *humates*, which, unlike *humins*, may be recovered if prior to extraction the sample is decalcified with dilute mineral acid. For the chromatographic method, Pfeiffer's original recommendations called for a standard 1:10 sample:solution extracting ration with no mention of differences in extraction efficiency (Pfeiffer 1959). It is therefore apparent that the amount of soluble organic matter applied to the chromatograms would differ widely between samples of varying origin, which clearly could bias the results. This implies that the extractability of the humus exerts a first-order effect on the appearance of the chromatograms. This trait of extactability is nonetheless a significant clue to the condition in which humus may exist. For example, compare a soil high in acidity and low in biological activity with an intensively managed agricultural one (Fig. 15.3). However, does a link exist between the appearance of the chromatogram and the quality of the humus, defined by its degree of *humification*, as originally purported (Pfeiffer 1959; Koepf 1964)?

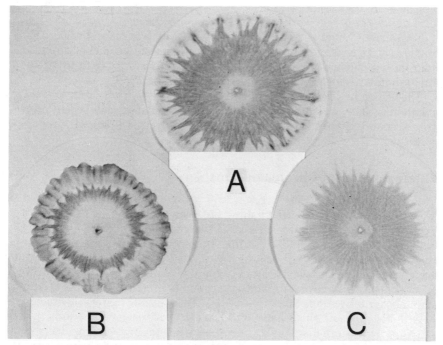

FIG. 15.3.   CHROMATOGRAMS OBTAINED FROM DIFFERENT SOIL SAMPLES: A= NEUTRAL COMPOST-FED GARDEN SOIL; B=CONIFEROUS, ACID FOREST SOIL; C= ALKALINE AGICULTURAL FIELD SOIL.

We investigated this point by adjusting the soil:solution ratio to eliminate any differences in humus extractability (determined in advance), and then ranking the subsequent chromatograms by appearance and statistically analyzing the connection to the *humic:fulvic acid* ratios by a rank-order correlation procedure (Goodman 1964; Norman 1975). These results gave evidence (> 95% significance) of a correlation between the appearance of the chromatograms and the soils' humic:fulvic acid ratios. The results suggest to us that in reading the chromatograms one must distinguish between the first-order effect (humus extractability) and the second-order effect (humus quality), as will be shown later. However, in order to avoid a bias associated with samples of either very high or very low organic content, we apply a correction factor in determining the actual soil:solution ratio for extracting the humus, as follows:

$$r = 0.10 \left/ \sqrt{\frac{\text{sample organic matter \%}}{5}} \right.$$

where r is the dilution ratio. This empirically formulated calculation, which assumes that a normal sample of 5% organic matter is ideal for the 1:10 extraction ratio, has worked excellently in our uses.

Six to eight hours extraction time is generally adequate. Periodic shaking, e.g, at 15 min and 1 hr, is advisable; and centrifugation before chromatographing is usually required, unless the solids are allowed to settle for many hours, as originally recommended (Pfeiffer 1959).

The use of the silver nitrate substrate in conjunction with humic extracts means that the chromatograph is a qualitative oxidation–reduction system, responding with varying degrees of coloration to the sample's reducing abilities.

Interpretation of Chromatograms

Chromatographs of varying soil and compost conditions are shown in Fig. 15.3 and 15.4. In distinguishing between them, it is helpful at first to recognize the three general zones of the chromatogram: *center,* usually light-colored or even blank; *middle,* the area in which the dark-colored spikes occur; and *outer,* extending beyond the spikes and varying in color from yellow to diffuse dark brown. This outer zone is of primary importance in evaluating the chromatograms. As conventional applications of humus chromatography show, three main fractions of humic materials are generally distinguished: the least mobile, most condensed compounds, which travel only a short distance in paper before stopping; intermediary compounds; and finally, highly mobile, *fulvic-acid* compounds, which migrate the furthest when chromatographed (Kononova 1966; Pospisil 1962). Of course, with this particular use of chromatography, the laws that govern rF

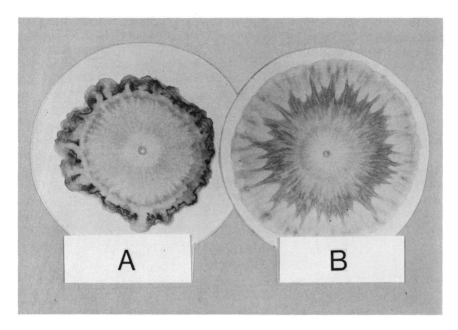

FIG. 15.4.   CHROMATOGRAMS OBTAINED FROM POULTRY MANURE: A=FRESH
POULTRY MANURE; B=POULTRY MANURE COMPOSTED 2 MONTHS.

factors of moving compounds will not be strictly obeyed, but nevertheless
the general relationships will hold. Therefore, we may expect that, where
the relative concentration of fulvic acid compounds is high in the extract, a
thick moving front will be established, leading to a dark outer zone as may
be typically observed in the chromatogram of the acid forest humus in Fig.
15.3. Where the proportion of these mobile compounds is lower in relation to
humic acid types, the outer zone becomes considerably lighter (see garden
soil, Fig. 15.3). Finally in an intensively cultivated agricultural soil, receiving virtually no fresh organic amendments, the more mobile compounds
may be absent and consequently the outer zone may disappear altogether
(see field soil, Fig. 15.3). Judging by the intensity of color between the three
chromatograms in Fig. 15.3, it is evident that the extractability has been
the highest in the acid forest soil and lowest in the field soil. The levels of
organic matter are not identical, of course. The type of gradation in soil
humus condition of which these chromatograms are suggestive may be
represented as in Fig. 15.5.

When the method described is applied to evaluation of composting materials, the basis for interpretation is similar. Here, fresh, undecomposed hen
manure gives strong coloration and a thick outer zone. After a period of
composting, the changes observed on the chromatograph point to a loss

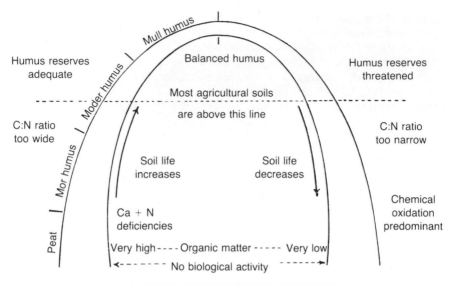

FIG. 15.5.   HUMUS TYPE IN RELATION TO SOIL CONDITION.

of mobile compounds associated with fresh materials and a decrease in extractability suggesting that otherwise extractable humic compounds have been complexed by inorganic constituents and thereby rendered more stable and insoluble. Such stabilization of organic materials is a fundamental goal of composting.

CONCLUSIONS

The use of the Pfeiffer circular chromatography as a complementary tool in soil and compost analysis provides a strictly qualitative means for interpreting the condition of humus-like compounds that may be present. The appearance of the chromatograms relates not so much to the absolute quantity of *organic matter* in a sample being tested as to its qualities— qualities that are first and foremost defined by the extracting solution. In view of this feature, chromatograms must be interpreted with care; the solutions of humus obtained by the sodium hydroxide extractant are generally not representative of the entire sample, and sodium hydroxide may arbitrarily select for some compounds over others (Waksman and Stevens 1930). However, similar research with sodium hydroxide extracts of soils has shown that qualities of the extracted compounds are characteristic of soil type, most particularly when humic:fulvic ratios are investigated (Kononova 1966; Tokudome and Kanno 1968; Harris 1979). It may also be apparent that those humus-related compounds of most immediate agricultural concern are the ones amenable to nondestructive extraction; these include the most physiologically active forms and those which are precursors to the stable, structure-conferring forms important in soils.

Organic materials applied to varying soils may not share common fates, particularly in view of moisture conditions, biological activity, acidity, and the soil's current use (Webber and Beauchamp 1977). Soil conditons of high acidity and low biological activity may select for mobility in organic materials, leading to ultimate loss as carbon dioxide or leaching of soluble organo–mineral products, contributing to podzolization (Kononova 1966; Franco 1968; Khantulev *et al.* 1968). However, under near-neutral soil conditions, humic-like compounds may be readily coagulated in polymer and organo–mineral (humate) forms, preserving them in the arable layer and conferring favorable structural effects on the soil (Alexandrova *et al.* 1968; Pauli 1967; Martin and Focht 1977).

From these points it may appear obvious that the efficiency of retention of added organic materials will vary appreciably depending on soil type, bringing into question generalized principles for organic waste application. For example, farming literature contains many assertions that sheet composting of organic material is equally effective as prior composting and subsequent soil application. However, the composting environment may select for stabilization of organic material through polymerization and complexation with minerals at characteristically higher pH levels (Springer 1949), whereas the same materials applied as sheet compost to an acid soil may never enjoy such a form of humification.

The fairly simple, qualitative chromatographic technique described in this paper can provide a means of distinguishing these features, whether from a soil or a composting point of view. As a nonquantitative technique, the method is challenging and may require collaborative data—for example, organic matter content and pH—to assist interpretation. Used for monitoring short-term changes in composts, the method provides clues to the progress of humification and may suggest probable effects the compost will have on a soil. Used in conjunction with soils, the method can reveal humus effects related to past and present soil-forming processes and agricultural management, contributing an important framework for understanding efficient soil utilization of organic materials.

ACKNOWLEDGMENT

The assistance of Robert Parnes in the research collaboration for this report is gratefully acknowledged.

REFERENCES

AINA, P.O.   1979.   Soil changes resulting from long-term management practices in western Nigeria.   Soil Sci. Soc. Am. J. *43*, 173–177.

ALEXANDROVA, L.N., ARSHAVSKAY, T.TH., DORFMAN, E.M., LYUZIN, M.F., and YURLOVA, O.V.   1968.   Humus acids and their organo-mineral derivatives in soil.   Trans. 9th Int. Cong.   Soil Sci. *3* , 143–152.

BRINTON, W.F. 1979. The effects of different fertilizer treatments on humus quality. Compost Sci. Land Util. *205*, 38−41.

ECKHOLM, E. 1976. Losing Ground: Environmental Stress and World Food Production. W.W. Norton, Co., New York.

FLAIG, W., NAGAR, B., SÖCHTIG, H., and TIETJEN, C. 1977. Organic Materials and Soil Productivity. Food and Agriculture Organization, Rome.

FRANCO, E.P.C. 1968. Some cases of podsolization under tropical conditions in Angola. Trans. Int. Cong. Soil Sci. *3*, 265−273.

FREYTAG, H. 1962. Über einige Analogien im Verlaufe pflanzlicher und synthetischer Humifizierungsprozesse. Symposium Humus and Plant, Czech. Acad. Sci., Prague.

GOODMAN, R. 1964. Modern Statistics. Arc Books, New York.

HARRIS, S.A. 1979. Humic acid: fulvic acid ratio. *In* The Encylopedia of Soil Science, Part 1. Dowden, Hutchinson & Ross, Stroudsburg, pp. 194−195.

HERTELENDY, K. 1973. Qualitäts Beurteilung von Kompost aus Siedlungsabfällen. Jahresbericht EAWAG.

KHANTULEV, A.A., GAGARINA, E.I., RASTVOROVA, O.G., SCHASTNAJA, L.S., TERESHENKOVA, I.A., and TSYPLENKOV, V.P. 1968. The structure and pedogenesis of complex humus profiles in the boreal forest zone. Trans. 9th Int. Cong. Soil Sci. *3*, 221−236.

KOEPF, H.H. 1964. Soil tests and chromatograms. Biodynamics *69*, 1−13.

KONONOVA, M.M. 1966. Soil Organic Matter: Its Nature, Its Role in Soil Formation and in Soil Fertility. 2nd Edition. Pergamon Press, London.

LUNIN, J. 1977. Introduction in Soils for Management of Organic Wastes and Waste Waters. Soil Sci. Soc. Am., Madison, Wisconsin.

MARTIN, J.P. and FOCHT, D.D. 1977. Biological properties of soils. *In* Soils for Management of Organic Wastes and Waste Waters. Soil Sci. Soc. Am., Madison, Wisconsin.

MARTIN, J.P., HAIDER, K., and LINHARES, L.F. 1979. Decomposition and stabilization of ring 14C-labeled catechol in soil. Soil Sci. Soc. Am. J. *43*, 100−104.

NAJMR, S. 1962. Ein Beitrag zur Kenntnis der Humine in den genetischen Bodentypen. Symposium Humus and Plant, Czech. Acad. Sci., Prague.

NORMAN, N. 1975. Statistical Package for the Social Sciences. McGraw Hill, New York, pp. 288−290.

PAULI, F.W. 1967. Soil Fertility: A Biodynamical Approach. Adam Hilger Ltd., London.

PFEIFFER, E.E. 1959. The art and science of composting. Biodynamics *49*, 1−20.

PFEIFFER, E.E. 1960. Qualitative chromatographic method for the determination of biological factors. Biodynamics *50*, 2−15.

POSPÍŠIL, F. 1962. Einige physikalisch−chemische Eigenschaften der Humusstoffe. Symposium Humus and Plant, Czech. Acad. Sci., Prague.

SABARTH, E. 1962. Chromatograms of soils: B.D. preparations and their source materials. Biodynamics *62*, 9−14.

SCHNITZER, M. and KAHN, S.U.   1972.   Humic Substances in the Environment.   Marcel Dekker, Inc., New York.

SMITH, M.J.   1973.   Further research into a chromatographic technique for
vitamin analysis.   Human Dimensions, 2 (1), 2−7.

SPRINGER, U.   1949.   In welchem Ausmass ist eine Humusvermehrung
durch Mineraldüngung, Stallmist- und Kompost-Düngung möglich?   Ztschr.
Pflanzener.   Bodenk. 46, 196−233.

STICKELBERGER, B.   1975.   Survey of city refuse composting.   In FAO
Soils Bulletin #27.   FAO, Rome, pp. 185−209.

TOKUDOME, S. and KANNO, I.   1968.   Nature of the humus of some Japanese soils.   Trans. 9th Int. Cong. Soil Sci. 3, 163−173.

WAKSMAN, S.A. and STEVENS, K.R.   1930.   Critical study of the methods
for determining the nature and abundance of soil organic matter.   Soil Sci.
30:97−115.

WEBBER, L.R. and BEAUCHAMP, E.G.   1977.   Land utilization and dis-
posal of organic wastes in cool subhumid and humid regions.   In Soils for
Management of Organic Wastes and Waste Waters.   Soil Sci. Soc. Am.,
Madison, Wisconsin, pp. 457−472.

16

Nutritional Considerations in Planning for Food Production

Olaf Mickelsen

FACTORS INFLUENCING CONSUMERS' FOOD PURCHASES

On only a few occasions have nutritional factors been considered in rational agricultural plans. A number of reasons explain why so little attention has been given to the human nutritional implications of agricultural practices. Perhaps one of the important reasons for this apparent neglect of the ultimate consumer's nutritional well-being is that the consumer, to a large extent, does not decide what to purchase on the basis of the nutrient content of foods. One may argue that the advent of nutrient content labelling of processed foods reflects the consumers' desire to know the nutritional value of their purchase. There is some question as to whether such labelling was the result of a recognized need or was the work of a group of zealous but misguided individuals who felt the program would be helpful in choosing

394

the most nutritious processed food in the retail market. To verify this, one has only to watch consumers in any supermarket rapidly filling their shopping carts with processed foods (Mickelsen 1972). Seldom does the purchaser examine the label to determine the nutrient content of a food. If any attention is given to the potential purchase, it is related to the coupons that offer a monetary discount when a specified item is purchased. Perhaps this behavior on the part of the consumer is an indication of faith in the quality standards maintained by food processors and the ability of the Food and Drug Administration to monitor the safety of our foods. Undoubtedly, a small segment of consumers depend upon and benefit from certain aspects of nutrient labelling. In most cases, they are individuals who are afflicted with a chronic disease that requires a limitation in the consumption of certain food items.

In developed countries, a number of food characteristics other than the nutrient content of processed foods are likely to influence the consumer's choice. These include taste, appearance, color, consistency, cooking facilities and time required for preparation, likes and dislikes of family members and, especially during an economic recession, the cost of the food. The last is attested to by the use of a tremendous number of coupons that allow a reduction in price of a specific product at the time of purchase.

From the farmers' and producers' standpoint, these factors are important, in an indirect way, in determining what and how much will be planted or how many animals will be raised. The overriding factor that determines what and how much of different foods will be produced is the financial profit from the harvested crop. That may depend to a large extent on the price of the food in the marketplace, but in some cases the market price may be supplemented by government subsidies to the farmer or processor. For crops, such as wheat or rice, that can be stored for relatively long periods, the size of the previous year's crop is not likely to affect the acreage that will be planted and/or the intensity with which fertilizers, herbicides, and the like are applied.

Perhaps, the raising of farm animals for the consumer market represents one area where nutritional requirements have influenced agricultural practices. A great deal of attention has been and is continually being bestowed on the nutritional requirements of farm animals, because the economic repercussions are so apparent they cannot be ignored. The rapid growth rate of farm animals and, consequently, their high nutritional requirements make any health disturbance associated with their rations apparent in a very short time.

CROPS FOR HUMAN NUTRITION

The absence of nutritional considerations directed to the ultimate consumer in the formulation of agricultural policies, among other things, may stem from the poor record of such attempts in the past. One of the early suggestions that the nutrient content of foods should determine their price at the retail market was made by W. O. Atwater, one of the early American nutritionists.

In the latter part of the previous century, Atwater was very impressed with the energy requirements of human subjects. He had spent some time working in Germany with Pettenkofer and Voit, who developed one of the first calorimeters for measuring energy metabolism (McCollum 1957, p. 130). On his return to the United States, Atwater and Rosa, a physicist, developed a calorimeter that could be used for the study of the energy expended in various forms of physical activity. The results so impressed Atwater with the importance of the fuel value of foods that he proposed that the cost of all foods be based on their caloric content. On that basis, there was little point in purchasing such fruits as oranges, which were composed mostly of water. Although Atwater was with the USDA, his suggestion for pricing foods was never attempted in this country.

The fallacy of Atwater's proposal became apparent shortly after he suggested it. Vitamins and deficiency diseases became recognized as such only a few years later. When Atwater suggested that foods be priced on the basis of their caloric content, Eijkman was just initiating his studies on the island of Java that led to the recognition that foods provided nutrients besides carbohydrates, fats, proteins, and minerals.

RUBNER AND WORLD WAR I

Another example of the perversion of nutritional information in agricultural planning occurred early in World War I. At that time, Max Rubner was one of the world's leading nutrition authorities. He was asked how German agricultural practices should be altered in order for that country to prepare for the war that had just started (Davidson *et al.* 1973, p. 58). Rubner was unduly intrigued by the role protein played in the body's functions. On that basis, he suggested that the production of meat, milk, and dairy products be continued. His reasoning was based on the assumption that physical activity involved the utilization of protein and that this effect was proportional to the effort expended. The soldiers, because of their greater activity, would require a continued high protein intake. The need for high protein foods would be increased by the more strenuous work that would have to be performed by the civilians during the war. On these bases, German agricultural practices were not changed.

It is difficult to understand the exaggerated importance Rubner attached to dietary protein, all the more because a Swiss physiologist and a chemist prior to World War I had definitely shown that such strenuous physical activity as mountain climbing produced no greater breakdown of body protein than the routine work in the laboratory (McCollum 1957, p. 125). On both a day in the laboratory and a following day of strenuous mountain climbing, these men avoided eating protein foods and limited their intake to carbohydrates and fats. They found that the urinary nitrogen excretion was the same for the day of increased physical activity as it was when they performed their usual tasks at the university. These investigators concluded that the fuel used by the body during physical activity was carbohydrate and fat. For such strenuous physical activity, there was no need to increase the protein intake.

Rubner's error in recommending a continuance of the production of high protein foods didn't become apparent until the Allied blockade restricted the importation of food to Germany. When food in Germany became limited, the tide of war rapidly went against that country. Had Rubner recommended a more vegetarian diet for the Germans, it is likely that there would have been an adequate amount of food and the outcome of the war might have been different (Lusk 1928, p. 756). This error on Rubner's part "probably did more than any army general to lose the war that then began . . ." (Davidson *et al.* 1973, p. 58).

ANIMAL FOODS IN HUMAN NUTRITION

The preceding historical sketch emphasizes the fact that the production of animal protein provides fewer calories per hectare than do plant products consumed directly by man. That difference is due to a considerable loss of energy when plant foods are cycled through animals. The reduction in caloric recovery varies from a high of almost 90% in the case of such meat as beef to a low of 50 – 75% in the case of milk and eggs. These figures obviously depend upon a number of factors such as the efficiency of the animals in converting feed to meat, milk, eggs, and so on; the kind of feed available to the animals; the environmental conditions under which the animals are raised; and possibly other additional factors. Some of this loss in caloric recovery is of minor importance because some meat-producing animals can secure adequate forage in parts of a country not physically adapted to tillage. Where this is the case, animal production appears to be more than justified.

Animal protein has had a very prominent place in the recommendations of American nutritionists. This largely stemmed from the fact that the laboratory rat played such an important role in nutrition research. Early in the development of nutrition science, the growth of the weanling rat was used as a measure of the quality of various protein foods, each of which served as the principal source of that nutrient in the experimental diet. On that basis, the scores assigned to the proteins of animal origin were far larger than those secured when different plant foods were assayed. Consequently, plant foods came to be considered primarily as contributors of carbohydrates to the diet and, in the early days of nutrition, as sources of roughage.

The superiority of the proteins in animal foods received additional experimental support from the observation that the proteins in plant foods could support growth in the weanling rat when supplemented with animal proteins. On that basis, milk was considered an excellent means of improving the biological value of the proteins in cereal products. This concept was adopted by the Food and Nutrition Board of the National Academy of Sciences. In the Recommended Dietary Allowances promulgated by the board, animal foods played a very prominent role, as evident in the statement that "The inclusion of a variety of foods, and especially products of animal origin, in the diet assures a satisfactory amino acid distribution as well as sources of other nutrients" (Food and Nutrition Board 1953).

GROWTH RATE AND MILK CONSUMPTION

Some British investigators early recognized that the growth rate of newborn animals was related to the energy and protein levels in their dams' milk (Widdowson 1968, p. 226). This was strikingly brought out by Widdowson, who indicated that, by 4 or 5 months of age, the rat had practically attained its adult weight, which was some 60-fold greater than its birth weight, whereas the human infant had only doubled or tripled its birth weight. The pig went on to increase its birth weight within one year by a factor of about 180. These tremendous differences in growth rates are reflected in the composition of the dam's milk for each species (see Table 16.1).

The almost 10-fold greater concentration of protein on an absolute basis in rat milk when compared with human milk is probably associated with a comparable increased concentration of other essential nutrients. The net result is that the newborn rat receives a diet that contains, in a concentrated form, all the essential nutrients needed for very rapid growth. This should not be interpreted to mean that human milk when used for the human infant is inferior to that of either animal species. Actually, the normal milk of each species is uniquely adapted to the physiological needs of its newborn and probably was not intended to be used by other species. That may explain the need to dilute cow's milk with water to reduce its protein concentration to the point where the kidneys of the human infant can excrete the urea resulting from the metabolism of the relatively high level of protein in cow's milk.

RAT MILK VERSUS HUMAN MILK

These factors led to a study of the growth rates of weanling rats fed a synthetic milk that simulated human milk in composition, and a comparable group fed a milk simulating rat's milk. That study showed the inability

TABLE 16.1.   COMPOSITION OF MILKS

Species	Protein (g/100 g)	kcal/100 g	Calories from protein (% of total calories)
Human	1.2	69	6.9%
Pig	5.8	122	19.0%
Rat	12.0	245	19.6%

Adapted from Widdowson 1968, p. 226.

of human milk to support good growth in rats, whereas those animals fed simulated rat's milk grew at a normal rate. Such an observation would never be interpreted to mean that the human infant should be fed rats' milk in order to benefit from optimum nutrition.

This is obviously an exaggerated situation, cited primarily to indicate the narrow approach that many investigators have followed in translating the results of their nutritional studies with the laboratory rat to human beings. There is no question but that the qualitative nutritional requirements of many species are similar, but their quantitative needs for the essential nutrients may differ. It is in the latter area where much of the misunderstanding about human nutrient needs resides.

BREAD PROTEIN: STUDIES WITH RATS

The significance of the just-mentioned limitation became obvious when one of my graduate students indicated that she would like to work on a problem that would benefit her countrymen on her return to Iran. Since about 70% of the people in Iran lived in villages where the diet provided some 80–90% of the calories from bread, she initiated research to improve nutritional value of the bread protein.

This research involved an evaluation of the growth rates of weanling rats fed Iranian bread as the primary source of their protein. The bread was purchased from bakers in Teheran. The rations fed the rats contained this bread or this bread supplemented with skim milk powder or dried legumes. In all cases, the rations contained an adequate amount of essential minerals and vitamins. Those animals fed the unsupplemented bread grew very poorly whereas the legumes or skim milk powder, as supplements to the bread, permitted an almost normal growth rate. One calculation indicated that an Iranian farmer consuming 2500 kcal per day would receive 1.8 g of lysine if 90% of his caloric intake came from 70% extraction flour. As Rose (1957) found that normal young men required 0.8 g of lysine per day, bread made with American white flour should provide the Iranian farmer with an adequate intake of the amino acid lysine, which was reported to limit the nutritional value of wheat products (Bolourchi 1963). That the Iranians received sufficient lysine from the bread in their diet was apparent from their old civilization and their extensive empire centuries ago.

These observations suggested that human subjects, at least those past their rapid growth stage, should be able to secure all their essential amino acids from bread. Calculations indicated that this was possible when bread provided about 40% of the caloric requirement. Similar calculations by Hegsted (1962) indicated that even a 7-year-old child should receive an adequate intake of lysine if most of its protein came from food made with white flour. Calculations such as these were largely ignored, as the few studies of human subjects fed large amounts of bread suggested that wheat products were unable to maintain the human body in nitrogen equilibrium. These investigations, beginning with that of Thomas (1909), covered periods of only a few days.

BREAD PROTEIN: STUDIES WITH YOUNG MEN

To secure a more precise evaluation of the adequacy of the amino acid content of wheat flour to supply human needs, a 70-day study was performed (Bolourchi *et al.* 1968A) with normal college men who received a diet that contained 70 g protein per day. During the experimental period, there was no animal protein in the diet, which provided 90–95% of that nutrient from commercial white flour. That experimental diet was served for 49 days. It was preceded by a 3-week control period, when the protein intake was the same as that in the experimental period but about half of the protein was of animal origin.

The results of that study showed that wheat, when it was the primary source of dietary protein, provided an adequate amount of the essential amino acids required by these subjects. This conclusion is based on the response seen among the subjects after the third week of the study. Prior to that, the 12 subjects had been in negative nitrogen balance. Actually, they were losing an average of almost 2 g of nitrogen per day during the first 10 days of the experimental period. Thereafter, the negative nitrogen balance rapidly decreased so that, by the 20th day, the subjects were in equilibrium. During the last 30 days of the study, the subjects retained enough nitrogen to make up for that lost during the first part of the experimental period.

The conversion of the negative nitrogen balance some time after the second week of the study indicates that most of the previous studies, which were limited to seven to ten days, did not provide an accurate indication of the ability of wheat flour products to provide the essential amino acids needed by human subjects (Vaghefi *et al.* 1974). This is supported by the physical status of the Iranian villagers who secure most of their protein from wheat. Their diet provides very little animal protein because the rainfall is so low that only very limited numbers of sheep and goats can be maintained on the meager forage.

WHEAT AND BLOOD UREA LEVELS

In addition to providing an adequate amount of essential amino acids, wheat may have some positive effects on the health of those who consume large amounts of it. The first indication of that became apparent in the reduction of the blood urea level of the subjects involved in the previously described wheat study (Bolourchi *et al.* 1968B). That occurred despite the fact that the protein intake during the 3-week control period was the same as that in the experimental period. The reduction in the blood urea level was contrary to the report of Addis and coworkers (1947). These clinicians reported that the level of blood urea was related to the amount of dietary protein. No distinction was made by Addis' group as to whether the protein was of plant or animal origin.

Subsequent work in our laboratory confirmed the reduction in blood urea level when wheat was the primary source of protein in the diet. This reduction in blood urea levels might have medical implications since, for many years, that parameter was used as an index of kidney function. As the kidneys began to fail, the blood urea level increased. Admittedly, such increase in urea level occurred only after there was considerable deterioration in the kidney. Normally, the kidney has a great deal of reserve functioning capacity for the excretion of metabolic waste products. On that basis, one might postulate that the reduction in blood urea to levels that were one-half of normal might indicate an improved functioning in the kidneys of these normal college men. Prior to the initiation of each study involving human subjects, they were given a physical examination to ascertain whether they had any disturbances of the heart and kidneys. Their medical records were also checked to make certain that, from a health standpoint, they were normal and free of detectable diseases. The reduction in blood urea implied that the kidneys of these normal subjects fed diets containing large amounts of wheat were functioning at a level that was better than normal.

A study devised specifically to determine the effect of the wheat diet on kidney function suggested that such a diet produced a marked improvement. For that test, a group of normal college men were fed a control diet providing 70 g of protein per day, with about half of it from animal sources. That diet was fed for three weeks. At the termination of the control period, urea and creatinine clearances were determined on all six subjects. These two tests are routinely used in evaluating the functioning of the kidneys. For that purpose, there are more elaborate tests, but from an ethical standpoint their use is justified primarily with patients. The results of both tests, at the end of the control period, indicated that the kidneys of our subjects were functioning normally.

The 3-week control period was followed by the high wheat diet, which was served for 7 weeks. Again, that diet contained no animal protein, and from 90 to 95% of its protein came from wheat. That produced the usual, approximately 50% reduction in blood urea levels. The results of the kidney function tests at the end of the experimental period indicated a 25% improvement in urea clearance and a 10% improvement in creatinine clearance. This change in kidney function probably explained the observed reduction in blood urea levels.

The implications of these observations are still to be determined. Unfortunately, the medical profession is so engrossed in treating ill patients and prescribing drugs that no effort, on a statistically sound basis, has been made to evaluate the use of a high wheat diet by individuals when they first manifest some abnormality in the functioning of their kidneys. However, reports from two patients who were undergoing renal dialysis suggest that the diet high in bread in one patient increased the number of days between dialysis treatments and in the other obviated the need for further dialysis. Both patients were prompted to request permission from their physicians to alter their diets after reading about the effect of wheat on kidney function.

It was largely to explore the incidence and nature of renal diseases among the people in Iran that we accepted an invitation to spend two years in that country. Unfortunately, the political upheaval that started shortly after we arrived prevented any definitive work in that area. Furthermore, we soon learned that the Iranian hospitals did not maintain any medical records. When a patient was discharged, the attending physician took the records back to his office. Consultation with some of the urologists indicated that very little kidney disturbance of a metabolic nature occurred among the village people. However, many of these individuals developed a variety of kidney infections, largely because of the poor sanitary facilities available. In contrast, the situation in the major cities such as Teheran, Shiraz, and Isphahan was just the opposite. In the urban centers, there was a considerable amount of metabolically related renal disease and relatively less of those diseases associated with infection. This difference may reflect the nature of the diet in the urban and rural areas. As previously mentioned, the village people in Iran consume a diet in which bread provides from 80 to 90% of the calories. On the other hand, most of the people in the urban centers were following a diet that began to resemble that in Western countries. Large amounts of meat were being imported; milk and cheese became common ingredients of practically every meal. Although bread still was eaten in large amounts compared to the situation in the United States, there were indications that rice was rapidly replacing a considerable amount of bread. This occurred despite the fact that the cost of bread was maintained at a low price by governmental subsidy.

OSTEOPOROSIS AND VEGETARIANISM

Another area where there is strong evidence that a vegetarian-type diet may enhance health relates to osteoporosis. The demineralization of the bones that occurs in a high proportion of Western women after the menopause may be diet-related. Suggestive evidence for that possibility came from the observation of Walker (Mickelsen 1976). He reported that older Bantu women on reservations in South Africa, who had a daily intake of 200 – 400 mg of calcium, had had some six to eight pregnancies and nursed their offspring for two to three years. Under such circumstances, these women should have lost a great deal of calcium both to their fetuses and in the milk they provided their offspring. Despite this, these Bantu women had thick, well-mineralized cortices; and osteoporosis was unknown among them. On the other hand, the white women in the urban centers of South Africa, with calcium intakes of 800 to 1200 mg, had had two pregnancies and, in many cases, fed their infants formulated milk. These procedures should have prevented the development of osteoporosis. That was not the case: The older white women in South Africa had an incidence of osteoporosis comparable to that seen among women in northern Europe and the United States.

In addition to the mentioned differences in calcium intake between the Bantu and white women in South Africa, there was a marked variation in the amount of animal foods in their diets. Reports suggest that the Bantu women on the reservations received no or only very limited amounts of animal foods. Their diet was based largely on corn. The white women, on the other hand, followed a diet similar to that of Western women, especially insofar as animal food intake was concerned. The migration of the Bantu women to the urban centers was associated with a dietary change resulting in an increased intake of animal foods. At the villages intermediate between the reservations and the urban centers, the dietary practices of the Bantus approached that of their kinfolk in the cities. With that dietary alteration, the incidence of osteoporosis increased among the older women, especially those who had been in the urban centers for one or more generations.

URINARY CALCIUM LOSS AND TITRATABLE ACIDITY

A possible explanation for the difference in the incidence of osteoporosis among vegetarians and those who are omnivorous probably relates to the differential effect of the diet on the titratable acidity of the urine. When the urine is slightly alkaline, such as occurs when a vegetarian diet is consumed, the skeleton retains its calcium and may actually show an increase in mineral content. On the other hand, an acidic urine, which usually accompanies the ingestion of animal foods, especially meat, enhances the loss of calcium. Because practically all the calcium in the body is found in teeth and bones, the production of an acidic urine ultimately results in the demineralization of the skeleton. As far as osteoporosis is concerned, there is some physiological mechanism that minimizes or perhaps eliminates the urinary acidity effects on calcium metabolism in women prior to menopause. This became obvious when a large number of Seventh-day Adventist women were studied.

SEVENTH-DAY ADVENTISTS AND OSTEOPOROSIS

The Seventh-day Adventists were studied because one of their important tenets stresses the avoidance of meat in their diet. Many of these people are lacto-ovo-vegetarians and so should provide an answer to the question: Is the inclusion of meat in the diet associated with demineralized skeletons, especially among older women?

That study (Marsh *et al.* 1980; Sanchez *et al.* 1980) showed good skeletal mineralization among the Seventh-day Adventist older women, some of whom were over 90 years of age. The Seventh-day Adventist women who were under 55 years of age (the average age of menopause among American women) had bone mineralization that was the same as that of omnivorous women. Such a finding suggested that, prior to the reduction in estrogen production associated with the menopause, skeletal mineralization is not influenced or only minimally influenced by the nature of the diet. However, among older women, there was a marked reduction in bone mineral content for the omnivorous women, whereas there was little change among comparably aged Seventh-day Adventist women.

Although all the data have not been collected, there are indications that osteoporosis is relatively rare among Seventh-day Adventist women. That study will attempt to determine the age when the women adopted the lacto-ovo-vegetarian regimen. Because members of that religious faith may choose the dietary program they will follow, this study is also probing the nature of the diet followed by the older women.

DIETARY FIBER

This discussion of vegetarianism would not be complete without some reference to the work of Dr. Dennis Burkitt and his English colleagues (1975). While Dr. Burkitt was a surgeon in Africa, he was impressed by the almost complete absence of certain types of cancer, especially of the gastro-intestinal tract, among the natives, whereas the white people in the same area had as many malignancies as the people in Europe. One of the important differences between the two groups of people in Africa was the nature of their diet. The Africans, in most cases, consumed a diet high in roughage whereas the people of European extraction ingested very little dietary fiber. The reduction in the fiber content of the diet, according to Burkitt, resulted in a slow movement of food through the intestine. One result of that was the increased time during which carcinogenic compounds were in contact with the cells lining the inner wall of the intestine. That provided a greater opportunity for the carcinogenic compounds to affect the mucosal cells and initiate the cancerous process.

The difference in what Burkitt called the transit time of food through the intestinal tract was a matter of days. For those individuals in Africa who consumed a vegetarian diet most of their lives, residues of their food appear in their feces within 24 hours or less. On the other hand, the transit time for omnivorous eaters is as long as 3 to 5 days.

According to Burkitt and coworkers, a variety of diseases common to Western people are associated with a reduction in the dietary fiber content. It will require more work before the validity of all these claims can be ascertained. There is, however, increasing evidence that diabetes may be related to a reduction in the dietary fiber intake. That was suggested by Trowell (1975) on the basis of both geographic and historical bases. Our own observations in Iran appeared to confirm this. Among the villagers, little if any diabetes occurred, whereas in Teheran, approximately 10% of the adults were reported to have this disease. More recent work along this line (Kiehm et al. 1976) indicates that the insulin requirement of diabetics requiring no more than 40 units per day can be obviated when the patient increases his or her daily bran intake to about 30 g.

WATER NEEDS OF DIFFERENT FOODS

This discussion of the effects of a vegetarian diet on human survival and health has been introduced to indicate that agricultural planning does not have to be based on the assumption that a large amount of animal food need appear in our diet. Actually, other considerations may favor the use of a vegetarian diet as our natural resources become more limited. One of the resources that may shortly become critical is water. In some parts of the world, it is already a critically scarce environmental factor.

There is a marked difference in the water required for the production of plant versus animal foods. Even among plant foods, there is considerable variation in the amount of water needed in their production (Table 16.2). It is impossible to know whether these values refer to the entire plant or only the edible portion. That it may be the former is suggested by Borgstrom (1972, p. 483). Under those circumstances, the requirement for wheat as used by human subjects would have to be increased by a factor of 1.6 to 4.2. Similar, if not greater, factors would have to be applied to some of the other foods. These values (Table 16.2) are primarily indicative of the fact that wheat production requires considerably less moisture than rice and somewhat less than potatoes. This fact may explain why wheat is an important crop in those parts of the world where rainfall is restricted.

The production of animal products, such as milk and meat, requires considerably more water on a calorically equivalent base than plant products. The 35-fold and greater amount of water needed to produce 1000 kcal in the form of milk or meat largely accounts for the fact that semi-arid regions of the world such as Iran (except along the Caspian) depend upon wheat to supply most of the calories used by their inhabitants.

Not only is the requirement for water greater for animal production, but the processing of the animals also requires large amounts of water. On the other hand, one might argue that for the conversion of the wheat kernel into flour, water to power the mills is needed. That was true for this country and partially explains why flour mills became so prominent on the falls of the Mississippi River in Minneapolis. The use of other forms of energy has reduced the dependence of the milling industry on water power. That change, however, has added another factor, energy, to those that must be considered by individuals responsible for determining agricultural policy.

TABLE 16.2.   WATER NEEDED TO PRODUCE 1000 KCAL FOOD

Crop	Water required (liters)
Wheat	53–133
Potatoes	148–205
Rice	372–490
Milk	1960
Meat	3310–5050

Adapted from Borgstrom 1972, p. 483.

ENERGY TO PROCESS AND STORE ENERGY

A great deal more energy is required, both in the form of processing equipment and for storage, for animal products than for plant foods, especially those that may be the major source of calories for large numbers of people. This is evident when one considers the refrigeration and other equipment needed for processing, storage, transportation, and sale of most animal products. In contrast, relatively little in the way of special equipment or energy is needed for the cereal grains. Relatively little has been done on the energy requirements needed to convert plant or animal products from the form in which they appear on the retail market to the food routinely consumed by human subjects. Here again, considerable variation is likely to occur, depending on the form in which the food is served and the nature of the heat to which it has been subjected. For instance, it would be difficult to compare the energy needed for frying meat on top of the stove with that used by an oven for baking bread. This area should be explored, not only as a means of assisting officials in underdeveloped countries to make rational agricultural policy decisions but also to provide a reasonable basis for conservation-minded individuals in the more developed countries to assess how they can economize on their energy costs.

PLANT FOODS FOR MAN'S SURVIVAL

This discussion was prepared to indicate that from a nutritional standpoint, there is no rational evidence to suggest that, in agricultural planning, provision must be made for the production or availability in the retail market of large amounts of animal foods. There is sufficient evidence, from both an economic and a health standpoint, to warrant the use of a diet in which a large fraction of the calories are of plant origin. Actually, such a program is advocated in the reports of the Select Committee on Nutrition and Human Needs of the United States Senate. One of their first reports was entitled "Towards a National Nutrition Policy" (1975). The second edition of that report, entitled "Dietary Goals for the United States" (1977), contains the statement by Senator McGovern that these goals "provide nutrition knowledge with which Americans can begin to take responsibility for maintaining their health and reducing their risk of illness."

A number of problems require caution in advocating complete reliance on a wholly vegetarian diet. Individuals who rely on such diets are called vegans. Some evidence suggests that, if they have followed a strictly vegetarian diet for many years, they are likely to manifest blood changes (Stewart et al. 1970; Rose, 1976). However, others (Sanders et al. 1978) claim the vegans they studied had normal hemoglobin levels. A deficiency of vitamin B_{12} associated with a metabolic disturbance that results in the absence of the intrinsic factor in the patient's intestinal tract appears to be involved in the etiology of pernicious anemia. As vitamin B_{12} occurs primarily in foods of animal origin, prudence suggests that such foods should not be completely eliminated from the diet.

Another dietary factor that requires some consideration in agricultural policy deliberations is the calcium needs of infants and small children. For them, milk is the ideal source of calcium as well as other nutrients and is an almost indispensable food in their dietary regimen. However, the situation may change as the child matures. It has only been within recent years that some attention has been directed to an evaluation of the role that foods play in regulating the titratable acidity of the urine and thus influencing the loss of calcium from the body. To avoid that situation, the primary emphasis in the United States has been on the inclusion of large amounts of dairy products in the diet as a means of overcoming the urinary loss of calcium associated with a meat diet.

This manner of rationalization is reminiscent of the adage, "If a little is good, then more must be better." Where the increased intake has no adverse effects on the body, such advice may not be dangerous. However, some people will interpret an intake lower than the recommended one as being harmful. That is how the person with a little nutrition knowledge is likely to react, especially if conscientiously attempting to follow the guidelines put forth by quasigovernmental groups. As far as calcium needs are concerned, one should remember Thoreau's (1973) encounter with a farmer plowing his field near Walden. This farmer said, "You cannot live on vegetable food solely, for it furnishes nothing to make bones with." Yet, as Thoreau notices, the oxen "with vegetable-made bones, jerk him and his lumbering plow along in spite of every obstacle." Now we can suggest that the oxen secured a small amount of calcium in their forage and that, because of the plant ration on which they subsisted, the little of this mineral they consumed was largely retained in their bones.

Animal foods, especially meat, will continue to play a prominent role in the human diet. This is especially true as the economic situation in a country improves. That was obvious in the large amounts of beef and lamb imported by Iran after the price of petroleum increased to the point where large numbers of Iranians could pay for that food.

There are many reasons that people want to include meat in their daily diet. One of these relates to the physiological and psychological reactions initiated in many people by the aroma of cooking meat. The taste of meat, cheese, and other animal foods appeals to most individuals.

It is for these and other subtle, nonnutritious reasons that, as the family income increases, the amount of animal food in the diet frequently becomes greater. That was clearly brought out when Friedrich Engels (1958) about 1845 studied the diets of the people in England, where his family had a weaving mill. On the basis of his inquiries, he stated that the poor people in England could afford very little meat and that which they purchased was of poor quality and frequently tainted. The better meat had been bought earlier in the day by the wealthier people who did not work as long hours as the poor. To secure sufficient food, the poor increased their consumption of bread. That was purchased from bakers who frequently adulterated the bread they sold. The wealthy ate little bread and that was made in their own homes.

From the standpoint of agricultural policy considerations, it should be recognized that a diet based to a large extent on plant foods not only provides a greater return in terms of calories than a regimen that includes large quantities of animal products, but it may also bestow health benefits upon the people who follow such a practice. This health improvement is likely to be associated with a reduction and, in some cases, the elimination of a few of the chronic diseases that afflict large numbers of individuals in the more developed countries. Furthermore, the proper choice of plant foods should provide a diet that, with the possible exception of vitamin B_{12}, contains all the nutrients in amounts adequate to supply the needs of everyone except for infants and very small children.

Far less equipment, and that of a less sophisticated nature, is necessary for the production, storage, and distribution of the food essential to feed large numbers of people a vegetarian-type diet than one that contains considerable amounts of animal foods. As the world's population continues to increase at its present rate, the land available for agricultural production will decrease. Not only will there be a reduction in the amount of land available for food production, but the remaining land is not well adapted to agricultural purposes. At some time in the near future, such conditions will raise the cost of food to an extent that a more nearly vegetarian diet will become a necessity for large groups of people. That will be brought about either by the development of rational agricultural policies or through economic factors that will spur most people to include more foods of plant origin in their daily fare.

REFERENCES

ADDIS, T., BARRETT, E., POO, L.J., and D.W. YUEN. 1947. The relation between the serum urea concentration and the protein consumption of normal individuals. J. Clin. Invest. 26, 869.

BOLOURCHI, S. 1963. A study of the biological value and composition of breads from various countries. Master's thesis, Michigan State University, East Lansing, Michigan.

BOLOURCHI, S., FRIEDEMANN, C.M., and MICKELSEN, O. 1968A. Wheat flour as a source of protein for adult human subjects. Am. J. Clin. Nutr. 21, 827.

BOLOURCHI, S., FEURIG, J.S., and MICKELSEN, O. 1968B. Wheat flour, blood urea concentrations and urea metabolism in adult human subjects. Am. J. Clin. Nutr. 21, 836.

BORGSTROM, G. 1972. The Hungry Planet. The Macmillan Co., New York.

BURKITT, D.P. 1975. Benign and malignant tumors of the large bowel. In Refined Carbohydrate Foods and Disease, Some Implications of Dietary Fibre. D.P. Burkitt and H.C. Trowell (Editors). Academic Press, London p. 117.

DAVIDSON, S., PASSMORE, R., and BROCK, J.F. 1973. Human Nutrition and Dietetics. The Williams and Wilkins Co., Baltimore.

ENGELS, F. 1958. The Condition of the Working Class in England. Translated and edited by W.O. Henderson and W.H. Chaloner. The Macmillan Co., New York.

FOOD AND NUTRITION BOARD. 1953. Recommended Dietary Allowances. National Academy of Sciences, Pub. 302, Washington, D.C.

HEGSTED, D.M. 1962. The potential of wheat for meeting man's nutrient needs. *In* Role of Wheat in World's Food Supply. Report of a conference, May 1962, Albany, California. USDA Western Regional Res. Lab.

KIEHM, T.G., ANDERSON, J.W., and WARD, K. 1976. Beneficial effects of a high carbohydrate, high fiber diet on hyperglycemic diabetic men. Am. J. Clin. Nutr. *29*, 895.

LUSK, G. 1928. The Elements of the Science of Nutrition. W.B. Saunders Co., Philadelphia.

MARSH, A.G., SANCHEZ, T.V., MICKELSEN, O., KEISER, J., and MAYOR, G. 1980. Cortical bone density of adult lacto-ovo-vegetarian and omnivorous women. J. Am. Diet. Assoc. *76*, 148.

McCOLLUM, E.V. 1957. A History of Nutrition. Houghton Mifflin Co., Boston.

MICKELSEN, O. 1972. Nutritional labeling. Omicron Nu *38*(3) 15.

MICKELSEN, O. 1976. The possible role of vitamins in the aging process. *In* Nutrition, Longevity and Aging. M. Rockstein and M.L. Sussman (Editors). Academic Press, New York, p. 123.

ROSE, M. 1976. Vitamin-B_{12} deficiency in Asian immigrants. Lancet 2, 681.

ROSE, W.C. 1957. The amino acid requirements of adult men. Nutr. Abst. Rev. *27*, 631.

SANCHEZ, T.V., MICKELSEN, O., MARSH, A.G., GARN, S.M., and G.H. MAYOR. 1980. Bone mineral in elderly vegetarian and omnivorous females. Proc. Fourth Intern. Cong. on Bone Measurement. U.S. Dept. Health and Human Services; PHS, NIH Pub. No. 80-1938, p. 94.

SANDERS, T.A.B., ELLIS, F.R., and DICKERSON, J.W.T. 1978. Hematological studies on vegans. Brit. J. Nutr. *40*, 9.

SELECT COMMITTEE ON NUTRITION AND HUMAN NEEDS OF THE UNITED STATES SENATE. 1975. Towards a national nutrition policy. 94th Congress, 1st Session. U.S. Government Printing Office, Washington, D.C.

SELECT COMMITTEE ON NUTRITION AND HUMAN NEEDS OF THE UNITED STATES SENATE. 1977. Dietary Goals for the United States. 95th Congress, 1st Session. U.S. Government Printing Office, Washington, D.C.

STEWART, J.S., ROBERTS, P.D., and HOFFRAND, A.V. 1970. Response of dietary vitamin B_{12} deficiency to physiological oral doses of cyanocobalamin. Lancet 2, 542.

THOMAS, K. 1909. Über die biologische Wertigkeit der Stickstoffsubstanz in verschieden Nahrungsmitteln. Arch. Physiol., p. 219.

THOREAU, H.D. 1973. The Illustrated Walden. Princeton University Press, Princeton, New Jersey, p. 9.

TROWELL, H.C.   1975.   Diabetes mellitus and obesity.   *In* Refined Carbohydrate Foods and Disease: Some Implications of Dietary Fibre.   D.P. Burkitt and H.C. Trowell (Editors).   Academic Press, London, p. 227.

VAGHEFI, S., MAKDANI, D.D., and MICKELSEN, O.   1974.   Lysine supplementation of wheat—A review.   Am. J. Clin. Nutr. *27*, 1231.

WIDDOWSON, E.M.   1968.   The place of experimental animals in the study of human nutrition.   *In* Calorie Deficiencies and Protein Deficiencies. R.A. McCance and E.M. Widdowson (Editors).   Little, Brown and Co., Boston.

Index

DATE DUE

MAY - 1 '90			
MAY 2 2 '90			
JUN 1 2 '90			
JUN 1 4 1995			
FEB 1 0 1995			
MAR 0 3 1995			
MAR 2 0 1995			
DEC 1 6 1996			
MAR 1 8 1999			
261-2500			Printed in USA